The Ultimate Ninja Foodi Cookbook

500
Fast & Delicious Air Fry, Broil, Pressure Cook, Slow Cook, Simple, Affordable, and Delicious Recipes for Beginners and Advanced Users

Beth Chaney

All Rights Reserved:

The content contained within this book may not be reproduced, duplicated, or transmitted without direct written permission from the author or the publisher. Under no circumstances will any blame or legal responsibility be held against the publisher, or author, for any damages, reparation, or monetary loss due to the information contained within this book, either directly or indirectly.

Legal Notice: This book is copyright protected. It is only for personal use. You cannot amend, distribute, sell, use, quote or paraphrase any part, or the content within this book, without the consent of the author or publisher.

Disclaimer Notice:

Please note the information contained within this document is for educational and entertainment purposes only. All effort has been executed to present accurate, up to date, reliable, complete information. No warranties of any kind are declared or implied. Readers acknowledge that the author is not engaged in the rendering of legal, financial, medical, or professional advice. The content within this book has been derived from various sources. Please consult a licensed professional before attempting any techniques outlined in this book. By reading this document, the reader agrees that under no circumstances is the author responsible for any losses, direct or indirect, that are incurred as a result of the use of the information contained within this document, including, but not limited to, errors, omissions, or inaccuracies.

Table of Contents

Table of Contents 3
Introduction 8
Prepare for Your Ninja Foodi Journey 8

What is the Ninja Foodi 8
How to Use the Ninja Foodi 9
Four Reasons to Use the Ninja Foodi 9
Frequently Asked Questions 10
How to clean Ninja foodi pressure cooker? 10

Snacks, Appetizers & Sides 11

Zucchini Muffins 11
Crispy Sesame Shrimp 11
Turkey Scotch Eggs 11
Sweet Pickled Cucumbers 11
Mexican Street Corn 11
Hot Crab Dip 12
Sweet Potato And Beetroot Chips 12
Herb Roasted Mixed Nuts 12
Fried Beef Dumplings 12
Bacon-wrapped Halloumi Cheese 13
Nutmeg Peanuts 13
Caribbean Chicken Skewers 13
Asparagus Fries With Chipotle Dip 13
Louisiana Crab Dip 14
Charred Broccoli With Mustard Cream Sauce 14
Pull Apart Cheesy Garlic Bread 14
Cheesy Fried Risotto Balls 14
Butter-flower Medley 15
Cheesy Tangy Arancini 15
Crispy Delicata Squash 15
Mini Steak Kebabs 16
Parmesan Stuffed Mushrooms 16
Crispy Cheesy Straws 16
South Of The Border Corn Dip 16
Sweet Potato Fries 16
Cashew Cream 17
Mini Shrimp Tacos 17
Zucchini Chips 17
Herbed Cauliflower Fritters 17
Buttery Chicken Meatballs 18
Enchilada Bites 18
Italian Pita Crisps 18
Zesty Brussels Sprouts With Raisins 18
Chicken Meatballs With Dill Dipping Sauce 18
Wrapped Asparagus In Bacon 19
Sweet Potato Skins 19
Cheesy Stuffed Mushroom 19
Dill Butter 19
Mini Crab Cakes 20
Zesty Meatballs 20
Honey Bourbon Wings 20
Cheesy Stuffed Onions 20
Rosemary Potato Fries 21
Popcorn Chicken 21
Cheesy Bacon Brussel Sprouts 21
Crispy Chicken Skin 21
Cumin Baby Carrots 22
Cheesy Chicken Dip 22
Parmesan Butternut Crisps 22
Cheeseburger Boats 22
Apple Pecan Cookie Bars 22
Spicy Black Bean Dip 23
Apricot Snack Bars 23
Herby Fish Skewers 23
Cauliflower Gratin 23
Chipotle-lime Chicken Wings 24
Tangy Jicama Chips 24
Pork Shank 24
Three-layer Taco Dip 24
Cauliflower Nuggets 25
Gingered Butternut Squash 25
Chicken Bites 25
Strawberry Snack Bars 25
Spinach Hummus 26
Chicken Lettuce Wraps 26
Jalapeno Salsa 26
Caponata 26
Almond Lover's Bars 27
Mushrooms Stuffed With Veggies 27
Caramelized Cauliflower With Hazelnuts 27

Breakfast 28

Banana Custard Oatmeal 28
Applesauce Pumpkin Muffins 28
Ham&Hash Brown Casserole 28
Chili Cheese Quiche 28
Quinoa Protein Bake 29
Cinnamon Sugar Donuts 29
Spinach Turkey Cups 29
Butternut Breakfast Squash 29
Pumpkin Steel Cut Oatmeal 30
Strawberry Oat Breakfast Bars 30
Almond Quinoa Porridge 30
Bacon&Egg Poppers 30
Cranberry Lemon Quinoa 30
Sausage Wrapped Scotch Eggs 31
Maple Dipped Asparagus 31
Prosciutto Egg Bake 31
Homemade Vanilla Yogurt 31
Ricotta Raspberry Breakfast Cake 32
Hearty Breakfast Muffins 32
Walnut Orange Coffee Cake 32
Bell Pepper Frittata 32
Bbq Chicken Sandwiches 33
Swiss Bacon Frittata 33
Nutmeg Pumpkin Porridge 33
Sweet Bread Pudding 33
Avocado Cups 34
Chicken Omelet 34
Glazed Lemon Muffins 34

Ninja Foodi Cookbook

Pumpkin Pecan Oatmeal 34	Cheesy Meat Omelet 38
Pumpkin Coconut Breakfast Bake 35	Cinnamon Apple Bread 38
Carrot Cake Oats 35	Banana Coconut Loaf 39
Grilled Broccoli 35	Cinnamon Bun Oatmeal 39
Cinnamon Sugar French Toast Bites 35	Sweet Potatoes&Fried Eggs 39
Sausage&Broccoli Frittata 36	Baked Eggs In Spinach 40
Banana Nut Muffins 36	Stuffed Baked Tomatoes 40
Morning Pancakes 36	Apple Walnut Quinoa 40
Breakfast Pies 36	Sweet Potato,Sausage,And Rosemary Quiche 40
Chocolate Chip And Banana Bread Bundt Cake 37	Cinnamon Crumb Donuts 41
Cranberry Vanilla Oatmeal 37	Glazed Carrots 41
Maple Giant Pancake 37	Cheesecake French Toast 41
Flaxseeds Granola 37	Bacon And Gruyère Egg Bites 41
Ham Breakfast Casserole 38	Spinach Casserole 42
Spanish Potato And Chorizo Frittata 38	Southern Grits Casserole 42
Breakfast Burrito Bake 38	Paprika Hard-boiled Eggs 42

Fish&Seafood 43

Pistachio Crusted Mahi Mahi 43	Crab Cakes 51
Salmon With Creamy Grits 43	Parmesan Tilapia 51
Tuscan Cod 43	Sweet&Spicy Shrimp 51
Italian Flounder 44	Blackened Salmon 52
Pistachio Crusted Salmon 44	Mussel Chowder With Oyster Crackers 52
Salmon With Dill Sauce 44	Haddock With Sanfaina 52
Farfalle Tuna Casserole With Cheese 44	Caramelized Salmon 52
Fried Salmon 45	Curried Salmon&Sweet Potatoes 53
Coconut Shrimp With Pineapple Rice 45	Spanish Steamed Clams 53
Tuna&Avocado Patties 45	Mustard And Apricot-glazed Salmon With Smashed
Shrimp Etouffee 45	Potatoes 53
Roasted Bbq Shrimp 46	Crab Cake Casserole 54
Citrus Glazed Halibut 46	Steamed Sea Bass With Turnips 54
Spicy"grilled"Catfish 46	Speedy Clams Pomodoro 54
New England Lobster Rolls 46	Clam&Corn Chowder 54
Arroz Con Cod 47	Seafood Gumbo 55
Shrimp Fried Rice 47	Sesame Tuna Steaks 55
Salmon,Cashew&Kale Bowl 47	Almond Crusted Haddock 55
Shrimp&Asparagus Risotto 47	Creamy Crab Soup 55
Salmon With Dill Chutney 48	Cajun Shrimp 56
Orange Glazed Cod&Snap Peas 48	Shrimp And Sausage Paella 56
Shrimp&Zoodles 48	Kung Pao Shrimp 56
Lemon Cod Goujons And Rosemary Chips 49	Flounder Oreganata 56
Flounder Veggie Soup 49	Spiced Red Snapper 57
Spicy Shrimp Pasta With Vodka Sauce 49	Simple Salmon&Asparagus 57
Fish Broccoli Stew 50	Spicy Grilled Shrimp 57
Penne All Arrabbiata With Seafood And Chorizo 50	Baked Cod Casserole 57
Salmon Chowder 50	Sweet&Spicy Shrimp Bowls 58
Teriyaki Salmon 50	Garlic Shrimp And Veggies 58
Garlic Shrimp 51	Poached Flounder With Mango Salsa 58
Classic Crab Imperial 51	

Vegan&Vegetable 59

Italian Baked Zucchini 59	Okra Stew 62
Stuffed Manicotti 59	Quinoa Pesto Bowls With Veggies 62
Hearty Veggie Soup 59	Pomegranate Radish Mix 62
Radish Apples Salad 59	Burrito Bowls 62
Crème De La Broc 60	Creamy Golden Casserole 62
Artichoke Lasagna Rolls 60	Cheesy Baked Spinach 63
Caprese Pasta Salad 60	Grilled Cheese 63
Baked Linguine 60	Veggie Lasagna 63
Tomato Bisque 61	Baked Cajun Turnips 64
Bell Peppers Mix 61	Italian Sausage With Garlic Mash 64
Spinach,Tomatoes,And Butternut Squash Stew 61	Bok Choy And Zoddle Soup 64
Vegan Split Pea Soup 61	Mushroom Goulash 64
Cauliflower Steaks&Veggies 61	Sesame Radish 65

Ninja Foodi Cookbook

Recipe	Page
Cheesy Squash Tart	65
Cauliflower Enchiladas	65
Paneer Cutlet	66
Baby Porcupine Meatballs	66
Veggie Loaded Pasta	66
Creamy Polenta&Mushrooms	66
Noodles With Tofu And Peanuts	67
Green Minestrone	67
Stir Fried Veggies	67
Southern Pineapple Casserole	67
Veggie Lover's Pizza	67
Mushroom Brown Rice Pilaf	68
Chorizo Mac And Cheese	68
Rosemary Sweet Potato Medallions	68
Potato Filled Bread Rolls	68
Asparagus With Feta	68
Carrot Gazpacho	69
Veggie Skewers	69
Pasta Veggie Toss	69
Roasted Vegetable Salad	69
Artichoke With Mayo	70
Cheesy Green Beans With Nuts	70
Spanish Rice	70
Cheesy Chilies	70
Pesto With Cheesy Bread	70
Quick Indian-style Curry	71
Minestrone With Pancetta	71
Olives And Rice Stuffed Mushrooms	71
Pumpkin Soup	72
Spinach Gratin&Eggs	72
Tasty Acorn Squash	72
Stuffed Mushrooms	72
Tofu&Carrot Toss	73
Artichoke&Spinach Casserole	73
Green Squash Gruyere	73
Cabbage With Bacon	73
Green Cream Soup	74
Stuffed Summer Squash	74
Sour Cream&Onion Frittata	74
Parsley Mashed Cauliflower	74
Steamed Artichokes With Lemon Aioli	74
Mashed Potatoes With Spinach	75
Palak Paneer	75
Broccoli Cauliflower	75
Pepper And Sweet Potato Skewers	75
Mashed Broccoli With Cream Cheese	76
Garlic Potatoes	76
Carrots Walnuts Salad	76
Eggplant Casserole	76

Poultry 77

Recipe	Page
Chicken Pasta With Pesto Sauce	77
Paprika Buttered Chicken	77
Chicken In Thai Peanut Sauce	77
Healthy Chicken Stew	77
Turkey Meatballs	78
Shredded Chicken And Wild Rice	78
Salsa Chicken With Feta	78
Hassel Back Chicken	78
Shredded Chicken With Lentils And Rice	79
Tuscan Chicken&Pasta	79
Crunchy Chicken Schnitzels	79
Cran-apple Turkey Cutlets	79
Buttermilk Chicken Thighs	79
Lettuce Carnitas Wraps	80
Paprika Chicken	80
Creamy Tuscan Chicken Pasta	80
Southwest Chicken Bake	80
Chicken With Tomatoes And Capers	81
Creamy Chicken Carbonara	81
Chicken Carnitas	81
Thyme Turkey Nuggets	82
Greek Chicken With Potatoes	82
Garlic Turkey Breasts	82
Bacon&Cranberry Stuffed Turkey Breast	82
Cheesy Chicken And Broccoli Casserole	83
Chicken With Prunes	83
Cheesy Chicken&Artichokes	83
Italian Turkey&Pasta Soup	83
Garlic-herb Roasted Chicken	84
Turkey Croquettes	84
Asian Chicken	84
Apple Butter Chicken	85
Chicken Cacciatore	85
Chicken Wings With Lemon	85
Thyme Chicken With Veggies	85
Buttermilk Fried Chicken	86
Fiesta Chicken Casserole	86
Chicken With Bacon And Beans	86
Pizza Stuffed Chicken	87
Honey Garlic Chicken And Okra	87
Chicken Meatballs Primavera	87
Moo Shu Chicken	88
Garlic Chicken And Bacon Pasta	88
Butternut Turkey Stew	88
Crunchy Chicken&Almond Casserole	88
Lemon Turkey Risotto	89
Chicken Cutlets In Dijon Sauce	89
Chicken And Quinoa Soup	89
Salsa Verde Chicken With Salsa Verde	89
Butter Chicken	90
Chicken With Mushroom Sauce	90
Country Chicken Casserole	90
Chipotle Raspberry Chicken	90
Chicken Stroganoff With Fetucini	91
Speedy Fajitas	91
Coq Au Vin	91
Chicken And Broccoli	92
Chicken Chickpea Chili	92
Turkey Enchilada Casserole	92
Lime Chicken Chili	92
Mexican Chicken Soup	93
Shredded Chicken&Black Beans	93
Bacon Lime Chicken	93
Chicken Meatballs In Tomato Sauce	93
Turkey Breakfast Sausage	93
Creamy Slow Cooked Chicken	94
Slow Cooked Chicken In White Wine And Garlic	94
Chicken Cordon Bleu	94
Quesadilla Casserole	95
Pesto Stuffed Chicken With Green Beans	95
Apricot Bbq Duck Legs	95
Buttered Turkey	95
Lemon,Barley&Turkey Soup	96
Chicken With Bbq Sauce	96

Chicken Tenders With Broccoli 96

Beef, Pork & Lamb 97

Asian Beef 97
Crunchy Cashew Lamb Rack 97
Tender Beef&Onion Rings 97
Cheese Burgers In Hoagies 97
Pork Chops With Broccoli 98
Beef Bourguignon(2) 98
Mongolian Beef 98
Flank Steak With Bell Pepper Salsa 98
Pesto Pork Chops&Asparagus 99
Cuban Pork 99
Sticky Barbeque Baby Back Ribs 99
Beef Broccoli 99
Honey Short Ribs With Rosemary Potatoes 100
Baked Bacon Macaroni And Cheese 100
Char Siew Pork Ribs 100
Pepper Crusted Tri Tip Roast 101
Beef Stew With Beer 101
Bacon-wrapped Hot Dogs 101
Pork Asado 101
Crusted Pork Chops 102
Beef Tips&Mushrooms 102
Beef Brisket 102
Carne Guisada 102
Pork Medallions With Dijon Sauce 103
Hamburger&Macaroni Skillet 103
Smoky Sausage&Potato Soup 103
Beef Brisket&Carrots 103
Baked Rigatoni With Beef Tomato Sauce 104
Teriyaki Pork Noodles 104
Ranch Pork With Mushroom Sauce 104
Beef Stroganoff 104
Sausage With Celeriac And Potato Mash 105
Bacon Strips 105
Swedish Meatballs With Mashed Cauliflower 105
Beef Sirloin Steak 105
Chunky Pork Meatloaf With Mashed Potatoes 106
Mexican Pot Roast 106
Beef And Cabbage Stew 106
Philippine Pork Chops 106
Braised Short Ribs With Mushrooms 107
Korean Pork Chops 107
Bolognese Pizza 107
Tex Mex Beef Stew 107
Beef Stir Fry 108
Hawaiian Pork Meal 108
Lamb Chops And Potato Mash 108
Maple Glazed Pork Chops 109
Bacon&Sauerkraut With Apples 109
Cheddar Cheeseburgers 109
Lime Glazed Pork Tenderloin 109
Mexican Pork Stir Fry 109
Ham,Ricotta&Zucchini Fritters 110
Lone Star Chili 110
Brisket Chili Verde 110
Beef&Broccoli Casserole 111
Cuban Marinated Pork 111
Bunless Burgers 111
Pork Sandwiches With Slaw 111
Chipotle Beef Brisket 112
Cauliflower&Bacon Soup 112
Korean-style Barbecue Meatloaf 112
Roasted Pork With Apple Gravy 112
Simple Beef&Shallot Curry 113
Beef Jerky 113
Southern Sweet Ham 113
Baby Back Ribs With Barbeque Sauce 113
Sour And Sweet Pork 114
Zucchini&Beef Lasagna 114
Beef Lasagna 114
Smoky Horseradish Spare Ribs 115
Spanish Lamb&Beans 115
Jamaican Pork 115
Healthier Meatloaf 115
Beef In Basil Sauce 116
Creole Dirty Rice 116
Italian Pot Roast 116
Beef And Pumpkin Stew 116
Pork And Ricotta Meatballs With Cheesy Grits 117
Meatballs With Spaghetti Sauce 117
Garlicky Pork Chops 117
Traditional Beef Stroganoff 118
Beef Mole 118
Pulled Pork Tacos 118
Beef Pho With Swiss Chard 118
Pork Chops With Squash Purée And Mushroom Gravy ... 119

Soups & Stews 120

Italian Sausage,Potato,And Kale Soup 120
Chickpea,Spinach,And Sweet Potato Stew 120
Coconut And Shrimp Bisque 120
Fish Chowder And Biscuits 120
Tex-mex Chicken Tortilla Soup 121
Chicken Potpie Soup 121
Butternut Squash,Apple,Bacon And Orzo Soup 122
Chicken Enchilada Soup 122
Lasagna Soup 122
Chicken Chili 123
Creamy Pumpkin Soup 123
Loaded Potato Soup 123
Jamaican Jerk Chicken Stew 124
Mushroom And Wild Rice Soup 124
Goulash(hungarian Beef Soup) 124

Desserts 125

Chocolate Cheesecake 125
Cinnamon Apple Cake 125
Portuguese Honey Cake 125
Poached Peaches 126
Coconut Lime Snack Cake 126
Pecan Pie Bars 126
Almond Milk 126
Maply Soufflés 126
Vanilla Cheesecake(1) 127
Pecan Stuffed Apples 127
Cheese Babka 127
Chocolate Chip Brownies 128

Vanilla Chocolate Spread 128	Blueberry Peach Crisp 134
Peach Cobbler 128	Molten Lava Cake 135
Cheat Apple Pie 128	Rhubarb,Raspberry,And Peach Cobbler 135
Pecan Apple Crisp 129	Almond Banana Dessert 135
Chocolate Fondue 129	Buttery Cranberry Cake 135
Strawberry Crumble 129	Carrot Raisin Cookie Bars 135
Coconut Rice Pudding 129	Banana Coconut Pudding 136
Lime Blueberry Cheesecake 129	Mixed Berry Cobbler 136
Coconut Cream Dessert Bars 130	Tres Leches Cake 136
Key Lime Pie 130	Milk Dumplings In Sweet Sauce 136
Fried Snickerdoodle Poppers 130	Yogurt Cheesecake 137
Chocolate Peanut Butter And Jelly Puffs 130	Brownie Bites 137
Lemon And Blueberries Compote 131	Red Velvet Cheesecake 137
Strawberry And Lemon Ricotta Cheesecake 131	Cranberry Cheesecake 138
Churro Bites 131	Chocolate Mousse 138
Coconut Cream"custard"Bars 132	Cinnamon Butternut Squash Pie 138
Flourless Chocolate Cake 132	Spiced Poached Pears 138
Cranberry Almond Rice Pudding 133	Chocolate Brownie Cake 138
Mini Vanilla Cheesecakes 133	Blueberry Lemon Pound Cake 139
Pumpkin Crème Brulee 133	Double Chocolate Cake 139
Filling Coconut And Oat Cookies 133	Caramel Apple Bread Pudding 139
Vanilla Hot Lava Cake 133	Strawberry Cheesecake 140
Peanut Butter Pie 134	Chocolate Cake 140
Vanilla Pound Cake 134	Citrus Steamed Pudding 140

RECIPE INDEX 141

Introduction

Imagine being able to sauté vegetables, steam rice, and cook the perfect steak in just one pot. That's right. You can prepare a meal that has all your daily nutritional requirements using only one appliance. Even better? You can make desserts like a cobbler and flan in the very same unit.

If you haven't heard about the Ninja Foodi, you should start reading this book, because not only will it offer some of the most sumptuous recipes that you can ever stumble into, but it will also offer you useful information that will help you understand the function of this new cooking appliance. So, if you are a Newbie in the use of the Ninja Foodi, don't get frustrated, because, in this book, you will just find everything you need and enough information that will help you understand this cooking appliance better.

It is a single machine that can do the work of four machines. It can do everything that is done by an Instant Pot. It can even do much more than that. Also, the Ninja Foodi costs you less than the amount you have to pay for buying all other machines individually. Ninja Foodi is very easy to use, and you don't need to put in a lot of effort into understand how it works. It's easy to learn its usage and does not bother you much. Apart from other aspects comes the cleaning of Ninja Foodi. It's easy to clean Ninja Foodi and clear it from the food particles and oily content of your food. One who uses it can quickly get the trick of its efficient cleaning.

In this book, you'll find 1ooo mouth-watering recipes for every occasion, from game day to Thanksgiving dinner, from breakfasts, lunches, and snacks to filling main courses and delectable desserts—all ready in less time than traditional cooking methods.

Along with delicious recipes , you'll find loads of cooking hacks and flavoring suggestions to make cooking even more convenient and fitted to your preferences—there are so many ways to cut corners in the kitchen without cutting down on flavor!

Throughout this book you'll learn everything you need to know about using an Ninja Foodi, as well as helpful ways to elevate your meals,even if you're completely new to cooking. So let's get started!

Are you hungry yet? Turn on your Ninja Foodi and let's get cooking. I am here to help you get started with this ultimate beginner's guide for this one-of-a-kind cooking adventure that is sure to have everyone leaving the table with happy taste buds and full bellies.

Prepare for Your Ninja Foodi Journey

What is the Ninja Foodi

The Ninja Foodi delivers a whole new way of cooking by combining the speed of a pressure cooker with the quick-crisping action of an air fryer to give you TenderCrisp Technology. Now, quick meals, made from real food and with great flavor and texture, can be on the table in no time. And did I mention there is only one pot to clean?

You've likely seen your social media feed flooded recently with pressure cooker recipes. This trend has taken over because it cooks food fast and, as you are using whole ingredients, it is inherently a healthier choice. But the truth is, pressure cooking only takes you so far. It makes juicy, tender food, but there is no texture. And, let's be honest, texture is just as important as flavor.

Each Ninja Foodi comes with the pressure lid, crisping lid, cooking pot, reversible rack, and cook & crisp basket. You can sauté just as you would on a stove, but with built in timers and controls that make sense. The crisping lid can broil a steak, just as I would in a professional kitchen, with ease. Broiling creates a crisp crust with a juicy interior. This leads to the aforementioned textural juxtaposition. I could talk about it all day, but the bottom line is this—human beings are hardwired to crave foods with multiple textures. It's good for our brains and makes us happy. In addition, the bottom heating element can effectively sear, which is a claim I don't make lightly. A sear is all or nothing, and it's the difference between crispy yummy skin on a piece of salmon or something that gets scraped off to the side of the plate. This is how you get a crisp skin on a juicy chicken, or an asparagus spear that is cooked, but not lifeless. It's what restaurants do all the time. In other pressure cookers, none of this is possible.

Ninja Foodi Cookbook

How to Use the Ninja Foodi

Before using the device, it is essential to check all its components, if the power cord is intact, all the valves are in their position, and the sealing ring is properly fixed, etc. If any of the components are not properly set, the device will not function well. Now that everything is in place, you can plug in your device. Once plugged in, the LED screen of the control panel lights up.

1. Add Ingredients to the Ninja Foodi Cooking Pot:
To start with the cooking, you can either remove the cooking pot from the vessel and add ingredients to it or leave it in the vessel to cook a meal in which we need to start by sautéing the ingredients; the inner pot is left inside of the vessels and ingredients are added gradually to the pot. The inner markings of the pot provide a good measurement for the food, and it also marks the limit, do not add anything above its 2/3 full limit. There must be enough space above the food so that it could easily boil or expand.

2. Seal and Secure the Lid:
For pressure cooking, the pressure lid with the valve attached needs to be installed, sealed, and locked on top of the vessel. For that, simply place the lid over the vessel and rotate it until it sounds clicks. When the arrow on the vessel aligns with the close marking of the lid, it means your lid is sealed. Whenever the lid is not properly closed, the timer does not initiate. This is one of the security features of the Ninja Foodi, which does not initiate cooking without proper locking of the lid. For Air Crisping, use the crisping lid.

3. Select the Appropriate Cooking Mode:
As a multipurpose Ninja Foodi cooker offers you several different cooking modes, each of these modes has its own preset or integrated settings to adjust both the time and pressure according to the requirement. To start the cooking process, select any of the desired programs by pressing their respective buttons or keys. Remember that each mode has its own settings; to make changes in time and pressure, use the adjustment keys. Every standard control panel of a Ninja Foodi pressure cooker gives you these many options: Steam, Air Crisp, Sear/Sauté, Pressure, Slow Cook, Bake/Roast, Broil, Dehydrate and Keep Warm.
Once the mode is selected, the Ninja Foodi will immediately switch to a Preheating State, which continues for 10 seconds. During this stage, the cooker sets its internal temperature and the internal pressure; then, it finally switches to the cooking state. Once the food is all cooked, the Ninja Foodi automatically switches to a standby mode where it is kept warm at low temperatures. The Keep Warm key allows you to either stop or cancel the operation or switch the appliance to the Warm mode. Once set, the warm mode will continue until the button is pressed again.
Once the mode is selected, use the time and temperature keys to increase or decrease the values. Then pressure the START/STOP button to initiate the cooking or stop it.

Four Reasons to Use the Ninja Foodi

For too long we have settled for convenience over flavor. Opting for takeout over a home-cooked meal or leaning on multi-cookers that don't deliver to answer the question, "What's for dinner?" With the Ninja Foodi Pressure Cooker, you no longer have to settle. TenderCrisp Technology unlocks unlimited possibilities for breakfast, lunch, dinner, dessert, and more.

TenderCrisp Technology
TenderCrisp Technology is quite simple. First, use the pressure function to quickly cook and tenderize food with superheated steam. Then, remove the pressure lid and lower the crisping lid to quickly crisp and caramelize for the perfect finishing touch. With TenderCrisp Technology, you can cook quickly and ensure your food is tender inside and crispy on the outside.

One Pot Meals
With the Foodi Pressure Cooker, you can transform boring, one-texture meals into one-pot wonders. Use the pressure function to quickly cook your favorite casseroles, stews, and chilis. Then top with cheese, biscuits, or a crust. Swap the top and use the crisping lid to broil the cheese, bake the biscuits, or crisp the crust. With everything prepared in one pot, your prep time is cut down, and you only have one pot to clean! Make the recipes that have been handed down from generation to generation—but with this unique twist, you can make them in half the time!

360 Meals
Make a delicious, restaurant-inspired meal in one pot. I'm talking a full meal complete with fluffy rice, roasted veggies, and perfectly cooked proteins—each with its own unique texture. Pile grains on the bottom of your cooking pot, add some veggies, pop in the Reversible Rack, and place your proteins on top. Use the recipes throughout the book, or go off book and try your own combination.

Frozen to Crispy

Ninja Foodi Cookbook

Perhaps the most convenient feature of the Ninja Foodi Pressure Cooker is the ability to cook food straight from frozen. There's no need to wait around for food to thaw. Use pressure to quickly defrost and tenderize frozen meat, then lower the crisping lid to sizzle and crisp the outside. No more uneven defrosting using the microwave or waiting hours for your food to defrost on the counter.

Frequently Asked Questions

1. Why does the Ninja Foodi come with two lids?
The Ninja Foodi is the only pressure cooker that crisps. For this reason, it comes with a Pressure Lid for the Pressure, Steam, Slow Cook, and Sear/Sauté functions, as well as a Crisping Lid for the Air Crisp, Bake/Roast, Broil, and Dehydrate functions. Use the lids individually or one right after the other to unlock a world of recipes you never knew you could make at home.
2. What is the difference between quick release and natural release?
Quick release is when you manually switch the pressure release valve to the Vent position. Quick release is used in the majority of this book's recipes. Natural release occurs when you let the Ninja Foodi decrease in pressure naturally after cooking is complete. This technique is most commonly used when cooking beans.
3. When doing a TenderCrisp recipe, should I remove the liquid after using the Pressure Lid, before switching to the Crisping Lid?
If you are following one of the TenderCrisp recipes in this book, there is no need to remove the liquid before switching to the Crisping Lid. These recipes are specifically designed to work with the amount of liquid in the bottom of the pot.
If you are creating your own recipe and would like to make sure the bottom of your food is browned in the Cook & Crisp Basket, make sure not to exceed the 3-cup mark (located on the inside of the pot) with liquid.

4. Can I cook frozen food in the Ninja Foodi?
Yes! One of the best things about the Ninja Foodi is that you can cook frozen food straight from the freezer without the need to defrost. Use Pressure to turn frozen chicken breasts into shredded chicken or ground beef into chili, or use the combination of Pressure and the Crisping Lid to roast a whole chicken from frozen or cook the perfect medium-rare steak.

How to clean Ninja foodi pressure cooker?

The popularity of the Ninja Foodi FD401 Programmable Pressure Cooker and Air Fryer has skyrocketed in recent years because it cooks meals quickly without using too much oil. It can be challenging to clean this appliance, but the following tips should help you get your Ninja looking new.
·First, disconnect the power from your pressure cooker.
·To clean the pressure cooker & air fryer, you need lemon, soapy water, a brush, and a sponge.
·Mix 4-5 pieces of lemon juice with water inside the cooker.
·Then, close the lead and boil the water.
·After boiling the water, open the lid.
·Now, on the lid, you can see grease, oil, which has boiled due to the warmth of the hot water.
·Then wipe the lead with a paper towel to remove the oil & grease.
·If you see food particles stuck after wiping, you can use a soft brush to remove the food particles.
·Then keep washing well with soapy water.
·After washing, wipe with a clean towel.
·Then leave to dry, but should not be allowed to dry in the sunlight.
·Use for cooking again after drying.

Pressure Lid
Quickly tenderize and cook ingredients.

Deluxe Reversible Rack
Use both layers to increase capacity to cook up to 8 chicken breasts or salmon fillets at once. Remove the top layer to steam or reverse to broil.

Cook & Crisp™ Basket
5-quart nonstick, ceramic-coated basket fits 4 lbs of French fries.

Crisping Lid
Use to finish off pressure cooked recipes or to air fry your food.

Cooking Pot
8-quart nonstick, ceramic-coated cooking pot serves 8-10.

14 Safety Features
Passed rigorous testing for certification, giving you peace of mind.

Snacks, Appetizers & Sides

Zucchini Muffins

Servings: 6
Cooking Time: 15 Minutes
Ingredients:
- 1 cup coconut flour
- 1 medium zucchini, finely chopped
- 1 teaspoon baking soda
- 1 tablespoon lemon juice
- ½ teaspoon salt
- ½ teaspoon black pepper
- 1 tablespoon butter
- ⅓ cup of coconut milk
- 1 teaspoon poppy seeds
- 2 tablespoons flax meal

Directions:
1. Place the chopped zucchini in a blender and mix until smooth.
2. Combine the salt, baking soda, lemon juice, poppy, coconut flour, butter, black pepper, and flax meal together.
3. Add the milk and blended zucchini.
4. Knead the dough until smooth. It can be a little bit sticky.
5. Place the muffins in the muffin's tins and transfer the zucchini muffins in the Ninja Foodi's insert.
6. Cook the muffins on the "Steam" mode for 15 minutes.
7. Once done, check if the dish is done using a toothpick.
8. If the muffins are cooked, remove them from the Ninja Foodi's insert and serve.

Nutrition:
- InfoCalories: 146; Fat: 8.9g; Carbohydrates: 13.5g; Protein: 4g

Crispy Sesame Shrimp

Servings: 10
Cooking Time: 10 Minutes
Ingredients:
- 1 cup flour
- ¼ tsp salt
- ¼ tsp cayenne pepper
- ¾ cup club soda
- Nonstick cooking spray
- 1 lb. medium shrimp, peel & devein
- 2 tsp sesame seeds

Directions:
1. In a medium bowl, combine flour, salt, and pepper.
2. Whisk in club soda until combined.
3. Spray fryer basket with cooking spray.
4. Dip shrimp, one at a time, in the batter and place in basket in a single layer. Sprinkle with sesame seeds.
5. Add tender-crisp lid and set cooker to air fryer function on 400°F. Cook shrimp 8-10 minutes or until golden brown. Serve immediately.

Nutrition:
- InfoCalories 81, Total Fat 1g, Total Carbs 10g, Protein 7g, Sodium 319mg.

Turkey Scotch Eggs

Servings: 6
Cooking Time: 20 Min
Ingredients:
- 10 oz. ground turkey/300g
- 4 eggs, soft boiled, peeled
- 2 garlic cloves, minced
- 2 eggs, lightly beaten
- 1 white onion; chopped
- ½ cup flour/65g
- ½ cup breadcrumbs/65g
- 1 tsp dried mixed herbs/5g
- Salt and pepper to taste
- Cooking spray

Directions:
1. Mix together the onion, garlic, salt, and pepper. Shape into 4 balls. Wrap the turkey mixture around each egg, and ensure the eggs are well covered.
2. Dust each egg ball in flour, then dip in the beaten eggs and finally roll in the crumbs, until coated. Spray with cooking spray.
3. Lay the eggs into your Ninja Foodi's basket. Set the temperature to 390°F or 199°C, close the crisping lid and cook for 15 minutes. After 8 minutes, turn the eggs. Slice in half and serve warm.

Sweet Pickled Cucumbers

Servings: 6
Cooking Time: 5 Min
Ingredients:
- 1 pound small cucumbers; sliced into rings/450g
- 1/4 cup green garlic, minced/32.5g
- 2 cups white vinegar/500ml
- 1 cup sugar/130g
- 1 cup water/250ml
- 2 tbsp Dill Pickle Seasoning/30g
- 2 tsp salt/10g
- 1 tsp cumin/5g

Directions:
1. Into the pot, add sliced cucumber, vinegar and pour water on top. Sprinkle sugar over cucumbers. Add cumin, dill pickle seasoning, and salt.
2. Stir well to dissolve the sugar. Seal the pressure lid, choose Pressure, set to High, and set the timer to 4 minutes. Press Start.
3. When ready, release the pressure quickly. Ladle cucumbers into a large storage container and pour cooking liquid over the top. Chill for 1 hour.

Mexican Street Corn

Servings: 3
Cooking Time: 14 Minutes
Ingredients:
- 3 ears corn, husked, rinsed, and dried
- Olive oil spray
- ¼ cup sour cream
- ¼ cup mayonnaise
- ¼ cup crumbled cotija cheese, plus more for garnish
- 1 teaspoon freshly squeezed lime juice
- ½ teaspoon garlic powder
- ¼ teaspoon chili powder, plus more as needed
- Fresh cilantro leaves, for garnish
- ½ teaspoon salt
- ½ teaspoon freshly ground black pepper

Directions:
1. Select AIR CRISP,set the temperature to 400°F,and set the time to 5 minutes to preheat.Select START/STOP to begin.
2. Lightly mist the corn with olive oil and place the corn in the Cook&Crisp Basket.Close the crisping lid.
3. Select AIR CRISP,set the temperature to 400°F,and set the time to 12 minutes.Select START/STOP to begin.After 7 minutes,flip the corn.Close the crisping lid and cook for 5 minutes more.
4. While the corn cooks,in a small bowl,stir together the sour cream,mayonnaise,cotija cheese,lime juice,garlic powder,and chili powder until blended.
5. When cooking is complete,carefully remove the corn and brush or spoon the sauce onto it.Sprinkle with cilantro,cotija cheese,and more chili powder.
6. If desired,return the corn to the basket.Close the crisping lid.Select BROIL and set the time for 2 minutes.Select START/STOP to begin.
7. Serve hot,seasoned with salt and pepper,as needed.
Nutrition:
- InfoCalories:280,Total Fat:15g,Sodium:701mg,Carbohydrates:35g,Protein:7g.

Hot Crab Dip
Servings:8
Cooking Time:30 Minutes
Ingredients:
- 8 oz.cream cheese,fat free,soft
- ¼lb.crabmeat,flaked
- ½tsp fresh lemon juice
- ½tsp onion powder
- 1 tbsp.fresh dill,chopped
- ¼tsp garlic powder

Directions:
1. Set to air fryer on 350°F.Place the rack in the cooking pot.
2. In a medium bowl,combine all ingredients until smooth.Transfer to a small baking dish.
3. Place the dish on the rack and add the tender-crisp lid.Bake 30-35 minutes until heated through and lightly browned on top.Serve warm.
Nutrition:
- InfoCalories 78,Total Fat 1g,Total Carbs 8g,Protein 10g,Sodium 201mg.

Sweet Potato And Beetroot Chips
Servings:1
Cooking Time:8 Hours
Ingredients:
- ½small beet,peeled and cut into⅛-inch slices
- ½small sweet potato,peeled and cut into⅛-inch slices
- ½tablespoon extra-virgin olive oil
- ½teaspoon sea salt

Directions:
1. In a large bowl,toss the beet slices with half the olive oil until evenly coated.Repeat,in a separate bowl,with the sweet potato slices and the rest of the olive oil(if you don't mind pink sweet potatoes,you can toss them together in one bowl).Season with salt.
2. Arrange the beet slices flat in a single layer in the bottom of the pot.Arrange the sweet potato slices flat in a single layer on the Reversible Rack in the lower position.Place rack in pot and close crisping lid.
3. Select DEHYDRATE,set temperature to 135°F,and set time to 8 hours.Select START/STOP to begin.
4. When dehydrating is complete,remove rack from pot.Transfer the beet and sweet potato chips to an airtight container.
Nutrition:
- InfoCalories:221,Total Fat:7g,Sodium:1057mg,Carbohydrates:36g,Protein:4g.

Herb Roasted Mixed Nuts
Servings:12
Cooking Time:15 Minutes
Ingredients:
- ½cup pecan halves
- ½cup raw cashews
- ½cup walnut halves
- ½cup hazelnuts
- ½cup Brazil nuts
- ½cup raw almonds
- 1 tbsp.fresh rosemary,chopped
- 1 tbsp.fresh thyme,chopped
- ½tbsp.fresh parsley,chopped
- 1 tsp garlic granules
- ½tsp paprika
- ½tsp salt
- ¼tsp pepper
- ½tbsp.olive oil

Directions:
1. Combine all ingredients in a large bowl and toss to coat thoroughly.
2. Pour the nuts in the fryer basket and place in the cooking pot.Add the tender-crisp lid and select air fry on 375°F.Cook 10 minutes,then stir the nuts around.
3. Cook another 5-10 minutes,stirring every few minutes and checking to make sure they don't burn.Serve warm.
Nutrition:
- InfoCalories 229,Total Fat 21g,Total Carbs 7g,Protein 5g,Sodium 99mg.

Fried Beef Dumplings
Servings:8
Cooking Time:45 Min
Ingredients:
- 8 ounces ground beef/240g
- 20 wonton wrappers
- 1 carrot,grated
- 1 large egg,beaten
- 1 garlic clove,minced
- ½cup grated cabbage/65g
- 2 tbsps olive oil/30ml
- 2 tbsps coconut aminos/30g
- ½tbsp melted ghee/7.5ml
- ½tbsp ginger powder/7.5g
- ½tsp salt/2.5g
- ½tsp freshly ground black pepper/2.5g

Directions:
1. Put the Crisping Basket in the pot.Close the crisping lid,choose Air Crisp,set the temperature to 400°F or 205°C,and the time to 5 minutes;press Start/Stop.In a large bowl,mix the beef,cabbage,carrot,egg,garlic,coconut aminos,ghee,ginger,salt,and black pepper.

2. Put the wonton wrappers on a clean flat surface and spoon 1 tbsp of the beef mixture into the middle of each wrapper.
3. Run the edges of the wrapper with a little water; fold the wrapper to cover the filling into a semi-circle shape and pinch the edges to seal. Brush the dumplings with olive oil.
4. Lay the dumplings in the preheated basket, choose Air Crisp, set the temperature to 400°F or 205°C, and set the time to 12 minutes. Choose Start/Stop to begin frying.
5. After 6 minutes, open the lid, pull out the basket and shake the dumplings. Return the basket to the pot and close the lid to continue frying until the dumplings are crispy to your desire.

Bacon-wrapped Halloumi Cheese

Servings: 8
Cooking Time: 10 Minutes
Ingredients:
- 1-pound halloumi cheese
- 8 oz bacon, sliced
- 1 teaspoon olive oil

Directions:
1. Cut the cheese into 8 sticks.
2. Wrap every cheese stick into the sliced bacon and sprinkle with olive oil.
3. Place the wrapped sticks in the cooker basket and lower the air fryer lid.
4. Cook the snack for 4 minutes from each side. Serve it warm.

Nutrition:
- InfoCalories: 365; Fat: 29.4g; Carbohydrates: 1.9g; Protein: 22.7g

Nutmeg Peanuts

Servings: 8
Cooking Time: 1.5 Hour
Ingredients:
- 3 cups peanuts in shells
- 1 tablespoon salt
- 4 cups of water
- ½ teaspoon nutmeg

Directions:
1. Combine the water, nutmeg, and salt together.
2. Stir the mixture well until salt is dissolved.
3. Transfer the water in the Ninja Foodi's insert.
4. Add peanuts in shells and Close the Ninja Foodi's lid.
5. Cook the dish on the "Pressure" mode for 90 minutes.
6. Once done, remove the peanuts from the Ninja Foodi's insert.
7. Let the peanuts cool before serving.

Nutrition:
- InfoCalories: 562; Fat: 36.8g; Carbohydrates: 8.57g; Protein: 28g

Caribbean Chicken Skewers

Servings: 8
Cooking Time: 30 Minutes
Ingredients:
- 2 tsp jerk seasoning
- 1 lime, juiced
- 1 tbsp. extra virgin olive oil
- 1 lb. chicken, boneless, skinless & cut in 1-inch cubes
- 1 red onion, cut in 1-inch pieces
- 1 cup cherry tomatoes
- 1 cup fresh pineapple, cut in 1-inch cubes
- 1 very ripe plantain, peel on, sliced
- ½ tsp salt
- ½ tsp pepper
- Nonstick cooking spray

Directions:
1. If using wood skewers, soak them in water for 30 minutes.
2. In a large bowl, combine jerk seasoning, lime juice, and olive oil.
3. Add the chicken, onions, and tomatoes and toss to coat. Cover and refrigerate 20 minutes.
4. Thread skewers with chicken, onion, tomatoes, pineapple, and plantains, leaving a little space at both ends. Sprinkle skewers with salt and pepper.
5. Lightly spray the rack with cooking spray and place in the cooking pot. Place the skewers on top.
6. Add the tender-crisp lid and set to air fry on 400°F. Cook skewers 25-30 minutes until chicken is cooked through. Baste with marinade and turn over halfway through cooking time. Serve.

Nutrition:
- InfoCalories 127, Total Fat 3g, Total Carbs 11g, Protein 13g, Sodium 173mg.

Asparagus Fries With Chipotle Dip

Servings: 4
Cooking Time: 10 Minutes
Ingredients:
- Nonstick cooking spray
- 1 lb. asparagus, ends trimmed
- 1/3 cup panko bread crumbs
- ¼ cup parmesan cheese
- ¼ tsp pepper
- ½ tsp salt, divided
- 1/8 tsp garlic powder
- 1/8 tsp cayenne pepper
- 3 tbsp. skim milk
- 1 cup Greek yogurt
- 1 tbsp. chipotle peppers, pureed
- 1 clove garlic, diced fine

Directions:
1. Lightly spray fryer basket with cooking spray.
2. In a small bowl, combine bread crumbs, parmesan, pepper, salt, garlic powder, and cayenne pepper, mix well.
3. Pour milk in a shallow dish.
4. Dip asparagus in the milk then dredge in crumb mixture, pressing crumbs to stick. Place asparagus in a single layer in the basket.
5. Place the basket in the cooking pot and add the tender-crisp lid. Select air fry on 425°F. Cook 8-10 minutes until golden brown, turning halfway through cooking time. Repeat with remaining asparagus.
6. In a small bowl, stir together yogurt, peppers, garlic, and remaining salt. Serve with fried asparagus for dipping.

Nutrition:
- InfoCalories 133, Total Fat 5g, Total Carbs 16g, Protein 8g, Sodium 505mg.

Louisiana Crab Dip

Servings:8
Cooking Time:50 Minutes
Ingredients:
- 2 tablespoons unsalted butter
- 3 garlic cloves,minced
- ½cup mayonnaise
- 1 pound whipped or room temperature cream cheese
- 2 teaspoons Worcestershire sauce
- 3 teaspoons hot sauce
- 3 teaspoons freshly squeezed lemon juice
- 2 teaspoons Creole seasoning
- ¾cup Parmesan cheese
- 1 pound lump crab meat

Directions:
1. Select SEAR/SAUTÉand set to MED.Select START/STOP to begin.Let preheat for 3 minutes.
2. Add the butter and garlic and sautéfor 2 minutes.
3. Add the mayonnaise,cream cheese,Worcestershire sauce,hot sauce,lemon juice,Creole seasoning,and Parmesan cheese.Stir well.
4. Add the crab meat and lightly fold to incorporate.Close crisping lid.
5. Select BAKE/ROAST,set temperature to 350°F,and set time to 40 minutes.Select START/STOP to begin
6. When cooking is complete,open lid.Let cool for 10 minutes before serving.

Nutrition:
- InfoCalories:391,Total Fat:39g,Sodium:976mg,Carbohydrates:4g,Protein:16g.

Charred Broccoli With Mustard Cream Sauce

Servings:4
Cooking Time:13 Minutes
Ingredients:
- 2 heads broccoli,trimmed into florets
- 2 tablespoons extra-virgin olive oil
- Sea salt
- ½cup heavy(whipping)cream
- 2 tablespoons brown mustard
- 1 tablespoon freshly squeezed lemon juice

Directions:
1. Place Cook&Crisp Basket in pot.Close crisping lid.Select AIR CRISP,set temperature to 390°F,and set time to 5 minutes.Select START/STOP to begin preheating.
2. In a large bowl,toss the broccoli with the oil.Season with salt.
3. Once unit has preheated,open lid and place the broccoli in the basket.Close crisping lid.
4. Select AIR CRISP,set temperature to 390°F,and set time to 13 minutes.Select START/STOP to begin.
5. In a medium bowl,whisk together the heavy cream,brown mustard,and lemon juice.Season with salt.
6. After 5 minutes,open lid,then lift basket and shake the broccoli or toss them with silicone-tipped tongs.Lower basket back into pot and close lid to continue cooking.
7. After 5 minutes,check for desired crispness.Continue cooking up to 3 minutes more if necessary.
8. When cooking is complete,serve the broccoli topped with the mustard cream sauce.

Nutrition:
- InfoCalories:421,Total Fat:19g,Sodium:206mg,Carbohydrates:16g,Protein:7g.

Pull Apart Cheesy Garlic Bread

Servings:6
Cooking Time:25 Minutes
Ingredients:
- ½pound store-bought pizza dough
- 3 tablespoons unsalted butter,melted
- 4 garlic cloves,minced
- ¼cup shredded Parmesan cheese
- ¼cup shredded mozzarella cheese
- ¼cup minced parsley
- ½teaspoon kosher salt
- ½teaspoon garlic powder
- Cooking spray
- Marinara sauce,for serving

Directions:
1. Cut the pizza dough into 1-inch cubes.Roll each cube into a ball.Place the dough balls in a large bowl.Add the butter,garlic,Parmesan cheese,mozzarella cheese,parsley,salt,and garlic powder.Toss,ensuring everything is evenly coated and mixed.Set aside.
2. Close crisping lid.Select BAKE/ROAST,set temperature to 325°F,and set time to 30 minutes.Select START/STOP to begin.Let preheat for 5 minutes.
3. Coat the Ninja Multi-Purpose Pan with cooking spray.Place the dough balls in the pan and place pan on Reversible Rack,making sure it is in the lower position.
4. Once unit has preheated,open lid and insert the rack in pot.Close lid and cook for 25 minutes.
5. Once cooking is complete,open lid and let the bread cool slightly.Serve with marinara sauce for dipping.

Nutrition:
- InfoCalories:182,Total Fat:10g,Sodium:514mg,Carbohydrates:20g,Protein:6g.

Cheesy Fried Risotto Balls

Servings:6
Cooking Time:45 Minutes
Ingredients:
- ½cup extra-virgin olive oil,plus 1 tablespoon
- 1 small yellow onion,diced
- 2 garlic cloves,minced
- 5 cups vegetable broth
- ½cup white wine
- 2 cups arborio rice
- ½cup shredded mozzarella cheese
- ½cup shredded fontina cheese
- ½cup grated Parmesan cheese,plus more for garnish
- 2 tablespoons chopped fresh parsley
- 1 teaspoon sea salt
- 1 teaspoon freshly ground black pepper
- 2 cups fresh bread crumbs
- 2 large eggs

Directions:
1. Select SEAR/SAUTÉand set to MD:HI.Select START/STOP to begin.Allow the pot to preheat for 5 minutes.
2. Add 1 tablespoon of oil and the onion to the preheated pot.Cook until soft and translucent,stirring occasionally.Add the garlic and cook for 1 minute.

3. Add the broth, wine, and rice to the pot; stir to incorporate. Assemble the pressure lid, making sure the pressure release valve is in the SEAL position.
4. Select PRESSURE and set to HI. Set the time to 7 minutes. Press START/STOP to begin.
5. When pressure cooking is complete, allow pressure to naturally release for 10 minutes. After 10 minutes, quick release any remaining pressure by turning the pressure release valve to the VENT position. Carefully remove the lid when the unit has finished releasing pressure.
6. Add the mozzarella, fontina, and Parmesan cheeses, the parsley, salt, and pepper. Stir vigorously until the rice begins to thicken. Transfer the risotto to a large mixing bowl and let cool.
7. Meanwhile, clean the pot. In a medium mixing bowl, stir together the bread crumbs and the remaining ½ cup of olive oil. In a separate mixing bowl, lightly beat the eggs.
8. Divide the risotto into 12 equal portions and form each one into a ball. Dip each risotto ball in the beaten eggs, then coat in the breadcrumb mixture.
9. Arrange half of the risotto balls in the Cook&Crisp Basket in a single layer.
10. Close the crisping lid. Select AIR CRISP, set the temperature to 400°F, and set the time to 10 minutes. Select START/STOP to begin.
11. Repeat steps 9 and 10 to cook the remaining risotto balls.

Nutrition:
- InfoCalories:722,Total Fat:33g,Sodium:1160mg,Carbohydrates:81g,Protein:23g.

Butter-flower Medley

Servings: 10
Cooking Time: 15 Minutes
Ingredients:
- 3 cups butternut squash, peel&cut in 1-inch cubes
- 1 head cauliflower, separated into florets
- 2 cloves garlic
- 1 tbsp. skim milk
- ½ tsp onion powder
- ¼ tsp thyme
- 1/8 tsp salt
- 1/8 tsp black pepper
- 1 tbsp. butter
- 1 tbsp. parmesan cheese, reduced fat

Directions:
1. Add the squash, cauliflower, and garlic to the cooking pot. Pour in ½ cup water. Add the lid and select pressure cooking on high. Set the timer for 8 minutes.
2. When timer goes off use natural release to remove the lid. Drain the vegetables and place in a large bowl.
3. Add remaining ingredients, except parmesan, and beat until smooth.
4. Transfer the squash mixture back to the cooking pot and sprinkle top with parmesan cheese. Add the tender-crisp lid and select air fry on 400°F. Cook 5-6 minutes or until top is lightly browned. Serve.

Nutrition:
- InfoCalories 47, Total Fat 1g, Total Carbs 8g, Protein 2g, Sodium 68mg.

Cheesy Tangy Arancini

Servings: 6
Cooking Time: 105 Min
Ingredients:
- ½ cup olive oil, plus 1 tbsp/140ml
- 2 large eggs
- 2 garlic cloves, minced
- 1 small white onion; diced
- ½ cup apple cider vinegar/125ml
- 2 cups short grain rice/260g
- 2 cups fresh panko bread crumbs/260g
- 5 cups chicken stock/1250ml
- 1½ cups grated Parmesan cheese, plus more for garnish/195g
- 1 cup chopped green beans/130g
- 1 tsp salt/5g
- 1 tsp freshly ground black pepper/5g

Directions:
1. Choose Sear/Sautéon the pot and set to Medium High. Choose Start/Stop to preheat the pot. Add 1 tbsp of oil and the onion, cook the onion until translucent, add the garlic and cook further for 2 minutes or until the garlic starts getting fragrant.
2. Stir in the stock, vinegar, and rice. Seal the pressure lid, choose pressure, set to High, and set the time to 7 minutes; press Start.
3. After cooking, perform a natural pressure release for 10 minutes, thenaquick pressure release and carefully open the pressure lid.
4. Stir in the Parmesan cheese, green beans, salt, and pepper to mash the rice until a risotto forms. Spoon the mixture intoabowl and set aside to cool completely.
5. Clean the pot and in a bowl, combine the breadcrumbs and the remaining olive oil. In another bowl, lightly beat the eggs.
6. Form 12 balls out of the risotto or as many as you can get. Dip each into the beaten eggs, and coat in the breadcrumb mixture.
7. Put half of the rice balls in the Crisping Basket inasingle layer. Close the crisping lid, hit Air Crisp, set the temperature to 400°F or 205°C, and set the time to 10 minutes; press Start. Leave to cool before serving.

Crispy Delicata Squash

Servings: 4
Cooking Time: 15 Minutes
Ingredients:
- 1 large delicata squash, seeds removed and sliced
- 1 tablespoon extra-virgin olive oil
- ¼ teaspoon sea salt

Directions:
1. Place Cook&Crisp Basket in pot. Close crisping lid. Select AIR CRISP, set temperature to 390°F, and set time to 5 minutes. Select START/STOP to begin preheating.
2. In a large bowl, toss the squash with the olive oil and season with salt.
3. Once unit has preheated, place the squash in the basket. Close crisping lid.
4. Select AIR CRISP, set temperature to 390°F, and set time to 15 minutes. Select START/STOP to begin.
5. After 7 minutes, open the lid, then lift the basket and shake the squash. Lower the basket back into pot. Close lid and continue cooking until the squash achieves your desired crispiness.

Nutrition:
- InfoCalories:75,Total Fat:4g,Sodium:117mg,Carbohydrates:10g,Protein:2g.

Ninja Foodi Cookbook

Mini Steak Kebabs

Servings: 12
Cooking Time: 10 Minutes
Ingredients:
- 1 lb. flank steak, cut in 24 thin slices
- ½ cup peanut butter, reduced fat
- 2 tbsp. light soy sauce
- 2 tsp sesame oil
- 1 tbsp. butter
- 1 tsp red pepper flakes

Directions:
1. Soak 24 6-inch wood skewers in water for 15 minutes.
2. Set cooker to air fryer function on 350°F. Lightly spray the fryer basket with cooking spray.
3. Thread sliced beef on prepared skewers.
4. In a small saucepan over low heat, combine remaining ingredients. Cook, stirring frequently, until butters are melted and sauce is smooth.
5. Place skewers in fryer basket in single layer, these will need to be cooked in batches. Brush sauce over them, making sure to coat them all.
6. Add tender-crisp lid and bake 8-10 minutes, turning over halfway through cooking time and brushing with sauce again. Repeat with remaining skewers. Serve.

Nutrition:
- InfoCalories 131, Total Fat 8g, Total Carbs 4g, Protein 11g, Sodium 178mg.

Parmesan Stuffed Mushrooms

Servings: 5
Cooking Time: 15 Minutes
Ingredients:
- 1 lb. button mushrooms, wash & remove stems
- 2 tbsp. olive oil, divided
- ¼ cup parmesan cheese, fat free
- 2 cloves garlic, diced fine
- ¼ cup cream cheese, fat free, soft
- ¼ cup whole wheat panko bread crumbs

Directions:
1. Place the rack in the cooking pot and top with a piece of parchment paper.
2. Brush the mushrooms with 1 tablespoon oil.
3. In a small bowl, combine parmesan, garlic, and cream cheese until smooth. Spoon 1 teaspoon of the mixture into each mushroom. Place mushrooms on parchment paper.
4. In a separate small bowl, stir together bread crumbs and remaining oil. Sprinkle over tops of mushrooms.
5. Add the tender-crisp lid and select bake on 375°F. Cook mushrooms 15 minutes, or until tops are nicely browned and mushrooms are tender. Serve immediately.

Nutrition:
- InfoCalories 121, Total Fat 6g, Total Carbs 10g, Protein 7g, Sodium 191mg.

Crispy Cheesy Straws

Servings: 8
Cooking Time: 45 Min
Ingredients:
- 2 cups cauliflower florets, steamed/260g
- 5 oz. cheddar cheese/150g
- 3½ oz. oats/105g
- 1 egg
- 1 red onion; diced
- 1 tsp mustard/5g
- Salt and pepper, to taste

Directions:
1. Add the oats in a food processor and process until they resemble breadcrumbs. Place the steamed florets in a cheesecloth and squeeze out the excess liquid.
2. Put the florets in a large bowl, and add the rest of the ingredients to the bowl.
3. Mix well with your hands, to combine the ingredients thoroughly.
4. Take a little bit of the mixture and twist it into a straw. Place in the lined Ninja Foodi basket; repeat with the rest of the mixture.
5. Close the crisping lid and cook for 10 minutes on Air Crisp mode at 350°F or 177°C. After 5 minutes, turn them over and cook for an additional 10 minutes.

South Of The Border Corn Dip

Servings: 8
Cooking Time: 2 Hours
Ingredients:
- 33 oz. corn with chilies
- 10 oz. tomatoes & green chilies, diced
- 8 oz. cream cheese, cubed
- ½ cup cheddar cheese, grated
- ¼ cup green onions, chopped
- ½ tsp garlic, diced fine
- ½ tsp chili powder

Directions:
1. Place all ingredients in the cooking pot and stir to mix.
2. Add the lid and set to slow cooking function on low heat. Set timer for 2 hours. Stir occasionally.
3. Dip is done when all the cheese is melted and it's bubbly. Stir well, then transfer to serving bowl and serve warm.

Nutrition:
- InfoCalories 225, Total Fat 13g, Total Carbs 24g, Protein 7g, Sodium 710mg.

Sweet Potato Fries

Servings: 4
Cooking Time: 20 Minutes
Ingredients:
- Nonstick cooking spray
- ½ tsp cumin
- ½ tsp chili powder
- ½ tsp pepper
- ½ tsp salt
- ¼ tsp cayenne pepper
- 2 sweet potatoes, peeled & julienned
- 1 tbsp. extra-virgin olive oil

Directions:
1. Lightly spray fryer basket with cooking spray.
2. In a small bowl, combine cumin, chili powder, pepper, salt, and cayenne pepper.
3. Place potatoes in a large bowl and sprinkle spice mix and oil over them. Toss well to coat.
4. Place the fries, in small batches, in the basket and place in the cooking pot.
5. Add the tender-crisp lid and select air fryer on 425°F. Cook fries 15-20 minutes, until crispy on the outside and tender inside, turning halfway through cooking time. Serve immediately.

Nutrition:
- InfoCalories 86, Total Fat 3g, Total Carbs 13g, Protein 1g, Sodium 327mg.

Ninja Foodi Cookbook

Cashew Cream

Servings: 10
Cooking Time: 10 Minutes
Ingredients:
- 3 cups cashew
- 2 cups chicken stock
- 1 teaspoon salt
- 1 tablespoon butter
- 2 tablespoons ricotta cheese

Directions:
1. Combine the cashews with the chicken stock in the Ninja Foodi's insert.
2. Add salt and close the Ninja Foodi's lid.
3. Cook the dish in the "Pressure" mode for 10 minutes.
4. Remove the cashews from the Ninja Foodi's insert and drain the nuts from the water.
5. Transfer the cashews to a blender, and add the ricotta cheese and butter.
6. Blend the mixture until it is smooth. When you get the texture you want, remove it from a blender.
7. Serve it immediately, or keep the cashew butter in the refrigerator.

Nutrition:
- InfoCalories: 252; Fat: 20.6g; Carbohydrates: 13.8g; Protein: 6.8 g

Mini Shrimp Tacos

Servings: 8
Cooking Time: 5 Minutes
Ingredients:
- Nonstick cooking spray
- 3 tsp chili powder
- ¼ tsp salt, divided
- 24 medium shrimp, peel, devein & remove tails
- Juice of 1 lime, divided
- 1 avocado, peeled & chopped
- 1/3 cup sour cream, fat free
- 1 tsp cumin
- 2 tbsp. cilantro, chopped, divided
- 24 multigrain tortilla chip scoops

Directions:
1. Spray fryer basket with cooking spray.
2. In a large Ziploc bag, combine chili powder and 1/8 teaspoon salt. Add shrimp and toss to coat evenly.
3. Place shrimp, in a single layer, in the fryer basket. Drizzle half the lime juice over shrimp.
4. Add the tender-crisp lid and set to air fryer function on 375°F. Cook shrimp 5-8 minutes or until they are all pink, stirring halfway through cooking time.
5. In a small bowl, combine avocado and remaining salt and lime juice. Mix well.
6. In a separate small bowl, whisk together sour cream, cumin, and 1 tablespoon cilantro.
7. To assemble: place 1 teaspoon of avocado mixture and ½ teaspoon of sour cream mixture in each chip. Top with a shrimp and sprinkle of cilantro. Serve.

Nutrition:
- InfoCalories 77, Total Fat 4g, Total Carbs 7g, Protein 4g, Sodium 235mg.

Zucchini Chips

Servings: 6
Cooking Time: 10 Minutes
Ingredients:
- Nonstick cooking spray
- 1/3 cup whole wheat bread crumbs
- ¼ cup parmesan cheese, reduced fat
- ½ tsp garlic powder
- 1/8 tsp cayenne pepper
- 3 tbsp. skim milk
- 1 zucchini, cut in 1/4-inch slices

Directions:
1. Spray the rack with cooking spray and place in the cooking pot.
2. In a medium bowl, combine bread crumbs, parmesan, garlic powder, and cayenne pepper.
3. Pour milk into a shallow dish.
4. Dip the zucchini first in the milk then the crumb mixture. Lay them in a single layer on the rack.
5. Add the tender-crisp lid and set to air fry on 400°F. Cook zucchini 10 minutes, or until crisp and lightly browned. Serve immediately.

Nutrition:
- InfoCalories 39, Total Fat 1g, Total Carbs 5g, Protein 2g, Sodium 111mg.

Herbed Cauliflower Fritters

Servings: 7
Cooking Time: 13 Minutes
Ingredients:
- 1-pound cauliflower
- 1 medium white onion
- 1 teaspoon salt
- ½ teaspoon ground white pepper
- 1 tablespoon sour cream
- 1 teaspoon turmeric
- ½ cup dill, chopped
- 1 teaspoon thyme
- 3 tablespoons almond flour
- 1 egg
- 2 tablespoons butter

Directions:
1. Wash the cauliflower and separate it into the florets.
2. Chop the florets and place them in a blender.
3. Peel the onion and dice it. Add the diced onion to a blender and blend the mixture.
4. When you get the smooth texture, add salt, ground white pepper, sour cream, turmeric, dill, thyme, and almond flour.
5. Add egg blend the mixture well until a smooth dough form.
6. Remove the cauliflower dough from a blender and form the medium balls.
7. Flatten the balls a little. Set the Ninja Foodi's insert to "Sauté" mode.
8. Add the butter to the Ninja Foodi's insert and melt it.
9. Add the cauliflower fritters in the Ninja Foodi's insert, and sauté them for 6 minutes.
10. Flip them once. Cook the dish in "Sauté" stew mode for 7 minutes.
11. Once done, remove the fritters from the Ninja Foodi's insert.
12. Serve immediately.

Nutrition:
- InfoCalories: 143; Fat: 10.6g; Carbohydrates: 9.9g; Protein: 5.6g

Ninja Foodi Cookbook

Buttery Chicken Meatballs

Servings: 6
Cooking Time: 90 Min
Ingredients:
- 1 pound ground chicken/450g
- 1 green bell pepper, minced
- 1 egg
- 2 celery stalks, minced
- ¼cup hot sauce/62.5ml
- ½cup water/125ml
- ¼cup panko bread crumbs/32.5g
- ¼cup crumbled queso fresco/32.5g
- 2 tbsps melted butter/30ml

Directions:
1. Choose Sear/Sauté on the pot and set to High. Choose Start/Stop to preheat the pot. Meanwhile, in a bowl, evenly combine the chicken, bell pepper, celery, queso fresco, hot sauce, breadcrumbs, and egg. Form meatballs out of the mixture.
2. Then, pour the melted butter into the pot and fry the meatballs in batches until lightly browned on all sides. Use a slotted spoon to remove the meatballs onto a plate.
3. Put the Crisping Basket in the pot. Pour in the water and put all the meatballs in the basket. Seal the pressure lid, choose Pressure, set to High, and set the timer to 5 minutes. Choose Start/Stop to begin cooking.
4. When done cooking, perform a quick pressure release and carefully open the lid. Close the crisping lid. Choose Air Crisp, set the temperature to 360°F, and set the time to 10 minutes; press Start.
5. After 5 minutes, open the lid, lift the basket and shake the meatballs. Return the basket to the pot and close the lid to continue cooking until the meatballs are crispy.

Enchilada Bites

Servings: 12
Cooking Time: 25 Minutes
Ingredients:
- ½lb. ground turkey
- ¾cup mild red enchilada sauce
- ½cup black beans, drained & rinsed
- ½tsp cumin
- 1 tbsp. cilantro, chopped
- Nonstick cooking spray
- 6 whole wheat tortillas, 6-inch
- 1 cup cheddar cheese, reduced fat, grated fine

Directions:
1. Add turkey to the cooking pot and set cooker to sautéon medium heat. Cook 8-10 minutes until no longer pink.
2. Add enchilada sauce, beans, cumin, and cilantro, stir to mix. Reduce heat to low and simmer 5 minutes. Transfer to a bowl.
3. Lightly spray fryer basket with cooking spray.
4. Spray both sides of the tortillas. Spread 2 tablespoons turkey mixture over each tortilla and top with 4 teaspoons cheese. Roll up tightly and secure with a toothpick. Cut each roll in half and place them in a single layer in the basket.
5. Add the tender-crisp lid and set to air fryer on 375°F. Bake 8-10 minutes, or until cheese has melted. Cut each roll in half and serve.

Nutrition:
- InfoCalories 135, Total Fat 4g, Total Carbs 15g, Protein 9g, Sodium 465mg.

Italian Pita Crisps

Servings: 8
Cooking Time: 15 Minutes
Ingredients:
- 4 whole wheat pita breads
- 1/3 cup finely chopped parsley
- 1 teaspoon Italian herb seasoning
- 1/3 cup finely grated fresh parmesan cheese

Directions:
1. With a sharp knife, cut away the outside edge of each pita. Open the pitas up into 2 halves. Cut each half into 4 wedges.
2. In a small bowl, combine parsley, seasoning, and parmesan.
3. Place pita wedges, in a single layer in the fryer basket, these will need to be cooked in batches. Sprinkle with some of the parmesan mixture.
4. Add the tender-crisp lid and set to air fryer function on 350°F. Bake 12-15 minutes or until golden brown. Repeat with remaining pitas and seasoning.

Nutrition:
- InfoCalories 103, Total Fat 4g, Total Carbs 18g, Protein 4g, Sodium 303mg.

Zesty Brussels Sprouts With Raisins

Servings: 4
Cooking Time: 45 Min
Ingredients:
- 14 oz. Brussels sprouts, steamed/420g
- 2 oz. toasted pine nuts/60g
- 2 oz. raisins/60g
- 1 tbsp olive oil/15ml
- Juice and zest of 1 orange

Directions:
1. Soak the raisins in the orange juice and let sit for about 20 minutes. Drizzle the Brussels sprouts with the olive oil, and place them in the basket of the Ninja Foodi.
2. Close the crisping lid and cook for 15 minutes on Air Crisp mode at 370°F or 188°C. Remove to a bowl and top with pine nuts, raisins, and orange zest.

Chicken Meatballs With Dill Dipping Sauce

Servings: 8
Cooking Time: 15 Minutes
Ingredients:
- Nonstick cooking spray
- 1 lb. lean ground chicken
- 1 tsp oregano
- 1 cup whole wheat panko bread crumbs
- 1 egg, beaten
- 1/3 cup milk
- 2 cloves garlic, diced fine
- 1/3 cup red onions, diced fine
- 1/3 cup fresh parsley, chopped fine
- ¾tsp salt, divided
- ¼tsp black pepper
- 1 cup plain Greek yogurt, low fat
- 1/3 cup fresh dill, chopped fine
- 1 lemon, zest and juice
- ½tsp cumin

- 1/8 tsp cayenne pepper

Directions:
1. Lightly spray the fryer basket with cooking spray.
2. In a large bowl,combine chicken,oregano,bread crumbs,egg,milk,garlic,onions,parsley,½teaspoon salt,and black pepper until thoroughly combined.Form into 1-inch meatballs.
3. Place meatballs in the basket in a single layer,do not over crowd.Add the tender crisp lid and set to air fry on 400°F.Cook meatballs 10-15 minutes until cooked through,turning over halfway through cooking time.
4. In a small bowl,stir together yogurt,dill,lemon zest and juice,remaining salt,cumin,and cayenne pepper until combined.
5. Serve meatballs with sauce for dipping.

Nutrition:
- InfoCalories 174,Total Fat 7g,Total Carbs 13g,Protein 14g,Sodium 386mg.

Wrapped Asparagus In Bacon

Servings:6
Cooking Time:30 Min
Ingredients:
- 1 lb.bacon;sliced/450g
- 1 lb.asparagus spears,trimmed/450g
- ½cup Parmesan cheese,grated/65g
- Cooking spray
- Salt and pepper,to taste

Directions:
1. Place the bacon slices out on a work surface,top each one with one asparagus spear and half of the cheese.Wrap the bacon around the asparagus.
2. Line the Ninja Foodi basket with parchment paper.Arrange the wraps into the basket,scatter over the remaining cheese,season with salt and black pepper,and spray with cooking spray.Close the crisping lid and cook for 8 to 10 minutes on Roast mode at 370°F or 188°C.If necessary,work in batches.Serve hot!

Sweet Potato Skins

Servings:4
Cooking Time:20 Minutes
Ingredients:
- 2 sweet potatoes,baked&halved lengthwise
- 1 tsp olive oil
- 2 cloves garlic,diced fine
- 1 tbsp.fresh lime juice
- 2 cups baby spinach
- ½cup chicken,cooked&shredded
- 1 tsp oregano
- 1 tsp cumin
- 2 tsp chili powder
- ½cup mozzarella cheese,grated
- ¼cup cilantro,chopped

Directions:
1. Scoop out the center of the potatoes,leaving some on the side to help keep the shape.
2. Set the cooker to sauté on med-high heat and add the oil.
3. Once the oil is hot,add garlic,lime juice,and spinach.Cook 2-3 minutes until spinach is wilted.
4. In a large bowl,mash the sweet potato centers until almost smooth.
5. Stir in chicken,oregano,cumin,and chili powder.Stir in spinach until combined.
6. Place the rack in the cooking pot and top with parchment paper.
7. Spoon the potato mixture into the skins and top with cheese.Place on the rack.
8. Add the tender-crisp lid and set to bake on 400°F.Bake 15-20 minutes until cheese is melted and lightly browned.Let cool slightly then cut each skin in 4 pieces and serve garnished with cilantro.

Nutrition:
- InfoCalories 132,Total Fat 2g,Total Carbs 20g,Protein 9g,Sodium 155mg.

Cheesy Stuffed Mushroom

Servings:7
Cooking Time:7 Minutes
Ingredients:
- 12 ounces Parmesan cheese
- 7 mushroom caps
- 2 teaspoons minced garlic
- ¼sour cream
- 1 teaspoon butter
- 1 teaspoon ground white pepper
- 2 teaspoons oregano

Directions:
1. Mix the minced garlic,sour cream,ground white pepper,and oregano,and stir the mixture.
2. Add grated parmesan to the minced garlic mixture.
3. Blend the mixture until smooth.
4. Stuff the mushrooms with the cheese mixture and place the dish in the Ninja Foodi's insert.
5. Set the Ninja Foodi's insert to"Pressure"mode,add butter,and close the Ninja Foodi's lid.
6. Cook the dish for 7 minutes.
7. Once done,remove it from the Ninja Foodi's insert,let it rest briefly,and serve.

Nutrition:
- InfoCalories:203;Fat:7.6g;Carbohydrates:8.35g;Protein:8g

Dill Butter

Servings:7
Cooking Time:5 Minutes
Ingredients:
- 1 cup butter
- 1 teaspoon minced garlic
- 1 teaspoon dried oregano
- 1 teaspoon dried cilantro
- 1 tablespoon dried dill
- 1 teaspoon salt
- ½teaspoon black pepper

Directions:
1. Set"Sauté"mode and place butter inside the Ninja Foodi's insert.
2. Add minced garlic,dried oregano,dried cilantro,butter,dried dill,salt,and black pepper.
3. Stir the mixture well and sauté it for 4-5 minutes or until the butter is melted.
4. Then switch off the cooker and stir the butter well.
5. Transfer the butter mixture into the butter mould and freeze it.

Nutrition:
- InfoCalories:235;Fat:26.3g;Carbohydrates:0.6g;Protein:0.4g

Mini Crab Cakes

Servings: 9
Cooking Time: 10 Minutes
Ingredients:
- Nonstick cooking spray
- 2/3 cup Italian seasoned bread crumbs
- ½ cup egg substitute
- ½ red bell pepper, chopped fine
- ½ red onion, chopped fine
- 1 stalk celery, chopped fine
- 3 tbsp. lite mayonnaise
- 2 tsp fresh lemon juice
- ½ tsp salt
- ¾ tsp pepper
- 1 tsp dried tarragon
- 2 cans lump crabmeat, drained

Directions:
1. Lightly spray fryer basket with cooking spray.
2. In a large bowl, combine all ingredients, except crab, until combined. Gently fold in crab. Form into 36 patties. Place them in a single layer in the fryer basket without overcrowding them.
3. Add the tender-crisp lid and set to air fry on 350°F. Cook patties 3-5 minutes per side until golden brown. Repeat with remaining patties. Serve warm.

Nutrition:
- InfoCalories 96, Total Fat 2g, Total Carbs 8g, Protein 10g, Sodium 543mg.

Zesty Meatballs

Servings: 12
Cooking Time: 15 Minutes
Ingredients:
- Nonstick cooking spray
- 1 lb. ground pork
- ½ cup plain bread crumbs
- ¼ cup water
- 1 onion, chopped
- ¼ cup fresh parsley, chopped
- 1 tsp fennel seed, crushed
- ½ tsp garlic powder
- ¼ tsp cayenne pepper
- ½ tsp salt
- ½ tsp black pepper

Directions:
1. Set to air fryer on 350°F. Lightly spray fryer basket with cooking spray and put in the cooking pot.
2. In a large bowl, combine all ingredients thoroughly. Form into 1-inch balls.
3. Place meatballs in a single layer in the fryer basket, these will need to be cooked in batches.
4. Add the tender-crisp lid and bake 15 minutes, or until no longer pink. Turn meatballs over halfway through cooking time. Transfer to serving plate.

Nutrition:
- InfoCalories 109, Total Fat 8g, Total Carbs 2g, Protein 7g, Sodium 127mg.

Honey Bourbon Wings

Servings: 6
Cooking Time: 11 Minutes
Ingredients:
- ¾ cup ketchup
- 1 tbsp. Liquid Smoke
- ½ cup brown sugar
- ¼ cup onion, chopped fine
- 2 cloves garlic, chopped fine
- ½ cup water
- ¼ cup bourbon
- 3 tbsp. honey
- 2 tsp paprika
- ¼ tsp cayenne pepper
- 1 tsp salt
- ½ tsp pepper
- 4-5 lb. chicken wings

Directions:
1. Set cooker to sauté on medium heat.
2. Add ketchup, liquid smoke, brown sugar, onion, and garlic to the cooking pot. Cook, stirring often, until sauce starts to thicken, about 5 minutes. Turn off the cooker.
3. Stir in water, bourbon, honey, and seasonings until combined.
4. Add the wings and stir to coat.
5. Secure the lid and set to pressure cooking on high for 5 minutes. When the timer goes off use quick release to remove the lid.
6. Line the fryer basket with foil.
7. Transfer the wings to the basket. Set cooker to sauté on medium again and cook sauce until thickened. Pour sauce into a large bowl.
8. Place the basket in the cooking pot and add the tender-crisp lid. Set to air fry on 400°F. Cook wings 6 minutes. Dunk in sauce to coat the wings, then air fry another 6 minutes. Serve with any remaining sauce for dipping.

Nutrition:
- InfoCalories 636, Total Fat 13g, Total Carbs 36g, Protein 84g, Sodium 972mg.

Cheesy Stuffed Onions

Servings: 6
Cooking Time: 1 Hour
Ingredients:
- 3 onions, peeled & cut in half horizontally
- 1 tbsp. olive oil
- ¼ cup cream cheese, reduced fat, soft
- 2 tbsp. sour cream, fat free
- 1 clove garlic, diced fine
- 1 tsp fresh rosemary, diced fine
- 1/8 tsp salt
- 1/8 tsp pepper
- 2 tbsp. panko bread crumbs
- 1 tbsp. butter, melted
- 1 tsp bacon bits

Directions:
1. Place onions, cut side up, in the cooking pot. Drizzle with oil.
2. Add the tender-crisp lid and select air fry on 400°F. Cook onions for 40 minutes. Transfer to wire rack and let cool enough to handle.
3. Carefully remove the center of the onion so you have a shell.
4. In a small bowl, combine cream cheese, sour cream, garlic, rosemary, salt, and pepper. Spread over and into the onions.
5. In a separate small bowl, combine bread crumbs, butter, and bacon.

Ninja Foodi Cookbook

6. Place the rack in the cooking pot and top with a sheet of parchment paper. Place the onions back in the pot and sprinkle the tops with bacon mixture.
7. Add the tender-crisp lid and set to bake on 400°F. Bake onions another 10-15 minutes or until golden brown. Serve.
Nutrition:
- InfoCalories 93, Total Fat 6g, Total Carbs 8g, Protein 2g, Sodium 127mg.

Rosemary Potato Fries

Servings: 4
Cooking Time: 30 Min
Ingredients:
- 4 russet potatoes, cut into sticks
- 2 garlic cloves, crushed
- 2 tbsp butter, melted/30ml
- 1 tsp fresh rosemary; chopped/5g
- Salt and pepper, to taste

Directions:
1. Add butter, garlic, salt, and pepper to a bowl; toss until the sticks are well-coated. Lay the potato sticks into the Ninja Foodi's basket. Close the crisping lid and cook for 15 minutes at 370°F or 188°C. Shake the potatoes every 5 minutes.
2. Once ready, check to ensure the fries are golden and crispy all over if not, return them to cook for a few minutes.
3. Divide standing up between metal cups lined with nonstick baking paper, and serve sprinkled with rosemary.

Popcorn Chicken

Servings: 4
Cooking Time: 15 Minutes
Ingredients:
- Nonstick cooking spray
- 1 cup cornflakes, crushed
- ½ cup Bisquick baking mix, reduced fat
- ½ tsp garlic powder
- ½ tsp salt
- ¼ tsp pepper
- ½ tsp paprika
- ¾ lb. chicken breasts, boneless, skinless & cut in 1-inch pieces

Directions:
1. Lightly spray fryer basket with cooking spray.
2. In a large Ziploc bag, combine cornflakes, baking mix, garlic powder, salt, pepper, and paprika, shake to mix.
3. Add chicken and shake to coat.
4. Place chicken in basket in single layer, spray lightly with cooking spray.
5. Add the tender-crisp lid and set to air fry on 400°F. Cook chicken 12-15 minutes until crispy on the outside and no longer pink on the inside, turning over halfway through cooking time. Serve immediately.
Nutrition:
- InfoCalories 179, Total Fat 3g, Total Carbs 17g, Protein 21g, Sodium 596mg.

Cheesy Bacon Brussel Sprouts

Servings: 6
Cooking Time: 15 Minutes
Ingredients:
- Nonstick cooking spray
- 3 slices turkey bacon, chopped
- 2 tsp olive oil
- 1 lb. Brussels sprouts, trimmed & cut in half
- 2 cloves garlic, diced fine
- ¼ cup water
- 3 oz. goat cheese, soft
- 2 tbsp. skim milk
- 1 tbsp. parmesan cheese
- ¼ tsp salt
- ¼ tsp pepper
- 1 tsp paprika

Directions:
1. Spray the cooking pot with cooking spray. Set to sauté on med-high heat.
2. Add bacon and cook until crisp, transfer to paper-towel line plate.
3. Add oil and let it get hot. Add Brussel sprouts and cook, stirring frequently, 5 minutes or until they start to brown.
4. Add water, cover and cook another 5 minutes or until fork-tender. Drain any water from the pot.
5. Add goat cheese, milk, parmesan, salt, and pepper. Cook, stirring frequently, until cheese has melted.
6. Stir in bacon and cook until heated through. Sprinkle with paprika and serve.
Nutrition:
- InfoCalories 106, Total Fat 6g, Total Carbs 8g, Protein 7g, Sodium 274mg.

Crispy Chicken Skin

Servings: 7
Cooking Time: 10 Minutes
Ingredients:
- 1 teaspoon red chili flakes
- 1 teaspoon black pepper
- 1 teaspoon salt
- 9 ounces of chicken skin
- 2 tablespoons butter
- 1 teaspoon olive oil
- 1 teaspoon paprika

Directions:
1. Combine the black pepper, chilli flakes, and paprika together.
2. Stir the mixture and combine it with the chicken skin.
3. Let the mixture rest for 5 minutes. Set the Ninja Foodi's insert to "Sauté" mode.
4. Add the butter to the Ninja Foodi's insert and melt it.
5. Add the chicken skin and sauté it for 10 minutes, stirring frequently.
6. Once the chicken skin gets crunchy, remove it from the Ninja Foodi's insert.
7. Place the chicken skin on the paper towel and drain.
8. Serve warm.
Nutrition:
- InfoCalories: 134; Fat: 11.5g; Carbohydrates: 0.98g; Protein: 7g

Ninja Foodi Cookbook

Cumin Baby Carrots

Servings: 4
Cooking Time: 25 Min
Ingredients:
- 1¼lb.baby carrots/562.5g
- 1 handful cilantro;chopped
- 2 tbsp olive oil/30ml
- ½tsp cumin powder/2.5g
- ½tsp garlic powder/2.5g
- 1 tsp cumin seeds/5g
- 1 tsp salt/5g
- ½tsp black pepper/2.5g

Directions:
1. Place the baby carrots in a large bowl.Add cumin seeds,cumin,olive oil,salt,garlic powder,and pepper,and stir to coat them well.
2. Put the carrots in the Ninja Foodi's basket,close the crisping lid and cook for 20 minutes on Roast mode at 370°F or 188°C.Remove to a platter and sprinkle with chopped cilantro,to serve.

Cheesy Chicken Dip

Servings: 6
Cooking Time: 2 Hours
Ingredients:
- 1 lb.cheddar cheese,cubed
- 2 cups chicken,cooked&shredded
- 4 oz.cream cheese,cubed
- 1 cup tomatoes,diced
- 1 cup black beans,drained&rinsed
- ½cup black olives,pitted&sliced
- 1 jalapeno,seeded&diced
- 2 tbsp.taco seasoning

Directions:
1. Place all ingredients in the cooking pot and stir to mix.
2. Add the lid and set to slow cooking on low heat.Set timer for 2 hours.Let dip cook,stirring occasionally until hot and bubbly and the cheese has melted.
3. Stir well then transfer to a serving dish and serve warm.

Nutrition:
- InfoCalories 507,Total Fat 35g,Total Carbs 12g,Protein 35g,Sodium 1022mg.

Parmesan Butternut Crisps

Servings: 4
Cooking Time: 20 Minutes
Ingredients:
- 1 butternut squash,peeled,seeded&halved lengthwise
- 1½tsp salt
- ½tsp fresh rosemary,chopped
- 1/8 tsp cayenne pepper
- 2 tbsp.extra-virgin olive oil
- ¼cup parmesan cheese,reduced fat

Directions:
1. Bring a large pot of water to a boil.
2. Cut the squash in 1/8-1/4-inch thick slices.When water is boiling,add squash and boil 1-2 minutes.Drain and rinse in cold water.Pat dry.
3. Place the rack in the cooking pot and line with parchment paper.
4. In a small bowl,combine salt,rosemary,and cayenne pepper.
5. Place the squash in a large bowl,sprinkle the spice mixture and oil over the top and toss well to coat.
6. Lay slices in a single layer on the parchment paper,these will need to be cooked in batches,and sprinkle with parmesan.
7. Add the tender-crisp lid,set to air fry on 350°F.Bake the chips 15-20 minutes or until golden brown.Store in an airtight container.

Nutrition:
- InfoCalories 108,Total Fat 8g,Total Carbs 8g,Protein 2g,Sodium 971mg.

Cheeseburger Boats

Servings: 9
Cooking Time: 20 Minutes
Ingredients:
- 3 bell peppers
- 1 lb.lean ground beef
- 1 onion,chopped fine
- ½tsp salt
- ½tsp pepper
- 2/3 cup ketchup,divided
- 1 tbsp.mustard
- 5 slices cheddar cheese,reduced fat

Directions:
1. Place the rack in the cooking pot and top with a sheet of parchment paper.
2. Cut peppers in 6 vertical pieces,using the indention lines as a guide.Remove ribs and seeds.
3. In a large bowl,combine beef,onion,salt,pepper,1/3 cup ketchup,and mustard.Spoon mixture into peppers.
4. Place peppers on parchment paper,these will need to be cooked in batches.Add the tender-crisp lid and select bake on 375°F.Bake 20 minutes,or until meat is no longer pink.
5. Drizzle with some of the remaining ketchup and top with ¼slice of cheese.Cook about 5 minutes more or until cheese has melted.Serve immediately.

Nutrition:
- InfoCalories 175,Total Fat 7g,Total Carbs 10g,Protein 18g,Sodium 479mg.

Apple Pecan Cookie Bars

Servings: 12
Cooking Time: 20 Minutes
Ingredients:
- Nonstick cooking spray
- 2/3 cup sugar
- 2 egg whites
- ½tsp vanilla
- ½cup flour
- 1 tsp baking powder
- 2 cups Granny Smith apples,chopped
- ¼cup pecans,chopped

Directions:
1. Lightly spray an 8-inch baking pan with cooking spray.
2. In a large bowl,whisk together egg whites,sugar,and vanilla until frothy.
3. Whisk in flour and baking powder until combined.
4. Fold in apples and nuts and pour into pan.
5. Place the rack in the cooking pot and place the pan on it.Add the tender-crisp lid and set to air fry on 350°F.Bake 18-20 minutes or until the cookies pass the toothpick test.
6. Let cool before cutting and serving.

Nutrition:
- InfoCalories 90,Total Fat 2g,Total Carbs 18g,Protein 1g,Sodium 10mg.

Ninja Foodi Cookbook

Spicy Black Bean Dip

Servings:12
Cooking Time:20 Minutes
Ingredients:
- 2 16 oz.cans black beans,rinsed&drained,divided
- 1 cup salsa,divided
- 1 tsp olive oil
- ¾onion,diced fine
- 1 red bell pepper,diced fine
- 3 cloves garlic,diced fine
- 1 tbsp.cilantro
- 2 tsp cumin
- ¼tsp salt
- ¼cup cheddar cheese,reduced fat,grated
- 1 tomato,chopped

Directions:
1. Add 1 can beans and¼cup salsa to a food processor or blender.Pulse until smooth.
2. Set cooker to sautéon medium heat.Add oil and let it get hot.
3. Add the onion,pepper,and garlic and cook,stirring occasionally,5-7 minutes,or until vegetables are tender.
4. Add the pureed bean mixture along with remaining ingredients except cheese and tomatoes,mix well.Reduce heat to low and bring to a simmer.Let cook 5 minutes,stirring frequently.
5. Transfer dip to serving bowl and top with cheese and tomato.Serve immediately.

Nutrition:
- InfoCalories 100,Total Fat 2g,Total Carbs 16g,Protein 6g,Sodium 511mg.

Apricot Snack Bars

Servings:16
Cooking Time:25 Minutes
Ingredients:
- Butter flavored cooking spray
- ¾cup oats
- ¾cup flour
- ¼cup brown sugar
- ¾tsp vanilla
- ¼cup butter
- ¾cup apricot preserves,sugar free

Directions:
1. Lightly spray an 8-inch baking pan with cooking spray.Place the rack in the cooking pot.
2. In a large bowl,combine oats,flour,sugar,and vanilla until combined.
3. With a pastry blender or a fork,cut the butter in until mixture is crumbly.Press half the mixture in the bottom of the pan.
4. Spread the preserves over the top of the oat mixture and sprinkle the remaining oat over the top,gently press down.
5. Place the pan on the rack and add the tender-crisp lid.Set to air fry on 350°F.Bake 25-30 minutes until golden brown and bubbly.
6. Transfer to a wire rack and let cool before cutting.

Nutrition:
- InfoCalories 100,Total Fat 3g,Total Carbs 18g,Protein 2g,Sodium 3mg.

Herby Fish Skewers

Servings:4
Cooking Time:75 Min
Ingredients:
- 1 pound cod loin,boneless,skinless;cubed/450g
- 2 garlic cloves,grated
- 1 lemon,juiced and zested
- 1 lemon,cut in wedges to serve
- 3 tbsp olive oil/45ml
- 1 tsp dill;chopped/5g
- 1 tsp parsley;chopped/5g
- Salt to taste

Directions:
1. In a bowl,combine the olive oil,garlic,dill,parsley,salt,and lemon juice.Stir in the cod and place in the fridge to marinate for 1 hour.Thread the cod pieces onto halved skewers.
2. Arrange into the oiled Ninja Foodi basket;close the crisping lid and cook for 10 minutes at 390°F or 199°C.Flip them over halfway through cooking.When ready,remove toaserving platter,scatter lemon zest and serve with wedges.

Cauliflower Gratin

Servings:6
Cooking Time:28 Minutes
Ingredients:
- 2 cups water
- 1 large head cauliflower,cut into 1-inch florets
- 3 tablespoons unsalted butter
- 3 tablespoons all-purpose flour
- 1½cups whole milk
- 1 cup heavy(whipping)cream
- 2 tablespoons capers,drained
- 1 tablespoon fresh thyme
- Kosher salt
- Freshly ground black pepper
- ¾cup shredded Swiss cheese
- ¼cup grated Parmesan cheese

Directions:
1. Pour the water in the pot.Place the Reversible Rack in the lower position in the pot.Place the cauliflower on the rack.Assemble pressure lid,making sure the pressure release valve is in the SEAL position.
2. Select PRESSURE and set to HI.Set time to 5 minutes.Select START/STOP to begin.
3. When pressure cooking is complete,quick release the pressure by turning the pressure release valve to the VENT position.Carefully remove lid when the unit has finished releasing pressure.
4. Remove rack and place the cauliflower in the Ninja Multi-Purpose Pan or 8-inch baking dish.Drain the water from the pot and wipe it dry.Reinsert pot into base.
5. Select SEAR/SAUTÉand set temperature to HI.Select START/STOP to begin.Let preheat for 5 minutes.
6. Add the butter.Once melted,add the onion and cook 3 minutes.Add the flour and cook,stirring constantly,1 minute.
7. Add the milk,cream,capers,and thyme.Season with salt and pepper.Bring to a boil and cook,about 4 minutes.
8. Pour the sauce over the cauliflower.Place the pan onto the Reversible Rack,making sure the rack is in the lower position.Place the rack with pan in the pot.Close crisping lid.
9. Select BAKE/ROAST,set temperature to 400°F,and set time to 20 minutes.Select START/STOP to begin.

Ninja Foodi Cookbook

10. After 15 minutes, open lid and sprinkle the cauliflower with the Swiss and Parmesan cheeses. Close lid and continue cooking.
11. Once cooking is complete, open lid. Let the gratin sit for 10 minutes before serving.
Nutrition:
- InfoCalories:341,Total Fat:27g,Sodium:263mg,Carbohydrates:16g,Protein:11g.

Chipotle-lime Chicken Wings
Servings:4
Cooking Time:28 Minutes
Ingredients:
- ½cup water
- 2 pounds frozen chicken wings
- ¼cup extra-virgin olive oil
- 2 tablespoons chipotle chiles in adobo sauce,chopped
- Juice of 2 limes
- Zest of 1 lime
- 1 tablespoon minced garlic
- Sea salt
- Freshly ground black pepper

Directions:
1. Pour the water in the pot. Place the wings in the Cook&Crisp Basket and insert basket in pot. Assemble pressure lid, making sure the pressure release valve is in the SEAL position.
2. Select PRESSURE and set to HI. Set time to 5 minutes. Select START/STOP to begin.
3. In a large bowl mix together the olive oil, chipotles in adobo sauce, lime juice, lime zest, and garlic. Season with salt and pepper.
4. When pressure cooking is complete, quick release the pressure by turning the pressure release valve to the VENT position. Carefully remove lid when unit has finished releasing pressure.
5. Transfer the chicken wings to the large bowl and toss to coat. Place the wings back in the basket. Close crisping lid.
6. Select AIR CRISP, set temperature to 375°F, and set time to 15 minutes. Select START/STOP to begin.
7. After 7 minutes, open lid, then lift the basket and shake the wings. Lower the basket back into pot. Close lid and continue cooking until the wings reach your desired crispiness.

Nutrition:
- InfoCalories:560,Total Fat:45g,Sodium:942mg,Carbohydrates:2g,Protein:38g.

Tangy Jicama Chips
Servings:8
Cooking Time:10 Minutes
Ingredients:
- Nonstick cooking spray
- 1 jicama, peeled&sliced very thin
- 2 tbsp.extra virgin olive oil
- 1½tsp lemon pepper seasoning

Directions:
1. Lightly spray the fryer basket with cooking spray.
2. Place the sliced jicama in a large bowl. Drizzle oil over the top and sprinkle with lemon pepper. Toss well to coat.
3. Place chips, in batches, in the basket. Place in cooker and add the tender-crisp lid. Set to air fry on 350°F. Cook 10 minutes until golden brown and crips, turning over halfway through cooking time. Repeat with remaining jicama. Serve.

Nutrition:
- InfoCalories 61,Total Fat 3g,Total Carbs 7g,Protein 1g,Sodium 3mg.

Pork Shank
Servings:6
Cooking Time:45 Minutes
Ingredients:
- 1-pound pork shank
- ½cup parsley,chopped
- 4 garlic cloves
- 1 teaspoon salt
- ½teaspoon paprika
- 2 tablespoons olive oil
- 1 teaspoon cilantro,chopped
- 1 tablespoon celery
- 1 carrot,grated
- 1 cup of water
- 1 red onion,chopped
- ⅓cup wine
- 2 tablespoons lemon juice

Directions:
1. Chop the parsley and slice the garlic cloves.
2. Combine the vegetables together and add salt, paprika, cilantro, wine, and lemon juice and stir the mixture.
3. Combine the pork shank and marinade together and leave the mixture.
4. Combine the sliced onion and grated carrot together.
5. Add celery and blend well. Add the vegetables to the pork shank mixture and stir using your hands.
6. Place the meat in the Ninja Foodi's insert and add water.
7. Close the Ninja Foodi's lid, and set the Ninja Foodi to"Pressure."
8. Cook for 45 minutes. Once done, remove the meat from the Ninja Foodi's insert and chill the dish well.
9. Slice the pork shank and serve.

Nutrition:
- InfoCalories:242;Fat:19.8g;Carbohydrates:5.38g;Protein: 11g

Three-layer Taco Dip
Servings:6
Cooking Time:15 Minutes
Ingredients:
- 2 cans pinto beans,rinsed and drained
- 1 white onion,chopped
- 8 garlic cloves,chopped
- 1 can diced tomatoes
- 1 serrano chile,seeded and chopped
- 1 teaspoon kosher salt
- 2 teaspoons ground cumin
- 2 teaspoons chili powder
- 2 cups shredded Mexican blend cheese
- 1 cup shredded iceberg lettuce

Directions:
1. Place the beans, onions, garlic, tomatoes, chile, salt, cumin, and chili powder in the pot. Assemble pressure lid, making sure the pressure release valve is in the SEAL position.
2. Select PRESSURE and set to HI. Set time to 5 minutes. Select START/STOP to begin.

Ninja Foodi Cookbook

3. When pressure cooking is complete,quick release the pressure by moving the pressure release valve to the VENT position.Carefully remove lid when unit has finished releasing pressure.
4. Using a silicone spatula,stir the mixture in the pot.Sprinkle shredded cheese across the top of the bean mixture.Close crisping lid.
5. Select BROIL and set time to 10 minutes.Select STOP/START to begin.
6. When cooking is complete,open lid.Let cool for 5 minutes,then add the shredded lettuce.Serve immediately.

Nutrition:
- InfoCalories:327,Total Fat:14g,Sodium:612mg,Carbohydrates:33g,Protein:19g.

Cauliflower Nuggets

Servings:8
Cooking Time:10 Minutes
Ingredients:
- 8 ounces cauliflower
- 1 big red onion,chopped
- 2 carrots
- ½cup almond flour
- ¼cup pork rinds
- 2 eggs
- 1 teaspoon salt
- ½teaspoon red pepper
- ⅓teaspoon ground white pepper
- 1 tablespoon olive oil
- 1 teaspoon dried dill

Directions:
1. Peel the red onion and carrots.Chop the vegetables roughly and transfer them to the food processor.
2. Wash the cauliflower and separate it into the florets.
3. Add the cauliflower florets to a food processor and puree until smooth.
4. Add the eggs and salt.Blend the mixture for 3 minutes,then transfer to a mixing bowl.
5. Add pork rinds,red pepper,ground white pepper,and dill.
6. Blend the mixture until smooth.Form the nuggets from the vegetable mixture and dip them in the almond flour.
7. Spray the Ninja Foodi's insert with olive oil inside.
8. Place the vegetable nuggets in the Ninja Foodi's insert and cook them on the"Sauté"mode for 10 minutes.
9. Once the nuggets are cooked,remove from the Ninja Foodi's insert and serve.

Nutrition:
- InfoCalories:85;Fat:5.1g;Carbohydrates:5.9g;Protein:5g

Gingered Butternut Squash

Servings:6
Cooking Time:15 Minutes
Ingredients:
- 8 cups butternut squash,peeled,seeded,&cut in 1-inch cubes
- 1 cup water
- ½tsp salt
- 4 tbsp.butter
- ¼cup half n half
- 3 tbsp.honey
- ½tsp ginger
- ¼tsp cinnamon

Directions:
1. Add the squash,water,and salt to the cooking pot,stir.
2. Add the lid and select pressure cooking on high.Set timer for 12 minutes.When the timer goes off,use quick release to remove the lid.
3. Drain the squash and place in a large bowl.
4. Add remaining ingredients.Set cooker to saute on medium heat.Cook until butter melts,stirring occasionally
5. Once the butter melts,pour the sauce over the squash and mash with a potato masher.Serve.

Nutrition:
- InfoCalories 198,Total Fat 9g,Total Carbs 31g,Protein 2g,Sodium 267mg.

Chicken Bites

Servings:4
Cooking Time:8 Minutes
Ingredients:
- ½cup Italian seasoned bread crumbs
- 2 tablespoons grated Parmesan cheese
- ¼teaspoon sea salt
- ¼teaspoon freshly ground black pepper
- 1 boneless,skinless chicken breast,cut into 1-inch pieces
- ½cup unsalted butter,melted
- Cooking spray

Directions:
1. Place Cook&Crisp Basket in pot.Close crisping lid.Select AIR CRISP,set temperature to 390°F,and set time to 5 minutes.Select START/STOP to begin preheating.
2. In a medium bowl,combine the bread crumbs,Parmesan cheese,salt,and pepper.In a separate medium bowl,toss the chicken in the butter until well coated.Move a few of the chicken pieces to the breadcrumb mixture and coat.Repeat until all the chicken is coated.
3. Once unit is preheated,open lid and place the chicken bites in the basket in a single layer.Coat well with cooking spray.Close lid.
4. Select AIR CRISP,set temperature to 390°F,and set time to 8 minutes.Select START/STOP to begin.
5. After 4 minutes,open lid,then lift basket and flip the chicken bites with silicone-tipped tongs.Coat well with cooking spray.Lower basket back into pot and close lid to continue cooking.
6. After 4 minutes,check for desired crispness.Cooking is complete when the internal temperature of the chicken reads at least 165°F on a food thermometer.

Nutrition:
- InfoCalories:279,Total Fat:25g,Sodium:246mg,Carbohydrates:5g,Protein:10g.

Strawberry Snack Bars

Servings:16
Cooking Time:30 Minutes
Ingredients:
- Butter flavored cooking spray
- 1 cup butter,soft
- 2 oz.stevia
- 1 tbsp.sour cream,reduced fat
- 1 egg
- 1 cup flour
- 1 cup whole wheat flour
- 1 cup strawberry jam,sugar free
- 1 tbsp.brown sugar
- 2 tbsp.walnuts,chopped

Directions:
1. Spray an 8-inch square pan with cooking spray.

2. In a medium bowl, beat butter and Stevia until creamy.
3. Beat in sour cream and egg until combined.
4. Stir in both flours, ½ cup at a time, until mixture forms a soft dough.
5. Press half the dough in the bottom of the prepared pan. Spread the jam over the top. Then spread the other half of the dough gently over the top. Sprinkle the brown sugar and nuts over the top.
6. Place the rack in the cooking pot and place the pan on it. Add the tender-crisp lid and set to bake on 375°F. Bake 25-30 minutes until bubbly and golden brown.
7. Transfer to wire rack to cool before cutting.

Nutrition:
- InfoCalories 195, Total Fat 13g, Total Carbs 22g, Protein 3g, Sodium 97mg.

Spinach Hummus

Servings: 12
Cooking Time: 1 Hr 10 Min
Ingredients:
- 2 cups spinach; chopped/260g
- ½ cup tahini/65g
- 2 cups dried chickpeas/260g
- 8 cups water/2000ml
- 5 garlic cloves, crushed
- 5 tbsp grapeseed oil/75ml
- 2 tsp salt; divided/10g
- 5 tbsp lemon juice/75ml

Directions:
1. In the pressure cooker, mix 2 tbsp oil, water, 1 tsp or 5g salt, and chickpeas. Seal the pressure lid, choose Pressure, set to High, and set the timer to 35 minutes. Press Start. When ready, release the pressure quickly. In a small bowl, reserve ½ cup of the cooking liquid and drain chickpeas.
2. Mix half the reserved cooking liquid and chickpeas in a food processor and puree until no large chickpeas remain; add remaining cooking liquid, spinach, lemon juice, remaining tsp salt, garlic, and tahini.
3. Process hummus for 8 minutes until smooth. Stir in the remaining 3 tbsp or 45ml of olive oil before serving.

Chicken Lettuce Wraps

Servings: 6
Cooking Time: 30 Minutes
Ingredients:
- 8 ounces chicken fillet
- ¼ cup tomato juice
- 5 tablespoon sour cream
- 1 teaspoon black pepper
- 8 ounces lettuce leaves
- 1 teaspoon salt
- ½ cup chicken stock
- 1 teaspoon butter
- 1 teaspoon turmeric

Directions:
1. Chop the chicken fillet roughly and sprinkle it with sour cream, tomato juice, black pepper, turmeric, and salt.
2. Mix up the meat mixture. Put the chicken spice mixture in the Ninja Foodi's insert and add chicken stock.
3. Close the Ninja Foodi's lid and cook the dish in the "Sauté" mode for 30 minutes.
4. Once the chicken is done, remove it from the Ninja Foodi's insert and shred it well.
5. Add the butter and blend well. Transfer the shredded chicken to the lettuce leaves.
6. Serve the dish warm.

Nutrition:
- InfoCalories:138; Fat:7.4g; Carbohydrates:12.63g; Protein:6g

Jalapeno Salsa

Servings: 10
Cooking Time: 7 Minutes
Ingredients:
- 8 ounces jalapeno pepper
- ¼ cup Erythritol
- 5 tablespoon water
- 2 tablespoons butter
- 1 teaspoon paprika

Directions:
1. Wash the jalapeno pepper and remove the seeds.
2. Slice it into thin circles. Sprinkle the sliced jalapeno pepper with paprika and Erythritol.
3. Put the butter and jalaeno mixture into the Ninja Foodi's insert and add water.
4. Set the Ninja Foodi's insert to "Sauté" mode.
5. Once the butter melts, add the sliced jalapeno in the Ninja Foodi's insert.
6. Close the Ninja Foodi's lid and sauté the dish for 7 minutes.
7. Once done, remove the dish from the Ninja Foodi's insert.
8. Cool it and serve.

Nutrition:
- InfoCalories:28; Fat:2.5g; Carbohydrates:7.5g; Protein:0.4g

Caponata

Servings: 10
Cooking Time: 30 Minutes
Ingredients:
- 2 tbsp. olive oil
- 1 eggplant, unpeeled & chopped
- 1 onion, chopped
- 2 tbsp. garlic powder
- ½ cup pimiento-stuffed green olives, chopped
- 3 stalks celery, chopped
- 8 oz. tomato sauce
- ¼ cup white vinegar
- 1/3 cup brown sugar, packed
- ¼ tsp hot pepper sauce

Directions:
1. Set cooker to sauté on med-high heat. Add oil and let it get hot.
2. Once oil is hot, add eggplant, onion, and garlic powder and cook 5 minutes, stirring occasionally, until eggplant starts to get soft.
3. Stir in remaining ingredients and reduce heat to low. Cook 25 minutes, or until all the vegetables are tender. Serve warm or cold.

Nutrition:
- InfoCalories 87, Total Fat 3g, Total Carbs 15g, Protein 1g, Sodium 16mg.

Almond Lover's Bars

Servings: 20
Cooking Time: 30 Minutes
Ingredients:
- 2 cups almond flour, sifted
- 1½ cups flour
- 1 tsp baking powder
- ½ tsp salt
- 10 tbsp. butter, soft
- 1 cup sugar
- 2 eggs
- 2 tsp vanilla
- 1 tbsp. powdered sugar

Directions:
1. Line an 8-inch square baking dish with parchment paper.
2. In a medium bowl, whisk together both flours, baking powder, and salt.
3. In a large bowl, beat butter and sugar until creamy.
4. Beat in eggs and vanilla. Then stir in dry ingredients until combined. Press firmly in prepared pan.
5. Place the rack in the cooking pot and place the pan on it. Add the tender-crisp lid and set to bake on 325°F. Bake 25-30 minutes until lightly browned and the bars pass the toothpick test.
6. Let cool before cutting into bars. Sprinkle with powdered sugar before serving.

Nutrition:
- InfoCalories 207, Total Fat 11g, Total Carbs 23g, Protein 3g, Sodium 83mg.

Mushrooms Stuffed With Veggies

Servings: 6
Cooking Time: 25 Minutes
Ingredients:
- 12 large mushrooms, washed
- 1 tbsp. olive oil
- 1 zucchini, grated
- ½ onion, chopped fine
- ½ red bell pepper, chopped fine
- ¼ cup bread crumbs
- ½ tsp garlic powder
- ¼ tsp salt
- ¼ tsp pepper

Directions:
1.
2.
3. Remove stems from mushroom and finely chop them.
4. Add oil to the cooking pot and set to sauté on medium heat.
5. Once oil is hot, add mushroom stems, zucchini, onion, and bell pepper. Cook, stirring occasionally, about 5 minutes or until vegetables are tender.
6. Stir in bread crumbs, garlic powder, salt, and pepper. Transfer mixture to a bowl.
7. Place the rack in the cooking pot and top with parchment paper.
8. Stuff each mushroom cap with vegetable mixture and place on the parchment.
9. Add the tender-crisp lid and set to air fry on 350°F. Bake 15-20 minutes or until mushrooms are tender. Serve immediately.

Nutrition:
- InfoCalories 56, Total Fat 3g, Total Carbs 6g, Protein 2g, Sodium 134mg.

Caramelized Cauliflower With Hazelnuts

Servings: 4
Cooking Time: 15 Minutes
Ingredients:
- 1 head cauliflower, cut in ½-inch thick slices
- 2 cups cold water
- 2 tbsp. olive oil
- 1 tbsp. honey
- ½ tsp fresh lemon juice
- ½ tsp salt
- ¼ tsp pepper
- 1 tbsp. fresh sage, chopped
- 1 tbsp. hazelnuts, toasted & chopped
- ¼ cup parmesan cheese, reduced fat

Directions:
1. Remove any core from the cauliflower slices. Lay them in a single layer in the cooking pot.
2. Add enough water to come halfway up the sides of the cauliflower. Add oil, honey, lemon, salt, and pepper.
3. Set cooker to sauté on high. Cover and cook cauliflower until the water has evaporated, about 6-8 minutes. When it begins to brown reduce heat to low.
4. Once water has evaporated, flip cauliflower over and cook another 5 minutes, or until bottom is golden brown.
5. Transfer to serving plates and top with sage, hazelnuts, and parmesan cheese. Serve.

Nutrition:
- InfoCalories 112, Total Fat 8g, Total Carbs 9g, Protein 3g, Sodium 407mg.

Ninja Foodi Cookbook

Breakfast

Banana Custard Oatmeal
Servings: 6
Cooking Time: 40 Minutes
Ingredients:
- Butter flavored cooking spray
- 1 2/3 cups vanilla almond milk, unsweetened
- 2 large bananas, mashed
- 1 cup bananas, sliced
- 1 cup steel cut oats
- 1/3 cup maple syrup
- 1/3 cup walnuts, chopped
- 2 eggs, beaten
- 1 tbsp. butter, melted
- 1½ tsp cinnamon
- 1 tsp baking powder
- 1 tsp vanilla extract
- ½ tsp nutmeg
- ¼ teaspoon salt
- 2½ cups water

Directions:
1. Spray a 1 1/2–quart baking dish with cooking spray.
2. In a large bowl, combine all ingredients thoroughly. Transfer to prepared baking dish.
3. Pour 1½ cups water into the cooking pot and add the trivet. Place dish on the trivet and secure the lid.
4. Select pressure cooking on high and set timer for 40 minutes.
5. When timer goes off, release pressure naturally for 10 minutes, then use quick release. Stir oatmeal well then serve.

Nutrition:
- InfoCalories 349, Total Fat 10g, Total Carbs 56g, Protein 10g, Sodium 281mg.

Applesauce Pumpkin Muffins
Servings: 8
Cooking Time: 15 Minutes
Ingredients:
- 4 eggs
- ½ cup applesauce, unsweetened
- ½ cup pumpkin
- ½ cup coconut flour
- 2 tbsp. cinnamon
- ¼ tsp cloves
- ¼ tsp ginger
- 1/8 tsp nutmeg
- ¼ tsp salt
- 1 tsp baking soda
- 2 tsp vanilla
- 4 tbsp. coconut oil, melted
- 1 tbsp. honey

Directions:
1. Set cooker to air fryer function on 375°F. Line 2 6-cup muffin tins with paper liners.
2. Add all ingredients to a blender or food processor and blend on low just until combined.
3. Pour batter evenly into prepared tins. Place muffin pans, one at a time, in the cooker and secure the tender-crisp lid. Bake 12-15 minutes or until muffins pass the toothpick test.
4. Let cool in pans 10 minutes, then transfer to wire rack to cool completely.

Nutrition:
- InfoCalories 122, Total Fat 9g, Total Carbs 11g, Protein 3g, Sodium 264mg.

Ham & Hash Brown Casserole
Servings: 12
Cooking Time: 7 Hours
Ingredients:
- Nonstick cooking spray
- 30 oz. hash browns, shredded & frozen
- 1 lb. ham, diced
- 1 onion, diced
- 1 red bell pepper, diced
- 1 orange bell pepper, diced
- 1½ cups cheddar cheese, grated
- 12 eggs
- 1 cup milk
- 4 oz. green chilies, diced
- 1 tbsp. Dijon mustard
- ½ tsp garlic powder
- ½ tsp pepper
- ¼ tsp salt

Directions:
1. Spray the cooking pot with cooking spray.
2. Layer half the hash browns, ham, onions, peppers, and cheese in the pot. Repeat layers.
3. In a large bowl, whisk together the eggs, milk, green chilies, and seasonings until combined. Pour over ingredients in the cooking pot.
4. Secure the lid and set to slow cooker function on low heat. Set the timer for 7 hours. Casserole is done when the eggs are set.

Nutrition:
- InfoCalories 348, Total Fat 18g, Total Carbs 22g, Protein 23g, Sodium 893mg.

Chili Cheese Quiche
Servings: 4
Cooking Time: 30 Minutes
Ingredients:
- Nonstick cooking spray
- 4 eggs
- 1 cup half-n-half
- 10 oz. green chilies, diced
- ½ tsp salt
- ½ tsp cumin
- 1 cup Mexican blend cheese, grated
- ¼ cup cilantro, chopped

Directions:
1. Spray a 6-inch baking pan with cooking spray.
2. In a mixing bowl, beat eggs then stir in half-n-half, chilies, salt, cumin, and half the cheese.
3. Pour into prepared pan and cover with foil.
4. Add 2 cups water to the cooking pot and add the rack. Place the pan on the rack and secure the lid.
5. Select pressure cooking on high and set timer for 20 minutes.

Ninja Foodi Cookbook

6. When timer goes off, release pressure naturally for 10 minutes, then use quick release.
7. Remove the foil and sprinkle remaining cheese over the top. Secure the tender-crisp lid and set to 375°F. Cook another 3-5 minutes or until cheese is melted and starts to brown. Serve garnished with cilantro.

Nutrition:
- InfoCalories 300, Total Fat 23g, Total Carbs 7g, Protein 16g, Sodium 1172mg.

Quinoa Protein Bake

Servings: 4
Cooking Time: 30 Minutes

Ingredients:
- Nonstick cooking spray
- 1 cup white quinoa, cooked
- 3 egg whites, lightly beaten
- ½ tsp salt
- ¼ cup red bell pepper, chopped
- ¼ cup spinach, chopped
- ½ cup mozzarella cheese, grated

Directions:
1. Spray the cooking pot with cooking spray.
2. In a large bowl, combine all ingredients thoroughly. Pour into pot.
3. Add the tender-crisp lid and select air fry on 350°F. Bake 25-30 minutes until lightly browned on top and eggs are completely set.
4. Let cool a few minutes before serving.

Nutrition:
- InfoCalories 191, Total Fat 3g, Total Carbs 28g, Protein 13g, Sodium 441mg.

Cinnamon Sugar Donuts

Servings: 4
Cooking Time: 10 Minutes

Ingredients:
- ⅔ cup all-purpose flour, plus additional for dusting
- 3 tablespoons granulated sugar, divided
- ½ teaspoon baking powder
- ¼ teaspoon, plus ½ tablespoon cinnamon
- ¼ teaspoon sea salt
- 2 tablespoons cold unsalted butter, cut into small pieces
- ¼ cup plus 1½ tablespoons whole milk
- Cooking spray

Directions:
1. In a medium bowl, mix together the flour, 1 tablespoon of sugar, baking powder, ¼ teaspoon of cinnamon, and salt.
2. Use a pastry cutter or two forks to cut in the butter, breaking it up into little pieces until the mixture resembles coarse cornmeal. Add the milk and continue to mix together until the dough forms a ball.
3. Place the dough on a lightly floured work surface and knead it until a smooth ball forms, about 30 seconds. Divide the dough into 8 equal pieces and roll each piece into a ball.
4. Place the Cook&Crisp Basket in the pot. Close crisping lid. Select AIR CRISP, set temperature to 350°F, and set time to 3 minutes. Press START/STOP to begin.
5. Once preheated, coat the basket with cooking spray. Place the dough balls in the basket, leaving room between each. Spray them with cooking spray. Close crisping lid.
6. Select AIR CRISP, set temperature to 350°F, and set time to 10 minutes. Press START/STOP to begin.
7. In a medium bowl, combine the remaining 2 tablespoons of sugar and ½ tablespoon of cinnamon.
8. When cooking is complete, open lid. Place the dough balls in the bowl with the cinnamon sugar and toss to coat. Serve immediately.

Nutrition:
- InfoCalories: 192, Total Fat: 7g, Sodium: 126mg, Carbohydrates: 31g, Protein: 3g.

Spinach Turkey Cups

Servings: 4
Cooking Time: 23 Minutes

Ingredients:
- 1 tablespoon unsalted butter
- 1-pound fresh baby spinach
- 4 eggs
- 7 ounces cooked turkey, chopped
- 4 teaspoons unsweetened almond milk
- Black pepper and salt, as required

Directions:
1. Select the "Sauté/Sear" setting of Ninja Foodi and place the butter into the pot.
2. Press the "Start/Stop" button to initiate cooking and heat for about 2-3 minutes.
3. Add the spinach and cook for about 3 minutes or until just wilted.
4. Press the "Start/Stop" button to pause cooking and drain the liquid completely.
5. Transfer the spinach into a suitable and set aside to cool slightly.
6. Set the "Air Crisp Basket" in the Ninja Foodi's insert.
7. Close the Ninja Foodi's lid with a crisping lid and select "Air Crisp."
8. Set its cooking temperature to 355°F for 5 minutes.
9. Press the "Start/Stop" button to initiate preheating.
10. Divide the spinach into 4 greased ramekins, followed by the turkey.
11. Crack 1 egg into each ramekin and drizzle with almond milk.
12. Sprinkle with black pepper and salt.
13. After preheating, Open the Ninja Foodi's lid.
14. Place the ramekins into the "Air Crisp Basket."
15. Close the Ninja Foodi's lid with a crisping lid and select "Air Crisp."
16. Set its cooking temperature to 355°F for 20 minutes.
17. Press the "Start/Stop" button to initiate cooking.
18. Open the Ninja Foodi's lid and serve hot.

Nutrition:
- InfoCalories: 200; Fat: 10.2g; Carbohydrates: 4.5g; Protein: 23.4g

Butternut Breakfast Squash

Servings: 4
Cooking Time: 15 Minutes

Ingredients:
- 1 tbsp. coconut oil
- 12 oz. butternut squash, cubed
- 1 tbsp. peanut butter
- ¼ tsp cinnamon
- ¼ tsp all-spice
- 2 tsp maple syrup

Directions:
1. Select sauté function on medium heat and add the coconut oil to the cooking pot.

2. Add the squash and cook until it starts to soften, about 8-10 minutes.
3. Add remaining ingredients and mix well. Cook 2-3 minutes longer until heated through. Serve warm.
Nutrition:
- InfoCalories 201, Total Fat 11g, Total Carbs 26g, Protein 3g, Sodium 9mg.

Pumpkin Steel Cut Oatmeal

Servings: 4
Cooking Time: 25 Min
Ingredients:
- ½cup pumpkin seeds, toasted/65g
- 1 cup pumpkin puree/250ml
- 2 cups steel cut oats/260g
- 3 cups water/750ml
- 1 tbsp butter/15g
- 3 tbsp maple syrup/45ml
- ¼tsp cinnamon/1.25g
- ½tsp salt/2.5g

Directions:
1. Melt butter on Sear/Sauté. Add in cinnamon, oats, salt, pumpkin puree and water. Seal the pressure lid, choose Pressure, set to High, and set the timer to 10 minutes; press Start. When cooking is complete, do a quick release.
2. Open the lid and stir in maple syrup and top with toasted pumpkin seeds to serve.

Strawberry Oat Breakfast Bars

Servings: 16
Cooking Time: 25 Minutes
Ingredients:
- 2 cups oats
- ¼cup oat flour
- 1 cup coconut flakes, unsweetened
- 2 tbsp. chia seeds, ground
- ½cup almonds, chopped
- ¼salt
- 2 bananas, mashed
- 2 tbsp. honey
- ¼cup coconut oil, melted
- 1 cup strawberries, chopped
- 1 tsp vanilla

Directions:
1. Set to bake function on 350°F. Line an 8-inch baking dish with parchment paper.
2. In a large bowl, combine dry ingredients.
3. Stir in remaining ingredients until thoroughly combined.
4. Press mixture into prepared pan and place in cooker. Add the tender-crisp lid and bake 25 minutes until golden brown.
5. Let cool before slicing into 2-inch squares.
Nutrition:
- InfoCalories 179, Total Fat 8g, Total Carbs 24g, Protein 5g, Sodium 53mg.

Almond Quinoa Porridge

Servings: 6
Cooking Time: 1 Minute
Ingredients:
- 1¼cups water
- 1 cup almond milk
- 1½cups uncooked quinoa, rinsed
- 1 tablespoon choc zero maple syrup
- 1 cinnamon stick
- Pinch of salt

Directions:
1. In the Ninja Foodi's insert, add all ingredients and stir to combine well.
2. Close the Ninja Foodi's lid with the pressure lid and place the pressure valve in the "Seal" position.
3. Select "Pressure" mode and set it to "High" for 1 minute.
4. Press the "Start/Stop" button to initiate cooking.
5. Now turn the pressure valve to "Vent" and do a "Quick" release.
6. Open the Ninja Foodi's lid, and with a fork, fluff the quinoa.
7. Serve warm.
Nutrition:
- InfoCalories: 186; Fat: 2.6 g; Carbohydrates: 4.8 g; Protein: 6 g

Bacon & Egg Poppers

Servings: 6
Cooking Time: 25 Minutes
Ingredients:
- 12 slices bacon
- 4 jalapeno peppers
- 3 oz. cream cheese, soft
- 8 eggs
- ½tsp garlic powder
- ½tsp onion powder
- Salt & pepper, to taste
- Nonstick cooking spray
- ½cup cheddar cheese, grated

Directions:
1. Select air fryer function and heat cooker to 375°F.
2. Heat a skillet over med-high heat and cook bacon until almost crisp but still pliable. Remove to paper towels to drain and reserve bacon fat for later.
3. Remove the seeds from 3 of the jalapenos and chop them. With the remaining jalapeno, slice into rings.
4. In a large bowl, beat together cream cheese, 1 tablespoon bacon fat, chopped jalapenos, eggs, and seasonings.
5. Spray 2 6-cup muffin tins with cooking spray. Place one slice bacon around the edges of each cup.
6. Pour egg mixture into cups, filling ¾full then top with cheddar cheese and a jalapeno ring.
7. Place muffin pan, one at a time, in the cooker, secure the tender-crisp lid and bake 20-25 minutes, or until eggs are cooked. Repeat with other pan and serve immediately.
Nutrition:
- InfoCalories 399, Total Fat 34g, Total Carbs 3g, Protein 19g, Sodium 666mg.

Cranberry Lemon Quinoa

Servings: 6
Cooking Time: 20 Minutes
Ingredients:
- 16 oz. quinoa
- 4½cups water
- ½cup brown sugar, packed
- 1 tsp lemon extract
- ½tsp salt

- ½ cup cranberries,dried

Directions:
1. Add all ingredients,except the cranberries,to the cooker and stir to mix.
2. Secure the lid and select pressure cooking on high.Set timer for 20 minutes.
3. When timer goes off,use natural release for 10 minutes.Then use quick release and remove the lid.
4. Stir in cranberries and serve.

Nutrition:
- InfoCalories 284,Total Fat 4g,Total Carbs 56g,Protein 8g,Sodium 152mg.

Sausage Wrapped Scotch Eggs

Servings:4
Cooking Time:55 Min
Ingredients:
- 12 ounces Italian sausage patties/360g
- 4 eggs
- 1 cup water/250ml
- 1 cup panko bread crumbs/130g
- Nonstick cooking spray;for preparing the rack
- 2 tbsps melted unsalted butter/30ml

Directions:
1. Pour 1 cup of water into the inner pot.Put the reversible rack in the pot at the bottom,and carefully place the eggs on top.Seal the pressure lid,choose Pressure,set the pressure to High,and the cook time to 3 minutes.Press Start.
2. While cooking the eggs,fill halfabowl with cold water and about a cup full of ice cubes to make an ice bath.
3. After cooking,performaquick pressure release,and carefully open the lid.Use tongs to pick up the eggs into the ice bath.Allow cooling for 3 to 4 minutes;peel the eggs.
4. Pour the water out of the inner pot and return the pot to the base.Grease the reversible rack with cooking spray,fix the rack in the upper position,and place in the pot.
5. Cover the crisping lid;choose Air Crisp,set the temperature to 360°F or 183°C and the timer to 4 minutes.Press Start to preheat.
6. While preheating the pot,place an egg on each sausage patty.Pull the sausage around the egg and seal the edges.
7. In a small bowl,mix the breadcrumbs with the melted butter.One atatime,dredge the sausage-covered eggs in the crumbs while pressing into the breadcrumbs for a thorough coat.
8. Open the crisping lid and place the eggs on the rack.Close the crisping lid;choose Air Crisp,adjust the temperature to 360°F or 183°C,and the cook time to 15 minutes.Press Start.
9. When the timer has ended,the crumbs should be crisp andadeep golden brown color.Remove the eggs and allow cooling for several minutes.Slice the eggs in half and serve.

Maple Dipped Asparagus

Servings:4
Cooking Time:15 Minutes.
Ingredients:
- 2-pounds asparagus,trimmed
- 1/2 teaspoon black pepper
- 1 teaspoon salt
- 1/4 cup choc zero maple syrup
- 2 tablespoons olive oil
- 4 tablespoons tarragon,minced

Directions:
1. Toss asparagus with salt,oil,choc zero maple syrup,black pepper,and tarragon.Toss well.
2. Take Ninja Foodi Grill,set it over your kitchen platform,and open the Ninja Foodi's lid.
3. Set the grill grate and close the Ninja Foodi's lid.
4. Select"Grill"mode and select the"MED"tempcrature.
5. Set the cooking time to about 8 minutes,and then press the"Start/Stop"button to initiate preheating.
6. Set the asparagus over the grill grate.
7. Close the Ninja Foodi's lid and cook for 4 minutes.
8. Now open the Ninja Foodi's lid,flip the asparagus.
9. Close the Ninja Foodi's lid and cook for 4 more minutes.
10. Serve warm.

Nutrition:
- InfoCalories:241;Fat:15g;Carbohydrates:31g;Protein:7.5g

Prosciutto Egg Bake

Servings:4
Cooking Time:45 Min
Ingredients:
- 8 ounces prosciutto;chopped/240g
- 1 cup shredded Monterey Jack cheese/130g
- 1 cup water/250ml
- 1 cup whole milk/250ml
- 1 orange bell pepper,seeded and chopped
- 4 eggs
- 1 tsp salt/5g
- 1 tsp freshly ground black pepper/5g

Directions:
1. Break the eggs intoabowl,pour in the milk,salt,and black pepper and whisk until combined.Stir in the Monterey Jack Cheese.
2. Put the bell pepper and prosciutto in the cake pan.Then,pour over the egg mixture,cover the pan with aluminum foil and put on the reversible rack.
3. Put the rack in the pot and pour in the water.Seal the pressure lid,choose pressure and set to High.Set the time to 20 minutes and choose Start/Stop.
4. When done cooking,do a quick pressure release and carefully remove the lid that is after the pressure has completely escaped.
5. When baking is complete,take the pan out of the pot and set it onaheatproof surface,and cool for 5 minutes.

Homemade Vanilla Yogurt

Servings:6
Cooking Time:8 Hours
Ingredients:
- ½ gallon whole milk
- 3 tablespoons plain yogurt with active live cultures
- ½ tablespoon vanilla extract
- ½ cup honey

Directions:
1. Pour the milk into the pot.Assemble pressure lid,making sure the pressure release valve is in the VENT position.
2. Select YOGURT and set time to 8 hours.Select START/STOP to begin.
3. After the milk has boiled,the display will read COOL.
4. Once cooled,the unit will beep and display ADD&STIR.Remove pressure lid.Add the plain yogurt and whisk until fully incorporated.Reassemble pressure

lid,making sure the pressure release valve is still in the VENT position.
5. When incubating is complete after 8 hours,transfer the yogurt to a glass container or bowl,cover,and refrigerate for a minimum of 8 hours.
6. Once the yogurt has chilled,stir in the vanilla and honey until well combined.Cover and place the glass bowl back in the refrigerator or divide the yogurt into airtight glass jars.The yogurt may be refrigerated up to 2 weeks.
Nutrition:
- InfoCalories:286,Total Fat:11g,Sodium:133mg,Carbohydrates:38g,Protein:11g.

Ricotta Raspberry Breakfast Cake

Servings:12
Cooking Time:40 Minutes
Ingredients:
- Nonstick cooking spray
- 1¼cups oat flour
- ½tsp xanthan gum
- ¼cup cornstarch
- ¼tsp baking soda
- 1½tsp baking powder
- ½tsp salt
- ½cup sugar
- 4 tbsp.butter,unsalted,soft
- 1 cup ricotta cheese,room temperature
- 3 eggs,room temperature,beaten
- 1 tsp vanilla
- 1 cup fresh raspberries

Directions:
1. Set to bake function on 350°F.Lightly spray an 8-inch round baking pan with cooking spray.
2. In a large bowl,combine dry ingredients.
3. Make a well in the center and add butter,ricotta,eggs,and vanilla and mix just until combined.
4. Gently fold in half the berries,being careful not to crush them.
5. Pour batter into prepared pan and sprinkle remaining berries on the top.Add the tender-crisp lid and bake 40 minutes,or until a light brown and only a few moist crumbs show on a toothpick when inserted in the center.
6. Let cool in the pan 10 minutes then transfer to a wire rack to cool completely before serving.
Nutrition:
- InfoCalories 170,Total Fat 8g,Total Carbs 20g,Protein 6g,Sodium 164mg.

Hearty Breakfast Muffins

Servings:12
Cooking Time:20 Minutes
Ingredients:
- ½cup brown sugar
- 3 eggs
- 1/3 cup coconut oil,melted
- 1/3 cup applesauce,unsweetened
- ¼cup orange juice
- 1 tsp vanilla
- 2 cups whole wheat flour
- 2 tsp baking soda
- 2 tsp cinnamon
- ¼tsp salt
- 1½cup carrots,grated
- 1 cup apple,grated
- ¼cup pecans,chopped

Directions:
1. Set to bake function on 375°F.Line 2 6-cup muffin tins with paper liners.
2. In a large bowl,whisk together sugar,eggs,oil,applesauce,orange juice,and vanilla.
3. Stir in flour,baking soda,cinnamon,and salt just until combined.
4. Fold in carrots,apple,and pecans and mix well.Divide evenly among prepared muffin tins.
5. Place tins,one at a time,in the cooker and add the tender-crisp lid.Bake 20-25 minutes,or until muffins pass the toothpick test.Repeat.
6. Let cool in pan 10 minutes,then transfer to wire rack to cool completely.
Nutrition:
- InfoCalories 206,Total Fat 9g,Total Carbs 28g,Protein 5g,Sodium 288mg.

Walnut Orange Coffee Cake

Servings:8
Cooking Time:25 Minutes
Ingredients:
- Butter flavor cooking spray
- 1 cup Stevia
- 1/4 cup butter,unsalted,soft
- 1 egg
- 2 tsp orange zest,grated
- ½tsp vanilla
- 1/8 tsp cinnamon
- 2 cups whole wheat flour
- 1 tsp baking soda
- ½cup orange juice,fresh squeezed
- ½cup water
- ½cup walnuts,chopped

Directions:
1. Select bake function and heat cooker to 350°F.Spray a 7-inch round pan with cooking spray.
2. In a medium bowl,beat Stevia and butter until smooth.
3. Add egg,zest,vanilla,and cinnamon and mix until combined.
4. In a separate bowl,combine dry ingredients.Add to butter mixture and mix until thoroughly combined.Stir in nuts.
5. Spread batter in prepared pan and place in the cooker.Secure the tender-crisp lid and bakke 20-25 minutes,or until it passes the toothpick test.
6. Let cool in pan 10 minutes,then invert onto wire rack.Serve warm.
Nutrition:
- InfoCalories 203,Total Fat 10g,Total Carbs 53g,Protein 6g,Sodium 170mg.

Bell Pepper Frittata

Servings:2
Cooking Time:18 Minutes
Ingredients:
- 1 tablespoon olive oil
- 1 chorizo sausage,sliced
- 1½cups bell peppers,seeded and chopped
- 4 large eggs

- Black pepper and salt, as required
- 2 tablespoons feta cheese, crumbled
- 1 tablespoon fresh parsley, chopped

Directions:
1. Select the "Sauté/Sear" setting of Ninja Foodi and place the butter into the pot.
2. Press the "Start/Stop" button to initiate cooking and heat for about 2-3 minutes.
3. Add the sausage and bell peppers and cook for 6-8 minutes or until golden brown.
4. Meanwhile, in a suitable bowl, add the eggs, salt, and black pepper and beat well.
5. Press the "Start/Stop" button to pasue cooking and place the eggs over the sausage mixture, followed by the cheese and parsley.
6. Close the Ninja Foodi's lid with a crisping lid and select "Air Crisp."
7. Set its cooking temperature to 355°F for 10 minutes.
8. Press the "Start/Stop" button to initiate cooking.
9. Open the Ninja Foodi's lid and transfer the frittata onto a platter.
10. Cut into equal-sized wedges and serve hot.

Nutrition:
- InfoCalories:398;Fat:31g;Carbohydrates:8g;Protein:22.9 g

Bbq Chicken Sandwiches

Servings:4
Cooking Time:45 Min
Ingredients:
- 4 chicken thighs, boneless and skinless
- 1½ cups iceberg lettuce, shredded/195g
- 2 cups barbecue sauce/500ml
- 1 onion, minced
- 2 garlic cloves, minced
- 4 burger buns
- 2 tbsp minced fresh parsley/30g
- 1 tbsp lemon juice/15ml
- 1 tbsp mayonnaise/15ml
- Salt to taste

Directions:
1. Season the chicken with salt, and transfer into the inner pot. Add in garlic, onion and barbeque sauce. Coat the chicken by turning in the sauce. Seal the pressure lid, choose Pressure, set to High, and set the timer to 15 minutes. Press Start.
2. When ready, do a natural pressure release for 10 minutes. Use two forks to shred the chicken and mix into the sauce. Press Sear/Sauté and let the mixture to simmer for 15 minutes to thicken the sauce, until desired consistency.
3. Meanwhile, using a large bowl, mix the lemon juice, mayonnaise, salt, and parsley; toss lettuce into the mixture to coat.
4. Separate the chicken in equal parts to match the sandwich buns; apply lettuce for topping and complete the sandwiches.

Swiss Bacon Frittata

Servings:6
Cooking Time:23 Minutes
Ingredients:
- 1 small onion, chopped
- 1/2 lb. of raw bacon, chopped
- 1 lb. of frozen spinach
- 10 eggs
- 1 cup cottage cheese
- 1/2 cup half and half cream
- 1 tsp salt
- 1 cup shredded swiss cheese

Directions:
1. Preheat your Ninja Foodi for 5 minutes at 350°F on Saute Mode.
2. Add bacon, and onion to the Foodi and saute for 10 minutes until crispy.
3. Stir in spinach and stir cook for 3 minutes.
4. Whisk eggs with cottage cheese, salt and half and half cream in a bowl.
5. Pour this mixture into the Ninja Foodi cooking pot.
6. Drizzle swiss cheese over the egg mixture.
7. Secure the Ninja Foodi lid and switch the Foodi to Bake/Roast mode for 20 minutes at 350°F.
8. Serve warm.

Nutrition:
- InfoCalories 139;Total Fat 10.1g;Total Carbs 2.3g;Protein 10.1 g

Nutmeg Pumpkin Porridge

Servings:8
Cooking Time:5 Hours
Ingredients:
- 1 cup unsweetened almond milk
- 2 pounds pumpkin, peeled and cubed into ½-inch size
- 6-8 drops liquid stevia
- ½ teaspoon ground allspice
- 1 tablespoon ground cinnamon
- 1 teaspoon ground nutmeg
- ¼ teaspoon ground cloves
- ½ cup walnuts, chopped

Directions:
1. In the Ninja Foodi's insert, place ½ cup of almond milk and remaining ingredients and stir to combine.
2. Close the Ninja Foodi's lid with a crisping lid and select "Slow Cooker."
3. Set on "Low" for 4-5 hours.
4. Press the "Start/Stop" button to initiate cooking.
5. Open the Ninja Foodi's lid and stir in the remaining almond milk.
6. With a potato masher, mash the mixture completely.
7. Divide the porridge into serving bowls evenly.
8. Serve warm with the topping of walnuts.

Nutrition:
- InfoCalories:96;Fat:5.5g;Carbohydrates:11.2g;Protein:3.3g

Sweet Bread Pudding

Servings:3
Cooking Time:45 Min
Ingredients:
- 8 slices of bread
- 2 eggs
- ¼ cup sugar/32.5g
- ¼ cup honey/62.5ml
- 1 cup milk/250ml
- ½ cup buttermilk/125ml
- 4 tbsp raisins/60g
- 2 tbsp chopped hazelnuts/30g
- 2 tbsp butter, softened/30g

- ½tsp vanilla extract/2.5ml
- Cinnamon for garnish

Directions:
1. Beat the eggs along with the buttermilk,honey,milk,vanilla,sugar,and butter.Stir in raisins and hazelnuts.Cut the bread into cubes and place it in a bowl.
2. Pour the milk mixture over the bread.Let soak for about 10 minutes.Close the crisping lid and cook the bread pudding for 25 minutes on Roast mode.Leave the dessert to cool for 5 minutes,then invert ontoaplate and sprinkle with cinnamon to serve.

Avocado Cups

Servings:2
Cooking Time:12 Minutes
Ingredients:
- 1 avocado,halved and pitted
- Black pepper and salt,as required
- 2 eggs
- 1 tablespoon Parmesan cheese,shredded
- 1 teaspoon fresh chives,minced

Directions:
1. Set a greased square piece of foil in"Air Crisp Basket."
2. Set the"Air Crisp Basket"in the Ninja Foodi's insert.
3. Close the Ninja Foodi's lid with a crisping lid and select"Bake/Roast."
4. Set its cooking temperature to 390°F for 5 minutes.
5. Press the"Start/Stop"button to initiate preheating.
6. Carefully scoop out about 2 teaspoons of flesh from each avocado half.
7. Crack 1 egg in each avocado half and sprinkle with salt,black pepper,and cheese.
8. After preheating,Open the Ninja Foodi's lid.
9. Place the avocado halves into the"Air Crisp Basket."
10. Close the Ninja Foodi's lid with a crisping lid and Select"Bake/Roast."
11. Set its cooking temperature to 390°F for about 12 minutes.
12. Press the"Start/Stop"button to initiate cooking.
13. Open the Ninja Foodi's lid and transfer the avocado halves onto serving plates.
14. Top with Parmesan and chives and serve.

Nutrition:
- InfoCalories:278;Fat:24.7g;Carbohydrates:9.1g;Protein:8.4g

Chicken Omelet

Servings:2
Cooking Time:16 Minutes
Ingredients:
- 1 teaspoon butter
- 1 small yellow onion,chopped
- ½jalapeño pepper,seeded and chopped
- 3 eggs
- Black pepper and salt,as required
- ¼cup cooked chicken,shredded

Directions:
1. Select the"Sauté/Sear"setting of Ninja Foodi and place the butter into the pot.
2. Press the"Start/Stop"button to initiate cooking and heat for about 2-3 minutes.
3. Add the onion and cook for about 4-5 minutes.
4. Add the jalapeño pepper and cook for about 1 minute.
5. Meanwhile,in a suitable,add the eggs,salt,and black pepper and beat well.
6. Press the"Start/Stop"button to pause cooking and stir in the chicken.
7. Top with the egg mixture evenly.
8. Close the Ninja Foodi's lid with a crisping lid and select"Air Crisp."
9. Set its cooking temperature to 355°F for 5 minutes.
10. Press the"Start/Stop"button to initiate cooking.
11. Open the Ninja Foodi's lid and transfer the omelette onto a plate.
12. Cut into equal-sized wedges and serve hot.

Nutrition:
- InfoCalories:153;Fat:9.1g;Carbohydrates:4g;Protein:13.8g

Glazed Lemon Muffins

Servings:12
Cooking Time:20 Minutes
Ingredients:
- 1 cup flour
- 1 tsp baking powder
- ½tsp baking soda
- ¼tsp salt
- ½cup of coconut oil,melted
- 2 eggs
- 2 tbsp.Stevia
- ¼cup honey
- 1 cup Greek yogurt,low-fat
- 1¼tsp vanilla,divided
- 3 tbsp.+2 tsp fresh lemon juice,divided
- 1½tsp lemon zest
- 2 tbsp.Stevia powdered sugar

Directions:
1. Select bake function and heat to 350°F.Line 2 6-cup muffin tins with paper liners.
2. In a medium bowl,stir together flour,baking powder,baking soda,and salt.
3. In a large bowl,whisk together oil and eggs until smooth.
4. Add Stevia,honey,and yogurt and mix until combined.
5. Whisk in 1 teaspoon vanilla,3 tablespoons lemon juice,and 1 teaspoon zest.Fold in dry ingredients just until combined.
6. Pour batter evenly into prepared muffin tins.Place tins,one at a time in the cooker.Secure the tender-crisp lid and bake 20 minutes or until muffins pass the toothpick test.Remove to wire rack to cool.
7. In a small bowl,whisk together Stevia confectioner's sugar and remaining vanilla,lemon juice,and zest until smooth.Drizzle over the tops of the muffins and serve.

Nutrition:
- InfoCalories 164,Total Fat 10g,Total Carbs 15g,Protein 4g,Sodium 120mg.

Pumpkin Pecan Oatmeal

Servings:4
Cooking Time:10 Minutes
Ingredients:
- 1 cup water
- 2 cups old fashioned oats
- 1¾cup milk
- ½cup pumpkin puree
- 1 tsp pumpkin pie spice
- ¼tsp vanilla

Ninja Foodi Cookbook

- ½ cup maple syrup
- 2 tbsp.pecans,chopped

Directions:
1. Add the water,oats,milk,pumpkin,spice,vanilla,and syrup to the cooking pot.Stir to combine.
2. Secure the lid and select pressure cooking on high.Set timer for 8 minutes.
3. When timer goes off,release pressure naturally for 5 minutes,then use quick release for remaining pressure.
4. Stir oatmeal then ladle into bowls and top with pecans.

Nutrition:
- InfoCalories 526,Total Fat 13g,Total Carbs 86g,Protein 17g,Sodium 54mg.

Pumpkin Coconut Breakfast Bake

Servings:8
Cooking Time:1 Hour 15 Minutes
Ingredients:
- Butter flavored cooking spray
- 5 eggs
- ½ cup coconut milk
- 2 cups pumpkin puree
- 1 banana,mashed
- 2 dates,pitted&chopped
- 1 tsp cinnamon
- 1 cup raspberries
- ¼ cup coconut,unsweetened&shredded

Directions:
1. Lightly spray an 8-inch baking dish with cooking spray.
2. In a large bowl,whisk together eggs and milk.
3. Whisk in pumpkin until combined.
4. Stir in banana,dates,and cinnamon.Pour into prepared dish.
5. Sprinkle berries over top.
6. Place the rack in the cooking pot and place the dish on it.Add the tender-crisp lid and select bake on 350°F.Bake 20 minutes.
7. Sprinkle coconut over the top and bake another 20-25 minutes until top is lightly browned and casserole is set.Slice and serve warm.

Nutrition:
- InfoCalories 113,Total Fat 5g,Total Carbs 14g,Protein 6g,Sodium 62mg.

Carrot Cake Oats

Servings:8
Cooking Time:13 Minutes
Ingredients:
- 2 cups oats
- 1 cup water
- 4 cups unsweetened vanilla almond milk
- 2 apples,diced
- 2 cups shredded carrot
- 1 cup dried cranberries
- ½ cup maple syrup
- 2 teaspoons cinnamon
- 2 teaspoons vanilla extract

Directions:
1. Place all the ingredients in the pot.Assemble pressure lid,making sure the pressure release valve is in the SEAL position.
2. Select PRESSURE and set to LO.Set time to 3 minutes.Select START/STOP to begin.
3. When pressure cooking is complete,allow pressure to naturally release for 10 minutes.Then quick release remaining pressure by moving the pressure release valve to the VENT position.Carefully remove lid when unit has finished releasing pressure.
4. Stir oats,allowing them to cool,and serve with toppings such as chopped walnuts,diced pineapple,or shredded coconut,if desired.

Nutrition:
- InfoCalories:252,Total Fat:3g,Sodium:112mg,Carbohydrates:54g,Protein:4g.

Grilled Broccoli

Servings:4
Cooking Time:10 Minutes.
Ingredients:
- 2 heads broccoli,cut into florets
- 4 tablespoons soy sauce
- 2 tablespoons canola oil
- 4 tablespoons balsamic vinegar
- 2 teaspoons choc zero maple syrup
- Sesame seeds,to garnish
- Red pepper flakes,to garnish

Directions:
1. In a mixing bowl,add the soy sauce,balsamic vinegar,oil,and maple syrup.Whisk well and add the broccoli;toss well.
2. Take Ninja Foodi Grill,set it over your kitchen platform,and open the Ninja Foodi's lid.
3. Set the grill grate and close the Ninja Foodi's lid.
4. Press"GRILL"and select the"MAX"grill function.Adjust the timer to 10 minutes and then press the"Start/Stop"button to initiate preheating.
5. After you hear a beep,open the Ninja Foodi's lid.
6. Set the broccoli over the grill grate.
7. Close the Ninja Foodi's lid and allow it to cook until the timer reads zero.
8. Divide into serving plates.
9. Serve warm with red pepper flakes and sesame seeds on top.

Nutrition:
- InfoCalories:141;Fat:7g;Carbohydrates:14g;Protein:4.5g

Cinnamon Sugar French Toast Bites

Servings:4
Cooking Time:10 Minutes
Ingredients:
- Butter flavored cooking spray
- 1/3 cup Stevia
- 1 tsp cinnamon
- 4 slices sourdough bread,sliced thick,remove crust
- 2 eggs
- 2 tbsp.milk
- 1 tsp vanilla

Directions:
1. Set to air fryer function on 350°F.Spray the fryer basket with cooking spray.
2. In a small bowl,combine Stevia and cinnamon.
3. In a medium bowl,whisk together eggs,milk,and vanilla until smooth.

4. Slice bread into bite-size cubes, about 8 pieces per slice. Dip in egg mixture to coat. Place in a single layer in the fryer basket and spray lightly with cooking spray.
5. Secure the tender-crisp lid and cook 3-5 minutes until golden brown, turning over halfway through cooking time.
6. Roll French toast bites in cinnamon mixture and serve. Repeat with remaining bread and egg mixture.
Nutrition:
- InfoCalories 219, Total Fat 4g, Total Carbs 34g, Protein 10g, Sodium 424mg.

Sausage & Broccoli Frittata

Servings: 10
Cooking Time: 25 Minutes
Ingredients:
- 1 tbsp. olive oil
- 1 lb. country-style pork sausage
- 4 cups broccoli florets
- 1 onion, chopped
- ½tsp salt
- ¼tsp pepper
- 14 eggs
- ½cup milk
- 2 cups cheddar cheese, grated

Directions:
1. Select sauté function on med-high heat.
2. Add olive oil, once it's hot, add sausage, broccoli, onions, salt, and pepper. Cook, stirring frequently, until sausage is no longer pink. Drain the fat.
3. In a large bowl, whisk together eggs, milk, and cheese. Pour over sausage mixture.
4. Set cooker to bake function on 350°F. Secure the tender-crisp lid and set timer to 20 minutes.
5. Frittata is done when eggs are set. Let cool 5-10 minutes before serving.
Nutrition:
- InfoCalories 374, Total Fat 27g, Total Carbs 4g, Protein 28g, Sodium 432mg.

Banana Nut Muffins

Servings: 12
Cooking Time: x
Ingredients:
- 1½cups flour
- 1 tsp baking powder
- 1 tsp baking soda
- ½tsp salt
- ½tsp cinnamon
- 1 egg
- 3 bananas, mashed
- ¾cup Stevia
- 1/3 cup coconut oil, melted
- 1 tsp vanilla
- ½cup walnuts, chopped

Directions:
1. Set cooker to air fryer function on 350°F. Line 2 6-cup muffin tins with paper liners.
2. In a medium bowl, combine flour, baking powder, baking soda, salt, and cinnamon.
3. In a large bowl, whisk together egg, banana, Stevia, oil, and vanilla until smooth.
4. Stir in dry ingredients just until combined. Fold in nuts and pour into prepared tins.
5. Add one at a time to the cooker and secure the tender-crisp lid. Bake 12-15 minutes or until muffins pass the toothpick test. Repeat.
6. Let cool in pan 10 minutes then transfer to wire rack to cool completely.
Nutrition:
- InfoCalories 174, Total Fat 10g, Total Carbs 34g, Protein 3g, Sodium 209mg.

Morning Pancakes

Servings: 4
Cooking Time: 10 Minutes
Ingredients:
- 2 cups cream cheese
- 2 cups almond flour
- 6 large whole eggs
- 1/4 teaspoon salt
- 2 tablespoons butter
- ¼teaspoon ground ginger
- ½teaspoon cinnamon powder

Directions:
1. Take a large bowl and add cream cheese, eggs, 1 tablespoon butter. Blend on high until creamy.
2. Slow add flour and keep beating.
3. Add salt, ginger, cinnamon.
4. Keep beating until fully mixed.
5. Select "Sauté" mode on your Ninja Foodi and grease stainless steel insert.
6. Add butter and heat it up.
7. Add ½cup batter and cook for 2-3 minutes, flip and cook the other side.
8. Repeat with the remaining batter. Enjoy.
Nutrition:
- InfoCalories: 432; Fat: 40g; Carbohydrates: 3g; Protein: 14g

Breakfast Pies

Servings: 4
Cooking Time: 20 Minutes
Ingredients:
- 1½cup mozzarella cheese, grated
- 2/3 cup almond flour, sifted
- 4 eggs, beaten
- 4 tbsp. butter
- 6 slices bacon, cooked crisp & crumbled

Directions:
1. Select air fryer function and heat cooker to 400°F.
2. In a microwave safe bowl, melt the mozzarella cheese until smooth.
3. Stir in flour until well combined.
4. Roll the dough out between 2 sheets of parchment paper. Use a sharp knife to cut dough into 4 equal rectangles.
5. Heat the butter in a skillet over medium heat. Add the eggs and scramble to desired doneness.
6. Divide eggs evenly between the four pieces of dough, placing them on one side. Top with bacon.
7. Fold dough over filling and seal the edges with a fork. Poke a few holes on the top of the pies.
8. Place the pies in the fryer basket in a single layer. Secure the tender-crisp lid and bake 20 minutes, turning over halfway through. Serve immediately.
Nutrition:
- InfoCalories 420, Total Fat 33g, Total Carbs 3g, Protein 28g, Sodium 663mg.

Chocolate Chip And Banana Bread Bundt Cake

Servings:8
Cooking Time:40 Minutes
Ingredients:
- 2 cups all-purpose flour
- 1 teaspoon baking soda
- ¼teaspoon cinnamon
- ¼teaspoon sea salt
- 1 stick(½cup)unsalted butter,at room temperature
- ½cup dark brown sugar
- ¼cup granulated sugar
- 2 eggs,beaten
- 1 teaspoon vanilla extract
- 3 ripe bananas,mashed
- 1 cup semisweet chocolate chips
- Cooking spray

Directions:
1. Close crisping lid.Select BAKE/ROAST,set temperature to 325°F,and set time to 5 minutes.Select START/STOP to begin preheating.
2. In a medium bowl,stir together the flour,baking soda,cinnamon,and salt.
3. In a large bowl,beat together the butter,brown sugar,and granulated sugar.Stir in the eggs,vanilla,and bananas.
4. Slowly add the dry mixture to wet mixture,stirring until just combined.Fold in chocolate chips.
5. Use cooking spray to grease the Ninja Tube Pan or a 7-inch Bundt pan.Pour the batter into the pan.
6. Once preheated,place pan on the Reversible Rack in the lower position.Close crisping lid.
7. Select BAKE/ROAST,set temperature to 325°F,and set time to 40 minutes.Select START/STOP to begin.
8. After 30 minutes,open lid and check doneness by inserting a toothpick into the cake.If it comes out clean,it is done.If not,continue baking until done.
9. When cooking is complete,remove pan from pot and place on a cooling rack for 30 minutes before serving.

Nutrition:
- InfoCalories:484,Total Fat:21g,Sodium:238mg,Carbohydrates:70g,Protein:6g.

Cranberry Vanilla Oatmeal

Servings:6
Cooking Time:8 Hours
Ingredients:
- Nonstick cooking spray
- 1½cups steel cut oats
- 4½cups water
- 1½tsp cinnamon
- 2½tsp vanilla
- 1½cups cranberries,dried

Directions:
1. Spray the cooking pot with cooking spray.
2. Add the oats,water,cinnamon,and vanilla and stir to combine.
3. Secure the lid and set to slow cooker on low heat.Set timer for 8 hours.
4. When timer goes off stir in cranberries and serve.

Nutrition:
- InfoCalories 250,Total Fat 3g,Total Carbs 51g,Protein 7g,Sodium 2mg.

Maple Giant Pancake

Servings:6
Cooking Time:30 Min
Ingredients:
- 3 cups flour/390g
- ⅓cup olive oil/84ml
- ⅓cup sparkling water/84ml
- ¾cup sugar/98g
- 5 eggs
- 2 tbsp maple syrup/30ml
- ⅓tsp salt/1.67g
- 1½tsp baking soda/7.5g
- A dollop of whipped cream to serve

Directions:
1. Start by pouring the flour,sugar,eggs,olive oil,sparkling water,salt,and baking soda intoafood processor and blend until smooth.Pour the batter into the Ninja Foodi and let it sit in there for 15 minutes.Close the lid and secure the pressure valve.
2. Select the Pressure mode on Low pressure for 10 minutes.Press Start/Stop.
3. Once the timer goes off,press Start/Stop,quick-release the pressure valve to let out any steam and open the lid.
4. Gently run a spatula around the pancake to let loose any sticking.Once ready,slide the pancake ontoaserving plate and drizzle with maple syrup.Top with the whipped cream to serve

Flaxseeds Granola

Servings:16
Cooking Time:2½Hours
Ingredients:
- ½cup sunflower kernels
- 5 cups mixed nuts,crushed
- 2 tablespoons ground flax seeds
- ¼cup olive oil
- ½cup unsalted butter
- 1 teaspoon ground cinnamon
- 1 cup choc zero maple syrup

Directions:
1. Grease the Ninja Foodi's insert.
2. In the greased Ninja Foodi's insert,add sunflower kernels,nuts,flax seeds,oil,butter,and cinnamon and stir to combine.
3. Close the Ninja Foodi's lid with a crisping lid and select"Slow Cooker."
4. Set on"High"for 2½hours.
5. Press the"Start/Stop"button to initiate cooking.
6. Stir the mixture after every 30 minutes.
7. Open the Ninja Foodi's lid and transfer the granola onto a large baking sheet.
8. Add the maple syrup and stir to combine.
9. Set aside to cool completely before serving.
10. You can preserve this granola in an airtight container.

Nutrition:
- InfoCalories:189;Fat:10 g;Carbohydrates:7.7 g;Protein:4.6 g

Ham Breakfast Casserole

Servings: 4
Cooking Time: 10 Minutes
Ingredients:
- 4 whole eggs
- 1 tablespoons milk
- 1 cup ham, cooked and chopped
- ½ cup cheddar cheese, shredded
- ¼ teaspoon salt
- ¼ teaspoon black pepper

Directions:
1. Take a baking pan small enough to fit into your Ninja Foodi bowl, and grease it well with butter.
2. Take a medium bowl and whisk in eggs, milk, salt, pepper and add ham, cheese, and stir.
3. Pour mixture into baking pan and lower the pan into your Ninja Foodi.
4. Set your Ninja Foodi Air Crisp mode and Air Crisp for 325°F for 7 minutes.
5. Remove pan from eggs and enjoy.

Nutrition:
- InfoCalories:169; Fat:13g; Carbohydrates:1g; Protein:12g

Spanish Potato And Chorizo Frittata

Servings: 4
Cooking Time: 20 Minutes
Ingredients:
- 4 eggs
- 1 cup milk
- Sea salt
- Freshly ground black pepper
- 1 potato, diced
- ½ cup frozen corn
- 1 chorizo sausage, diced
- 8 ounces feta cheese, crumbled
- 1 cup water

Directions:
1. In a medium bowl, whisk together the eggs and milk. Season with salt and pepper.
2. Place the potato, corn, and chorizo in the Multi-Purpose Pan or an 8-inch baking pan. Pour the egg mixture and feta cheese over top. Cover the pan with aluminum foil and place on the Reversible Rack. Make sure it's in the lower position.
3. Pour the water into the pot. Assemble pressure lid, making sure the pressure release valve is in the SEAL position.
4. Select PRESSURE and set to HI. Set time to 20 minutes. Select START/STOP to begin.
5. When pressure cooking is complete, quick release the pressure by moving the pressure release valve to the VENT position. Carefully remove lid when unit has finished releasing pressure.
6. Remove the pan from pot and place it on a cooling rack for 5 minutes, then serve.

Nutrition:
- InfoCalories:361, Total Fat:24g, Sodium:972mg, Carbohydrates:17g, Protein:21g.

Breakfast Burrito Bake

Servings: 8
Cooking Time: 40 Minutes
Ingredients:
- 14 oz. pinto beans, drain & rinse
- 2 cups mild salsa
- 2 cups baby spinach, chopped
- 1 tsp cumin
- 1 tsp oregano
- Nonstick cooking spray
- 8 corn tortillas, gluten-free
- 1½ cups sharp cheddar cheese, grated
- 6 eggs
- ½ cup skim milk

Directions:
1. In a large bowl, combine the beans, salsa, spinach, cumin and oregano.
2. Spray an 8-inch baking dish with cooking spray.
3. Spread ¼ cup bean mixture in the bottom of the dish. Top with 4 tortillas, overlapping as necessary.
4. Top tortillas with half the remaining bean mixture and sprinkle with half the cheese.
5. On top of the cheese lay the remaining tortillas and cover with remaining bean mixture.
6. In a medium bowl, whisk together eggs and milk. Pour over casserole. Cover and refrigerate overnight.
7. Place the baking dish in the cooking pot and add the tender-crisp lid. Select air fryer function on 350°F. Bake 25-30 minutes, or until eggs are set and top starts to brown.
8. Sprinkle remaining cheese over the top and bake another 5 minutes until cheese melts. Let cool slightly before cutting and serving.

Nutrition:
- InfoCalories 277, Total Fat 12g, Total Carbs 27g, Protein 16g, Sodium 790mg.

Cheesy Meat Omelet

Servings: 2
Cooking Time: 20 Min
Ingredients:
- 1 beef sausage; chopped
- 4 slices prosciutto; chopped
- 1 cup grated mozzarella cheese/130g
- 4 eggs
- 3 oz. salami; chopped/90g
- 1 tbsp chopped onion/15g
- 1 tbsp ketchup/15ml

Directions:
1. Preheat the Ninja Foodi to 350°F or 177°C on Air Crisp mode. Whisk the eggs with the ketchup, in a bowl. Stir in the onion. Spritz the inside of the Ninja Foodi basket with a cooking spray. Add and brown the sausage for about 2 minutes.
2. Meanwhile, combine the egg mixture, mozzarella cheese, salami and prosciutto. Pour the egg mixture over the sausage and stir it. Close the crisping lid and cook for 10 minutes. Once the timer beeps, ensure the omelet is just set. Serve immediately.

Cinnamon Apple Bread

Servings: 10
Cooking Time: 55 Minutes
Ingredients:
- Butter flavored cooking spray
- ½ cup coconut flour
- 1½ cup almond flour, sifted
- ¾ cup Stevia

Ninja Foodi Cookbook

- 1 tsp baking soda
- 2 tbsp.cinnamon
- 5 eggs
- 1 cup applesauce,unsweetened

Directions:
1. Set to bake function on 350°F.Lightly spray a loaf pan with cooking spray.
2. In a large bowl,combine both flours,Stevia,cinnamon,and baking soda.
3. In a medium bowl,whisk the eggs and applesauce together.Add to dry ingredients and stir to combine.
4. Pour into prepared pan and place in the cooker.Add the tender-crisp lid and bake 45-55 minutes,or until bread passes the toothpick test.
5. Let cool 15 minutes,then invert onto serving plate and slice.

Nutrition:
- InfoCalories 189,Total Fat 10g,Total Carbs 30g,Protein 7g,Sodium 162mg.

Banana Coconut Loaf

Servings:8
Cooking Time:35 Minutes
Ingredients:
- Nonstick cooking spray
- 1¼cup whole wheat flour
- ½cup coconut flakes,unsweetened
- 2 tsp baking powder
- ½tsp baking soda
- ½tsp salt
- 1 cup banana,mashed
- ¼cup coconut oil,melted
- 2 tbsp.honey

Directions:
1. Select the bake function on heat cooker to 350°F.Spray an 8-inch loaf pan with cooking spray.
2. In a large bowl,combine flour,coconut,baking powder,baking soda,and salt.
3. In a separate bowl,combine banana,oil,and honey.Add to dry ingredients and mix well.Spread batter in prepared pan.
4. Secure the tender-crisp lid and bake 30-35 minutes or until loaf passes the toothpick test.
5. Remove pan from the cooker and let cool 10 minutes.Invert loaf to a wire rack and cool completely before slicing.

Nutrition:
- InfoCalories 201,Total Fat 11g,Total Carbs 26g,Protein 3g,Sodium 349mg.

Cinnamon Bun Oatmeal

Servings:6
Cooking Time:26 Minutes
Ingredients:
- 1 cup gluten-free steel-cut oats
- 3½cups water
- ¼teaspoon sea salt
- 1 teaspoon nutmeg
- 2 teaspoons cinnamon,divided
- ½cup all-purpose flour
- ½cup rolled oats
- ⅔cup brown sugar
- ⅓cup cold unsalted butter,cut into pieces
- 2 tablespoons granulated sugar
- ¾cup raisins
- 2 ounces cream cheese,at room temperature
- 2 tablespoons confectioners'sugar
- 1 teaspoon whole milk

Directions:
1. Place the steel-cut oats,water,salt,nutmeg,and 1 teaspoon of cinnamon in the pot.Assemble pressure lid,making sure the pressure release valve is in the SEAL position.
2. Select PRESSURE and set to HI.Set time to 11 minutes.Select START/STOP to begin.
3. In a medium bowl,combine the flour,rolled oats,brown sugar,butter,remaining 1 teaspoon of cinnamon,and granulated sugar until a crumble forms.
4. When pressure cooking is complete,allow pressure to naturally release for 5 minutes.After 5 minutes,quick release any remaining pressure by moving the pressure release valve to the VENT position.Carefully remove lid when unit has finished releasing pressure.
5. Stir the raisins into the oatmeal.Cover and let sit 5 minutes to thicken.
6. Evenly spread the crumble topping over the oatmeal.Close crisping lid.
7. Select AIR CRISP,set temperature to 400°F,and set time to 10 minutes.Select START/STOP to begin.
8. In a small bowl,whisk together the cream cheese,confectioners'sugar,and milk.Add more milk or sugar,as needed,to reach your desired consistency.
9. When crumble topping is browned,cooking is complete.Open lid and serve the oatmeal in individual bowls topped with a swirl of cream cheese topping.

Nutrition:
- InfoCalories:454,Total Fat:16g,Sodium:117mg,Carbohydrates:73g,Protein:8g.

Sweet Potatoes&Fried Eggs

Servings:4
Cooking Time:x
Ingredients:
- 2 large sweet potatoes,peel&cut in 1-inch cubes
- 1 tbsp.apple cider vinegar
- 1½tsp salt,divided
- 3 tbsp.extra virgin olive oil,divided
- 1 cup red onion,chopped
- 1 cup green bell pepper,chopped
- 2 cloves garlic,diced fine
- ½tsp pepper
- ½tsp cumin
- ½tsp paprika
- 4 eggs
- 2 tbsp.cilantro,chopped

Directions:
1. Add potatoes,vinegar,and one teaspoon salt to the cooking pot.Add just enough water to cover potatoes.
2. Secure the lid and set to pressure cooking on high.Set timer for 5 minutes.When timer goes off,use quick release to remove the lid.Potatoes should be slightly soft.Drain and set aside.
3. Add one tablespoon oil to the cooking pot and set to sautéfunction on medium heat.When oil is hot,add onions and bell pepper,cook about 5 minutes or until tender.Add garlic and cook 1 minute more.Transfer to a bowl and keep warm.

4. Add remaining oil to the pot. When hot, add potatoes, remaining salt, pepper, cumin, and paprika and decrease heat to medium-low. Cook, stirring occasionally, until potatoes are nicely browned on the outside and tender.
5. Stir in the onion mixture and create 4 "wells" in the mixture. Crack an egg in each one.
6. Secure the tender-crisp lid and set to air fryer function on 350°F. Bake until whites are set. Sprinkle with cilantro and serve.

Nutrition:
- InfoCalories 239, Total Fat 15g, Total Carbs 18g, Protein 8g, Sodium 982mg.

Baked Eggs In Spinach

Servings: 4
Cooking Time: 20 Minutes
Ingredients:
- 2 tsp olive oil
- 2 cloves garlic, diced fine
- 4 cups baby spinach
- ½cup parmesan cheese, reduced fat
- 4 eggs
- 1 tomato, diced fine

Directions:
1. Select sauté function on medium heat. Add oil to the pot and heat.
2. Add the spinach and garlic and cook, stirring, about 2 minutes, or until spinach has wilted. Drain off excess liquid.
3. Stir in parmesan cheese. Make 4 small indents in the spinach. Crack an egg into each indent.
4. Set to air fryer function at 350°F. Secure the tender-crisp lid and bake 15-20 minutes or until egg whites are cooked and yolks are still slightly runny.
5. Let cool 5 minutes, serve topped with tomatoes.

Nutrition:
- InfoCalories 139, Total Fat 10g, Total Carbs 3g, Protein 12g, Sodium 280mg.

Stuffed Baked Tomatoes

Servings: 4
Cooking Time: 25 Minutes
Ingredients:
- 4 large tomatoes
- 4 slices turkey bacon, chopped
- ¼cup green pepper, chopped
- 3 tbsp. mushroom, chopped
- 2 eggs
- 4 egg whites
- 2 tbsp. skim milk
- ¼tsp salt
- ½cup cheddar cheese, reduced fat, grated

Directions:
1. Cut off the tops of the tomatoes and scoop out the inside, do not cut the bottom or sides. Set aside.
2. Set cooker to sauté on medium heat. Add bacon and cook until almost crisp.
3. Add the peppers and mushrooms and cook until bacon is crisp and peppers are tender. Spoon into tomatoes.
4. In a medium bowl, whisk together eggs, egg whites, milk, and salt. Pour into tomatoes leaving ¼inch space at the top.
5. Place tomatoes in the cooking pot and top with cheese. Set to air fryer function on 350°F. Secure the tender-crisp lid and bake 15-20 minutes or until eggs are cooked through. Let rest 5 minutes before serving.

Nutrition:
- InfoCalories 165, Total Fat 8g, Total Carbs 9g, Protein 15g, Sodium 483mg.

Apple Walnut Quinoa

Servings: 2
Cooking Time: 15 Minutes
Ingredients:
- ½cup quinoa, rinsed
- 1 apple, cored&chopped
- 2 cups water
- ½cup apple juice, unsweetened
- 2 tsp maple syrup
- 1 tsp cinnamon
- ¼cup walnuts, chopped&lightly toasted

Directions:
1. Set the cooker to sauté on med-low heat. Add the quinoa and apples and cook, stirring frequently, 5 minutes.
2. Add water and apple juice and stir to mix. Secure the lid and set to pressure cooking on high. Set timer for 10 minutes.
3. When timer goes off use quick release to remove the lid. Quinoa should be tender and the liquid should be absorbed, if not cook another 5 minutes.
4. When quinoa is done, stir in syrup and cinnamon. Sprinkle nuts over top and serve.

Nutrition:
- InfoCalories 348, Total Fat 12g, Total Carbs 54g, Protein 9g, Sodium 7mg.

Sweet Potato, Sausage, And Rosemary Quiche

Servings: 6
Cooking Time: 38 Minutes
Ingredients:
- 6 eggs
- ¼cup sour cream
- ½pound ground Italian sausage
- 1 tablespoon fresh rosemary, chopped
- 2 medium sweet potatoes, cut into½-inch cubes
- 2 teaspoons kosher salt
- ½teaspoon freshly ground black pepper
- 1 store-bought refrigerated pie crust

Directions:
1. In a medium bowl, whisk together the eggs and sour cream until well combined. Set aside.
2. Select SEAR/SAUTÉ and set to HI. Select START/STOP to begin. Let preheat for 5 minutes.
3. Add the sausage and rosemary and cook, stirring frequently, for about 5 minutes. Add the sweet potatoes, salt, and pepper and cook, stirring frequently, for about 5 minutes. Transfer this mixture to a bowl.
4. Place the pie crust in the pan, using your fingers to gently push onto the bottom and sides of the pan. Place pan with pie crust on the Reversible Rack, making sure it is in the lower position. Place rack with pan in pot. Close crisping lid.
5. Select BAKE/ROAST, set temperature to 400°F, and set time to 8 minutes. Select START/STOP to begin.
6. Stir the sausage and sweet potatoes in to the egg mixture.
7. When cooking is complete, open lid and pour the egg mixture into the browned crust. Close crisping lid.
8. Select BAKE/ROAST, set temperature to 360°F, and set time to 15 minutes. Select START/STOP to begin.

9. When cooking is complete,carefully remove pan from pot.Let cool for 10 minutes before removing from pan.
Nutrition:
- InfoCalories:344,Total Fat:22g,Sodium:743mg,Carbohydrates:22g,Protein:14g.

Cinnamon Crumb Donuts
Servings:6
Cooking Time:10 Minutes
Ingredients:
- Butter flavored cooking spray
- ¼cup Stevia,granulated
- 1 cup+3½tbsp.flour,divided
- ¼tsp cinnamon
- ¼cup butter,cut in cubes
- ½cup Stevia brown sugar,packed
- ½tsp salt
- 1 tsp baking powder
- ½cup sour cream
- 2½tbsp.butter,melted
- 1 egg,room temperature
- ½cup Stevia confectioners'sugar
- ½tbsp.milk
- ½tsp vanilla

Directions:
1. Select air fryer function and heat cooker to 350°F.Spray a 6 mold donut pan with cooking spray.
2. In a small bowl,combine¼cup granulated Stevia,3½tablespoons flour,and¼teaspoon cinnamon.
3. With a pastry cutter,or fork,cut in the cold butter until mixture resembles coarse crumbs.Cover and chill until ready to use.
4. In a large bowl,stir together 1 cup flour,the Stevia brown sugar,salt,and baking powder.
5. In a separate bowl,whisk together sour cream,melted butter,and egg.Stir into dry ingredients just until combined.
6. Spoon dough into prepared pan.Sprinkle chilled crumb topping evenly over the tops.
7. Place the pan in the cooker and secure the tender-crisp lid.Cook 10-11 minutes or donuts pass the toothpick test.Cool in the pan 10 minutes then transfer to a wire rack.
8. In a small bowl,whisk together Stevia powdered sugar substitute,milk,and vanilla.Drizzle donuts with glaze and serve.

Nutrition:
- InfoCalories 250,Total Fat 18g,Total Carbs 21g,Protein 4g,Sodium 366mg.

Glazed Carrots
Servings:4
Cooking Time:4 Minutes
Ingredients:
- 2 pounds carrots,washed,peeled and sliced
- Pepper,to taste
- 1 cup of water
- 1 tablespoon butter
- 1 tablespoon choc zero maple syrup

Directions:
1. Add carrots,water to the Instant Pot.
2. Lock and secure the Ninja Foodi's lid,then cook on"HIGH"pressure for 4 minutes.
3. Quick-release Pressure.
4. Strain carrots.
5. Add butter,maple syrup to the warm mix,stir it gently.
6. Transfer strained carrots back to the pot and stir.
7. Coat well with maple syrup.
8. Sprinkle a bit of pepper and serve.
9. Enjoy.

Nutrition:
- InfoCalories:358;Fat:12g;Carbohydrates:20g;Protein:2g

Cheesecake French Toast
Servings:6
Cooking Time:50 Minutes
Ingredients:
- Butter flavored cooking spray
- 4 eggs
- ½cup sugar
- 1 cup milk
- 1½tsp vanilla,divided
- 1/8 tsp salt
- ½lb.challah bread,cut in 1-inch cubes
- ½cup strawberries,chopped
- 2 oz.cream cheese,soft
- ¼cup powdered sugar

Directions:
1. Select bake function and heat the cooker to 350°F.Spray a baking dish with cooking spray.
2. In a large bowl,whisk together eggs,sugar,milk,1 teaspoon vanilla,and salt until smooth.
3. Add bread and strawberries and fold until the bread is thoroughly coated with the egg mixture.
4. In another bowl,beat cream cheese,powdered sugar,and remaining vanilla until smooth.
5. Place half the bread mixture in the prepared baking dish.Drop half the cheese mixture by teaspoons over bread.Repeat.
6. Carefully place the dish into the cooker and secure the tender-crisp lid.Bake 45-50 minutes,or until golden brown and a toothpick inserted in center comes out clean.
7. Remove the dish and let cool 10 minutes before serving.

Nutrition:
- InfoCalories 259,Total Fat 9g,Total Carbs 35g,Protein 9g,Sodium 337mg.

Bacon And Gruyère Egg Bites
Servings:6
Cooking Time:26 Minutes
Ingredients:
- 5 slices bacon,cut into½-inch pieces
- 5 eggs
- 1 teaspoon kosher salt
- ¼cup sour cream
- 1 cup shredded Gruyère cheese,divided
- Cooking spray
- 1 cup water
- 1 teaspoon chopped parsley,for garnish

Directions:
1. Select SEAR/SAUTÉand set temperature to HI.Select START/STOP and let preheat for 5 minutes.
2. Add the bacon and cook,stirring frequently,about 5 minutes,or until the fat is rendered and bacon starts to brown.Transfer the bacon to a paper towel-lined plate to drain.Wipe the pot clean of any remaining fat.
3. In a medium bowl,whisk together the eggs,salt,and sour cream until well combined.Fold in¾cup of cheese and the bacon.

4. Spray egg molds or Ninja Silicone Mold with the cooking spray. Ladle the egg mixture into each mold, filling them halfway.
5. Pour the water in the pot. Carefully place the egg molds in the pot. Assemble pressure lid, making sure the pressure release valve is in the SEAL position.
6. Select PRESSURE and set to LO. Set time to 10 minutes. Select START/STOP to begin.
7. When pressure cooking is complete, natural release the pressure for 6 minutes, then quick release the remaining pressure by moving the pressure release valve to the VENT position.
8. Carefully remove the lid. Using mitts or a towel, carefully remove egg molds. Top with the remaining ¼ cup of cheese, then place the mold back into the pot. Close the crisping lid.
9. Select AIR CRISP, set temperature to 390°F, and set time to 5 minutes. Select START/STOP to begin.
10. Once cooking is complete, carefully remove the egg molds and set aside to cool for 5 minutes. Using a spoon, carefully remove the egg bites from the molds. Top with chopped parsley and serve immediately.

Nutrition:
- InfoCalories: 230, Total Fat: 18g, Sodium: 557mg, Carbohydrates: 2g, Protein: 16g.

Spinach Casserole

Servings: 4
Cooking Time: 5 Minutes

Ingredients:
- 4 whole eggs
- 1 tablespoons milk
- 1 tomato, diced
- ½ cup spinach
- ¼ teaspoon salt
- ¼ teaspoon black pepper

Directions:
1. Take a baking pan small enough to fit Ninja Foodi and grease it with butter.
2. Take a medium bowl and whisk in eggs, milk, salt, pepper, add veggies to the bowl and stir.
3.
4. Pour egg mixture into the baking pan and lower the pan into the Ninja Foodi.
5. Close Air Crisping lid and Air Crisp for 325 degrees for 7 minutes.
6. Remove the pan from eggs, and enjoy hot.

Nutrition:
- InfoCalories: 78; Fat: 5g; Carbohydrates: 1 g; Protein: 7 g

Southern Grits Casserole

Servings: 8
Cooking Time: 45 Minutes

Ingredients:
- 3 cups water
- 2 cups milk or heavy (whipping) cream, divided
- 2 cups stone ground grits
- Kosher salt
- Freshly ground black pepper
- 4 tablespoons unsalted butter
- 1 pound cooked breakfast sausage, casing removed and chopped
- 6 eggs
- 2 cups shredded Cheddar cheese

Directions:
1. Pour the water, 1½ cups of milk, and grits in the pot. Season with salt and pepper. Stir well. Assemble pressure lid, making sure the pressure release valve is in the SEAL position.
2. Select PRESSURE and set to HI. Set time to 10 minutes. Select START/STOP to begin.
3. When pressure cooking is complete, allow pressure to naturally release for 15 minutes. Then quick release remaining pressure by moving the pressure release valve to the VENT position. Carefully remove lid when unit has finished releasing pressure.
4. Stir in the butter and sausage.
5. In a large bowl, whisk together the eggs and remaining ½ cup of milk. Fold the eggs and cheese into the grits. Close crisping lid.
6. Select BAKE/ROAST, set temperature to 375°F, and set time to 25 minutes. Select START/STOP to begin.
7. Once cooking is complete, open lid. Let cool for 10 minutes before slicing to serve.

Nutrition:
- InfoCalories: 551, Total Fat: 36g, Sodium: 692mg, Carbohydrates: 31g, Protein: 27g.

Paprika Hard-boiled Eggs

Servings: 3
Cooking Time: 25 Min

Ingredients:
- 6 eggs
- 1 cup water/250ml
- 1 tsp sweet paprika/5g
- Salt and ground black pepper, to taste

Directions:
1. In the Foodi, add water and place a reversible rack on top. Lay your eggs on the rack. Seal the pressure lid, choose Pressure, set to High, and set the timer to 5 minutes. Press Start.
2. Once ready, do a natural release for 10 minutes. Transfer the eggs to ice cold water to cool completely. When cooled, peel and slice. Season with salt and pepper. Sprinkle with sweet paprika before serving.

Fish & Seafood

Pistachio Crusted Mahi Mahi

Servings: 6
Cooking Time: 20 Minutes
Ingredients:
- Nonstick cooking spray
- 6 fresh Mahi Mahi filets
- 2 tbsp. fresh lemon juice
- ½ tsp nutmeg
- ¼ tsp pepper
- ¼ tsp salt
- ½ cup pistachio nuts, chopped
- 2 tbsp. butter, melted

Directions:
1. Place the rack in the cooking pot. Lightly spray a small baking sheet with cooking spray.
2. Place the fish on the prepared pan. Season with lemon juice and spices. Top with pistachios and drizzle melted butter over the tops.
3. Place the pan on the rack and add the tender-crisp lid. Set to bake on 350°F. Cook fish 15-20 minutes or until it flakes easily with a fork. Serve immediately.

Nutrition:
- InfoCalories 464, Total Fat 14g, Total Carbs 3g, Protein 77g, Sodium 405mg.

Salmon With Creamy Grits

Servings: 4
Cooking Time: 100 Min
Ingredients:
- 4 salmon fillets, skin removed
- 1½ cups vegetable stock/375ml
- ¾ cup corn grits/98g
- 1½ cups coconut milk/375ml
- 3 tbsps Cajun/45g
- 1 tbsp packed brown sugar/15g
- 3 tbsps butter; divided/45g
- 2 tsp s salt/10g
- Cooking spray

Directions:
1. Pour the grits into a heatproof bowl. Add the coconut milk, stock, 1 tbsp or 15g of butter, and ½ tsp or 2.5g of salt. Stir and cover the bowl with foil. Pour the water into the inner pot. Put the reversible rack in the pot and place the bowl on top.
2. Seal the pressure lid, choose Pressure; adjust the pressure to High and the cook time to 15 minutes. Press Start to begin cooking.
3. In a bowl combine the Cajun, brown sugar, and remaining salt.
4. Oil the fillets on one side with cooking spray and place one or two at a time with sprayed-side down into the spice mixture. Oil the other sides and turn over to coat that side in the seasoning. Repeat the process with the remaining fillets.
5. Once the grits are ready, perform a natural pressure release for 10 minutes. Remove the rack and bowl from the pot.
6. Add the remaining butter to the grits and stir to combine well. Cover again with aluminum foil and return the bowl to the pot (without the rack).
7. Fix the rack in the upper position of the pot and put the salmon fillets on the rack.
8. Close the crisping lid and Choose Bake/Roast; adjust the temperature to 400°F and the cook time to 12 minutes. Press Start. After 6 minutes, open the lid and use tongs to turn the fillets over. Close the lid and continue cooking.
9. When the salmon is ready, take out the rack. Remove the bowl of grits and take off the foil. Stir and serve immediately with the salmon.

Tuscan Cod

Servings: 4
Cooking Time: 32 Minutes
Ingredients:
- 2 tablespoons canola oil, divided
- 1½ pounds baby red potatoes, cut into ½-inch pieces
- 2½ teaspoons kosher salt, divided
- 1 teaspoon freshly ground black pepper, divided
- 1 cup panko bread crumbs
- 6 tablespoons unsalted butter, divided
- 2 teaspoons poultry seasoning
- Juice of 1 lemon
- 1 medium onion, thinly sliced
- 1½ cups cherry tomatoes, halved
- 4 garlic cloves, quartered lengthwise
- ⅓ cup Kalamata olives, roughly chopped
- 4 fresh cod fillets
- 1 teaspoon fresh mint, finely chopped
- 1 lemon, cut into wedges

Directions:
1. Select SEAR/SAUTÉ and set to HI. Select START/STOP to begin. Let preheat for 5 minutes.
2. Add 1 tablespoon of oil and the potatoes. Season with 1½ teaspoons of salt and ½ teaspoon of pepper. Sauté for about 15 minutes, stirring occasionally, until the potatoes are golden brown.
3. While potatoes are cooking, combine the bread crumbs, 4 tablespoons of butter, poultry seasoning, the remaining 1 teaspoon of salt and ½ teaspoon of pepper, and lemon juice in a medium bowl. Stir well.
4. Once the potatoes are browned, carefully remove them from the pot and set aside. Add the remaining 1 tablespoon of oil, then the onion. Sauté for 2 to 3 minutes, until the onions are lightly browned. Add the tomatoes, garlic, and olives and cook for about 2 minutes more, stirring occasionally. Return the potatoes to the pot, stir. Select START/STOP to pause cooking. Close crisping lid to retain heat.
5. Coat the cod on both sides with the remaining 2 tablespoons of butter. Evenly distribute the breadcrumb mixture on top of the cod, pressing the crumbs down firmly.
6. Open lid and place the Reversible Rack in the pot over the potato mixture, making sure it is the higher position. Place the cod fillets on the rack, bread-side up. Close crisping lid.
7. Select BAKE/ROAST, set temperature to 375°F, and set time to 12 minutes. Select START/STOP to begin.
8. When cooking is complete, leave the cod in the pot with the crisping lid closed for 5 minutes to rest before serving. After resting, the internal temperature of the cod should be at least 145°F and the bread crumbs should be golden brown. Serve with potato mixture and garnish with chopped mint and lemon wedges.

Nutrition:
- InfoCalories: 583, Total Fat: 28g, Sodium: 815mg, Carbohydrates: 48g, Protein: 37g.

Ninja Foodi Cookbook

Italian Flounder

Servings: 4
Cooking Time: 70 Min
Ingredients:
- 4 flounder fillets
- 3 slices prosciutto;chopped
- 2 bags baby kale/180g
- ½small red onion;chopped
- ½cup whipping cream/125ml
- 1 cup panko breadcrumbs/130g
- 2 tbsps chopped fresh parsley/30g
- 3 tbsps unsalted butter,melted and divided/45g
- ¼tsp fresh ground black pepper/1.25g
- ½tsp salt;divided/2.5g

Directions:
1. On the Foodi,choose Sear/Sautéand adjust to Medium.Press Start to preheat the inner pot.Add the prosciutto and cook until crispy,about 6 minutes.Stir in the red onions and cook for about 2 minutes or until the onions start to soften.Sprinkle with half of the salt.
2. Fetch the kale into the pot and cook,stirring frequently until wilted and most of the liquid has evaporated,about 4-5 minutes.Mix in the whipping cream.
3. Lay the flounder fillets over the kale in a single layer.Brush 1 tbsp or 15ml of the melted butter over the fillets and sprinkle with the remaining salt and black pepper.
4. Close the crisping lid and choose Bake/Roast.Adjust the temperature to 300°F or 149°C and the cook time to 3 minutes.Press Start.
5. Combine the remaining butter,the parsley and breadcrumbs inabowl.
6. When done cooking,open the crisping lid.Spoon the breadcrumbs mixture on the fillets.
7. Close the crisping lid and Choose Bake/Roast.Adjust the temperature to 400°F or 205°Cand the cook time to 6 minutes.Press Start.
8. After about 4 minutes,open the lid and check the fish.The breadcrumbs should be golden brown and crisp.If not,close the lid and continue to cook for an additional two minutes.

Pistachio Crusted Salmon

Servings: 1
Cooking Time: 15 Min
Ingredients:
- 1 salmon fillet
- 3 tbsp pistachios/45g
- 1 tsp grated Parmesan cheese/5g
- 1 tsp lemon juice/5ml
- 1 tsp mustard/5g
- 1 tsp olive oil/5ml
- Pinch of sea salt
- Pinch of garlic powder
- Pinch of black pepper

Directions:
1. Whisk the mustard and lemon juice together.Season the salmon with salt,pepper,and garlic powder.Brush the olive oil on all sides.
2. Brush the mustard-lemon mixture on top of the salmon.Chop the pistachios finely,and combine them with the Parmesan cheese.
3. Sprinkle them on top of the salmon.Place the salmon in the Ninja Foodi basket with the skin side down.
4. Close the crisping lid and cook for 10 minutes on Air Crisp mode at 350°F or 177°C.

Salmon With Dill Sauce

Servings: 4
Cooking Time: 20-25 Minutes
Ingredients:
- 4 salmon,each of 6 ounces
- 2 teaspoons olive oil
- 1 pinch salt
- Dill Sauce
- 1/2 cup non-Fat:Greek Yogurt
- 1/2 cup sour cream
- Pinch of salt
- 2 tablespoons dill,chopped

Directions:
1. Preheat Ninja Foodi by pressing the"AIR CRISP"option and setting it to"270°F"and timer to 25 minutes.
2. Wait until the appliance beeps.
3. Drizzle cut pieces of salmon with 1 teaspoon olive oil.
4. Season with salt.
5. Take the cooking basket out and transfer salmon to basket,cook for 20-23 minutes.
6. Take a suitable and stir in sour cream,salt,chopped dill,yogurt and mix well to prepare the dill sauce.
7. Serve cooked salmon by pouring the sauce all over.
8. Garnish with chopped dill and enjoy.

Nutrition:
- InfoCalories:600;Fat:45g;Carbohydrates:5g;Protein:60g

Farfalle Tuna Casserole With Cheese

Servings: 4
Cooking Time: 60 Min
Ingredients:
- 6 ounces farfalle/180g
- 1 can full cream milk;divided/360ml
- 2 cans tuna,drained/180g
- 1 medium onion;chopped
- 1 large carrot;chopped
- 1 cup vegetable broth/250ml
- 2 cups shredded Monterey Jack cheese/260g
- 1 cup chopped green beans/130g
- 2½cups panko bread crumbs/325g
- 3 tbsps butter,melted/45ml
- 1 tbsp olive oil/15ml
- 1 tsp salt/5g
- 2 tsp s corn starch/10g

Directions:
1. On the Foodi,Choose Sear/Sautéand adjust to Medium.Press Start to preheat the pot.
2. Heat the oil until shimmering and sautéthe onion and carrots for 3 minutes,stirring,until softened.
3. Add the farfalle,¾cup or 188ml of milk,broth,and salt to the pot.Stir to combine and submerge the farfalle in the liquid withaspoon.
4. Seal the pressure lid,choose pressure;adjust the pressure to Low and the cook time to 5 minutes;press Start.After cooking,do a quick pressure release and carefully open the pressure lid.
5. Choose Sear/Sautéand adjust to Less for low heat.Press Start.Pour the remaining milk on the farfalle.

Ninja Foodi Cookbook

6. In a medium bowl, mix the cheese and cornstarch evenly and add the cheese mixture by large handfuls to the sauce while stirring until the cheese melts and the sauce thickens. Add the tuna and green beans, gently stir. Heat for 2 minutes.
7. In another bowl, mix the crumbs and melted butter well. Spread the crumbs over the casserole. Close the crisping lid and press Broil. Adjust the cook time to 5 minutes; press Start. When ready, the topping should be crisp and brown. If not, broil for 2 more minutes. Serve immediately.

Fried Salmon

Servings: 1
Cooking Time: 13 Min
Ingredients:
- 1 salmon fillet.
- ¼ tsp garlic powder/1.25g
- 1 tbsp soy sauce/15ml
- Salt and pepper

Directions:
1. Combine the soy sauce with the garlic powder, salt, and pepper. Brush the mixture over the salmon. Place the salmon onto a sheet of parchment paper and inside the Ninja Foodi.
2. Close the crisping lid and cook for 10 minutes on Air Crisp at 350°F or 177°C, until crispy on the outside and tender on the inside.

Coconut Shrimp With Pineapple Rice

Servings: 4
Cooking Time: 45 Minutes
Ingredients:
- 2 tablespoons canola oil
- 1 can diced pineapple
- 1 yellow onion, diced
- 1 cup long-grain white rice
- 1½ cups chicken stock
- ½ cup freshly squeezed lime juice
- ¾ cup all-purpose flour
- 1 tablespoon kosher salt
- ½ teaspoon freshly ground black pepper
- 2 large eggs
- ½ cup coconut flakes
- ½ cup plain panko bread crumbs
- 10 ounces, deveined shrimp, tails removed
- Cooking spray

Directions:
1. Select SEAR/SAUTÉ and set temperature to HI. Select START/STOP to begin. Let preheat for 5 minutes.
2. Add the oil and heat for 1 minute. Add the pineapple and onion. Cook, stirring frequently, for about 8 minutes, or until the onion is translucent.
3. Add the rice, chicken stock, and lime juice. Assemble pressure lid, making sure the pressure release valve is in the SEAL position.
4. Select PRESSURE and set to HI. Set time to 2 minutes. Select START/STOP to begin.
5. When pressure cooking is complete, allow press to naturally release for 10 minutes. After 10 minutes, quick release remaining pressure by turning the pressure release valve to the VENT position. Carefully remove lid when unit has finished releasing pressure.
6. Transfer the rice mixture to a bowl and cover to keep warm. Clean the cooking pot and return to the unit.

7. Create a batter station with three medium bowls. In the first bowl, mix together the flour, salt and pepper. In the second bowl, whisk the eggs. In the third bowl, combine the coconut flakes and bread crumbs. Dip each shrimp into the flour mixture. Next dip it in the egg. Finally, coat in the coconut mixture, shaking off excess as needed. Once all the shrimp are battered, spray them with cooking spray.
8. Place Cook&Crisp Basket into pot. Place the shrimp in basket and close crisping lid.
9. Select AIR CRISP, set temperature to 390°F, and set time to 10 minutes. Select START/STOP to begin.
10. After 5 minutes, open lid, then lift basket and shake the shrimp. Lower basket back into the pot and close the lid to continue cooking until the shrimp reach your desired crispiness.
11. When cooking is complete, serve the shrimp on top of the rice.

Nutrition:
- InfoCalories: 601, Total Fat: 15g, Sodium: 784mg, Carbohydrates: 88g, Protein: 28g.

Tuna & Avocado Patties

Servings: 6
Cooking Time: 20 Minutes
Ingredients:
- Nonstick cooking spray
- 1 avocado, peeled & pitted
- 10 oz. Albacore tuna, drained
- ¼ cup whole wheat bread crumbs
- ¼ cup red onion, chopped fine
- 2 tbsp. cilantro, chopped
- 1 tbsp. fresh lime juice
- 1 tsp hot sauce
- ½ tsp garlic powder
- ½ tsp salt
- 1 egg

Directions:
1. Spray the fryer basket with cooking spray.
2. In a large bowl, mash the avocado. Add the remaining ingredients and mix well. Form into 6 patties.
3. Place the patties in the basket. Add the tender-crisp lid and set to air fry on 400°F. Cook patties 15 minutes or until crisp and cooked through, turning over halfway through cooking time. Serve.

Nutrition:
- InfoCalories 102, Total Fat 5g, Total Carbs 6g, Protein 10g, Sodium 269mg.

Shrimp Etouffee

Servings: 6
Cooking Time: 30 Minutes
Ingredients:
- ¼ cup olive oil
- ¼ cup flour
- 1 stalk celery, chopped
- 1 green bell pepper, chopped
- 2 jalapeno peppers, chopped
- ½ onion, chopped
- 4 cloves garlic, chopped
- 2 cups clam juice
- 1 tbsp. Cajun seasoning
- ½ tsp celery seed
- 1 tbsp. paprika

- 2 pounds shrimp, shell on, deveined
- 3 green onions, chopped
- Hot sauce to taste

Directions:
1. Add the oil to the cooking pot and set to sauté on medium heat. Whisk in the flour until smooth. Cook until a deep brown, whisking frequently, about 10 minutes.
2. Add celery, bell pepper, jalapeno, and onion and cook 4 minutes, stirring occasionally. Add the garlic and cook 2 minutes more.
3. Slowly stir in clam juice, a little at a time, until combined. The sauce should resemble syrup, add more juice if needed.
4. Add Cajun seasoning, celery seed, and paprika and mix well. Add the shrimp. Cover, reduce heat to low and cook 10 minutes.
5. Stir in green onions and hot sauce. Serve over rice.

Nutrition:
- InfoCalories 83, Total Fat 3g, Total Carbs 6g, Protein 7g, Sodium 395mg.

Roasted Bbq Shrimp

Servings: 2
Cooking Time: 7 Minutes

Ingredients:
- 3 tablespoons chipotle in adobo sauce, minced
- 1/4 teaspoon salt
- 1/4 cup BBQ sauce
- 1/2 orange, juiced
- 1/2-pound large shrimps

Directions:
1. Toss shrimp with chipotles and rest of the ingredients in a suitable bowl.
2. Preheat Ninja Foodi by pressing the "Bake/Roast" mode and setting it to "400°F" and timer to 7 minutes.
3. Let it preheat until you hear a beep.
4. Set shrimps over Grill Grate and lock lid, cook until the timer runs out.
5. Serve and enjoy.

Nutrition:
- InfoCalories:173;Fat:2g;Carbohydrates:21g;Protein:17g

Citrus Glazed Halibut

Servings: 4
Cooking Time: 10 Minutes

Ingredients:
- Nonstick cooking spray
- 1 onion, chopped
- 1 clove garlic, chopped fine
- 4 halibut steaks
- ½tsp salt
- ¼tsp lemon-pepper
- ½cup fresh orange juice
- 1 tbsp. fresh lemon juice
- 2 tbsp. fresh parsley, chopped fine

Directions:
1. Spray the cooking pot with cooking spray. Set to sauté on medium heat.
2. Add the onion and garlic and cook 2-3 minutes until onion starts to soften.
3. Add the halibut and season with salt and pepper. Drizzle the orange and lemon juices over the fish and sprinkle with parsley.
4. Add the lid and reduce heat to med-low. Cook 10-12 minutes until fish flakes easily with a fork. Serve immediately.

Nutrition:
- InfoCalories 131, Total Fat 2g, Total Carbs 6g, Protein 22g, Sodium 370mg.

Spicy "grilled" Catfish

Servings: 4
Cooking Time: 10 Minutes

Ingredients:
- Nonstick cooking spray
- 1 tbsp. fresh basil, chopped
- 1 tsp crushed red pepper flakes
- 1 tsp garlic powder
- ½tsp salt
- ½tsp pepper
- 4 catfish fillets
- 2 tbsp. olive oil

Directions:
1. Spray the rack with cooking spray and add to the cooking pot.
2. In a small bowl, combine all the spices and mix well.
3. Pat the fish dry with a paper towel. Rub both sides of the fish with the oil and coat with the seasoning mix.
4. Place the fish on the rack and add the tender-crisp lid. Set to roast on 350°F. Cook 7-9 minutes until fish flakes with a fork, turning over halfway through cooking time. Serve immediately.

Nutrition:
- InfoCalories 211, Total Fat 11g, Total Carbs 0g, Protein 26g, Sodium 359mg.

New England Lobster Rolls

Servings: 4
Cooking Time: 20 Minutes

Ingredients:
- 4 lobster tails
- ¼cup mayonnaise
- 1 celery stalk, minced
- Zest of 1 lemon
- Juice of 1 lemon
- ¼teaspoon celery seed
- Kosher salt
- Freshly ground black pepper
- 4 split-top hot dog buns
- 4 tablespoons unsalted butter, at room temperature
- 4 leaves butter lettuce

Directions:
1. Insert Cook&Crisp Basket into the pot and close the crisping lid. Select AIR CRISP, set temperature to 375°F, and set time to 15 minutes. Select START/STOP to begin. Let preheat for 5 minutes.
2. Once unit has preheated, open lid and add the lobster tails to the basket. Close the lid and cook for 10 minutes.
3. In a medium bowl, mix together the mayonnaise, celery, lemon zest and juice, and celery seed, and add salt and pepper.
4. Fill a large bowl with a tray of ice cubes and enough water to cover the ice.
5. When cooking is complete, open lid. Transfer the lobster into the ice bath for 5 minutes. Close lid to keep unit warm.
6. Spread butter on the hot dog buns. Open lid and place the buns in the basket. Close crisping lid.

Ninja Foodi Cookbook

7. Select AIR CRISP, set temperature to 375°F, and set time to 4 minutes. Select START/STOP to begin.
8. Remove the lobster meat from the shells and roughly chop. Place in the bowl with the mayonnaise mixture and stir.
9. When cooking is complete, open lid and remove the buns. Place lettuce in each bun, then fill with the lobster salad.
Nutrition:
- InfoCalories: 408, Total Fat: 24g, Sodium: 798mg, Carbohydrates: 22g, Protein: 26g.

Arroz Con Cod

Servings: 4
Cooking Time: 30 Minutes
Ingredients:
- ¼ cup olive oil
- 2 tbsp. garlic, chopped
- ½ cup red onion, chopped
- ½ cup red bell pepper, chopped
- ½ cup green bell pepper, chopped
- 2 cups long grain rice
- 3 tbsp. tomato paste
- 2 tsp turmeric
- 2 tbsp. cumin
- ½ tsp salt
- ¼ tsp pepper
- 4 cups chicken broth
- 1 bay leaf
- 1 lb. cod, cut in bite-size pieces
- ½ cup peas, cooked
- 4 tbsp. pimento, chopped
- 4 tsp cilantro, chopped

Directions:
1. Add the oil to the cooking pot and set to sauté on med-high.
2. Add the garlic, onion, and peppers, and cook, stirring frequently for 2 minutes.
3. Stir in rice, tomato paste, and seasonings, and cook another 2 minutes.
4. Add the broth and bay leaf and bring to a boil. Reduce heat, cover, and let simmer 5 minutes.
5. Add the fish, recover the pot and cook 15-20 minutes until all the liquid is absorbed. Turn off the cooker and let sit for 5 minutes.
6. To serve: spoon onto plates and top with cooked peas, pimento and cilantro.

Nutrition:
- InfoCalories 282, Total Fat 15g, Total Carbs 35g, Protein 4g, Sodium 1249mg.

Shrimp Fried Rice

Servings: 6
Cooking Time: 15 Minutes
Ingredients:
- 2 tbsp. sesame oil
- 2 tbsp. olive oil
- 1 lb. medium shrimp, peeled & deveined
- 1 cup frozen peas & carrots
- 1/2 cup corn
- 3 cloves garlic, chopped fine
- ½ tsp ginger
- 3 eggs, lightly beaten
- 4 cups brown rice, cooked
- 3 green onions, sliced
- 3 tbsp. tamari
- ½ tsp salt
- ½ tsp pepper

Directions:
1. Add the sesame and olive oils to the cooking pot and set to sauté on med-high heat.
2. Add the shrimp and cook 3 minutes, or until they turn pink, turning shrimp over halfway through. Use a slotted spoon to transfer shrimp to a plate.
3. Add the peas, carrots, and corn to the pot and cook 2 minutes until vegetables start to soften, stirring occasionally. Add the garlic and ginger and cook 1 minute more.
4. Push the vegetables to one side and add the eggs, cook to scramble, stirring frequently. Add the shrimp, rice, and onions and stir to mix all ingredients together.
5. Drizzle with tamari and season with salt and pepper, stir to combine. Cook 2 minutes or until everything is heated through. Serve immediately.

Nutrition:
- InfoCalories 361, Total Fat 13g, Total Carbs 38g, Protein 24g, Sodium 1013mg.

Salmon, Cashew & Kale Bowl

Servings: 6
Cooking Time: 15 Minutes
Ingredients:
- 12 oz. salmon filets, skin off
- 2 tbsp. olive oil, divided
- ½ tsp salt
- ¼ tsp pepper
- 2 cloves garlic, chopped fine
- 4 cups kale, stems removed & chopped
- ½ cup carrot, grated
- 2 cups quinoa, cooked according to package directions
- ¼ cup cashews, chopped

Directions:
1. Place the rack in the cooking pot and set to bake on 400°F. Place a sheet of parchment paper on the rack.
2. Brush the salmon with 1 tablespoon of oil and season with salt and pepper. Place the fish on the parchment paper.
3. Add the tender-crisp lid and cook 15 minutes or until salmon reaches desired doneness. Transfer the fish to a plate and keep warm.
4. Set the cooker to sauté on medium heat and add the remaining oil. Once the oil is hot, add garlic, kale, and carrot and cook, stirring frequently, until kale is wilted and soft, about 2-3 minutes.
5. Add the quinoa and cashews and cook just until heated through. Spoon mixture evenly into bowl and top with a piece of salmon. Serve immediately.

Nutrition:
- InfoCalories 294, Total Fat 17g, Total Carbs 18g, Protein 17g, Sodium 243mg.

Shrimp & Asparagus Risotto

Servings: 4
Cooking Time: 25 Minutes
Ingredients:
- 1 tbsp. butter
- ½ onion, chopped fine
- 1 clove garlic, chopped fine
- 1 cup Arborio rice
- 5 cups water, divided

- 1 cup clam juice
- 1 tbsp.olive oil
- ½lb.small shrimp,peeled&deveined
- ½bunch asparagus,cut in 1-inch pieces
- ¼cup parmesan cheese

Directions:
1. Add butter to cooking pot and set to sautéon medium heat.Once butter melts,add onion and garlic and cook 5 minutes,stirring frequently.
2. Add the rice and stir to coat with butter mixture.Transfer mixture to a 1-quart baking dish.
3. Pour 1 cup water and clam juice over rice mixture and cover tightly with foil.
4. Pour 2 cups water in the cooking pot and add the rack.Place the rice mixture on the rack,secure the lid and set to pressure cooking on high.Set timer for 10 minutes.
5. When timer goes off release the pressure quickly and remove the baking dish carefully.Drain out any remaining water.
6. Set the cooker back to sautéon med-high and heat the oil.Add the shrimp and asparagus and cook,stirring,just until shrimp start to turn pink.
7. Add the shrimp and asparagus to the rice and stir to mix well.Recover tightly with foil.Pour 2 cups water back in the pot and add the rack.
8. Place the rice mixture back on the rack and secure the lid.Set to pressure cooking on high and set the timer for 4 minutes.
9. When the timer goes off,release the pressure quickly.Remove the foil and stir.Serve immediately sprinkled with parmesan cheese.

Nutrition:
- InfoCalories 362,Total Fat 11g,Total Carbs 45g,Protein 20g,Sodium 623mg.

Salmon With Dill Chutney

Servings:2
Cooking Time:15 Min
Ingredients:
- 2 salmon fillets
- Juice from½lemon
- 2 cups water/500ml
- ¼tsp paprika/1.25g
- salt and freshly ground pepper to taste
- For Chutney:
- ¼cup extra virgin olive oil/62.5ml
- ¼cup fresh dill/32.5g
- Juice from½lemon
- Sea salt to taste

Directions:
1. Inafood processor,blend all the chutney Ingredients until creamy.Set aside.To your Foodi,add the water and place a reversible rack.
2. Arrange salmon fillets skin-side down on the steamer basket.Drizzle lemon juice over salmon and applyaseasoning of paprika.
3. Seal the pressure lid,choose Pressure,set to High,and set the timer to 3 minutes;press Start.When ready,release the pressure quickly.Season the fillets with pepper and salt,transfer to a serving plate and top with the dill chutney.

Orange Glazed Cod&Snap Peas

Servings:4
Cooking Time:15 Minutes
Ingredients:
- 2 tsp olive oil
- 1 tsp ginger
- 2 cloves garlic,chopped fine
- 1 bunch green onions,sliced
- 2/3 cup orange juice,unsweetened
- 1/3 cup water
- 2 tsp soy sauce,low sodium
- 1 tbsp.sugar
- 4 cod fillets,1-inch thick
- 2 cups sugar snap peas

Directions:
1. Add oil to the cooking pot and set to sautéon med-high heat.
2. Once oil is hot,add ginger,garlic,and half the green onions.Cook,stirring occasionally,3 minutes or until garlic is soft.
3. Add orange juice,water,soy sauce,and sugar and mix well.
4. Add the rack to the pot.Place the fish in the baking pan and place on rack.Set to bake on 325°F.Add the tender-crisp lid and cook 5 minutes.
5. Add the peas on top of the fish.Recover and cook another 3-5 minutes or until fish flakes easily with a fork.
6. Transfer fish and peas to serving plates and top with sauce and the remaining green onions.Serve immediately.

Nutrition:
- InfoCalories 157,Total Fat 3g,Total Carbs 13g,Protein 20g,Sodium 439mg.

Shrimp&Zoodles

Servings:6
Cooking Time:x
Ingredients:
- 2 tbsp.olive oil,divided
- 1 lb.shrimp,peel&devein
- 2 cloves garlic,chopped fine
- 3 zucchini,peel&spiralize
- ½tsp salt
- ¼tsp pepper
- ½tsp red pepper flakes
- 1 tbsp.fresh lemon juice
- 1 cup cherry tomatoes,halved

Directions:
1. Add 1 tablespoon oil to the cooking pot and set to sautéon medium heat.Add shrimp and cook until pink 2-3 minutes.Transfer to a plate and cover.
2. Add remaining oil to the pot with the garlic.Cook 1 minute,stirring.
3. Add the zucchini,salt,pepper,red pepper flakes,lemon juice,and tomatoes and toss to combine.Cook until zucchini is tender,about 5-7 minutes,stirring occasionally.
4. Place shrimp on top of the zucchini mixture,cover,and turn off heat.Let sit for 1 minute.Serve immediately.

Nutrition:
- InfoCalories 153,Total Fat 7g,Total Carbs 5g,Protein 19g,Sodium 283mg.

Lemon Cod Goujons And Rosemary Chips

Servings:4
Cooking Time:100 Min
Ingredients:
- 4 cod fillets,cut into strips
- 2 potatoes,cut into chips
- 4 lemon wedges to serve
- 2 eggs
- 1 cup arrowroot starch/130g
- 1 cup flour/130g
- 2 tbsps olive oil/30ml
- 3 tbsp fresh rosemary;chopped/45g
- 1 tbsp cumin powder/15g
- ½tbsp cayenne powder/7.5g
- 1 tsp black pepper,plus more for seasoning/5g
- 1 tsp salt,plus more for seasoning/5g
- Zest and juice from 1 lemon
- Cooking spray

Directions:
1. Fix the Crisping Basket in the pot and close the crisping lid.Choose Air Crisp,set the temperature to 375°F or 191°C,and the time to 5 minutes.Choose Start/Stop to preheat the pot.
2. In a bowl,whisk the eggs,lemon zest,and lemon juice.In another bowl,combine the arrowroot starch,flour,cayenne powder,cumin,black pepper,and salt.
3. Coat each cod strip in the egg mixture,and then dredge in the flour mixture,coating well on all sides.Grease the preheated basket with cooking spray.Place the coated fish in the basket and oil with cooking spray.
4. Close the crisping lid.Choose Air Crisp,set the temperature to 375°F or 191°C,and the time to 15 minutes;press Start/Stop.Toss the potatoes with oil and season with salt and pepper.
5. After 15 minutes,check the fish making sure the pieces are as crispy as desired.Remove the fish from the basket.
6. Pour the potatoes in the basket.Close the crisping lid;choose Air Crisp,set the temperature to 400°F or 205°C,and the time to 24 minutes;press Start/Stop.
7. After 12 minutes,open the lid,remove the basket and shake the fries.Return the basket to the pot and close the lid to continue cooking until crispy.
8. When ready,sprinkle with fresh rosemary.Serve the fish with the potatoes and lemon wedges.

Flounder Veggie Soup

Servings:10
Cooking Time:20 Minutes
Ingredients:
- 2 cups water,divided
- 14 oz.chicken broth,low sodium
- 2 lbs.potatoes,peeled&cubed
- 1 onion,chopped
- 2 stalks celery,chopped
- 1 carrot,chopped
- 1 bay leaf
- 2 12 oz.cans evaporated milk,fat free
- 4 tbsp.butter
- 1 lb.flounder filets,cut in 1/2-inch pieces
- ½tsp thyme
- ¼tsp salt
- ¼tsp pepper

Directions:
1. Add 1½cups water,broth,potatoes,onion,celery,carrot,and the bay leaf to the cooking pot.Stir to mix.
2. Add the lid and set to pressure cooker on high.Set the timer for 8 minutes.When the timer goes off,use quick release to remove the lid.
3. Set cooker to sauté on med-low.Stir in milk,butter,fish,thyme,salt and pepper and bring to a boil.
4. In a small bowl,whisk together remaining water and cornstarch until smooth.Add to the soup and cook,stirring,until thickened.Discard the bay leaf and serve.

Nutrition:
- InfoCalories 213,Total Fat 6g,Total Carbs 25g,Protein 14g,Sodium 649mg.

Spicy Shrimp Pasta With Vodka Sauce

Servings:6
Cooking Time:11 Minutes
Ingredients:
- 2 tablespoons extra-virgin olive oil
- 2 tablespoons minced garlic
- 1 teaspoon crushed red pepper flakes
- 1 small red onion,diced
- Kosher salt
- Freshly ground black pepper
- ¾cup vodka
- 2¾cups vegetable stock
- 1 can crushed tomatoes
- 1 box penne pasta
- 1 pound frozen shrimp,peeled and deveined
- 1 package cream cheese,cubed
- 4 cups shredded mozzarella cheese

Directions:
1. Select SEAR/SAUTÉ and set to MD:HI.Select START/STOP to begin.Let preheat for 5 minutes.
2. Add the olive oil,garlic,and crushed red pepper flakes.Cook until garlic is golden brown,about 1 minute.Add the onions and season with salt and pepper and cook until translucent,about 2 minutes.
3. Stir in the vodka,vegetable stock,crushed tomatoes,penne pasta,and frozen shrimp.Assemble pressure lid,making sure the pressure release valve is in the SEAL position.
4. Select PRESSURE and set temperature to HI.Set time to 6 minutes.Select START/STOP to begin.
5. When pressure cooking is complete,quick release the pressure by turning the pressure release valve to the VENT position.Carefully remove lid when unit has finished releasing pressure.
6. Stir in the cream cheese until it has melted.Layer the mozzarella on top of the pasta.Close crisping lid.
7. Select AIR CRISP,set temperature to 400°F,and set time to 5 minutes.Select START/STOP to begin.
8. When cooking is complete,open lid and serve.

Nutrition:
- InfoCalories:789,Total Fat:35g,Sodium:1302mg,Carbohydrates:63g,Protein:47g.

Fish Broccoli Stew

Servings: 4
Cooking Time: 20 Minutes
Ingredients:
- 1-pound white fish fillets, chopped
- 1 cup broccoli, chopped
- 3 cups fish stock
- 1 onion, diced
- 2 cups celery stalks, chopped
- 1 cup heavy cream
- 1 bay leaf
- 1 and 1/2 cups cauliflower, diced
- 1 carrot, sliced
- 2 tablespoons butter
- 1/4 teaspoon garlic powder
- 1/2 teaspoon salt
- 1/4 teaspoon black pepper

Directions:
1. Select "Sauté" mode on your Ninja Foodi.
2. Add butter, and let it melt.
3. Stir in onion and carrots, cook for 3 minutes.
4. Stir in remaining ingredients.
5. Close the Ninja Foodi's lid.
6. Cook for 4 minutes on High.
7. Release the pressure naturally over 10 minutes.
8. Remove the bay leave once cooked.
9. Serve and enjoy.

Nutrition:
- InfoCalories: 298g; Fat: 18g; Carbohydrates: 6g; Protein: 24g

Penne All Arrabbiata With Seafood And Chorizo

Servings: 4
Cooking Time: 50 Min
Ingredients:
- 16 ounces penne/480g
- 8 ounces shrimp, peeled and deveined/240g
- 8 ounces scallops/240g
- 12 clams, cleaned and debearded
- 1 jar Arrabbiata sauce/720ml
- 1 onion; diced
- 3 cups fish broth/750ml
- 1 chorizo; sliced
- 1 tbsp olive oil/15ml
- ½tsp freshly ground black pepper/2.5g
- ½tsp salt/2.5g

Directions:
1. Choose Sear/Sauté on the pot and set to Medium High. Choose Start/Stop to preheat the pot. Heat the oil and add the chorizo, onion, and garlic; sauté them for about 5 minutes. Stir in the penne, Arrabbiata sauce, and broth.
2. Season with the black pepper and salt and mix. Seal the pressure lid, choose Pressure, set to High and set the time to 2 minutes; press Start. When the time is over, do a quick pressure release and carefully open the lid.
3. Choose Sear/Sauté and set to Medium High. Choose Start/Stop. Stir in the shrimp, scallops, and clams. Put the pressure lid together and set to the Vent position.
4. Cover and cook for 5 minutes, until the clams have opened and the shrimp and scallops are opaque and cooked through.
5. Discard any unopened clams. Spoon the seafood and chorizo pasta into serving bowls and serve warm.

Salmon Chowder

Servings: 8
Cooking Time: 30 Minutes
Ingredients:
- 3 tbsp. butter
- ½cup celery, chopped
- ½cup onion, chopped
- ½cup green bell pepper, chopped
- 1 clove garlic, chopped fine
- 14½oz. chicken broth, low sodium
- 1 cup potatoes, peeled & cubed
- 1 cup carrots, chopped
- 1 tsp salt
- ½tsp pepper
- 1 tsp fresh dill, chopped
- 1 can cream-style corn
- 2 cups half and half
- 2 cups salmon, cut in 1-inch pieces

Directions:
1. Add the butter to the cooking pot and set to sauté on med-high heat.
2. Add the celery, onion, green pepper, and garlic and cook, stirring frequently, until vegetables start to soften.
3. Add the broth, potatoes, carrots, salt, pepper and dill and stir to mix.
4. Add the lid and set to pressure cook on high. Set the timer for 10 minutes. When the timer goes off, release the pressure with quick release.
5. Set back to sauté on medium and add the corn, cream, and salmon. Bring to a simmer and cook 15 minutes, or until salmon is cooked through. Serve.

Nutrition:
- InfoCalories 244, Total Fat 10g, Total Carbs 21g, Protein 18g, Sodium 905mg.

Teriyaki Salmon

Servings: 4
Cooking Time: 15 Minutes
Ingredients:
- ½cup brown sugar
- ½cup soy sauce, low sodium
- ¼cup cider vinegar
- 2 cloves garlic, chopped fine
- ¼tsp pepper
- ½tsp salt
- ½tsp sesame oil
- 1 tbsp. water
- 1 tbsp. cornstarch
- 4 salmon filets
- 2 tbsp. green onions, sliced thin
- 2 tbsp. sesame seeds

Directions:
1. Set to sauté on medium heat. Add the brown sugar, soy sauce, vinegar, garlic, pepper, salt, and oil to the cooking pot. Stir until smooth.
2. In a small bowl, whisk together the water and cornstarch until smooth. Slowly whisk it into the sauce. Bring to a boil and cook 1-2 minutes until it starts to thicken. Reserve ¼cup sauce.

Ninja Foodi Cookbook

3. Set cooker to bake on 400°F.Add the salmon to the pot and spoon sauce over the top.Add the tender-crisp lid and bake 15 minutes until salmon is firm to the touch but flakes easily.
4. Transfer salmon to serving plates and brush tops with reserved sauce.Garnish with green onion and sesame seeds and serve.
Nutrition:
- InfoCalories 309,Total Fat 14g,Total Carbs 34g,Protein 38g,Sodium 2090mg.

Garlic Shrimp

Servings:8
Cooking Time:5 Minutes
Ingredients:
- Nonstick cooking spray
- 1 lb.large shrimp,peeled&deveined
- 2 tbsp.butter,melted
- 4 cloves garlic,chopped fine
- ¼cup fresh parsley,chopped
- ¼tsp salt
- 1 tbsp.fresh lemon juice

Directions:
1. Spray the fryer basket with cooking oil.
2. Add the shrimp to the basket.
3. In a small bowl,combine remaining ingredients and pour over shrimp.Toss to coat.
4. Add the tender-crisp lid and set to air fry on 350°F.Cook 3-5 minutes until all the shrimp turn pink,stirring them after 2 minutes.Serve immediately.
Nutrition:
- InfoCalories 68,Total Fat 3g,Total Carbs 1g,Protein 8g,Sodium 417mg.

Classic Crab Imperial

Servings:6
Cooking Time:20 Minutes
Ingredients:
- 1 cup mayonnaise
- 2 eggs,lightly beaten
- 2 tsp sugar
- 2 tsp Old Bay seasoning
- 1 tsp lemon juice
- 2 tsp parsley,chopped fine
- 2 lb.jumbo lump crab meat

Directions:
1. In a medium bowl,combine mayonnaise,eggs,sugar,Old Bay,lemon juice,and parsley and mix well.
2. Gently fold in crab.Divide evenly between 6 ramekins and place in the cooking pot.
3. Add the tender-crisp lid and set to bake on 350°F.Bake 20-25 minutes until the top is golden brown.Let cool slightly before serving.
Nutrition:
- InfoCalories 382,Total Fat 18g,Total Carbs 10g,Protein 43g,Sodium 1201mg.

Crab Cakes

Servings:4
Cooking Time:55 Min
Ingredients:
- ½cup cooked crab meat/65g
- ¼cup breadcrumbs/32.5g
- ¼cup chopped celery/32.5g
- ¼cup chopped red pepper/32.5g
- ¼cup chopped red onion/32.5g
- Zest of½lemon
- 3 tbsp mayonnaise/45mk
- 1 tbsp chopped basil/15g
- 2 tbsp chopped parsley/30g
- Old Bay seasoning,as desired
- Cooking spray

Directions:
1. Place all Ingredients inalarge bowl and mix well until thoroughly incorporated.Make 4 large crab cakes from the mixture and place on a lined sheet.Refrigerate for 30 minutes,to set.
2. Spay the air basket with cooking spray and arrange the crab cakes in it.
3. Close the crisping lid and cook for 7 minutes on each side on Air Crisp at 390°F or 199°C.

Parmesan Tilapia

Servings:4
Cooking Time:15 Min
Ingredients:
- ¾cup grated Parmesan cheese/98g
- 4 tilapia fillets
- 1 tbsp olive oil/15ml
- 1 tbsp chopped parsley/15g
- ¼tsp garlic powder/1.25g
- 2 tsp paprika/10g
- ¼tsp salt/1.25g

Directions:
1. Mix parsley,Parmesan,garlic,salt,and paprika,in a shallow bowl.Brush the olive oil over the fillets,and then coat them with the Parmesan mixture.
2. Place the tilapia ontoalined baking sheet,and then into the Ninja Foodi.
3. Close the crisping lid and cook for about 4 to 5 minutes on all sides on Air Crisp mode at 350°F or 177°C.

Sweet&Spicy Shrimp

Servings:4
Cooking Time:5 Minutes
Ingredients:
- ¾cup pineapple juice,unsweetened
- 1 red bell pepper,sliced
- 1½cups cauliflower,grated
- ¼cup dry white wine
- ½cup water
- 2 tbsp.soy sauce
- 2 tbsp.Thai sweet chili sauce
- 1 tbsp.chili paste
- 1 lb.large shrimp,frozen
- 4 green onions,chopped,white&green separated
- 1½cups pineapple chunks,drained

Directions:
1. Add¾cup pineapple juice along with remaining ingredients,except the pineapple chunks and green parts of the onion,to the cooking pot.Stir to mix.
2. Add the lid and set to pressure cook on high.Set timer for 2 minutes.When the timer goes off,release pressure 10 minutes before opening the pot.
3. Add the green parts of the onions and pineapple chunks and stir well.Serve immediately.
Nutrition:
- InfoCalories 196,Total Fat 1g,Total Carbs 22g,Protein 26g,Sodium 764mg.

Blackened Salmon

Servings: 4
Cooking Time: 10 Minutes
Ingredients:
- 1 tbsp.plus 1 tsp sweet paprika
- 1 tsp garlic powder
- 1 tsp oregano
- 1 tsp salt
- ¾tsp cayenne pepper
- 2 tbsp.olive oil
- 4 salmon filets,skin on
- 1 lemon,cut in wedges

Directions:
1. In a shallow dish,combine all the seasonings.Press the salmon filets,flesh side down,into the seasonings to coat well.
2. Set to sear on medium heat and add the oil.Place the salmon,skin side up,in the pot and cook until blackened,about 3 minutes.
3. Turn the filets over and cook another 5-7 minutes or until they reach desired doneness.Serve immediately with lemon wedges.

Nutrition:
- InfoCalories 313,Total Fat 18g,Total Carbs 3g,Protein 34g,Sodium 368mg.

Mussel Chowder With Oyster Crackers

Servings: 4
Cooking Time: 75 Min
Ingredients:
- 1 pound parsnips,peeled and cut into chunks/450g
- 3 cans chopped mussels,drained,liquid reserved/180g
- 1½cups heavy cream/375ml
- 2 cups oyster crackers/260g
- ¼cup white wine/62.5ml
- ¼cup finely grated Pecorino Romano cheese/32.5g
- 1 cup clam juice/130g
- 2 thick pancetta slices,cut into thirds
- 1 bay leaf
- 2 celery stalks;chopped
- 1 medium onion;chopped
- 1 tbsp flour/15g
- 2 tbsps chopped fresh chervil/30g
- 2 tbsps melted ghee/30g
- ½tsp garlic powder/2.5g
- 1 tsp salt;divided/5g
- 1 tsp dried rosemary/5g

Directions:
1. To preheat the Foodi,close the crisping lid and Choose Air Crisp;adjust the temperature to 375°F or 191°C and the time to 2 minutes;press Start.In a bowl,pour in the oyster crackers.Drizzle with the melted ghee,add the cheese,garlic powder,and½tsp or 2.5g of salt.Toss to coat the crackers.Transfer to the crisping basket.
2. Once the pot is ready,open the pressure lid and fix the basket in the pot.Close the lid and Choose Air Crisp;adjust the temperature to 375°F or 191°C and the cook time to 6 minutes;press Start.
3. After 3 minutes,carefully open the lid and mix the crackers with a spoon.Close the lid and resume cooking until crisp and lightly browned.Take out the basket and set aside to cool.
4. On the pot,choose Sear/Sautéand adjust to Medium.Press Start.Add the pancetta and cook for 5 minutes,turning once or twice,until crispy.
5. Remove the pancetta toapaper towel-lined plate to drain fat;set aside.
6. Sautéthe celery and onion in the pancetta grease for 1 minute or until the vegetables start softening.Mix the flour into the vegetables to coat evenly and pour the wine over the veggies.Cook for about 1 minute or until reduced by about one-third.
7. Pour in the clam juice,the reserved mussel liquid,parsnips,remaining salt,rosemary,and bay leaf.Seal the pressure lid,choose Pressure;adjust the pressure to High and the cook time to 4 minutes.Press Start.
8. After cooking,perform a natural pressure release for 5 minutes.Stir in the mussels and heavy cream.Choose Sear/Sautéand adjust to Medium.Press Start to simmer to the chowder and heat the mussels.Carefully remove and discard the bay leaf after.
9. Spoon the soup into bowls and crumble the pancetta over the top.Garnish with the chervil andahandful of oyster crackers,serving the remaining crackers on the side.

Haddock With Sanfaina

Servings: 4
Cooking Time: 40 Min
Ingredients:
- 4 haddock fillets
- 1 can diced tomatoes,drained/435g
- ½small onion;sliced
- 1 small jalapeño pepper,seeded and minced
- 2 large garlic cloves,minced
- 1 eggplant;cubed
- 1 bell pepper;chopped
- 1 bay leaf
- ⅓cup sliced green olives/44g
- ¼cup chopped fresh chervil;divided/32.5g
- 3 tbsps olive oil/45ml
- 3 tbsps capers;divided/45g
- ½tsp dried basil/2.5g
- ¼tsp salt/1.25g

Directions:
1. Season the fish on both sides with salt,place in the refrigerator,and make the sauce.Press Sear/Sautéand set to Medium.Press Start.Melt the butter until no longer foaming.Add onion,eggplant,bell pepper,jalapeño,and garlic;sautéfor 5 minutes.
2. Stir in the tomatoes,bay leaf,basil,olives,half of the chervil,and half of the capers.Remove the fish from the refrigerator and lay on the vegetables in the pot.
3. Seal the pressure lid,choose Pressure;adjust the pressure to Low and the cook time to 3 minutes;press Start.After cooking,doaquick pressure release and carefully open the lid.Remove and discard the bay leaf.
4. Transfer the fish to a serving platter and spoon the sauce over.Sprinkle with the remaining chervil and capers.Serve.

Caramelized Salmon

Servings: 4
Cooking Time: 10 Minutes
Ingredients:
- 1 tbsp.coconut oil,melted
- 1/3 cup Stevia brown sugar,packed
- 3 tbsp.fish sauce

Ninja Foodi Cookbook

- 1½ tbsp. soy sauce
- 1 tsp fresh ginger, peeled & grated
- 2 tsp lime zest, finely grated
- 1 tbsp. fresh lime juice
- ½ tsp pepper
- 4 salmon fillets
- 1 tbsp. green onions, sliced
- 1 tbsp. cilantro chopped

Directions:
1. Add the oil, brown sugar, fish sauce, soy sauce, ginger, zest, juice, and pepper to the cooking pot. Stir to mix.
2. Set to sauté on medium heat and bring mixture to a simmer, stirring frequently. Turn heat off.
3. Add the fish to the sauce making sure it is covered. Add the lid and set to pressure cooking on low. Set the timer for 1 minute.
4. When the timer goes off let the pressure release naturally for 5 minutes, the release it manually. Fish is done when it flakes with a fork.
5. Transfer fish to a serving dish with the caramelized side up.
6. Set cooker back to sauté on medium and cook sauce 3-4 minutes until it's thickened. Spoon over fish and garnish with chopped green onions and scallions. Serve.

Nutrition:
- InfoCalories 316, Total Fat 18g, Total Carbs 5g, Protein 35g, Sodium 1514mg.

Curried Salmon & Sweet Potatoes

Servings: 4
Cooking Time: 20 Minutes
Ingredients:
- Nonstick cooking spray
- 2 sweet potatoes, peeled & cubed
- 1 tbsp. + 1 tsp olive oil, divided
- ½ tsp salt
- 1 tsp thyme
- 1 tsp curry powder
- 1 tsp honey
- ½ tsp lime zest
- 1/8 tsp crushed red pepper flakes
- 4 salmon filets

Directions:
1. Spray the cooking pot with cooking spray.
2. In a large bowl, combine potatoes, 1 tablespoon oil, salt, and thyme and toss to coat the potatoes. Place in the cooking pot.
3. Add the tender-crisp lid and set to roast on 400°F. Cook potatoes 10 minutes.
4. In a small bowl, whisk together remaining oil, curry powder, honey, zest, and pepper flakes. Lay the salmon on a sheet of foil and brush the curry mixture over the top.
5. Open the lid and stir the potatoes. Add the rack to the cooking pot and place the salmon, with the foil, on the rack. Close the lid and continue to cook another 10-15 minutes until potatoes are tender and fish flakes easily with a fork. Serve.

Nutrition:
- InfoCalories 239, Total Fat 8g, Total Carbs 15g, Protein 25g, Sodium 347mg.

Spanish Steamed Clams

Servings: 6
Cooking Time: 20 Minutes
Ingredients:
- 3 tbsp. olive oil
- 1 onion, chopped fine
- 3 oz. prosciutto, chopped
- ¼ cup dry sherry
- 36 littleneck clams

Directions:
1. Add the oil to the cooking pot and set to sauté on med-high heat.
2. Add the onion and cook, stirring, 1 minutes. Reduce heat to low, add the lid and cook 10-15 minutes until onion is soft.
3. Stir in remaining ingredients and increase heat to medium. Add the lid and cook 5 minutes, or until the clams open.
4. Discard any unopened clams and serve immediately.

Nutrition:
- InfoCalories 166, Total Fat 9g, Total Carbs 5g, Protein 15g, Sodium 657mg.

Mustard And Apricot-glazed Salmon With Smashed Potatoes

Servings: 4
Cooking Time: 25 Minutes
Ingredients:
- 20 ounces baby potatoes, whole
- 1½ cups water
- 4 frozen skinless salmon fillets
- ¼ cup apricot preserves
- 2 teaspoons Dijon mustard
- 2 tablespoons extra-virgin olive oil
- ½ teaspoon kosher salt
- ½ teaspoon freshly ground black pepper

Directions:
1. Place the potatoes and water in the pot. Put Reversible Rack in pot, making sure it is in the higher position. Place salmon on the rack. Assemble pressure lid, making sure the pressure release valve is in the SEAL position.
2. Select PRESSURE and set to HI. Set time to 5 minutes. Select START/STOP to begin.
3. Mix together the apricot preserves and mustard in a small bowl.
4. When pressure cooking is complete, quick release the pressure by turning the pressure release valve to the VENT position. Carefully remove lid when unit has finished releasing pressure.
5. Carefully remove rack with salmon. Remove potatoes from pot and drain. Place the potatoes on a cutting board and, using the back of a knife, carefully press down to flatten each. Drizzle the flattened potatoes with the olive oil and season with salt and pepper.
6. Place Cook&Crisp Basket in the pot. Place the potatoes into the basket and close crisping lid.
7. Select AIR CRISP, set temperature to 390°F, and set time to 15 minutes. Select START/STOP to begin.
8. After 8 minutes, open lid, and using silicone-tipped tongs, gently flip the potatoes. Lower basket back into pot and close lid to resume cooking.
9. When cooking is complete, remove basket from pot. Return the rack with the salmon to the pot, making sure

the rack is in the higher position.Gently brush the salmon with the apricot and mustard mixture.
10. Close crisping lid.Select BROIL and set time to 5 minutes.Select START/STOP to begin.
11. When cooking is complete,remove salmon and serve immediately with the potatoes.
Nutrition:
- InfoCalories:359,Total Fat:11g,Sodium:711mg,Carbohydrates:36g,Protein:31g.

Crab Cake Casserole
Servings:8
Cooking Time:17 Minutes
Ingredients:
- 2 tablespoons canola oil
- 1 large onion,chopped
- 2 celery stalks,chopped
- 1 red bell pepper,chopped
- 1½cups basmati rice,rinsed
- 2 cups chicken stock
- ¼cup mayonnaise
- ¼cup Dijon mustard
- 3 cans lump crab meat
- 1 cup shredded Cheddar cheese,divided
- 1 sleeve butter crackers,crumbled

Directions:
1. Select SEAR/SAUTÉand set to HI.Select START/STOP to begin.Let preheat for 5 minutes.
2. Add the oil.Once hot,add the onion,celery,and bell pepper and stir.Cook for 5 minutes,stirring occasionally.
3. Stir in the rice and chicken stock.Assemble pressure lid,making sure the pressure release valve is in the SEAL position.
4. Select PRESSURE and set to HI.Set time to 2 minutes.Select START/STOP to begin.
5. When pressure cooking is complete,allow pressure to naturally release for 10 minutes.After 10 minutes,quick release any remaining pressure by moving the pressure release valve to the VENT position.Carefully remove lid when unit has finished releasing pressure.
6. Stir in the mayonnaise,mustard,crab,and½cup of Cheddar cheese.Top evenly with the crackers,then top with remaining½cup of cheese.Close crisping lid.
7. Select BAKE/ROAST,set temperature to 350°F,and set time to 10 minutes.Select START/STOP to begin.
8. When cooking is complete,open lid and serve immediately.
Nutrition:
- InfoCalories:448,Total Fat:25g,Sodium:819mg,Carbohydrates:46g,Protein:22g.

Steamed Sea Bass With Turnips
Servings:4
Cooking Time:15 Min
Ingredients:
- 4 sea bass fillets
- 4 sprigs thyme
- 1 lemon;sliced
- 2 turnips;sliced
- 1 white onion;sliced into thin rings
- 1½cups water/375ml
- 2 tsp olive oil/30ml
- 2 pinches salt
- 1 pinch ground black pepper

Directions:
1. Add water to the Foodi.Setareversible rack into the pot.Line a parchment paper to the bottom of steamer basket.Place lemon slices inasingle layer on the reversible rack.
2. Arrange fillets on the top of the lemons,cover with onion and thyme sprigs and top with turnip slices.
3. Drizzle pepper,salt,and olive oil over the mixture.Put steamer basket onto the reversible rack.Seal lid and cook on Low for 8 minutes;press Start.
4. When ready,release pressure quickly.Serve over the delicate onion rings and thinly sliced turnips.

Speedy Clams Pomodoro
Servings:4
Cooking Time:10 Minutes
Ingredients:
- 2 dozen clams
- 14½oz.stewed tomatoes,chopped&undrained
- ¼cup dry white wine
- 2 tbsp.fresh basil,chopped
- ¼tsp pepper
- 1 lemon,cut in wedges

Directions:
1. Set cooker to sautéon med-high heat.
2. Add all the ingredients to the cooking pot and stir to mix.
3. Add the lid and bring mixture to a boil.Reduce heat to low and simmer 6-8 minutes or until the clams open.
4. Discard any unopened clams and serve immediately with lemon wedges.
Nutrition:
- InfoCalories 123,Total Fat 1g,Total Carbs 12g,Protein 14g,Sodium 715mg.

Clam&Corn Chowder
Servings:4
Cooking Time:5 Hours
Ingredients:
- 1 cup chicken broth,fat free
- 2 cups potatoes,peeled&cubed
- 1 cup corn
- 1 onion,peeled&chopped
- 1 bay leaf
- ½tsp marjoram
- ½tsp salt
- ¼tsp pepper
- 1 cup skim milk
- 10½oz.minced clams,undrained
- 2 tsp cornstarch

Directions:
1. Add the chicken broth,potatoes,corn,onion,bay leaf,marjoram,salt and pepper to the cooking pot,stir to mix.
2. Add the lid and set to slow cooking on high.Cook 4-5 hours or until potatoes are tender.Discard the bay leaf.
3. Transfer the mixture to a food processor and pulse until smooth.Return to the cooking pot.
4. Stir in¾cup milk and clams.Cover and cook another 15 minutes.
5. In a glass measuring cup,whisk together remaining milk and cornstarch until smooth.Stir into chowder and cook,stirring 2-3 minutes or until thickened.Serve.
Nutrition:
- InfoCalories 267,Total Fat 4g,Total Carbs 34g,Protein 23g,Sodium 348mg.

Seafood Gumbo

Servings: 4
Cooking Time: 90 Min
Ingredients:
- 1 pound jumbo shrimp/450g
- 8 ounces lump crabmeat/240g
- 1 medium onion;chopped
- 2 green onions,finely sliced
- 1 small banana pepper,seeded and minced
- 1 small red bell pepper;chopped(about⅔cup)
- 2 celery stalks;chopped
- 2 garlic cloves,minced
- 3 cups chicken broth/750ml
- ¼cup olive oil,plus 2 tsp s/72.5ml
- ⅓cup all-purpose flour/44g
- 1 cup jasmine rice/130g
- ¾cup water/375ml
- 1½tsp s Cajun Seasoning/7.5g
- 1½tsp s salt divided/7.5g

Directions:
1. Lay the shrimp in the Crisping Basket.Season with½tsp or 2.5g of salt and 2 tsp s or 10ml of olive oil.Toss to coat and fix the basket in the inner pot.Close the crisping lid and Choose Air Crisp;adjust the temperature to 400°F or 205°C and the cook time to 6 minutes.Press Start.
2. After 3 minutes,open the lid and toss the shrimp.Close the lid and resume cooking.When ready,the shrimp should be opaque and pink.Remove the basket and set aside.
3. Choose Sear/Sautéand adjust to High.Press Start.Heat the remaining¼cup of olive oil.Whisk in the flour withawooden spoon and cook the roux that forms for 3 to 5 minutes,stirring constantly,until the roux has the color of peanut butter.Turn the pot off.
4. Stir in the Cajun,onion,bell pepper,celery,garlic,and banana pepper for about 5 minutes until the mixture slightly cools.Add the chicken broth and crabmeat,stir.
5. Put the rice into a heatproof bowl.Add the water and the remaining salt.Cover the bowl with foil.Put the reversible rack in the lower position of the pot and set the bowl in the rack.
6. Seal the pressure lid,choose Pressure;adjust the pressure to High and the cook time to 6 minutes;press Start.After cooking,perform a natural pressure for 8 minutes.Take out the rack and bowl and set aside.Stir the shrimp into the gumbo to heat it up for 3 minutes.
7. Fluff the rice withafork and divide into the center of four bowls.Spoon the gumbo around the rice and garnish with the green onions.

Sesame Tuna Steaks

Servings: 4
Cooking Time: 10 Minutes
Ingredients:
- Nonstick cooking spray
- 2 tsp sesame oil
- 1 clove garlic,chopped fine
- 4 tuna steaks
- 1/8 tsp salt
- ½tsp pepper
- ½cup sesame seeds

Directions:
1. Place the rack in the cooking pot and spray it with cooking spray.
2. In a small bowl combine the oil and garlic.Rub it on both sides of the fish.Season with salt and pepper.
3. Place the sesame seeds in a shallow dish.Press the fish in the sesame seeds to coat completely.Place them on the rack.
4. Add the tender-crisp lid and set to roast on 350°F.Cook 8-10 minutes,turning over halfway through cooking time,until fish flakes with a fork.Serve immediately.

Nutrition:
- InfoCalories 263,Total Fat 14g,Total Carbs 3g,Protein 32g,Sodium 60mg.

Almond Crusted Haddock

Servings: 4
Cooking Time: 30 Minutes
Ingredients:
- 1 tbsp.sugar
- ¾tsp cinnamon
- ¼tsp red pepper
- ½tsp salt
- 1½lbs.haddock filets
- 1 egg white,beaten
- 2 cups almonds,sliced
- 2 tbsp.butter
- ½cup Amaretto liqueur

Directions:
1. In a small bowl,combine sugar,cinnamon,red pepper,and salt until combined.Use 1 teaspoon of the mixture to season the fish.
2. Spray the fryer basket with cooking spray and place it in the cooking pot.
3. In a shallow dish,beat the egg white.
4. In a separate shallow dish,place the almonds.Dip each filet in the egg white then coat with almonds.Place them in the fryer basket and spray them lightly with cooking spray.
5. Add the tender-crisp lid and set to air fry on 350°F.Cook the fish 5 minutes,then turn over and spray with cooking spray again.Cook another 2-3 minutes until golden brown.Transfer to serving plate and keep warm.
6. In a small saucepan over medium heat,melt the butter.Add the remaining sugar mixture and Amaretto to the pan.Reduce heat to low,and cook,stirring,1-2 minutes until sauce has thickened.Pour over fish and serve immediately.

Nutrition:
- InfoCalories 576,Total Fat 30g,Total Carbs 26g,Protein 38g,Sodium 715mg.

Creamy Crab Soup

Servings: 4
Cooking Time: 45 Min
Ingredients:
- 2 lb.Crabmeat Lumps/900g
- 2 celery stalk;diced
- 1 white onion;chopped
- ¾cup heavy cream/188ml
- ½cup Half and Half cream/125ml
- 1½cup chicken broth/375ml
- ¾cup Muscadet/98g
- 6 tbsp butter/90g
- 6 tbsp flour/90g
- 3 tsp Worcestershire sauce/15ml
- 3 tsp old bay Seasoning/15ml
- 2 tsp Hot sauce/10ml

- 3 tsp minced garlic/15g
- Salt to taste
- Lemon juice to serve
- Chopped dill to serve

Directions:
1. Melt the butter on Sear/Sauté mode,and mix in the all-purpose flour,in a fast motion to make a rue.Add celery,onion,and garlic.
2. Stir and cook until soft and crispy;for 3 minutes.While stirring,gradually add the half and half cream,heavy cream,and broth.
3. Let simmer for 2 minutes.Add Worcestershire sauce,old bay seasoning,Muscadet,and hot sauce.Stir and let simmer for 15 minutes.Add the crabmeat and mix it well into the sauce.
4. Close the crisping lid and cook on Broil mode for 10 minutes to soften the meat.
5. Dish into serving bowls,garnish with dill and drizzle squirts of lemon juice over.Serve with a side of garlic crusted bread.

Cajun Shrimp

Servings:4
Cooking Time:7 Minutes
Ingredients:
- 1¼ pound shrimp
- 1/4 teaspoon cayenne pepper
- 1/2 teaspoon old bay seasoning
- 1/4 teaspoon smoked paprika
- 1 pinch of salt
- 1 tablespoon olive oil

Directions:
1. Preheat Ninja Foodi by pressing the"AIR CRISP"option and setting it to"390°F"and timer to 10 minutes.
2. Dip the shrimp into a spice mixture and oil.
3. Transfer the prepared shrimp to your Ninja Foodi Grill cooking basket and cook for 5 minutes.
4. Serve and enjoy.

Nutrition:
- InfoCalories:170;Fat:2g;Carbohydrates:5g;Protein:23g

Shrimp And Sausage Paella

Servings:4
Cooking Time:70 Min
Ingredients:
- 1 pound andouille sausage;sliced/450g
- 1 pound baby squid,cut into¼-inch rings/450g
- 1 pound jumbo shrimp,peeled and deveined/450g
- 1 white onion;chopped
- 4 garlic cloves,minced
- 1 red bell pepper;diced
- 2 cups Spanish rice/260g
- 4 cups chicken stock/1000ml
- ½ cup dry white wine/125ml
- 1 tbsp melted butter/15ml
- 1 tsp turmeric powder/5g
- 1½ tsp s sweet paprika/7.5g
- ½ tsp freshly ground black pepper/5g
- ½ tsp salt/5g

Directions:
1. Choose Sear/Sauté on the pot and set to Medium High.Choose Start/Stop to preheat the pot.Melt the butter and add the sausage.Cook until browned on both sides,about 3 minutes while stirring frequently.Remove the sausage to a plate and set aside.
2. Sauté the onion and garlic in the same fat for 3 minutes until fragrant and pour in the wine.Use a wooden spoon to scrape the bottom of the pot of any brown bits and cook for 2 minutes or until the wine reduces by half.
3. Stir in the rice and water.Season with the paprika,turmeric,black pepper,and salt.Seal the pressure lid,choose Pressure and set to High.Set the time to 5 minutes,then Choose Start/Stop.When done cooking,do a quick pressure release and carefully open the lid.
4. Choose Sear/Sauté,set to Medium High,and choose Start/Stop.Add the squid and shrimp to the pot and stir gently without mashing the rice.
5. Seal the pressure lid again and cook for 6 minutes,until the shrimp are pink and opaque.Return the sausage to the pot and mix in the bell pepper.Warm through for 2 minutes.Dish the paella and serve immediately.

Kung Pao Shrimp

Servings:4
Cooking Time:15 Minutes
Ingredients:
- 1 tbsp.olive oil
- 1 red bell pepper,seeded&chopped
- 1 green bell pepper,seeded&chopped
- 3 cloves garlic,chopped fine
- 1 lb.large shrimp,peeled&deveined
- ¼ cup soy sauce
- 1 tsp sesame oil
- 1 tsp brown sugar
- 1 tsp Sriracha
- 1/8 tsp red pepper flakes
- 1 tsp cornstarch
- 1 tbsp.water
- ¼ cup peanuts
- ¼ cup green onions,sliced thin

Directions:
1. Add oil to the cooking pot and set to sauté on med-high heat.
2. Add the bell peppers and garlic and cook,3-5 minutes,until pepper is almost tender.
3. Add the shrimp and cook until they turn pink,2-3 minutes.
4. In a small bowl,whisk together soy sauce,sesame oil,brown sugar,Sriracha,and pepper flakes until combined.
5. In a separate small bowl,whisk together cornstarch and water until smooth.Whisk into sauce and pour over shrimp mixture.Add the peanuts.
6. Cook,stirring,until the sauce has thickened,about 2-3 minutes.Serve garnished with green onions.

Nutrition:
- InfoCalories 212,Total Fat 11g,Total Carbs 10g,Protein 20g,Sodium 1729mg.

Flounder Oreganata

Servings:4
Cooking Time:15 Minutes
Ingredients:
- 1/3 cup rolled oats
- ¼ cup panko bread crumbs
- 2 cloves garlic,chopped fine
- 2 tbsp.fresh parsley,chopped,divided
- ½ tsp oregano

- 4 tsp fresh lemon juice
- 1 tsp lemon zest
- 1 tbsp.olive oil
- 1 tsp salt,divided
- ½tsp pepper
- 4 flounder fillets
- Lemon wedges

Directions:
1. Place the rack in the cooking pot and top with a piece of parchment paper.
2. Add the oats to a food processor and pulse until they are finely ground.
3. In a small bowl,combine oats,bread crumbs,garlic,1½tablespoons parsley,oregano,lemon juice,zest,oil and½tsp salt.
4. Lay the fish on the parchment paper and season with salt and pepper.Spoon bread crumb mixture over the fish,pressing lightly.
5. Add the tender-crisp lid and set to bake on 450°F.Bake 10-12 minutes until topping is golden brown and fish flakes easily with a fork.Serve garnished with parsley and lemon wedges.

Nutrition:
- InfoCalories 261,Total Fat 9g,Total Carbs 14g,Protein 30g,Sodium 1459mg.

Spiced Red Snapper

Servings:6
Cooking Time:20 Minutes
Ingredients:
- Nonstick cooking spray
- 1 onion,sliced
- 14½oz.stewed tomatoes,undrained,chopped
- 1/3 cup dry white wine
- 3 tbsp.fresh lemon juice
- 1 tsp cumin
- 1/8 tsp cinnamon
- 6 red snapper fillets

Directions:
1. Spray the cooking pot with cooking spray.
2. Set to sautéon med-high heat and add the onion.Cook,stirring,3-4 minutes or until onions are soft.
3. Add tomatoes,wine,lemon juice,cumin,,and cinnamon and cook about 5 minutes or until sauce has thickened slightly.
4. Add the fish and spoon sauce over the top.Add the lid and reduce heat to medium.Cook 8-10 minutes until fish flakes with a fork.
5. Transfer fish to serving plates and top with sauce.Serve immediately.

Nutrition:
- InfoCalories 155,Total Fat 2g,Total Carbs 8g,Protein 25g,Sodium 201mg.

Simple Salmon&Asparagus

Servings:4
Cooking Time:15 Minutes
Ingredients:
- 4 salmon filets
- 1 tsp rosemary
- ½tsp pepper,divided
- 14 oz.vegetable broth,low sodium
- 1 tbsp.lemon juice
- ½lb.asparagus,trimmed&cut in 2-inch pieces

Directions:
1. Season the fish with rosemary and¼teaspoon pepper and add to cooking pot.
2. In a small bowl,whisk together broth,lemon juice,and remaining pepper until smooth.Pour over fish.
3. Add the lid and set to sautéon medium heat.Once mixture reaches a boil,reduce heat to low and simmer 5 minutes.
4. Add the asparagus around the salmon,recover,and cook another 5 minutes until asparagus is fork-tender and fish flakes easily.Serve immediately..

Nutrition:
- InfoCalories 163,Total Fat 5g,Total Carbs 3g,Protein 25g,Sodium 454mg.

Spicy Grilled Shrimp

Servings:4
Cooking Time:6 Minutes
Ingredients:
- 1 teaspoon garlic salt
- 1/2 teaspoon black pepper
- 1 tablespoon paprika
- 1 tablespoon garlic powder
- 2 tablespoons olive oil
- 1-pound jumbo shrimps,peeled and deveined
- 2 tablespoons brown erythritol

Directions:
1. Take a mixing bowl and stir in the listed ingredients to mix well.
2. Let it chill and marinate for 30-60 minutes.
3. Preheat Ninja Foodi by pressing the"GRILL"option and setting it to"MED"and timer to 6 minutes.
4. Let it preheat until you hear a beep.
5. Set prepared shrimps over grill grate,Lock and secure the Ninja Foodi's lid and cook for 3 minutes,flip and cook for 3 minutes more.
6. Serve and enjoy.

Nutrition:
- InfoCalories:370;Fat:27g;Carbohydrates:23g;Protein:6g

Baked Cod Casserole

Servings:6
Cooking Time:20 Minutes
Ingredients:
- Nonstick cooking spray
- 1 lb.mushrooms,chopped
- 1 onion,chopped
- ½cup fresh parsley,chopped
- ½tsp salt,divided
- ½tsp pepper,divided
- 6 cod fillets
- ¾cup dry white wine
- ¾cup plain bread crumbs
- 2 tbsp.butter,melted
- 1 cup Swiss cheese,grated

Directions:
1. Spray the cooking pot with cooking spray.
2. In a medium bowl,combine mushrooms,onion,parsley,¼teaspoon salt,and¼teaspoon pepper and mix well.Spread evenly on the bottom of the cooking pot.
3. Place the fish on top of the mushroom mixture and pour the wine over them.

4. In a separate medium bowl, combine remaining ingredients and mix well. Sprinkle over the fish.
5. Add the tender-crisp lid and set to bake on 450°F. Bake 15-20 minutes or until golden brown and fish flakes easily with a fork. Serve immediately.

Nutrition:
- InfoCalories 284, Total Fat 10g, Total Carbs 16g, Protein 27g, Sodium 693mg.

Sweet & Spicy Shrimp Bowls

Servings: 8
Cooking Time: 5 Minutes

Ingredients:
- ½ cup green onions, chopped
- 1 jalapeno pepper, seeded & chopped
- 1 tsp red chili flakes
- 8 oz. crushed pineapple, drained
- 2 tbsp. honey
- 1 lime, zested & juiced
- 1 tbsp. olive oil
- 2 lbs. large shrimp, peeled & deveined
- ¼ tsp salt
- 2 cups brown rice, cooked

Directions:
1. In a small bowl, combine green onions, jalapeno, chili flakes, pineapple, honey, lime juice, and zest and mix well.
2. Add the oil to the cooking pot and set to saute on medium heat.
3. Sprinkle the shrimp with salt and cook, 3-5 minutes or until they turn pink.
4. Add the shrimp to the pineapple mixture and stir to coat.
5. Spoon rice into bowls and top with shrimp mixture. Serve immediately.

Nutrition:
- InfoCalories 188, Total Fat 3g, Total Carbs 23g, Protein 17g, Sodium 644mg.

Garlic Shrimp And Veggies

Servings: 4
Cooking Time: 5 Minutes

Ingredients:
- 2 tablespoons unsalted butter
- 1 shallot, minced
- 3 garlic cloves, minced
- ¼ cup white wine
- ½ cup chicken stock
- Juice of ½ lemon
- ½ teaspoon sea salt
- ½ teaspoon freshly ground black pepper
- 1 ½ pounds frozen shrimp, thawed
- 1 large head broccoli, cut into florets

Directions:
1. Add the butter. Select SEAR/SAUTÉ and set to MED. Select START/STOP to begin.
2. Once the butter is melted, add the shallots and cook for 3 minutes. Add the garlic and cook for 1 minute.
3. Deglaze the pot by adding the wine and using a wooden spoon to scrape the bits of garlic and shallot off the bottom of the pot. Stir in the chicken stock, lemon juice, salt, pepper, and shrimp.
4. Place the broccoli florets on top of the shrimp mixture. Assemble pressure lid, making sure the pressure release valve is in the SEAL position.
5. Select PRESSURE and set to HI. Set time to 0 minutes. Select START/STOP to begin.
6. When pressure cooking is complete, quick release the pressure by moving the pressure release valve to the VENT position. Carefully remove lid when the unit has finished releasing pressure. Serve immediately.

Nutrition:
- InfoCalories: 281, Total Fat: 8g, Sodium: 692mg, Carbohydrates: 9g, Protein: 39g.

Poached Flounder With Mango Salsa

Servings: 6
Cooking Time: 10 Minutes

Ingredients:
- 1 mango, peeled, pitted & chopped
- 1 red bell pepper, seeded & chopped
- ½ red onion, chopped fine
- 8 ¼ oz. pineapple tidbits, drain & reserve juice
- ¼ tsp salt, divided
- ½ tsp red pepper, divided
- 6 flounder filets
- ½ cup water

Directions:
1. In a medium bowl, combine mango, bell pepper, onion, pineapple, 1/8 teaspoon salt, and ¼ teaspoon pepper, mix well. Cover and refrigerate at least one hour.
2. Season fish with remaining salt and pepper and place in the cooking pot. Pour reserved pineapple juice and water over the fish.
3. Add the lid and set to sauté on med-high heat. Bring to a boil then reduce heat to low and cook 7-8 minutes or until fish flakes easily with a fork.
4. Transfer to fish to serving plates and top with mango salsa. Serve immediately.

Nutrition:
- InfoCalories 200, Total Fat 4g, Total Carbs 17g, Protein 24g, Sodium 1092mg.

Vegan & Vegetable

Italian Baked Zucchini

Servings: 6
Cooking Time: 45 Minutes
Ingredients:
- Nonstick cooking spray
- 2 tsp olive oil
- 2 lbs. zucchini, sliced ¼-inch thick
- ¼ cup onion, chopped
- 3 plum tomatoes, cut in ½-inch pieces
- 1 tbsp. parmesan cheese
- ½ cup Italian blend cheese, grated
- 1 tsp garlic powder
- 1 tsp Italian seasoning
- ¼ tsp pepper
- 1 tbsp. Italian bread crumbs

Directions:
1. Spray the cooking pot with cooking spray.
2. Add the oil to the cooking pot and set to sauté on med-high heat.
3. Add the zucchini and onion and cook, stirring occasionally, 5 minutes, until softened.
4. Stir in tomatoes, parmesan, Italian blend cheese, garlic powder, Italian seasonings, and pepper. Cook 3 minutes, stirring occasionally. Sprinkle bread crumbs over the top.
5. Add the tender-crisp lid and set to bake on 375°F. Bake 25-30 minutes until golden brown. Serve.

Nutrition:
- InfoCalories 91, Total Fat 4g, Total Carbs 8g, Protein 7g, Sodium 146mg.

Stuffed Manicotti

Servings: 4
Cooking Time: 50 Minutes
Ingredients:
- Nonstick cooking spray
- 8 manicotti shells, cooked & drained
- ½ onion, chopped
- 1 cloves garlic, chopped fine
- 1 cup mushrooms, chopped
- 16 oz. ricotta cheese, fat free
- ½ cup mozzarella cheese, grated
- 1 egg
- 1 cup spinach, chopped
- ¾ tsp Italian seasoning
- ¼ tsp pepper
- 1 cups light spaghetti sauce
- 1 tbsp. parmesan cheese, grated

Directions:
1. Spray the cooking pot and an 8x8-inch baking pan with cooking spray.
2. Set cooker to sauté on med-high heat. Add onion and garlic and cook until tender, about 3-4 minutes.
3. Add mushrooms and cook until browned. Turn off the heat.
4. In a large bowl, combine ricotta and mozzarella cheeses, egg, spinach, Italian seasoning, and pepper, mix well.
5. Add the mushroom mixture to the cheese mixture and stir to combine. Spoon into manicotti shells and lay in the prepared pan.
6. Pour the spaghetti sauce over the top and sprinkle with parmesan cheese. Cover with foil.
7. Place the rack in the cooking pot and add the manicotti. Add the tender-crisp lid and set to bake on 400°F. Bake 30-35 minutes or until heated through. Serve immediately.

Nutrition:
- InfoCalories 367, Total Fat 19g, Total Carbs 27g, Protein 24g, Sodium 308mg.

Hearty Veggie Soup

Servings: 12
Cooking Time: 15 Minutes
Ingredients:
- 2 cups water
- 3½ cups vegetable broth, low sodium
- 15 oz. red kidney beans, drained & rinsed
- 16 oz. cannellini beans, drained & rinsed
- 28 oz. tomatoes, crushed
- 10 oz. spinach, chopped
- 1 onion, chopped
- 10 oz. mixed vegetables, frozen
- 1 tsp garlic powder
- ½ tsp pepper
- 1 cup elbow macaroni

Directions:
1. Set the cooker to sauté on med-high heat.
2. Add all the ingredients, except macaroni, and stir to combine. Bring to a boil.
3. Stir in macaroni. Add the lid and set to pressure cook on high. Set timer for 10 minutes. When timer goes off, use natural release to remove the pressure. Stir well and serve.

Nutrition:
- InfoCalories 181, Total Fat 1g, Total Carbs 34g, Protein 10g, Sodium 478mg.

Radish Apples Salad

Servings: 4
Cooking Time: 15 Minutes
Ingredients:
- 1-pound radishes, roughly cubed
- 2 apples, cored and cut into wedges
- ¼ cup chicken stock
- 2 spring onions, chopped
- 3 tablespoons tomato paste
- Juice of 1 lime
- Cooking spray
- 1 tablespoon cilantro, chopped

Directions:
1. In your Ninja Foodi, combine the radishes with the apples and the other ingredients.
2. Put the Ninja Foodi's lid on and cook on High for 15 minutes.
3. Release the pressure quickly for 5 minutes, divide everything between plates and serve.

Nutrition:
- InfoCalories: 122; Fat: 5g; Carbohydrates: 4.5g; Protein: 3g

Ninja Foodi Cookbook

Crème De La Broc

Servings: 6
Cooking Time: 25 Min
Ingredients:
- 1½ cups grated yellow and white Cheddar cheese+extra for topping/195g
- 1½ oz. cream cheese/195g
- 1 medium Red onion; chopped
- 3 cloves garlic, minced
- 4 cups chopped broccoli florets, only the bushy tops/520g
- 3 cups heavy cream/750ml
- 3 cups vegetable broth/750ml
- 4 tbsp butter/60g
- 4 tbsp flour/60g
- 1 tsp Italian Seasoning/5g
- Salt and black pepper to taste

Directions:
1. Select Sear/Sauté mode, adjust to High and melt the butter once the pot is ready. Add the flour and use a spoon to stir until it clumps up. Gradually pour in the heavy cream while stirring until white sauce forms. Fetch out the butter sauce into a bowl and set aside.
2. Press Stop and add the onions, garlic, broth, broccoli, Italian seasoning, and cream cheese. Use a wooden spoon to stir the mixture.
3. Seal the lid, and select Pressure mode on High pressure for 12 minutes. Press Start/Stop. Once the timer has ended, do a quick pressure release.
4. Add in butter sauce and cheddar cheese, salt, and pepper. Close the crisping lid and cook on Broil mode for 3 minutes. Dish the soup into serving bowls, top it with extra cheese, to serve.

Artichoke Lasagna Rolls

Servings: 10
Cooking Time: 55 Minutes
Ingredients:
- 2 tsp olive oil
- ½ cup onion, chopped fine
- 24 oz. tomato and basil pasta sauce
- 1 cup ricotta cheese, low fat
- 1 egg
- 3 cloves garlic, chopped fine
- 14 oz. artichoke hearts, drained, quartered
- 2 tbsp. fresh basil, chopped
- 2 tbsp. parmesan cheese
- 10 lasagna noodles, cooked & drained

Directions:
1. Add oil to the cooking pot and set to sauté on med-high heat.
2. Add the onion and cook 5 minutes until soft. Stir in tomato sauce and cook another 5 minutes. Transfer all but 1 cup of the sauce to a bowl.
3. In a large bowl, combine ricotta cheese, egg, garlic, artichokes, basil, and parmesan cheese, mix well.
4. Lay lasagna noodles on a work surface and spoon cheese mixture over noodles. Roll up tightly and stand up in the cooking pot.
5. Pour remaining sauce over the top. Add the tender-crisp lid and set to bake on 350°F. Bake 40-45 minutes. Serve.

Nutrition:
- InfoCalories 172, Total Fat 6g, Total Carbs 23g, Protein 8g, Sodium 330mg.

Caprese Pasta Salad

Servings: 8
Cooking Time: 3 Minutes
Ingredients:
- 1 box elbow pasta
- 4 cups water
- 1 tablespoon sea salt
- 2 tablespoons extra-virgin olive oil
- ½ cup red bell pepper, diced
- 1 cup cherry tomatoes, sliced
- ¼ cup black olives, sliced
- ½ pound fresh mozzarella, diced
- ½ cup chopped fresh basil
- ½ cup Italian dressing

Directions:
1. Place the pasta, water, and salt in the pot. Assemble pressure lid, making sure the pressure release valve is in the SEAL position.
2. Select PRESSURE and set to HI. Set time to 3 minutes. Select START/STOP to begin.
3. When pressure cooking is complete, allow pressure to naturally release for 10 minutes. After 10 minutes, quick release remaining pressure by moving the pressure release valve to the VENT position. Carefully remove lid when unit has finished releasing pressure.
4. Drain the pasta in a colander. Place the pasta in a large bowl and toss with the olive oil. Set aside to cool for 20 minutes.
5. Stir in the bell pepper, cherry tomatoes, olives, mozzarella, and basil. Gently fold in the Italian seasoning.
6. Serve immediately or cover and refrigerate for later.

Nutrition:
- InfoCalories: 377, Total Fat: 15g, Sodium: 694mg, Carbohydrates: 45g, Protein: 14g.

Baked Linguine

Servings: 8
Cooking Time: 30 Minutes
Ingredients:
- 1 tbsp. olive oil
- 1 zucchini, cut in 1-inch pieces
- 1 red bell pepper, cut in 1-inch pieces
- 1 eggplant, cut in 1-inch pieces
- 26 oz. light spaghetti sauce
- 1 cup salsa
- 1 lb. linguine, cooked & drained
- ¾ cup mozzarella cheese, grated

Directions:
1. Add the oil to the cooking pot and set to sauté on med-high heat.
2. Add the zucchini, pepper, and eggplant and cook, stirring occasionally, until tender, about 6-8 minutes.
3. Stir in spaghetti sauce and salsa until combined. Add linguine and mix well. Sprinkle cheese over the top.
4. Add the tender-crisp lid and set to bake on 350°F. Bake 25-30 minutes until cheese is melted and linguine is heated through. Serve.

Nutrition:
- InfoCalories 200, Total Fat 4g, Total Carbs 33g, Protein 9g, Sodium 698mg.

Tomato Bisque

Servings: 6
Cooking Time: 3 Hours
Ingredients:
- 2 28 oz. cans tomatoes, crushed
- 1 tbsp. sugar
- 1 tbsp. fresh basil, chopped
- 1 tsp garlic powder
- 1 tsp onion powder
- ½ tsp pepper
- 12 oz. evaporated milk, low fat

Directions:
1. Place the tomatoes, sugar, basil, garlic powder, onion powder, and pepper in the cooking pot, stir to mix.
2. Add the lid and set to slow cook on high. Cook 2½ hours.
3. Stir in evaporated milk and let cook another 30 minutes. Serve.

Nutrition:
- InfoCalories 141, Total Fat 1g, Total Carbs 29g, Protein 9g, Sodium 558mg.

Bell Peppers Mix

Servings: 4
Cooking Time: 16 Minutes
Ingredients:
- 1-pound red bell peppers, cut into wedges
- ½ teaspoon curry powder
- ½ cup tomato sauce
- Black pepper and salt to the taste
- 1 tablespoon olive oil
- 2 garlic cloves, minced
- 1 tablespoon parsley, chopped

Directions:
1. Put the reversible rack in the Foodi, add the baking pan inside and grease it with the oil.
2. Add the peppers, curry powder and the other ingredients except for the parsley, toss a bit.
3. Cook on Baking mode at 380°F for 16 minutes.
4. Divide cooked peppers between plates and serve with the parsley sprinkled on top.

Nutrition:
- InfoCalories:150; Fat:3.5g; Carbohydrates:3.1g; Protein:1.2g

Spinach, Tomatoes, And Butternut Squash Stew

Servings: 6
Cooking Time: 65 Min
Ingredients:
- 2 lb. butternut squash, peeled and cubed/900g
- 1 can sundried tomatoes, undrained/450g
- 2 cans chickpeas, drained/450g
- 1 white onion; diced
- 4 garlic cloves, minced
- 4 cups baby spinach/520g
- 4 cups vegetable broth/1000ml
- 1 tbsp butter/15g
- ½ tsp smoked paprika/2.5g
- 1 tsp coriander powder/5g
- 1½ tsp s cumin powder/7.5g
- ½ tsp salt/2.5g
- ½ tsp freshly ground black pepper/2.5g

Directions:
1. Choose Sear/Sauté, set to Medium High, and the timer to 5 minutes; press Start/Stop to preheat the pot. Combine the butter, onion, and garlic in the pot. Cook, stirring occasionally; for 5 minutes or until soft and fragrant.
2. Add the butternut squash, vegetable broth, tomatoes, chickpeas, cumin, paprika, coriander, salt, and black pepper to the pot. Put the pressure lid together and lock in the Seal position.
3. Choose Pressure, set to High, and set the time to 8 minutes; press Start/Stop.
4. When the timer is done reading, performa quick pressure release. Stir in the spinach to wilt, adjust the taste with salt and black pepper, and serve warm.

Vegan Split Pea Soup

Servings: 8
Cooking Time: 8 Hours
Ingredients:
- 16 oz. dried split peas
- 2 cups carrots, chopped
- 1 cup onion, chopped
- 1 cup celery, chopped
- 3 cups water
- ½ tsp salt
- ½ tsp pepper
- 4 cups vegetable broth, low sodium
- 1 bay leaf

Directions:
1. Place all ingredients in the cooking pot and stir to mix.
2. Add the lid and set to slow cook on low. Cook 8 hours or until peas are tender and soup has thickened.
3. Discard the bay leaf and serve immediately.

Nutrition:
- InfoCalories 225, Total Fat 1g, Total Carbs 42g, Protein 14g, Sodium 655mg.

Cauliflower Steaks & Veggies

Servings: 6
Cooking Time: 45 Minutes
Ingredients:
- ¼ cup butter, melted
- 1 tbsp. olive oil
- 3 tbsp. lemon juice
- 2 tsp fresh parsley, chopped
- ¾ tsp onion powder
- ¾ tsp garlic powder
- ½ tsp salt
- ¼ tsp pepper
- 1 head cauliflower, cut in ½-inch thick slices
- 12 baby carrots
- 6 small potatoes, halved
- 1 zucchini, cut in 1-inch pieces

Directions:
1. In a large bowl, whisk together butter, oil, lemon juice, parsley, onion powder, garlic powder, salt, and pepper.
2. Line a baking sheet with foil. Brush both sides of cauliflower steaks with butter mixture and place on baking sheet.
3. Add remaining vegetables to the butter mixture and toss to coat. Place in the cooking pot. Add the rack and place the cauliflower on the rack.

Ninja Foodi Cookbook

4. Add the tender-crisp lid and set to roast on 400°F. Bake 40-45 minutes until vegetables are tender and starting to brown, turning over halfway through cooking time. Serve.
Nutrition:
- InfoCalories 260, Total Fat 11g, Total Carbs 38g, Protein 6g, Sodium 313mg.

Okra Stew

Servings: 4
Cooking Time: 12 Minutes
Ingredients:
- 1-pound okra, trimmed
- 2 leeks, sliced
- Black pepper and salt to the taste
- 1 cup tomato sauce
- ¼ cup pine nuts, toasted
- 1 tablespoon cilantro, chopped

Directions:
1. In your Ninja Foodi, mix the okra with the leeks and the other ingredients except the cilantro.
2. Put the Ninja Foodi's lid on and cook on High for 12 minutes.
3. Release the pressure quickly for 5 minutes, divide the okra mix into bowls and serve with the cilantro sprinkled on top.
Nutrition:
- InfoCalories:146;Fat:3g;Carbohydrates:4g;Protein:3g

Quinoa Pesto Bowls With Veggies

Servings: 2
Cooking Time: 30 Min
Ingredients:
- 1 cup quinoa, rinsed/130g
- 1 cup broccoli florets/130g
- ¼ cup pesto sauce/62.5ml
- 2 cups water/500ml
- ½ pound Brussels sprouts/225g
- 2 eggs
- 1 small beet, peeled and cubed
- 1 carrot, peeled and chopped
- 1 avocado, thinly sliced
- lemon wedges; for serving
- salt and ground black pepper to taste

Directions:
1. In the pot, mix water, salt, quinoa and pepper. Set the reversible rack to the pot over quinoa. To the reversible rack, add eggs, Brussels sprouts, broccoli, beet cubes, carrots, pepper and salt.
2. Seal the pressure lid, choose Pressure, set to High, and set the timer to 1 minute. Press Start. Release pressure naturally for 10 minutes, then release any remaining pressure quickly.
3. Remove reversible rack from the pot and set the eggs to a bowl of ice water. Peel and halve the eggs. Use a fork to fluff quinoa.
4. Separate quinoa, broccoli, avocado, carrots, beet, Brussels sprouts, eggs, and a dollop of pesto into two bowls. Serve alongside lemon wedge.

Pomegranate Radish Mix

Servings: 4
Cooking Time: 8 Minutes
Ingredients:
- 1-pound radishes, roughly cubed
- Black pepper and salt to the taste
- 2 garlic cloves, minced
- ½ cup chicken stock
- 2 tablespoons pomegranate juice
- ¼ cup pomegranate seeds

Directions:
1. In your Ninja Foodi, combine the radishes with the stock and the other ingredients.
2. Put the Ninja Foodi's lid on and cook on High for 8 minutes.
3. Release the pressure quickly for 5 minutes, divide everything between plates and serve.
Nutrition:
- InfoCalories:133;Fat:2.3g;Carbohydrates:2.4g;Protein:2g

Burrito Bowls

Servings: 4
Cooking Time: 30 Min
Ingredients:
- 1 can diced tomatoes/435g
- 1 can black beans, drained and rinsed/435g
- 1½ cups vegetable stock/375ml
- 1 cup frozen corn kernels/130g
- 1 cup quinoa, rinsed/130g
- 1 avocado; sliced
- 1 onion
- 2 garlic cloves, minced
- 2 tbsp chopped cilantro/30g
- 1 tbsp roughly chopped fresh coriander/15g
- 2 tbsp olive oil/30ml
- 1 tbsp chili powder/15g
- 2 tsp ground cumin/10g
- 2 tsp paprika/10g
- 1 tsp salt/5g
- ½ tsp black pepper/2.5g
- ¼ tsp cayenne pepper/1.25g
- Cheddar cheese, grated for garnish

Directions:
1. Warm oil on Sear/Sauté. Add in onion and cook for 3 to 5 minutes until fragrant. Add garlic and cook for 2 more minutes until soft and golden brown. Add in chili powder, paprika, cayenne pepper, salt, cumin, and black pepper and cook for 1 minute until spices are soft.
2. Pour quinoa into onion and spice mixture and stir to coat quinoa completely in spices. Add diced tomatoes, black beans, vegetable stock, and corn; stir to combine.
3. Seal the pressure lid, choose Pressure, set to High, and set the timer to 7 minutes. Press Start. When ready, release the pressure quickly. Open the lid and let sit for 6 minutes until flavors combine. Use a fork to fluff quinoa and season with pepper and salt if desired.
4. Into quinoa and beans mixture, stir in cilantro and divide among plates. Top with cheese and avocado slices.

Creamy Golden Casserole

Servings: 6
Cooking Time: 40 Minutes
Ingredients:
- Nonstick cooking spray
- 2 lbs. summer squash, cut in 1-inch pieces
- ¾ cup sharp cheddar cheese, reduced fat, grated & divided
- ¼ cup light mayonnaise

Ninja Foodi Cookbook

- 2 eggs
- ¼ tsp salt
- ¼ tsp pepper

Directions:
1. Spray a 2-qt baking dish with cooking spray.
2. Add the squash to the cooking pot along with just enough water to cover. Set to saute on high heat and bring to a boil.
3. Reduce heat to medium and cook 8-10 minutes or until squash is tender. Drain.
4. Place the squash in a large bowl and add ½ cup cheese, mayonnaise, eggs, salt, and pepper and mix well. Spoon into prepared dish and sprinkle with remaining cheese.
5. Place the rack in the cooking pot and add the dish. Add the tender-crisp lid and set to bake on 375°F. Bake 30 minutes until heated through and top is golden brown. Serve.

Nutrition:
- InfoCalories 120, Total Fat 8g, Total Carbs 6g, Protein 7g, Sodium 303mg.

Cheesy Baked Spinach

Servings: 8
Cooking Time: 30 Minutes

Ingredients:
- Nonstick cooking spray
- 15 oz. spinach, thawed, chopped & drained well
- 1 cup wild rice, cooked
- 1½ cup cheddar cheese, reduced fat, grated
- 10½ oz. cream of mushroom soup, low fat
- 1 tbsp. butter, melted
- 1 tsp onion powder
- ¼ tsp nutmeg

Directions:
1. Place the rack in the cooking pot. Spray a casserole dish with cooking spray.
2. In a large bowl, combine all ingredients and mix well. Spoon into prepared dish and place on the rack.
3. Add the tender-crisp lid and set to bake on 350°F. Bake 30 minutes or until heated through. Serve.

Nutrition:
- InfoCalories 113, Total Fat 5g, Total Carbs 10g, Protein 8g, Sodium 492mg.

Grilled Cheese

Servings: 2
Cooking Time: 40 Minutes

Ingredients:
- 1 small cauliflower, cut in florets
- ½ cup mozzarella cheese, low fat, grated
- 1 egg
- ¼ tsp onion powder
- ¼ tsp pepper
- ½ cup sharp cheddar cheese, low fat, grated
- 1 tbsp. butter, soft, divided

Directions:
1. Place the cauliflower in a food processor and pulsed until finely chopped.
2. Place in a microwave safe bowl and microwave 8-9 minutes or until soft. Place in a strainer and press out any excess water.
3. Add the cauliflower to a large bowl and add mozzarella, egg, onion powder, salt, and pepper and mix well.
4. Add the rack to the cooking pot. Lay out a sheet of parchment paper and spread cauliflower mixture on it. Shape into 4 equal squares.
5. Place the parchment paper on the rack and add the tender-crisp lid. Set to bake on 400°F. Bake 15-20 minutes or until golden brown. Remove from cooking pot.
6. Add 1 teaspoon to the cooking pot and set to sauté on med-low heat.
7. Sprinkle cheese evenly on 2 cauliflower squares and top with remaining squares. Place in the cooking pot and spread remaining butter over top.
8. Cook 2-4 minutes until golden brown, flip and cook another 2-4 minutes until cheese is melted. Serve.

Nutrition:
- InfoCalories 394, Total Fat 28g, Total Carbs 9g, Protein 28g, Sodium 696mg.

Veggie Lasagna

Servings: 4
Cooking Time: 35 Minutes

Ingredients:
- Nonstick cooking spray
- 2 Portobello mushrooms, sliced ¼-inch thick
- 1 eggplant, cut lengthwise in 6 slices
- 1 yellow squash, cut lengthwise in 4 slices
- 1 red bell pepper, cut in ½-inch strips
- ½ tsp garlic powder
- ½ tsp salt
- ½ tsp black pepper
- ½ cup ricotta cheese, fat free, divided
- 2 tbsp. fresh basil, chopped, divided
- ¾ cup mozzarella cheese, grated fine, divided
- ¼ cup tomato sauce

Directions:
1. Spray the cooking pot and rack with cooking spray.
2. Place a single layer of vegetables in the cooking pot. Add the rack and place remaining vegetables on it. Season vegetables with garlic powder, salt, and pepper.
3. Add the tender-crisp lid and set to roast on 425°F. Cook vegetables 15-20 minutes until tender, stirring halfway through cooking time. Transfer to a large plate.
4. Spray an 8x8-inch baking pan with cooking spray.
5. Line the bottom of the pan with 3 slices of eggplant. Spread ¼ cup ricotta cheese, 1 tablespoon basil, and ¼ cup mozzarella over eggplant.
6. Layer with remaining vegetables, then remaining ricotta, basil and ¼ cup mozzarella on top. End with 3 slices of eggplant and pour tomato sauce over then sprinkle remaining cheese over the top.
7. Add the rack back to the cooking pot and place the lasagna on it. Add the tender-crisp lid and set to bake on 350°F. Bake 15-20 minutes until cheese is melted and lasagna is heated through, serve.

Nutrition:
- InfoCalories 145, Total Fat 3g, Total Carbs 18g, Protein 14g, Sodium 490mg.

Baked Cajun Turnips

Servings:4
Cooking Time:85 Min
Ingredients:
- 4 small turnips,scrubbed clean
- 4 green onions;chopped;divided
- ¼cup whipping cream/62.5ml
- ¼cup sour cream/62.5ml
- ½cup chopped roasted red bell pepper/65g
- 1½cups shredded Monterey Jack cheese/195g
- ⅓cup grated Parmesan cheese/44g
- 1 tsp Cajun seasoning mix/5g

Directions:
1. Pour 1 cup of water into the inner pot.Put the reversible rack in the pot and place the turnips on top.Seal the pressure lid,choose Pressure,adjust the pressure to High,and the cook time to 10 minutes;press Start.After cooking,performanatural pressure release for 5 minutes.
2. Remove the turnips to a cutting board and allow cooling.Slice offa½-inch piece from the top and the longer side of each turnip.Scoop the pulp into a bowl,including the flesh from the sliced tops making sure not to rip the skin of the turnip apart.
3. In the bowl with the pulp,add the whipping cream and sour cream and useapotato mash to break the pulp and mix the Ingredients until fairly smooth.Stir in the roasted bell pepper,Cajun seasoning,and Monterey Jack cheese.Fetch out 2 tbsps of green onions and stir the remaining into the mashed turnips.
4. Next,fill the turnip skins with the mashed mixture and sprinkle with the Parmesan.Pour the water into the inner pot and return the pot to the base.
5. Put the Crisping basket into the pot.Close the crisping lid;choose Air Crisp,adjust the temperature to 375°F or 191°C,and the time to 2 minutes.Press Start.
6. When the timer is done,open the lid and put the turnips in the basket.Close the crisping lid;choose Air Crisp,adjust the temperature to 375°F or 191°C,and the cook time to 15 minutes.Press Start.Cool for a few minutes and garnish with the reserved onions.

Italian Sausage With Garlic Mash

Servings:6
Cooking Time:30 Min
Ingredients:
- 6 Italian sausages
- 4 large potatoes,peeled and cut into 1½-inch chunks
- 2 garlic cloves,smashed
- ⅓cup butter,melted/44ml
- ¼cup milk;at room temperature,or more as needed/62.5ml
- 1½cups water/375ml
- 1 tbsp olive oil/15ml
- 1 tbsp chopped chives/15g
- salt and ground black pepper to taste

Directions:
1. Select Sear/Sauté,set to Medium High,and choose Start/Stop to preheat the pot and heat olive oil.Cook for 8-10 minutes,turning periodically until browned.Set aside.Wipe the pot with paper towels.Add in water and set the reversible rack over water.Place potatoes onto the reversible rack.
2. Seal the pressure lid,choose Pressure,set to High,and set the timer to 12 minutes.Press Start.
3. When ready,release the pressure quickly.Remove reversible rack from the pot.Drain water from the pot.Return potatoes to pot.Add in salt,butter,pepper,garlic,and milk and useahand masher to mash until no large lumps remain.
4. Using an immersion blender,blend potatoes on Low for 1 minute until fluffy and light.Avoid over-blending to ensure the potatoes do not become gluey!
5. Transfer the mash to a serving plate,top with sausages and scatter chopped chives over to serve.

Bok Choy And Zoddle Soup

Servings:6
Cooking Time:35 Min
Ingredients:
- 1 lb.baby bok choy,stems removed/450g
- 2 zucchinis,spiralized
- 6 oz.Shitake mushrooms,stems removed and sliced to a 2-inch thickness/180g
- 2-inch ginger;chopped
- 2 cloves garlic,peeled
- 3 carrots,peeled and sliced diagonally
- 2 sweet onion;chopped
- 6 cups water/1500ml
- 2 tbsp sesame oil/30ml
- 2 tbsp soy sauce/30ml
- 2 tbsp chili paste/30g
- Salt to taste
- Sesame seeds to garnish
- Chopped green onion to garnish

Directions:
1. Inafood processor,add the chili paste,ginger,onion,and garlic;and process them until they are pureed.Turn on the Ninja foodi and select Sear/Sautémode to High.
2. Pour in the sesame oil,once it has heated add the onion puree and cook for 3 minutes while stirring constantly to prevent burning.Add the water,mushrooms,soy sauce,and carrots.
3. Close the lid,secure the pressure valve,and select Pressure mode on High pressure for 5 minutes.Press Start/Stop.
4. Once the timer has ended,do a quick pressure release and open the lid.Add the zucchini noodles and bok choy,and stir to ensure that they are well submerged in the liquid.
5. Adjust the taste with salt,cover the pot with the crisping lid,and let the vegetables cook for 10 minutes on Broil mode.
6. Useasoup spoon to dish the soup with veggies into soup bowls.Sprinkle with green onions and sesame seeds.Serve as a complete meal.

Mushroom Goulash

Servings:6
Cooking Time:40 Minutes
Ingredients:
- 2 tbsp.olive oil,divided
- ½onion,sliced thin
- 1 red bell pepper,chopped
- 2 lbs.mushrooms,chopped
- ½tsp salt
- ¼tsp pepper
- 14 oz.tomatoes,diced
- 2 cups vegetable broth,low sodium

Ninja Foodi Cookbook

- 1 tsp garlic powder
- 1½ tbsp. paprika
- 5-6 sprigs fresh thyme

Directions:
1. Add half the oil to the cooking pot and set to sautéon med-high.
2. Add the onion and cook until they start to get soft, about 4 minutes. Add the red pepper and cook 3-5 minutes or until onions start to caramelize. Transfer to a plate.
3. Add the remaining oil to the pot and let it get hot. Add the mushrooms and cook until liquid is almost evaporated, stirring occasionally. Season with salt and pepper.
4. Add the peppers and onions back to the pot along with tomatoes, broth, garlic powder, paprika, and thyme, stir to mix well. Bring to a boil, cover, reduce heat to med-low and let simmer 20 minutes. Serve.

Nutrition:
- InfoCalories 115, Total Fat 5g, Total Carbs 14g, Protein 6g, Sodium 544mg.

Sesame Radish

Servings: 4
Cooking Time: 15 Minutes
Ingredients:
- 2 leeks, sliced
- ½ pound radishes, sliced
- 2 scallions, chopped
- 2 tablespoons black sesame seeds
- 1/3 cup chicken stock
- 1 tablespoon ginger, grated
- 1 tablespoon chives, minced

Directions:
1. In your Ninja Foodi, combine the leeks with the radishes and the other ingredients.
2. Put the Ninja Foodi's lid on and cook on High for 15 minutes more.
3. Release the pressure quickly for 5 minutes, divide everything between plates and serve.

Nutrition:
- InfoCalories:112; Fat:2g; Carbohydrates:4.2g; Protein:2g

Cheesy Squash Tart

Servings: 8
Cooking Time: 45 Minutes
Ingredients:
- 1 spaghetti squash
- 2 tbsp. olive oil
- 2 eggs
- 1/3 cup+2 tbsp. parmesan cheese, divided
- 1 cup ricotta cheese, fat free
- 1 clove garlic, chopped fine
- 2 tsp Italian seasoning
- ¼ tsp salt
- 1 cup light spaghetti sauce
- ½ cup mozzarella cheese, low fat, grated

Directions:
1. Place enough water in the cooking pot to reach 1-inch up sides. Add the squash, whole. Add the lid and set to pressure cook on high. Set timer for 13 minutes.
2. When timer goes off, use natural release to remove the pressure. Squash should be tender. Transfer to a cutting board and let cool 15-20 minutes.
3. Add the rack to the cooking pot. Spray an 8-inch deep-dish pie plate with cooking spray.
4. In a large bowl, combine oil, eggs, and 1/3 cup parmesan cheese, mix well.
5. Cut the squash in half lengthwise and remove the seeds. Use a fork to scrape out the flesh and add it to the egg mixture, mix well.
6. Pour the squash mixture into the prepared pie dish and press on the bottom and up sides to form a "crust".
7. In a small bowl, combine the ricotta, garlic, Italian seasoning, and salt and mix well. Spread evenly in the crust and top with spaghetti sauce.
8. Place the dish on the rack and add the tender-crisp lid. Set to bake on 325°F. Bake 25 minutes. Open the lid and sprinkle the remaining cheese over the top. Bake another 5 minutes or until the cheese melts. Let tart rest 10 minutes before serving.

Nutrition:
- InfoCalories 170, Total Fat 9g, Total Carbs 13g, Protein 10g, Sodium 277mg.

Cauliflower Enchiladas

Servings: 5
Cooking Time: 25 Minutes
Ingredients:
- 2 tablespoons canola oil
- 1 large head cauliflower, cut into 1-inch florets
- 2 teaspoons ground cumin
- 1 teaspoon ground chili pepper
- 2 teaspoons kosher salt
- ½ teaspoon freshly ground black pepper
- 1 can diced tomatoes, drained
- 5 flour tortillas
- 1 can red enchilada sauce
- 1½ cups shredded Mexican blend cheese
- ½ cup chopped cilantro, for garnish

Directions:
1. In a medium bowl, toss together the oil, cauliflower, cumin, chili pepper, salt, and black pepper. Place the cauliflower in the Cook&Crisp Basket and place the basket in pot. Close crisping lid.
2. Select AIR CRISP, set temperature to 390°F, and set time to 15 minutes. Select START/STOP to begin.
3. After 8 minutes, open lid, then lift the basket and shake the cauliflower. Lower basket back into pot and close lid. Continue cooking, until the cauliflower reaches your desired crispiness.
4. When cooking is complete, remove basket from pot. Place the cauliflower in a bowl and mix with the tomatoes.
5. Lay the tortillas on a work surface. Divide the cauliflower-
6. tomato mixture between the tortillas and roll them up. Place the filled tortillas seam-side down in the pot. Pour the enchilada sauce on top.
7. Close crisping lid. Select BROIL and set time to 10 minutes. Select START/STOP to begin.
8. After 5 minutes, open lid and add the cheese on top. Close lid and continue cooking until cheese is golden brown.
9. When cooking is complete, add cilantro and serve.

Nutrition:
- InfoCalories:315, Total Fat:19g, Sodium:822mg, Carbohydrates:28g, Protein:13g.

Paneer Cutlet

Servings: 1
Cooking Time: 15 Min
Ingredients:
- 1 small onion, finely chopped
- 2 cup grated paneer/260g
- 1 cup grated cheese/130g
- ½tsp chai masala/2.5g
- 1 tsp butter/5g
- ½tsp garlic powder/2.5g
- ½tsp oregano/2.5g
- ½tsp salt/2.5g

Directions:
1. Preheat the Ninja Foodi to 350°F or 177°C. Oil the Ninja Foodi basket. Mix all Ingredients in a bowl, until well incorporated.
2. Make cutlets out of the mixture and place them on the greased baking dish. Place the baking dish in the Ninja Foodi and cook the cutlets for 10 minutes.

Baby Porcupine Meatballs

Servings: 4
Cooking Time: 30 Min
Ingredients:
- 1 lb. of ground beef/450g
- 1 onion; chopped
- 1 green bell pepper, finely chopped
- 1 garlic clove, minced
- 1 cup rice/130g
- 2 cups of tomato juice/500ml
- 2 tbsp Worcestershire sauce/30ml
- 1 tsp celery salt/5g
- 1 tsp oregano/5g

Directions:
1. Combine the rice, ground beef, onion, celery, salt, green peppers, and garlic. Shape into balls of 1 inch each. Arrange the balls in the basket of the Ninja Foodi. Close the crisping lid and cook for 15 minutes at 320°F or 160°C.
2. After 8 minutes, shape the balls. Heat the tomato juice, cloves, oregano, and Worcestershire sauce in a saucepan over medium heat.
3. Pour in the meatballs, bring to a boil, reduce the heat and simmer for 10 minutes, stirring often. Serve warm.

Veggie Loaded Pasta

Servings: 8
Cooking Time: 2 Minutes
Ingredients:
- 1 box dry pasta, such as rigatoni or penne
- 4 cups water
- 2 tablespoons extra-virgin olive oil, divided
- 2 teaspoons kosher salt, divided
- 3 avocados
- Juice of 2 limes
- 2 tablespoons minced cilantro
- 1 red onion, chopped
- 1 cup cherry tomatoes, halved
- 4 heaping cups spinach, half an 11-ounce container
- ¼cup shredded Parmesan cheese, divided
- Freshly ground black pepper, for serving

Directions:
1. Place the pasta, water, 1 tablespoon of olive oil, and 1 teaspoon of salt in the pot. Stir to incorporate. Assemble pressure lid, making sure the pressure release valve is in the SEAL position.
2. Select PRESSURE and set to LO. Set time to 2 minutes. Select START/STOP to begin.
3. While pasta is cooking, place the avocados in a medium-sized mixing bowl and mash well with a wooden spatula until a thick paste forms. Add all remaining ingredients to the bowl and mix well to combine.
4. When pressure cooking is complete, allow pressure to naturally release for 10 minutes. After 10 minutes, quick release remaining pressure by moving the pressure release valve to the VENT position. Carefully remove lid when unit has finished releasing pressure.
5. If necessary, strain pasta to remove any residual water and return pasta to pot. Add avocado mixture to pot and stir.
6. Garnish pasta with Parmesan cheese and black pepper, as desired, then serve.

Nutrition:
- InfoCalories: 372, Total Fat: 16g, Sodium: 149mg, Carbohydrates: 49g, Protein: 11g.

Creamy Polenta & Mushrooms

Servings: 2
Cooking Time: 40 Minutes
Ingredients:
- 3 tbsp. olive oil
- 1 lb. assorted mushrooms, rinsed & chopped
- 1 clove garlic, chopped fine
- 1 tsp salt, divided
- 3/8 tsp pepper, divided
- 2½cups water, divided
- 3 tbsp. butter
- 1½tbsp. fresh lemon juice
- 1 tbsp. fresh parsley, chopped
- ½cup stone-ground white grits
- 1/8 cup heavy cream
- 3 tbsp. parmesan cheese, grated, divided
- ¼cup mascarpone

Directions:
1. Add oil to the cooking pot and set to sauté on medium heat.
2. Add mushrooms, garlic, ½teaspoon salt, and ¼teaspoon pepper and cook, stirring occasionally, until mushrooms are nicely browned and liquid has evaporated, about 6-8 minutes.
3. Add ¼cup water, butter, lemon juice, and parsley and cook, stirring, until butter melts. Cook 1-2 minutes. Transfer to a large bowl and keep warm.
4. Add the remaining water to the pot and increase heat to med-high. Bring just to a boil.
5. Whisk in grits slowly until combined. Reduce heat to med-low and simmer, stirring occasionally, about 30 minutes, or until liquid is absorbed. Turn off the heat.
6. Stir in cream, 1 tablespoon cheese, and remaining salt and pepper and mix well. Ladle polenta onto serving plates. Top with mushrooms, mascarpone, and remaining parmesan cheese. Serve immediately.

Nutrition:
- InfoCalories 102, Total Fat 7g, Total Carbs 8g, Protein 2g, Sodium 215mg.

Ninja Foodi Cookbook

Noodles With Tofu And Peanuts

Servings:4
Cooking Time:20 Min
Ingredients:
- 1 package tofu;cubed
- 8 ounces egg noodles/240g
- 2 bell peppers;sliced
- 3 scallions,thinly sliced
- ¼cup roasted peanuts/32.5g
- ¼cup soy sauce/62.5ml
- ¼cup orange juice/62.5ml
- 1 tbsp fresh ginger,peeled and minced/15g
- 2 tbsp vinegar/30ml
- 1 tbsp sesame oil/15ml
- 1 tbsp sriracha/15ml

Directions:
1. In the pressure cooker,mix tofu,bell peppers,orange juice,sesame oil,ginger,egg noodles,soy sauce,vinegar,and sriracha;cover with enough water.
2. Seal the pressure lid,choose Pressure,set to High,and set the timer to 2 minutes.Press Start.When ready,release the pressure quickly.Place the mixture into four plates;applyatopping of scallions and peanuts before serving.

Green Minestrone

Servings:4
Cooking Time:30 Min
Ingredients:
- 1 head broccoli,cut into florets
- 1 zucchini;chopped
- 2 cups chopped kale/260g
- 1 cup green beans/130g
- 2 cups vegetable broth/260g
- 4 celery stalks;sliced thinly
- 1 leek;sliced thinly
- 3 whole black peppercorns
- 2 tbsp olive oil/30ml
- water to cover
- salt to taste

Directions:
1. Into the pressure cooker,add broccoli,leek,green beans,salt,peppercorns,zucchini,and celery.Mix in vegetable broth,oil,and water.
2. Seal the pressure lid,choose Pressure,set to High,and set the timer to 4 minutes.Press Start.
3. Release pressure naturally for 5 minutes,then release the remaining pressure quickly.Add kale into the soup and stir;set to Keep Warm and cook until tender.

Stir Fried Veggies

Servings:6
Cooking Time:5 Minutes
Ingredients:
- 1 tbsp.olive oil
- 2 bell peppers,cut in strips
- 1 cup sugar snap peas
- 1 cup carrots,sliced thin
- 1 cup mushrooms,sliced thin
- 2 cups broccoli,separate into small florets
- 1 cup baby corn
- ½cup water chestnuts
- ¼cup soy sauce
- 3 cloves garlic,chopped fine
- 3 tbsp.brown sugar
- 1 tsp sesame oil
- ½cup vegetable broth
- 1 tbsp.cornstarch
- ¼cup green onions,sliced

Directions:
1. Add oil to the cooking pot and set to saute on med-high heat.
2. Add bell pepper,peas,carrots,mushrooms,broccoli,corn,and water chestnuts.Cook,stirring frequently,2-3 minutes until almost tender.
3. In a small bowl,whisk together soy sauce,garlic,brown sugar,sesame oil,broth,and cornstarch until combined.
4. Pour over vegetables and cook,stirring,until sauce has thickened.Spoon onto serving plates and garnish with green onions.

Nutrition:
- InfoCalories 150,Total Fat 5g,Total Carbs 26g,Protein 5g,Sodium 738mg.

Southern Pineapple Casserole

Servings:8
Cooking Time:35 Minutes
Ingredients:
- Nonstick cooking spray
- 1/3 cup butter,soft
- 1/4 cup Stevia
- 2 eggs
- 2 egg whites
- 1 tsp vanilla
- 2 tbsp.flour
- 20 oz.crushed pineapple in juice,drained;reserve 1 cup liquid
- 5 slices whole-wheat bread,cubed

Directions:
1. Spray the cooking pot with cooking spray.
2. In a large bowl,beat butter and Stevia until smooth and creamy.
3. Beat in eggs,egg whites,and vanilla until combined.
4. Stir in flour,pineapple,and reserved juice and mix well.
5. Add bread and toss to coat.Pour into cooking pot.
6. Add tender-crisp lid and set to bake on 350°F.Bake 30-35 minutes or until a knife inserted in center comes out clean.Serve warm.

Nutrition:
- InfoCalories 191,Total Fat 10g,Total Carbs 29g,Protein 5g,Sodium 183mg.

Veggie Lover's Pizza

Servings:1
Cooking Time:8 Minutes
Ingredients:
- 1 store-bought pizza dough,rolled into an 8-inch circle
- ¼cup traditional pizza sauce
- 1 teaspoon minced garlic
- ⅔cup shredded mozzarella cheese
- ¼cup chopped green bell pepper
- ¼cup sliced mushrooms
- Crushed red pepper flakes,for garnish

Ninja Foodi Cookbook

Directions:
1. Select BAKE/ROAST, set the temperature to 400°F, and set time to 5 minutes to preheat. Select START/STOP to begin.
2. Place the rolled dough in the Ninja Cook&Crisp Basket. Spread the pizza sauce over the crust, leaving about a 1-inch border uncovered. Sprinkle on the garlic, top with the mozzarella cheese, and evenly distribute the green bell pepper and mushrooms over the pizza.
3. Place the Cook&Crisp Basket into the pot and close the crisping lid.
4. Select BAKE/ROAST, set the temperature to 400°F, and set the time to 8 minutes. Select START/STOP to begin.
5. When cooking is complete, carefully open the lid and remove the pizza. Serve, garnished with red pepper flakes, if using.

Nutrition:
- InfoCalories:636,Total Fat:20g,Sodium:1150mg,Carbohydrates:95g,Protein:33g.

Mushroom Brown Rice Pilaf

Servings:4
Cooking Time:15 Min
Ingredients:
- 2 cups brown rice, rinsed/260g
- 1 cup Portobello mushrooms, thinly sliced/130g
- ¼cup Romano cheese, grated/32.5g
- 2 sprigs parsley, to garnish
- 4 cups vegetable broth/1000ml
- 3 tsp s olive oil/15ml
- Salt to taste

Directions:
1. Heat the oil on Sear/Sautéon Medium, and stir-fry the mushrooms for 3 minutes until golden. Season with salt, and add rice and broth.
2. Close the lid, secure the pressure valve, and select Pressure mode on High pressure for 5 minutes. Press Start/Stop to start cooking.
3. Once the timer has ended, do a quick pressure release and open the lid.
4. Spread the cheese over and close the crisping lid. Select Bake/Roast, adjust to 375°F or 191°C and the timer to 2 minutes. Press Start/Stop to start cooking. To serve, plate the pilaf and top with freshly chopped parsley.

Chorizo Mac And Cheese

Servings:6
Cooking Time:30 Min
Ingredients:
- 1 pound macaroni/450g
- 3 ounces chorizo; chopped/90g
- 2 cups milk/500ml
- 2 cups Cheddar cheese, shredded/260g
- 3 cups water/750ml
- 2 tbsp minced garlic/30g
- 1 tbsp garlic powder/15g
- salt to taste

Directions:
1. Put chorizo in the pot of your Foodi, select Sear/Sautéand stir-fry until crisp, about 5 minutes. Press Start. Set aside. Wipe the pot with kitchen paper. Add in water, macaroni, and salt to taste. Seal lid and cook on for 5 minutes High Pressure. Press Start.
2. When ready, release the pressure quickly. Stir in cheese and milk until the cheese melts. Divide the mac and cheese between serving bowls. Top with chorizo and serve.

Rosemary Sweet Potato Medallions

Servings:4
Cooking Time:25 Min
Ingredients:
- 4 sweet potatoes, scrubbed clean and dried
- 1 cup water/250ml
- 2 tbsp butter/30g
- 1 tbsp fresh rosemary/15g
- 1 tsp garlic powder/5g
- salt to taste

Directions:
1. Into the pot, add water and place the reversible rack over the water. Use a fork to prick sweet potatoes all over and set onto the reversible rack.
2. Seal the pressure lid, choose Pressure, set to High, and set the timer to 12 minutes. Press Start. When ready, release the pressure quickly. Transfer sweet potatoes toacutting board and slice into 1/2-inch medallions and ensure they are peeled.
3. Melt butter in the pressure cooker on Sear/Sauté. Add in the medallions and cook each side for 2 to 3 minutes until browned. Apply salt and garlic powder to season. Serve topped with fresh rosemary.

Potato Filled Bread Rolls

Servings:4
Cooking Time:25 Min
Ingredients:
- 8 slices of bread
- 2 green chilies, deseeded; chopped
- 5 large potatoes, boiled, mashed
- 2 sprigs curry leaf
- 1 medium onion; chopped
- 1 tbsp olive oil/15ml
- ½tsp mustard seeds/2.5g
- ½tsp turmeric/2.5g
- Salt, to taste

Directions:
1. Combine the olive oil, onion, curry leaves, and mustard seed, in the Ninja Foodi basket. Cook for 5 minutes. Mix the onion mixture with the mashed potatoes, chilies, turmeric, and some salt. Divide the dough into 8 equal pieces.
2. Trim the sides of the bread, and wet it with some water. Make sure to get rid of the excess water. Take one wet bread slice in your palm and place one of the potato pieces in the center.
3. Roll the bread over the filling, sealing the edges. Place the rolls onto a prepared baking dish, close the crisping lid and cook for 12 minutes on Air Crisp at 350°F or 177°C.

Asparagus With Feta

Servings:4
Cooking Time:15 Min
Ingredients:
- 1-pound asparagus spears, ends trimmed/450g
- 1 lemon, cut into wedges
- 1 cup feta cheese; cubed/130g
- 1 cup water/250ml
- 1 tbsp olive oil/15ml
- salt and freshly ground black pepper to taste

Directions:
1. Into the pot,add water and set trivet over the water.Place steamer basket on the trivet.Place the asparagus into the steamer basket.Seal the pressure lid,choose Pressure,set to High,and set the timer to 1 minute.Press Start.
2. When ready,release the pressure quickly.Add olive oil inabowl and toss in asparagus until well coated;season with pepper and salt.Serve alongside feta cheese and lemon wedges.

Carrot Gazpacho
Servings:4
Cooking Time:2 Hr 30 Min
Ingredients:
- 1 pound trimmed carrots/450g
- 1 pound tomatoes;chopped/450g
- 1 red onion;chopped
- 2 cloves garlic
- 1 cucumber,peeled and chopped
- 1/4 cup extra-virgin olive oil/62.5ml
- 1 pinch salt
- 2 tbsp lemon juice/30ml
- 2 tbsp white wine vinegar/30ml
- salt and freshly ground black pepper to taste

Directions:
1. To the Foodi add carrots,salt and enough water.Seal the pressure lid,choose Pressure,set to High,and set the timer to 20 minutes.Press Start.
2. Once ready,do a quick release.Set the beets toabowl and place in the refrigerator to cool.
3. In a blender,add carrots,cucumber,red onion,pepper,garlic,olive oil,tomatoes,lemon juice,vinegar,and salt.
4. Blend until very smooth.Place gazpacho toaserving bowl,chill while covered for 2 hours.

Veggie Skewers
Servings:4
Cooking Time:20 Min
Ingredients:
- 2 boiled and mashed potatoes
- ¼cup chopped fresh mint leaves/32.5g
- ⅔cup canned beans/88g
- ⅓cup grated carrots/44g
- ½cup paneer/65g
- 1 green chili
- 1-inch piece of fresh ginger
- 3 garlic cloves
- 2 tbsp corn flour/30g
- ½tsp garam masala powder/2.5g
- Salt,to taste

Directions:
1. Soak 12 skewers until ready to use.Place the beans,carrots,garlic,ginger,chili,paneer,and mint,in a food processor and process until smooth;transfer toabowl.
2. Add the mashed potatoes,corn flour,some salt,and garam masala powder to the bowl.Mix until fully incorporated.Divide the mixture into 12 equal pieces.
3. Shape each of the pieces around a skewer.Close the crisping lid and cook the skewers for 10 minutes on Air Crisp mode at 390°F or 199°C.

Pasta Veggie Toss
Servings:8
Cooking Time:10 Minutes
Ingredients:
- 2 tbsp.olive oil
- ½red onion,chopped
- ½lb.asparagus,trimmed&cut in 1-inch pieces
- ½lb.mushrooms,sliced
- 2 cloves garlic,chopped fine
- ¼cup dry white win
- 3 oz.sun dried tomatoes,reconstituted&sliced
- ½tsp salt
- ½tsp pepper
- ½cup half and half
- 10 oz.baby spinach,chopped
- 1 tbsp.fresh basil,chopped
- 8 oz.bow tie pasta,cooked&drained

Directions:
1. Add the oil to the cooking pot and set to sautéon med-high heat.
2. Add the onions and asparagus and cook,stirring occasionally,3 minutes.
3. Add the mushrooms and garlic and cook 2-3 minutes until softened.
4. Stir in the wine,tomatoes,salt,and pepper and cook 2-3 minutes until heated through.
5. Add the half and half and cook until heated through again.
6. Place the pasta in a large bowl and add sauce,spinach,and basil and toss to coat.Serve immediately.

Nutrition:
- InfoCalories 192,Total Fat 5g,Total Carbs 34g,Protein 7g,Sodium 218mg.

Roasted Vegetable Salad
Servings:1
Cooking Time:25 Min
Ingredients:
- 1 potato,peeled and chopped
- 1 cup cherry tomatoes/130g
- 1 carrot;sliced diagonally
- ½small beetroot;sliced
- ¼onion;sliced
- Juice of 1 lemon
- A handful of rocket salad
- A handful of baby spinach
- 2 tbsp olive oil/30ml
- 3 tbsp canned chickpeas/45g
- ½tsp cumin/2.5g
- ½tsp turmeric/2.5g
- ¼tsp sea salt/1.25g
- Parmesan shavings

Directions:
1. Combine the onion,potato,cherry tomatoes,carrot,beetroot,cumin,seas salt,turmeric,and 1 tbsp olive oil,inabowl.Place in the Ninja Foodi,close the crisping lid and cook for 20 minutes on Air Crisp mode at 370°F or 188°C;let cool for 2 minutes.
2. Place the rocket,salad,spinach,lemon juice,and 1 tbsp olive oil,into a serving bowl.Mix to combine;stir in the roasted veggies.Top with chickpeas and Parmesan shavings.

Artichoke With Mayo

Servings: 4
Cooking Time: 20 Min
Ingredients:
- 2 large artichokes
- 2 garlic cloves, smashed
- ½ cup mayonnaise/125ml
- 2 cups water/500ml
- Juice of 1 lime
- Salt and black pepper to taste

Directions:
1. Using a serrated knife, trim about 1 inch from the artichokes' top. Into the pot, add water and set trivet over. Lay the artichokes on the trivet. Seal lid and cook for 14 minutes. Press Start.
2. When ready, release the pressure quickly. Mix the mayonnaise with garlic and lime juice; season with salt and pepper. Serve artichokes in a platter with garlic mayo on the side.

Cheesy Green Beans With Nuts

Servings: 6
Cooking Time: 15 Min
Ingredients:
- 2 pounds green beans, trimmed/900g
- 1 cup chopped toasted pine nuts/130g
- 1 cup feta cheese, crumbled/130g
- 1½ cups water/375ml
- Juice from 1 lemon
- 6 tbsp olive oil/90ml
- ½ tsp salt/2.5g
- freshly ground black pepper to taste

Directions:
1. Add water to the pot. Set the reversible rack over the water. Loosely heap green beans into the reversible rack.
2. Seal lid and cook on High Pressure for 5 minutes. Press Start. When the cooking cycle is complete, When ready, release pressure quickly. Drop green beans into a salad bowl; top with the olive oil, feta cheese, pepper, and pine nuts.

Spanish Rice

Servings: 4
Cooking Time: 50 Min
Ingredients:
- 1 small onion; chopped
- 1 can pinto beans, drained and rinsed/480g
- 2 garlic cloves, minced
- 1 banana pepper, seeded and chopped
- ¼ cup stewed tomatoes/32.5g
- ½ cup vegetable stock/125ml
- 1 cup jasmine rice/130g
- ⅓ cup red salsa/88g
- 3 tbsps ghee/45g
- 1 tbsp chopped fresh parsley/15g
- 1 tsp Mexican Seasoning Mix/5g
- 1 tsp salt/5g

Directions:
1. On your Foodi, choose Sear/Sauté and adjust to Medium. Press Start to preheat the inner pot. Add the ghee to melt until no longer foaming and cook the onion, garlic, and banana pepper in the ghee. Cook for 2 minutes or until fragrant.
2. Stir in the rice, salsa, tomato sauce, vegetable stock, Mexican seasoning, pinto beans, and salt. Seal the pressure lid, choose Pressure and adjust the pressure to High and the cook time to 6 minutes; press Start.
3. After cooking, do a natural pressure release for 10 minutes. Stir in the parsley, dish the rice, and serve.

Cheesy Chilies

Servings: 4
Cooking Time: 25 Minutes
Ingredients:
- Nonstick cooking spray
- 2 poblano chilies, halved, seeded, stems on
- 1 cup cottage cheese, drained
- ¼ cup green onion, chopped
- ½ cup Colby-Jack cheese, grated

Directions:
1. Spray the fryer basket with cooking spray.
2. Place the chilies in the basket and add the tender-crisp lid. Set to broil. Cook chilies until skin is charred on all sides. Transfer to a bag and let cool. When cool, remove the skin.
3. Spray an 8x8-inch baking pan with cooking spray.
4. Place chilies in the prepared pan. Spoon cottage cheese in the chilies and sprinkle with green onion and Colby Jack cheese.
5. Place the rack in the cooking pot and add the baking pan. Add the tender-crisp lid and set to bake on 350°F. Bake 15-20 minutes until hot and cheese is melted. Serve immediately.

Nutrition:
- InfoCalories 119, Total Fat 7g, Total Carbs 5g, Protein 10g, Sodium 313mg.

Pesto With Cheesy Bread

Servings: 4
Cooking Time: 60 Min
Ingredients:
- 1 medium red onion; diced
- 1 celery stalk; diced
- 1 large carrot, peeled and diced
- 1 small yellow squash; diced
- 1 can chopped tomatoes/420g
- 1 can cannellini beans, rinsed and drained/810g
- 1 bay leaf
- 1 cup chopped zucchini/130g
- ¼ cup shredded Pecorino Romano cheese/32.5g
- ⅓ cup olive oil based pesto/88ml
- 3 cups water/750ml
- 1 Pecorino Romano rind
- 1 garlic clove, minced
- 4 slices white bread
- 3 tbsps butter; at room temperature/45g
- 3 tbsps ghee/45g
- 1 tsp mixed herbs/5g
- ¼ tsp cayenne pepper/1.25g
- ½ tsp salt/2.5g

Directions:
1. On your Foodi, choose Sear/Sauté, and adjust to Medium to preheat the inner pot. Press Start. Add the ghee to the pot to melt and sauté the onion, celery, and carrot for 3 minutes or until the vegetables start to soften.

Ninja Foodi Cookbook 70

2. Stir in the yellow squash,tomatoes,beans,water,zucchini,bay leaf,mixed herbs,cayenne pepper,salt,and Pecorino Romano rind.
3. Seal the pressure lid,choose Pressure,adjust to High,and set the time to 4 minutes.Press Start.Inabowl,mix the butter,shredded cheese,and garlic.Spread the mixture on the bread slices.
4. After cooking the soup,perform a natural pressure release for 2 minutes,thenaquick pressure release and carefully open the lid.
5. Adjust the taste of the soup with salt and black pepper,and remove the bay leaf.Put the reversible rack in the upper position of the pot and lay the bread slices in the rack with the buttered-side up.
6. Close the crisping lid.Choose Broil;adjust the cook time to 5 minutes,and Press Start/Stop to begin broiling.
7. When the bread is crispy,carefully remove the rack,and set aside.Ladle the soup into serving bowls and drizzle the pesto over.Serve with the garlic toasts.

Quick Indian-style Curry

Servings:8
Cooking Time:35 Minutes
Ingredients:
- 1 tablespoon vegetable oil
- 1 small onion,diced
- 1 small bell pepper,diced
- 1 large potato,cut into 1-inch cubes
- 1 teaspoon ground turmeric
- 1 teaspoon cumin seeds
- 1 teaspoon ground cumin
- 1 teaspoon garam masala(optional)
- 1 teaspoon curry powder
- 1 jar curry sauce,plus 1 jar water
- 1 can diced tomatoes
- 1 cup dried red lentils
- 8 ounces paneer,cubed(optional)
- 1 cup fresh cilantro,roughly chopped(optional)
- Salt
- Freshly ground black pepper

Directions:
1. Select SEAR/SAUTÉand set temperature to HI.Select START/STOP to begin and allow to preheat for 5 minutes.
2. Add the oil to the pot and allow to heat for 1 minute.Add the onion and bell pepper and sautéfor 3 to 4 minutes.
3. Add the potato,turmeric,cumin seeds,cumin,garam masala,and curry powder.Stir and cook for 5 minutes.
4. Stir in the curry sauce,water,tomatoes,and lentils.
5. Assemble the pressure lid,making sure the pressure release valve is in the SEAL position.
6. Select PRESSURE and set to HI.Set the time to 15 minutes.Select START/STOP to begin.
7. When pressure cooking is complete,allow the pressure to naturally release for 10 minutes.After 10 minutes,quick release any remaining pressure by moving the pressure release valve to the VENT position.Carefully remove the lid when the unit has finished releasing pressure.
8. Stir in the paneer(if using)and cilantro.Taste and season with salt and pepper,as needed.

Nutrition:
- InfoCalories:217,Total Fat:6g,Sodium:27mg,Carbohydrates:33g,Protein:8g.

Minestrone With Pancetta

Servings:6
Cooking Time:40 Min
Ingredients:
- 2 ounces pancetta;chopped/60g
- 1 can diced tomatoes/450g
- 1 can chickpeas,rinsed and drained/450g
- 1 onion;diced
- 1 parsnip,peeled and chopped
- 2 carrots,peeled and sliced into rounds
- 2 celery stalks,
- 2 garlic cloves,minced
- 6 cups chicken broth/1500ml
- ½cup grated Parmesan cheese/65g
- 2 cups green beans,trimmed and chopped/260g
- 1½cups small shaped pasta/195g
- 1 tbsp dried basil/15g
- 1 tbsp dried oregano/15g
- 2 tbsp olive oil/30ml
- 1 tbsp dried thyme/15g
- salt and ground black pepper to taste

Directions:
1. Warm oil on Sear/Sauté.Add onion,carrots,garlic,pancetta,celery,and parsnip,and cook for 5 minutes until they become soft.
2. Stir in basil,oregano,green beans,broth,tomatoes,pepper,salt,thyme,vegetable broth,chickpeas,and pasta.
3. Seal the pressure lid,choose Pressure,set to High,and set the timer to 6 minutes.Press Start.
4. Release pressure naturally for 10 minutes then release the remaining pressure quickly.Ladle the soup into bowls and serve garnished with grated parmesan cheese.

Olives And Rice Stuffed Mushrooms

Servings:4
Cooking Time:70 Min
Ingredients:
- 4 large Portobello mushrooms,stems and gills removed
- 1 green bell pepper,seeded and diced
- 1 lemon,juiced
- 1 tomato,seed removed and chopped
- ½cup brown rice,cooked/65g
- ¼cup black olives,pitted and chopped/32.5g
- ½cup feta cheese,crumbled/65g
- 2 tbsps melted butter/30ml
- ½tsp salt/2.5g
- ½tsp ground black pepper/2.5g
- Minced fresh cilantro;for garnish

Directions:
1. Put the Crisping Basket in the pot.Close the crisping lid,choose Air Crisp,setting the temperature to 375°F or 191°C,and setting the time to 5 minutes.Press Start/Stop to preheat the pot.
2. Brush the mushrooms with the melted butter.Open the crisping lid and arrange the mushrooms,open-side up and in a single layer in the preheated basket.
3. Close the crisping lid.Choose Air Crisp,set the temperature to 375°F or 191°C,and set the time to 20 minutes.Choose Start/Stop.

4. In a bowl, combine the brown rice, tomato, olives, bell pepper, feta cheese, lemon juice, salt, and black pepper.
5. Open the crisping lid and spoon the rice mixture equally into the 4 mushrooms. Close the lid.
6. Choose Air Crisp, set the temperature to 350°F or 177°C, and set the time to 8 minutes. Press Start/Stop to commence cooking.
7. When the mushrooms are ready, remove to a plate, garnish with fresh cilantro and serve immediately.

Pumpkin Soup

Servings: 8
Cooking Time: 8 Hours
Ingredients:
- 15 oz. pumpkin
- 1 cup celery, chopped
- ½ cup carrots, chopped fine
- ½ cup onion, chopped fine
- ¼ tsp salt
- ½ tsp oregano
- ½ tsp rosemary
- ¼ tsp red pepper
- ¼ tsp ginger
- 28 oz. vegetable broth
- ¼ cup whipped cream
- 3 tbsp. pumpkin seeds, toasted

Directions:
1. Add all ingredients, except whipped cream and pumpkin seeds, to the cooking pot, mix well.
2. Add the lid and set to slow cook on low. Cook 6-8 hours.
3. Stir in whipped cream until thoroughly combined. Ladle into bowls and top with pumpkin seeds. Serve.

Nutrition:
- InfoCalories 78, Total Fat 5g, Total Carbs 8g, Protein 3g, Sodium 500mg.

Spinach Gratin & Eggs

Servings: 6
Cooking Time: 1 Hour
Ingredients:
- 3 lbs. fresh spinach, blanched & drained well
- 2 cups milk
- 2 tbsp. butter
- 2 tbsp. flour
- ¾ tsp nutmeg
- 1/8 tsp pepper
- ¼ cup Gruyere cheese, grated
- 6 eggs, hard boiled & cut in half
- 4 tbsp. seasoned bread crumbs
- 1 tbsp. extra virgin olive oil

Directions:
1. Chop the spinach and place in a large bowl, Season with salt and pepper.
2. In a small saucepan, over medium heat, heat milk until steamy.
3. Add butter to the cooking pot and set to sauté on medium heat.
4. Once butter has melted, whisk in flour until smooth, cook, whisking 1-2 minutes. Slowly whisk in the hot milk and continue whisking until no lumps remain. Add nutmeg and pepper and cook until thickened, about 1-2 minutes.
5. Add the spinach and mix well. Sprinkle the Gruyere over the top. Arrange the eggs, cut side up, on the top of the spinach, press lightly so the eggs are even with the top of the spinach.
6. Sprinkle the bread crumbs over the top and drizzle with olive oil. Add the tender-crisp lid and set to bake on 375°F. Bake 25-30 minutes until top is nicely browned and casserole is heated through. Serve.

Nutrition:
- InfoCalories 74, Total Fat 4g, Total Carbs 5g, Protein 5g, Sodium 90mg.

Tasty Acorn Squash

Servings: 4
Cooking Time: 30 Min
Ingredients:
- 1 lb. acorn squash, peeled and cut into chunks/450g
- ½ cup water/125ml
- 2 tbsp butter/30g
- 1 tbsp dark brown sugar/15g
- 1 tbsp cinnamon/15g
- 3 tbsp honey; divided 45ml
- salt and ground black pepper to taste

Directions:
1. In a small bowl, mix 1 tbsp honey and water; pour into the pressure cooker's pot. Add in squash. Seal the and cook on High pressure for 4 minutes. Press Start. When ready, release the pressure quickly.
2. Transfer the squash to a serving dish. Turn Foodi to Sear/Sauté.
3. Mix brown sugar, cinnamon, the remaining 2 tbsp honey and the liquid in the pot; cook as you stir for 4 minutes to obtain a thick consistency and starts to turn caramelized and golden. Spread honey glaze over squash; add pepper and salt for seasoning.

Stuffed Mushrooms

Servings: 4
Cooking Time: 40 Min
Ingredients:
- 10 large white mushrooms, stems removed
- 1 red bell pepper, seeded and chopped
- 1 small onion; chopped
- 1 green onion; chopped
- ¼ cup roasted red bell peppers; chopped/32.5g
- ¼ cup grated Parmesan cheese/32.5g
- ½ cup water/125ml
- 1 tbsp butter/15g
- ½ tsp dried oregano/2.5g
- Salt and black pepper to taste

Directions:
1. Turn on the Ninja Foodi and select Sear/Sauté mode on Medium. Put in the butter to melt and add the roasted and fresh peppers, green onion, onion, oregano, salt, and pepper. Use a spoon to mix and cook for 2 minutes.
2. Spoon the bell pepper mixture into the mushrooms and use a paper towel to wipe the pot and place the stuffed mushrooms in it, 5 at a time. Pour in water.
3. Close the lid, secure the pressure valve, and select pressure mode on High pressure for 5 minutes. Press Start/Stop. Once the timer has ended, do a quick pressure release and open the lid.

4. Sprinkle with parmesan cheese and close the crisping lid.Select Bake/Roast,adjust the temperature to 380°F or 194°C and the time to 2 minutes and press Start/Stop button.
5. Useaset of tongs to remove the stuffed mushrooms onto a plate and repeat the cooking process for the remaining mushrooms.Serve hot withaside of steamed green veggies and a sauce.

Tofu&Carrot Toss

Servings:4
Cooking Time:20 Minutes
Ingredients:
- 1 tbsp.coconut oil
- 1 lb.carrots,grated
- 1 lb.extra firm tofu,drained,pressed&crumbled
- 1/3 cup soy sauce
- 1/3 cup sesame seeds
- 1 tsp dark sesame oil
- 1/4 cup cilantro,chopped

Directions:
1. Add oil to the cooking pot and set to sautéon med-high heat.
2. Add carrots and cook 15 minutes,stirring occasionally.
3. Add tofu and cook until carrots are tender,about 5 minutes.Stir in soy sauce and sesame seeds and cook 1 minute more,stirring constantly.
4. Turn the heat off and stir in sesame oil and cilantro.Serve over rice.

Nutrition:
- InfoCalories 279,Total Fat 20g,Total Carbs 16g,Protein 17g,Sodium 851mg.

Artichoke&Spinach Casserole

Servings:6
Cooking Time:30 Minutes
Ingredients:
- Nonstick cooking spray
- 2 tsp olive oil
- ½cup onion,chopped
- 3 cloves garlic,chopped fine
- 1 cup quinoa,cooked
- 14 oz.artichoke hearts,drained&chopped
- 10 oz.spinach,thawed&chopped
- ¾cup mozzarella cheese,grated,divided
- ½tsp nutmeg
- ¼tsp pepper
- 2 eggs
- ¾cup plain Greek yogurt

Directions:
1. Spray cooking pot with cooking spray.
2. Add oil and set to sautéon medium heat.
3. Add onion and garlic and cook,stirring frequently,3-5 minutes until onion is soft.Turn off heat.
4. In a large bowl,combine quinoa,artichokes,spinach,½cup mozzarella,nutmeg,and pepper,mix well.
5. In a medium bowl,whisk together egg and yogurt and stir into quinoa mixture.Sprinkle remaining cheese over the top.
6. Add the tender-crisp lid and set to bake on 375°F.Bake 25-30 minutes until heated through and cheese is melted and starting to brown.Serve.

Nutrition:
- InfoCalories 160,Total Fat 4g,Total Carbs 19g,Protein 14g,Sodium 216mg.

Green Squash Gruyere

Servings:4
Cooking Time:70 Min
Ingredients:
- 1 large green squash;sliced
- 2 cups tomato sauce/500ml
- 1 cup shredded mozzarella cheese/130g
- 1½cups panko breadcrumbs/195g
- ⅓cup grated Gruyere cheese/44g
- 3 tbsps melted unsalted butter/45ml
- 2 tsp s salt/10g

Directions:
1. Season the squash slices on both sides with salt and place the slices onawire rack to drain liquid for 5 to 10 minutes.In a bowl,combine the melted butter,breadcrumbs,and Gruyere cheese and set aside.
2. Rinse the squash slices with water and blot dry with paper towel.After,arrange the squash in the inner pot inasingle layer as much as possible and pour the tomato sauce over the slices.
3. Seal the pressure lid,choose Pressure,set to High,and the time to 5 minutes.Press Start to commence cooking.When the timer has read to the end,perform a quick pressure release.Sprinkle the squash slices with the mozzarella cheese.
4. Close the crisping lid.Choose Bake/Roast;adjust the temperature to 375°F or 191°C and the cook time to 2 minutes.Press Start to broil.
5. After,carefully open the lid and sprinkle the squash with the breadcrumb mixture.Close the crisping lid again,choose Bake/Roast,adjust the temperature to 375°F,and the cook time to 8 minutes.Press Start to continue broiling.Serve immediately.

Cabbage With Bacon

Servings:4
Cooking Time:20 Minutes
Ingredients:
- 4 cups red cabbage,shredded
- ¼cup veggie stock
- A pinch of black pepper and salt
- 1 tablespoon olive oil
- 1 cup canned tomatoes,crushed
- Zest of 1 lime,grated
- 2 ounces bacon,cooked and crumbled

Directions:
1. Put the reversible rack in the Foodi,add the baking pan inside and grease it with the oil.
2. Add the cabbage,the stock and the other ingredients into the pan.
3. Cook on Baking mode at 380°F for 20 minutes.
4. Divide the mix between plates and serve.

Nutrition:
- InfoCalories:144;Fat:3g;Carbohydrates:4.5g;Protein:4.4g

Green Cream Soup

Servings: 4
Cooking Time: 22 Min
Ingredients:
- ½lb.kale leaves;chopped/225g
- ½lb.Swiss chard leaves;chopped/225g
- ½lb.spinach leaves;chopped/225g
- 1 onion;chopped
- 4 cloves garlic,minced
- 4 cups vegetable broth/1000ml
- 1¼cup heavy cream/312.5ml
- 1 tbsp olive oil/15ml
- 1½tbsp white wine vinegar/22.5ml
- Salt and pepper,to taste
- Chopped Peanuts to garnish

Directions:
1. Turn on the Ninja Foodi and select Sear/Sautémode on Medium.Add the olive oil,once it has heated add the onion and garlic and sautéfor 2-3 minutes until soft.Add greens and vegetable broth.
2. Close the lid,secure the pressure valve,and select Pressure mode on High pressure for 10 minutes.Press Start/Stop.Once the timer has ended,doaquick pressure release.
3. Add the white wine vinegar,salt,and pepper.Use a stick blender to puree the Ingredients in the pot.Close the crisping lid and cook for 3 minutes on Broil mode.Stir in the heavy cream.Spoon the soup into bowls,sprinkle with peanuts,and serve.

Stuffed Summer Squash

Servings: 4
Cooking Time: 25 Minutes
Ingredients:
- 2 yellow squash,halved lengthwise&seeded
- 1 cup brown rice,cooked
- 2 tbsp.liquid egg substitute
- 2 tbsp.parmesan cheese,divided
- ½tsp onion powder
- 2 tsp fresh parsley,chopped
- ¼tsp pepper
- Nonstick cooking spray

Directions:
1. Add enough water to cover½inch up the sides of the cooking pot.Add the squash.
2. Add the lid and set to pressure cook on high.Set timer for 5 minutes.When timer goes off,use manual release to remove the pressure.Drain.
3. In a small bowl,combine rice,egg substitute,1 tablespoon parmesan,parsley,onion powder,and pepper and mix well.
4. Place squash,cut side up,in the cooking pot.Divide the rice mixture evenly between the squash halves.Sprinkle remaining cheese over the top.Spray lightly with cooking spray.
5. Add the tender-crisp lid and set to bake on 350°F.Bake 15-20 minutes until cheese is melted and starting to brown.Serve.

Nutrition:
- InfoCalories 84,Total Fat 1g,Total Carbs 15g,Protein 3g,Sodium 66mg.

Sour Cream&Onion Frittata

Servings: 6
Cooking Time: 15 Minutes
Ingredients:
- 1 lb.new potatoes,boiled peeled&sliced¼-inch thick
- 1½tbsp.olive oil
- 1½tbsp.butter
- 1 onion,sliced thin
- 10 eggs
- ¾cup cheddar cheese
- ½tsp salt
- ¼tsp pepper
- ½cup sour cream

Directions:
1. Add oil and butter to the cooking pot and set to sautéon med-high heat.
2. Add the onions and cook 3-5 minutes until soft.Add the potatoes and cook until golden brown,about 5 minutes,stirring occasionally.
3. In a large bowl,beat eggs.Stir in cheese,salt and pepper.Pour over the onion mixture.Spoon sour cream over the eggs and swirl it evenly around the frittata.Reduce heat to medium and cook 2-4 minutes until edges are set,do not stir.
4. Add the tender-crisp lid and set to bake on 400°F.Bake frittata 10-12 minutes until eggs are completely set.
5. Use a knife to loosen the edges and invert onto a cutting board.Let cool slightly before serving.

Nutrition:
- InfoCalories 330,Total Fat 23g,Total Carbs 16g,Protein 15g,Sodium 248mg.

Parsley Mashed Cauliflower

Servings: 4
Cooking Time: 15 Min
Ingredients:
- 1 head cauliflower
- 1/4 cup heavy cream/62.5g
- 2 cups water/500ml
- 1 tbsp fresh parsley,finely chopped/15g
- 1 tbsp butter/15g
- ¼tsp celery salt/1.25g
- ⅛tsp freshly ground black pepper/0.625g

Directions:
1. Into the pot,add water and set trivet on top and lay cauliflower head onto the trivet.Seal the pressure lid,choose Pressure,set to High,and set the timer to 8 minutes.Press Start.
2. When ready,release the pressure quickly.Remove the trivet and drain liquid from the pot before returning to the base.
3. Take back the cauliflower to the pot alongside the pepper,heavy cream,salt and butter;use an immersion blender to blend until smooth.Top with parsley and serve.

Steamed Artichokes With Lemon Aioli

Servings: 4
Cooking Time: 20 Min
Ingredients:
- 4 artichokes,trimmed
- 1 small handful parsley;chopped
- 1 lemon,halved

Ninja Foodi Cookbook

- 3 cloves garlic,crushed
- ½cup mayonnaise/125ml
- 1 cup water/250ml
- 1 tsp lemon zest/5g
- 1 tbsp lemon juice/15ml
- Salt to taste

Directions:
1. On the artichokes cut ends,rub with lemon.Add water into the pot of pressure cooker.Set the reversible rack over the water,
2. Place the artichokes into the steamer basket with the points upwards;sprinkle each with salt.Seal lid and cook on High pressure for 10 minutes.Press Start.When ready,release the pressure quickly.
3. Inamixing bowl,combine mayonnaise,garlic,lemon juice,and lemon zest.Season to taste with salt.Serve with warm steamed artichokes sprinkled with parsley.

Mashed Potatoes With Spinach

Servings:6
Cooking Time:30 Min
Ingredients:
- 3 pounds potatoes,peeled and quartered/1350g
- 2 cups spinach;chopped/260g
- ½cup milk/125ml
- ⅓cup butter/44g
- 1½cups water/375ml
- 2 tbsp chopped fresh chives/30g
- ½tsp salt/2.5g
- fresh black pepper to taste

Directions:
1. In the cooker,mix water,salt and potatoes.Seal the pressure lid,choose Pressure,set to High,and set the timer to 8 minutes.Press Start.When ready,release the pressure quickly.Drain the potatoes,and reserve the liquid in a bowl.Inalarge bowl,mash the potatoes.
2. Mix with butter and milk;season with pepper and salt.With reserved cooking liquid,thin the potatoes to attain the desired consistency.
3. Put the spinach in the remaining potato liquid and stir until wilted;season with salt and pepper.Drain and serve with potato mash.Garnish with black pepper and chives.

Palak Paneer

Servings:4
Cooking Time:20 Min
Ingredients:
- 1 pound spinach;chopped/450g
- 1 tomato;chopped
- 2 cups paneer;cubed/260g
- 1 cup water/250ml
- ¼cup milk/62.5ml
- 2 tbsp butter/30g
- 1 tsp minced fresh ginger/5g
- 1 tsp minced fresh garlic/5g
- 1 red onion;chopped
- 1 tsp cumin seeds/5g
- 1 tsp coriander seeds/5g
- 1 tsp salt,or to taste/5g
- 1 tsp chilli powder/5g

Directions:
1. Warm butter on Sear/Sauté,set to Medium High,and choose Start/Stop to preheat the pot.Press Start.
2. Add in garlic,cumin seeds,coriander seeds,chilli powder,ginger,and garlic and fry for 1 minute until fragrant;add onion and cook for 2 more minutes until crispy.Add in salt,water and chopped spinach.
3. Seal the pressure lid,choose Pressure,set to High,and set the timer to 1 minute.Press Start.
4. When ready,release the pressure quickly.Add spinach mixture toablender and blend to obtain a smooth paste.Mix paneer and tomato with spinach mixture.

Broccoli Cauliflower

Servings:4
Cooking Time:15 Minutes
Ingredients:
- 2 cups broccoli florets
- 1 cup cauliflower florets
- 2 tablespoons lime juice
- 1 tablespoon avocado oil
- 1/3 cup tomato sauce
- 2 teaspoons ginger,grated
- 2 teaspoons garlic,minced
- 1 tablespoon chives,chopped

Directions:
1. Set the Foodi on Sautémode,stir in the oil,heat it up,add the garlic and the ginger and sautéfor 2 minutes.
2. Stir in the broccoli,cauliflower and the rest of the ingredients.
3. Put the Ninja Foodi's lid on and cook on High for 13 minutes.
4. naturally Release the pressure for 10 minutes,divide everything between plates and serve.

Nutrition:
- InfoCalories:118;Fat:1.5g;Carbohydrates:4.3g;Protein:6 g

Pepper And Sweet Potato Skewers

Servings:1
Cooking Time:20 Min
Ingredients:
- 1 large sweet potato
- 1 green bell pepper
- 1 beetroot
- 1 tbsp olive oil/15ml
- 1 tsp chili flakes/5g
- ¼tsp black pepper/1.25g
- ½tsp turmeric/2.5g
- ¼tsp garlic powder/2.5g
- ¼tsp paprika/2.5g

Directions:
1. Soak 3 to 4 skewers until ready to use.Peel the veggies and cut them into bite-sized chunks.Place the chunks inabowl along with the remaining Ingredients Mix until fully coated.Thread the veggies in this order:potato,pepper,beetroot.
2. Place in the Ninja Foodi,close the crisping lid and cook for 15 minutes on Air Crisp mode at 350°F or 177°C;flip skewers halfway through.

Ninja Foodi Cookbook

Mashed Broccoli With Cream Cheese

Servings: 4
Cooking Time: 12 Min
Ingredients:
- 3 heads broccoli;chopped
- 2 cloves garlic,crushed
- 6 oz.cream cheese/180g
- 2 cups water/500ml
- 2 tbsp butter,unsalted/30g
- Salt and black pepper to taste

Directions:
1. Turn on the Ninja Foodi and select Sear/Sautémode,adjust to High.Drop in the butter,once it melts add the garlic and cook for 30 seconds while stirring frequently to prevent the garlic from burning.
2. Then,add the broccoli,water,salt,and pepper.Close the lid,secure the pressure valve,and select Pressure mode on High pressure for 5 minutes.Press Start/Stop.
3. Once the timer has ended,doaquick pressure release and use a stick blender to mash the Ingredients until smooth to your desired consistency and well combined.
4. Stir in Cream cheese.Adjust the taste with salt and pepper.Close the crisping lid and cook for 2 minutes on Broil mode.Serve warm.

Garlic Potatoes

Servings: 4
Cooking Time: 30 Min
Ingredients:
- 1½pounds potatoes/675g
- ½cup vegetable broth/125ml
- 3 cloves garlic,thinly sliced
- 3 tbsp butter/45g
- 2 tbsp fresh rosemary;chopped/30g
- ½tsp fresh parsley;chopped/2.5g
- ½tsp fresh thyme;chopped/2.5g
- 1/4 tsp ground black pepper 1.25g

Directions:
1. Use a small knife to pierce each potato to ensure there are no blowouts when placed under pressure.Melt butter on Sear/Sauté.Add in potatoes,rosemary,parsley,pepper,thyme,and garlic,and cook for 10 minutes until potatoes are browned and the mixture is aromatic.
2. Inabowl,mix miso paste and vegetable stock;stir into the mixture in the pressure cooker.
3. Seal the pressure lid,choose Pressure,set to High,and set the timer to 5 minutes.Press Start.Do a pressure quickly.

Carrots Walnuts Salad

Servings: 4
Cooking Time: 15 Minutes
Ingredients:
- 4 carrots,roughly shredded
- ½cup walnuts,sliced
- 3 tablespoons balsamic vinegar
- 1 cup chicken stock
- Black pepper and salt to the taste
- 1 tablespoon olive oil

Directions:
1. In your Ninja Foodi,mix the carrots with the vinegar and the other ingredients except for the walnuts.
2. Put the pressure cooking lid on and cook on High for 15 minutes.
3. Release the pressure quickly for 5 minutes,divide the mix between plates and serve with the walnuts sprinkled on top.

Nutrition:
- InfoCalories:120;Fat:4.5g;Carbohydrates:5.3g;Protein:1.3g

Eggplant Casserole

Servings: 8
Cooking Time: 1 Hour
Ingredients:
- Nonstick cooking spray
- 1 lb.eggplant,peeled,cubed
- ½cup seasoned bread crumbs,divided
- 2 eggs
- ¼tsp Italian seasoning
- ½tsp garlic powder
- 1/8 tsp salt
- 1/8 tsp pepper
- 2 tomatoes,sliced

Directions:
1. Spray an 8x8-inch baking dish with cooking spray.
2. Add enough water to the cooking pot to come 2 inches up the sides.Set to sautéon high heat and bring to a boil.
3. Add the eggplant,reduce heat to medium,cover and cook 20-30 minutes until soft.Drain.
4. Add the eggplant to a large bowl and mash with a fork.Stir in¼cup bread crumbs,eggs,Italian seasoning,garlic,salt,and pepper and mix well.
5. Add the rack to the cooking pot.Spread the eggplant mixture in the prepared dish.Top with sliced tomatoes.Sprinkle tomatoes with remaining bread crumbs and spray with cooking spray.Place the dish on the rack.
6. Add the tender-crisp lid and set to bake on 350°F.Bake 25-30 minutes or until tomatoes are tender and starting to brown around the edges.Serve.

Nutrition:
- InfoCalories 67,Total Fat 2g,Total Carbs 10g,Protein 3g,Sodium 181mg.

Poultry

Chicken Pasta With Pesto Sauce

Servings: 8
Cooking Time: 30 Min
Ingredients:
- 4 chicken breast, boneless, skinless; cubed
- 8 oz. macaroni pasta/240g
- 1 garlic clove; minced
- 1/4 cup Asiago cheese, grated/32.5g
- 2 cups fresh collard greens, trimmed/260g
- ¼ cup cream cheese, at room temperature/32.5g
- 1 cup cherry tomatoes, halved/130g
- ½ cup basil pesto sauce/125ml
- 3½ cups water/875ml
- 1 tbsp butter/15g
- 1 tbsp salt; divided/15g
- 1 tsp freshly ground black pepper to taste/5g
- Freshly chopped basil for garnish

Directions:
1. To the inner steel pot of the Foodi, add water, chicken, 2 tsp salt, butter, and macaroni, and stir well to mix and be submerged in water.
2. Seal the pressure lid, choose Pressure, set to High, and set the timer to 2 minutes. Press Start. When ready, release the pressure quickly. Press Start/Stop, open the lid, get rid of ¼ cup water from the pot.
3. Set on Sear/Sauté. Into the pot, mix in collard greens, pesto sauce, garlic, remaining 1 tsp o 5g salt, cream cheese, tomatoes, and black pepper. Cook, for 1 to 2 minutes as you stir, until sauce is creamy.
4. Place the pasta into serving plates; top with asiago cheese and basil before serving.

Paprika Buttered Chicken

Servings: 6
Cooking Time: 45 Min
Ingredients:
- 3.5-pound whole chicken/1575g
- ½ onion, thinly sliced
- 2 cloves garlic; minced
- 1 cup chicken stock/250ml
- ½ cup white wine/125ml
- 3 tbsp butter, melted/45ml
- ½ tsp paprika/2.5g
- ½ tsp ground black pepper/2.5g
- ½ tsp dried thyme/2.5g
- 1 tsp salt/5g

Directions:
1. Into the Foodi, add onion, chicken stock, white wine, and garlic. Over the mixture, place the reversible rack. Apply pepper, salt, and thyme to the chicken; lay onto reversible rack breast-side up.
2. Seal the pressure lid, choose Pressure, set to High, and set the timer to 26 minutes. Press Start. When ready, release the pressure quickly.
3. While pressure releases, preheat oven broiler. In a bowl, mix paprika and butter.
4. Remove the reversible rack with chicken from your pot. Get rid of onion and stock.
5. Onto the chicken, brush butter mixture and take the reversible rack back to the pot. Cook under the broiler for 5 minutes until chicken skin is crispy and browned.
6. Set chicken to a cutting board to cool for about 5 minutes, then carve and transfer to a serving platter.

Chicken In Thai Peanut Sauce

Servings: 8
Cooking Time: 10 Minutes
Ingredients:
- 2 tbsp. oil
- 2 lbs. chicken thighs, boneless & skinless
- ½ cup chicken broth, low sodium
- ¼ cup soy sauce, low sodium
- 3 tbsp. cilantro, chopped
- 2 tbsp. lime juice
- ¼ tsp red pepper flakes
- 1 tsp ginger
- ¼ cup peanut butter
- 1 tbsp. corn starch
- 2 tbsp. water
- ¼ cup peanuts, chopped
- 2 green onions, sliced

Directions:
1. Add the oil to the cooking pot and set to sauté on med-high heat.
2. Add the chicken, in batches, and cook to brown all sides. Transfer to a plate.
3. Add the broth, soy sauce, cilantro, lime juice, pepper flakes, and ginger to the pot, stir to scrape up any brown bits on the bottom of the pot.
4. Stir in the peanut butter until melted. Return the chicken back to the pot and stir to coat with sauce.
5. Add the lid and set to pressure cook on high. Set the timer for 10 minutes. Once the timer goes off, use quick release to remove the pressure. Transfer chicken back to a plate.
6. In a small bowl, whisk together cornstarch and water until smooth. Stir mixture into the sauce and set the cooker back to sauté on medium heat.
7. Bring sauce to a boil, stirring constantly, and cook until sauce thickens, about 2-3 minutes. Add chicken and stir to coat wall. Serve garnished with peanuts and green onions.

Nutrition:
- InfoCalories 679, Total Fat 40g, Total Carbs 8g, Protein 72g, Sodium 2421mg.

Healthy Chicken Stew

Servings: 4
Cooking Time: 4 Hours
Ingredients:
- 1 large potato, peeled & chopped
- 2 carrots, peeled & sliced
- ½ tsp salt
- ¼ tsp pepper
- 2 cloves garlic, chopped fine
- 3 cups chicken broth, low sodium
- 2 bay leaves
- 2 chicken breasts, boneless, skinless & cut in pieces
- ½ tsp thyme
- ¼ tsp basil
- 1 tsp paprika
- 2 tbsp. cornstarch
- ½ cup water

- 1 cup green peas

Directions:
1. Add the potatoes,carrots,salt,pepper,garlic,broth,bay leaves,chicken,thyme,basil,and paprika to the cooking pot,stir to mix.
2. Add the lid and set to slow cook on high.Cook 4 hours or until vegetables and chicken are tender.
3. In a small bowl,whisk together cornstarch and water until smooth.Stir into the cooking pot along with the peas.
4. Recover and cook another 15 minutes.Stir well before serving.

Nutrition:
- InfoCalories 187,Total Fat 2g,Total Carbs 25g,Protein 17g,Sodium 1038mg.

Turkey Meatballs

Servings:4
Cooking Time:4 Minutes
Ingredients:
- 1-pound ground turkey
- 1 cup onion,shredded
- 1/4 cup heavy whip cream
- 2 teaspoon salt
- 1 cup carrots,shredded
- 1/2 teaspoon ground caraway seeds
- 1 and 1/2 teaspoons black pepper
- 1/4 teaspoon ground allspice
- 1 cup almond meal
- 1/2 cup almond milk
- 2 tablespoons unsalted butter

Directions:
1. Transfer meat to a suitable.
2. Add cream,almond meal,onion,carrot,1 teaspoon salt,caraway,1/2 teaspoon pepper,allspice,and mix well.
3. Refrigerate the mixture for 30 minutes.
4. Once the mixture is cooled,use your hands to scoop the mixture into meatballs.
5. Place the turkey balls in your Ninja Foodi pot.
6. Add milk,pats of butter and sprinkle 1 teaspoon salt,1 teaspoon black pepper.
7. Lock and secure the Ninja Foodi's lid,then cook on"HIGH"pressure for 4 minutes.
8. Quick-release pressure.
9. Unlock and secure the Ninja Foodi's lid and serve.
10. Enjoy.

Nutrition:
- InfoCalories:338;Fat:23g;Carbohydrates:7g;Protein:23g

Shredded Chicken And Wild Rice

Servings:6
Cooking Time:45 Min
Ingredients:
- 6 chicken thighs,skinless
- 3 cups chicken broth;divided/750ml
- 1½cups wild rice/195g
- 1 cup pumpkin,peeled and cubed/130g
- 2 celery stalks;diced
- 2 onions;diced
- 2 garlic cloves,crushed
- 2 tbsp olive oil/30ml
- 1/8 tsp smoked paprika/0.625g
- ½tsp ground white pepper/2.5g
- ½tsp onion powder/2.5g
- 1 tsp Cajun seasoning/5g
- 1 tsp salt/5g
- ½tsp ground red pepper/2.5g

Directions:
1. Season the chicken with salt,onion powder,Cajun seasoning,ground white pepper,ground red pepper,and smoked paprika.Warm oil on Sear/Sauté.
2. Stir in celery and pumpkin and cook for 5 minutes until tender;set the vegetables on a plate.In batches,sear chicken in oil for 3 minutes each side until golden brown;set onaplate.
3. In the Foodi,add 1/4 cup or 62.5ml chicken stock to deglaze the pan,scrape away any browned bits from the bottom;add garlic and onion and cook for 2 minutes until fragrant.
4. Take back the celery and pumpkin to Foodi;add the wild rice and remaining chicken stock.Place the chicken over the rice mixture.
5. Seal the pressure lid,choose Pressure,set to High,and set the timer to 10 minutes.Press Start.When ready,release the pressure quickly.Place rice and chicken pieces in serving plates and serve.

Salsa Chicken With Feta

Servings:6
Cooking Time:30 Min
Ingredients:
- 2 pounds boneless skinless chicken drumsticks/900g
- 1 cup feta cheese,crumbled/130g
- 1½cups hot tomato salsa/375ml
- 1 onion;chopped
- ¼tsp salt/1.25g

Directions:
1. Sprinkle salt over the chicken;set in the inner steel pot of Foodi.Stir in salsa to coat the chicken.Seal the pressure lid,choose Pressure,set to High,and set the timer to 15 minutes.Press Start.When ready,do a quick pressure release.
2. Press Sear/Sautéand cook for 5 to 10 minutes as you stir until excess liquid has evaporated.Top with feta cheese and serve.

Hassel Back Chicken

Servings:4
Cooking Time:60 Minutes
Ingredients:
- 4 tablespoons butter
- Black pepper and salt to taste
- 2 cups fresh mozzarella cheese,sliced
- 8 large chicken breasts
- 4 large Roma tomatoes,sliced

Directions:
1. Make few deep slits in chicken breasts,season with black pepper and salt.
2. Stuff mozzarella cheese slices and tomatoes in chicken slits.
3. Grease Ninja Foodi pot with butter and set stuffed chicken breasts.
4. Lock and secure the Ninja Foodi's lid and"Bake/Roast"for 1 hour at 365°F.
5. Serve and enjoy.

Nutrition:
- InfoCalories:278;Fat:15g;Carbohydrates:3.8g;Protein:15g

Shredded Chicken With Lentils And Rice

Servings: 4
Cooking Time: 45 Min
Ingredients:
- 4 boneless, skinless chicken thighs
- 1 garlic clove; minced
- 1 small yellow onion; chopped
- 1 cup white rice/130g
- ½ cup dried lentils/65g
- 3 cups chicken broth; divided/750ml
- 1 tsp olive oil/5ml
- Chopped fresh parsley for garnish
- Salt and ground black pepper to taste

Directions:
1. Set your Foodi to Sear/Sauté, set to Medium High, and choose Start/Stop to preheat the pot. Warm oil. Add in onion and garlic and cook for 3 minutes until soft; add in broth, rice, lentils, and chicken.
2. Season with pepper and salt. Seal the pressure lid, choose Pressure, set to High, and set the timer to 15 minutes. Press Start.
3. Once ready, do a quick release. Remove and shred the chicken in a large bowl. Set the lentils and rice into serving plates, top with shredded chicken and parsley and serve.

Tuscan Chicken & Pasta

Servings: 8
Cooking Time: 2½ Hours
Ingredients:
- 2½ cups chicken broth, low sodium
- 1 tbsp. Italian seasoning
- ½ tsp salt
- ½ cup mushrooms, sliced
- ¼ tsp crushed red pepper flakes
- 1½ lbs. chicken thighs, boneless, skinless & cut in 1-inch pieces
- ½ lb. macaroni
- ½ cup sun-dried tomatoes with herbs, chopped
- 8 oz. cream cheese, cubed
- 1 cup parmesan cheese
- 1½ cups fresh baby spinach

Directions:
1. Spray the cooking pot with cooking spray.
2. Add the broth, Italian seasoning, mushrooms, salt, and pepper flakes to the pot and stir to mix.
3. Stir in chicken. Add the lid and set to slow cook on high. Cook 1½-2 hours or until chicken is cooked through.
4. Add the pasta and tomatoes and stir to mix. Recover and cook another 25-30 minutes or until pasta is tender, stirring occasionally.
5. Add cream cheese and parmesan and stir until cheeses melt. Stir in spinach and recover. Cook another 5-10 minutes until spinach is wilted and tender. Stir well and serve hot.

Nutrition:
- Info Calories 438, Total Fat 20g, Total Carbs 27g, Protein 35g, Sodium 788mg.

Crunchy Chicken Schnitzels

Servings: 4
Cooking Time: 25 Min
Ingredients:
- 4 chicken breasts, boneless
- 2 eggs, beaten
- 4 slices cold butter
- 4 slices lemon
- 1 cup flour/130g
- 1 cup breadcrumbs/130g
- 2 tbsp fresh parsley; chopped 30g
- Cooking spray
- Salt and pepper to taste

Directions:
1. Combine the breadcrumbs with the parsley in a dish and set aside. Season the chicken with salt and pepper. Coat in flour; shake off any excess. Dip the coated chicken into the beaten egg followed by breadcrumbs. Spray the schnitzels with cooking spray.
2. Put them into the Foodi basket, close the crisping lid and cook for 10 minutes at 380°F or 194°C. After 5 minutes, turn the schnitzels over. Arrange the schnitzels on a serving platter and place the butter and lemon slices over to serve.

Cran-apple Turkey Cutlets

Servings: 4
Cooking Time: 10 Minutes
Ingredients:
- Nonstick cooking spray
- 4 turkey breast cutlets
- 1 Granny Smith apple, chopped fine
- 2 tbsp. cranberries, dried
- 2 tsp orange peel, grated fine
- 2 tbsp. orange juice

Directions:
1. Spray the cooking pot with cooking spray. Set to sauté on medium heat.
2. Add the turkey cutlets and cook 3-4 minutes per side or until no longer pink. Transfer to serving plate and keep warm.
3. Add remaining ingredients to the pot and stir to mix. Cook, stirring occasionally, about 4 minutes or until apples are tender. Spoon over turkey and serve.

Nutrition:
- Info Calories 175, Total Fat 2g, Total Carbs 12g, Protein 27g, Sodium 129mg.

Buttermilk Chicken Thighs

Servings: 6
Cooking Time: 4 Hours 40 Min
Ingredients:
- 1½ lb. chicken thighs/675g
- 2 cups buttermilk/500ml
- 2 cups flour/260g
- 1 tbsp paprika/15g
- 1 tbsp baking powder/15g
- 2 tsp black pepper/10g
- 1 tsp cayenne pepper/5g
- 3 tsp salt divided/15g

Directions:
1. Rinse and pat dry the chicken thighs. Place the chicken thighs in a bowl. Add cayenne pepper, 2 tsp or 10g salt, black pepper, and buttermilk, and stir to coat well.
2. Refrigerate for 4 hours. Preheat the Foodi to 350°F or 177°C. In another bowl, mix the flour, paprika, 1 tsp or 5g salt, and baking powder.
3. Dredge half of the chicken thighs, one at a time, in the flour, and then place on a lined dish. Close the crisping lid and cook for 18 minutes on Air Crisp mode, flipping once halfway through. Repeat with the other batch.

Ninja Foodi Cookbook

Lettuce Carnitas Wraps

Servings: 6
Cooking Time: 50 Min
Ingredients:
- 2 pounds chicken thighs,boneless;skinless/900g
- 12 large lettuce leaves
- 2 cups canned pinto beans,rinsed and drained/260g
- 1 cup pineapple juice/250ml
- ⅓cup water/88ml
- ¼cup soy sauce/62.5ml
- 3 tbsp cornstarch/45g
- 2 tbsp maple syrup/30ml
- 2 tbsp canola oil/30ml
- 1 tbsp rice vinegar/15ml
- 1 tsp chili-garlic sauce/5ml
- salt and freshly ground black pepper to taste

Directions:
1. Warm oil on Sear/Sauté.In batches,sear chicken in the oil for 5 minutes until browned.Set aside inabowl.Into your pot,mix chili-garlic sauce,pineapple juice,soy sauce,vinegar,maple syrup,and water;stir in chicken to coat.
2. Seal the pressure lid,choose Pressure,set to High,and set the timer to 7 minutes.Press Start.Release pressure naturally for 10 minutes.Shred the chicken with two forks.Take¼cup liquid from the pot to a bowl;stir in cornstarch to dissolve.
3. Mix the cornstarch mixture with the mixture in the pot and return the chicken.
4. Select Sear/Sautéand cook for 5 minutes until the sauce thickens;add pepper and salt for seasoning.Transfer beans into lettuce leaves;applyatopping of chicken carnitas and serve.

Paprika Chicken

Servings: 4
Cooking Time: 5 Minutes
Ingredients:
- 4 chicken breasts,skin on
- Black pepper and salt,to taste
- 1 tablespoon olive oil
- ½cup sweet onion,chopped
- ½cup heavy whip cream
- 2 teaspoons smoked paprika
- ½cup sour cream
- 2 tablespoons fresh parsley,chopped

Directions:
1. Season the four chicken breasts with black pepper and salt.
2. Select"Sauté"mode on your Ninja Foodi and add oil;let the oil heat up.
3. Add chicken and sear both sides until properly browned,should take about 15 minutes.
4. Remove chicken and transfer them to a plate.
5. Take a suitable skillet and place it over medium heat;stir in onion.
6. Sautéfor 4 minutes until tender.
7. Stir in cream,paprika and bring the liquid to a simmer.
8. Return chicken to the skillet and alongside any juices.
9. Transfer the whole mixture to your Ninja Foodi and lock lid,cook on"HIGH"pressure for 5 minutes.
10. Release pressure naturally over 10 minutes.
11. Stir in sour cream,serve and enjoy.

Nutrition:
- InfoCalories:389;Fat:30g;Carbohydrates:4g;Protein:25g

Creamy Tuscan Chicken Pasta

Servings: 8
Cooking Time: 6 Minutes
Ingredients:
- 32 ounces chicken stock
- 1 jar oil-packed sun-dried tomatoes,drained
- 2 teaspoons Italian seasoning
- 3 garlic cloves,minced
- 1 pound chicken breast,cubed
- 1 box penne pasta
- 4 cups spinach
- 1 package cream cheese,cubed
- 1 cup shredded Parmesan cheese
- Kosher salt
- Freshly ground black pepper

Directions:
1. Place the chicken stock,sun-dried tomatoes,Italian seasoning,garlic,chicken breast,and pasta and stir.Assemble pressure lid,making sure the pressure release valve is in the SEAL position.
2. Select PRESSURE and set to HI.Set time to 6 minutes.Select START/STOP to begin.
3. When pressure cooking is complete,quick release the pressure by turning the pressure release valve to the VENT position.Carefully remove lid when unit has finished releasing pressure.
4. Add the spinach and stir,allowing it to wilt with the residual heat.Add the cream cheese,Parmesan cheese,salt and pepper and stir until melted.Serve.

Nutrition:
- InfoCalories:429,Total Fat:21g,Sodium:567mg,Carbohydrates:32g,Protein:29g.

Southwest Chicken Bake

Servings: 8
Cooking Time: 20 Minutes
Ingredients:
- 1 tablespoon extra-virgin olive oil
- 2 boneless,skinless chicken breasts,cut into 1-inch cubes
- ½red onion,diced
- ½red bell pepper,diced
- 1 cup white rice
- 1 can fire-roasted tomatoes with chiles
- 1 can black beans,rinsed and drained
- 1 can corn,rinsed
- 1 packet taco seasoning
- 2 cups chicken broth
- Kosher salt
- Freshly ground black pepper
- 2 cups shredded Cheddar cheese

Directions:
1. Select SEAR/SAUTÉand set to MD:HI.Select START/STOP to begin.Let preheat for 5 minutes.
2. Place the olive oil and chicken into the pot and cook,stirring occasionally,until the chicken is cooked through,2 to 3 minutes.Add the onion and bell pepper and cook until softened,about 2 minutes.
3. Add the rice,tomatoes,beans,corn,taco seasoning,broth,salt,and pepper and stir.Assemble pressure lid,making sure the pressure release valve is in the SEAL position.

Ninja Foodi Cookbook

4. Select PRESSURE and set to HI.Set time to 7 minutes.Select START/STOP to begin.
5. When complete,quick release the pressure by turning the pressure release valve to the VENT position.Carefully remove lid when unit has finished releasing pressure.
6. Add the cheese on top of the mixture.Close crisping lid.
7. Select BROIL and set time to 8 minutes.Select START/STOP to begin.
8. When cooking is complete,serve along with your choice of toppings,such as chopped cilantro,diced avocado,diced fresh tomatoes,sour cream,and sliced scallions.

Nutrition:
- InfoCalories:333,Total Fat:17g,Sodium:630mg,Carbohydrates:27g,Protein:25g.

Chicken With Tomatoes And Capers

Servings:4
Cooking Time:45 Min
Ingredients:
- 4 chicken legs
- 1 onion;diced
- 2 garlic cloves;minced
- ⅓cup red wine/84ml
- 2 cups diced tomatoes/260g
- ⅓cup capers/44g
- ¼cup fresh basil/32.5g
- 2 pickles;chopped
- 2 tbsp olive oil/30ml
- sea salt and fresh ground black pepper to taste

Directions:
1. Sprinkle pepper and salt over the chicken.Warm oil on Sear/Sauté.Add in onion and cook for 3 minutes until fragrant;add in garlic and cook for 30 seconds until softened.
2. Mix the chicken with vegetables and cook for 6 to 7 minutes until lightly browned.
3. Add red wine to the pan to deglaze,scrape the pan's bottom to get rid of any browned bits of food;stir in tomatoes.Seal the pressure lid,choose Pressure,set to High,and set the timer to 12 minutes;press Start.
4. When ready,release the pressure quickly.To the chicken mixture,add basil,capers and pickles.Serve the chicken in plates covered with the tomato sauce mixture.

Creamy Chicken Carbonara

Servings:4
Cooking Time:15 Minutes
Ingredients:
- 4 strips bacon,chopped
- 1 medium onion,diced
- 1½pounds chicken breast,cut into¾inch-cubes
- 6 garlic cloves,minced
- 2 cups chicken stock
- 8 ounces dry spaghetti,with noodles broken in half
- 2 cups freshly grated Parmesan cheese,plus more for serving
- 2 eggs
- Sea salt
- Freshly ground black pepper

Directions:
1. Select SEAR/SAUTÉand set to HI.Select START/STOP to begin.Let preheat for 5 minutes.
2. Add the bacon and cook,stirring frequently,for about 6 minutes,or until crispy.Using a slotted spoon,transfer the bacon to a paper towel-lined plate to drain.Leave any bacon fat in the pot.
3. Add the onion,chicken,and garlic and sautéfor 2 minutes,until the onions start to become translucent and the garlic is fragrant.
4. Add the chicken stock and spaghetti noodles.Assemble pressure lid,making sure the pressure release valve is in the SEAL position.
5. Select PRESSURE and set to HI.Set time to 6 minutes.Select START/STOP to begin.
6. When pressure cooking is complete,allow pressure to naturally release for 5 minutes.After 5 minutes,quick release remaining pressure by moving the pressure release valve to the VENT position.Carefully remove lid when unit has finished releasing pressure.
7. Add the cheese and stir to fully combine.Close the crisping lid,leaving the unit off,to keep the heat inside and allow the cheese to melt.
8. Whisk the eggs until full beaten.
9. Open lid,select SEAR/SAUTÉ,and set to LO.Select START/STOP to begin.Add the eggs and stir gently to incorporate,taking care to ensure the eggs are not scrambling while you work toward your desired sauce consistency.If your pot gets too warm,turn unit off.
10. Add the bacon back to the pot and season with salt and pepper.Stir to combine.Serve,adding more cheese as desired.

Nutrition:
- InfoCalories:732,Total Fat:28g,Sodium:1518mg,Carbohydrates:47g,Protein:70g.

Chicken Carnitas

Servings:6
Cooking Time:25 Minutes
Ingredients:
- 1 tbsp.cumin
- ½tsp chili powder
- ½tsp oregano
- ¼tsp salt,divided
- ¼tsp pepper
- 2 lb.chicken thighs,boneless&skinless
- 2 tbsp.olive oil
- 1 onion,quartered
- 5 cloves garlic,chopped
- 1 tbsp.orange zest
- ¼cup orange juice
- ¼cup lime juice
- ¼cup chicken broth
- 4 chipotle peppers,divided
- 3 tbsp.adobo sauce,divided
- 1 bay leaf
- ½bunch cilantro,chopped
- ½cup mayonnaise
- 1 tbsp.milk
- ¼tsp garlic powder

Directions:
1. In a small bowl,combine cumin,chili powder,oregano,1/8 teaspoon salt,and pepper,mix well.
2. Sprinkle the chicken with the seasonings on both sides.
3. Add the oil to the pot and set to sear on medium heat.Add the chicken and sear both sides,about 1 minute per side.Transfer to a plate.

4. Add the onions and garlic and cook 2 minutes or until onions are lightly browned on all sides. Return the chicken to the pot along with orange zest, orange juice, lime juice, broth, 2 peppers, 2 tablespoons adobo sauce, bay leaf and cilantro, stir to mix.
5. Add the lid and set to pressure cook on high. Set the timer for 10 minutes. When the timer goes off release the pressure naturally.
6. Add the mayonnaise, milk, remaining peppers and adobo sauce, garlic powder and remaining salt to a blender. Process until smooth.
7. Transfer the chicken to a work surface and shred using 2 forks. Place in a large bowl and mix in ¼ cup of the cooking liquid. Place in the fryer basket and return to the pot.
8. Add the tender-crisp lid and set to broil. Cook 5 minutes, then add the chipotle sauce and stir to mix. Broil another 5-6 minutes, if chicken gets too dry and a little of the cooking liquid. Serve with your favorite fixings.

Nutrition:
- InfoCalories 372, Total Fat 22g, Total Carbs 6g, Protein 35g, Sodium 568mg.

Thyme Turkey Nuggets

Servings: 2
Cooking Time: 20 Min
Ingredients:
- 8 oz. turkey breast, boneless and skinless/240g
- 1 cup breadcrumbs/130g
- 1 egg, beaten
- 1 tbsp dried thyme/15g
- ½tsp dried parsley/2.5g
- Salt and pepper, to taste

Directions:
1. Mince the turkey in a food processor. Transfer to a bowl. Stir in the thyme and parsley, and season with salt and pepper.
2. Take a nugget-sized piece of the turkey mixture and shape it into a ball, or another form. Dip it in the breadcrumbs, then egg, then in the breadcrumbs again. Place the nuggets onto a prepared baking dish. Close the crisping lid and cook for 10 minutes on Air Crisp mode at 350°F or 177°C

Greek Chicken With Potatoes

Servings: 4
Cooking Time: 40 Min
Ingredients:
- 4 potatoes, peeled and quartered
- 4 boneless skinless chicken drumsticks
- 2 lemons, zested and juiced
- 1 cucumber, thinly sliced
- 2 Serrano peppers, stemmed, cored, and chopped
- 1 cup packed watercress/130g
- ½cup cherry tomatoes, quartered/65g
- ¼cup Kalamata olives, pitted/32.5g
- ¼cup hummus/32.5g
- ¼cup feta cheese, crumbled/32.5g
- 4 cups water/1000ml
- 3 tbsp finely chopped parsley/45g
- 1 tbsp olive oil/15ml
- 2 tsp fresh oregano/10g
- ¼tsp freshly ground black pepper/1.25g
- Lemon wedges; for serving
- Salt to taste

Directions:
1. In the cooker, add water and potatoes. Set trivet over them. In a baking bowl, mix lemon juice, olive oil, black pepper, oregano, zest, salt, and red pepper flakes. Add chicken drumsticks in the marinade and stir to coat.
2. Set the bowl with chicken on the trivet in the inner pot. Seal the lid, select Pressure and set the time to 15 minutes on High pressure. Press Start.
3. When ready, do a quick pressure release. Take out the bowl with chicken and the trivet from the pot. Drain potatoes and add parsley and salt.
4. Split the potatoes among four serving plates and top with watercress, cucumber slices, hummus, cherry tomatoes, chicken, olives, and feta cheese. Each bowl should be garnished with a lemon wedge.

Garlic Turkey Breasts

Servings: 4
Cooking Time: 17 Minutes
Ingredients:
- ½teaspoon garlic powder
- 4 tablespoons butter
- ¼teaspoon dried oregano
- 1-pound turkey breasts, boneless
- 1 teaspoon pepper
- ½teaspoon salt
- ¼teaspoon dried basil

Directions:
1. Season turkey on both sides generously with garlic, dried oregano, dried basil, black pepper and salt.
2. Select "Sauté" mode on your Ninja Foodi and stir in butter; let the butter melt.
3. Add turkey breasts and sauté for 2 minutes on each side.
4. Lock the lid and select the "Bake/Roast" setting; bake for 15 minutes at 355°F.
5. Serve and enjoy once done.

Nutrition:
- InfoCalories: 223; Fat: 13g; Carbohydrates: 5g; Protein: 19g

Bacon & Cranberry Stuffed Turkey Breast

Servings: 4
Cooking Time: 1 Hour
Ingredients:
- ¼oz. porcini mushrooms, dried
- 1 slice bacon, thick cut, chopped
- ¼cup shallot, chopped fine
- 2 tbsp. cranberries, dried, chopped
- 1 tsp fresh sage, chopped fine
- ½cup bread crumbs
- 1 tbsp. fresh parsley, chopped
- 3 tbsp. chicken broth, low sodium
- 2 lb. turkey breast, boneless
- 2 tbsp. butter, soft
- ½tsp salt

Directions:
1. In a small bowl, add the mushrooms and enough hot water to cover them. Let sit 15 minutes, then drain and chop them.
2. Set the cooker to sauté on medium heat. Add the bacon and cook until crisp. Transfer to a paper-towel lined plate.

Ninja Foodi Cookbook

3. Add the shallots and cook until they start to brown, about 3-5 minutes. Add the cranberries, sage, and mushrooms and cook, stirring frequently, 2-3 minutes.
4. Stir in bread crumbs, parsley, bacon, and broth and mix well. Transfer to a bowl to cool.
5. Remove the skin from the turkey, in one piece, do not discard. Butterfly the turkey breast and place between 2 sheets of plastic wrap. Pound out to ¼-inch thick.
6. Spread the stuffing over the turkey, leaving a ¾-inch border. Start with a short end and roll up the turkey. Wrap the skin back around the roll.
7. Use butcher string to tie the turkey. Place in the cooking pot and rub with butter. Sprinkle with salt.
8. Add the tender-crisp lid and set to roast on 400°F. Cook 20 minutes, then decrease the heat to 325°F. Cook another 10-15 minutes or until juices run clear. Let rest 10 minutes before slicing and serving.

Nutrition:
- InfoCalories 159, Total Fat 7g, Total Carbs 3g, Protein 19g, Sodium 120mg.

Cheesy Chicken And Broccoli Casserole

Servings: 6
Cooking Time: 30 Minutes
Ingredients:
- 4 boneless, skinless chicken breasts
- 2 cups chicken stock
- 1 cup whole milk
- 1 cans condensed Cheddar cheese soup
- 1 teaspoon paprika
- 2 cups shredded Cheddar cheese
- Kosher salt
- Freshly ground black pepper
- 2 cups crushed buttered crackers

Directions:
1. Place the chicken and stock in the pot. Assemble pressure lid, making sure the pressure release valve is in the SEAL position.
2. Select PRESSURE and set to HI. Set timer to 20 minutes. Select START/STOP to begin.
3. When pressure cooking is complete, quick release the pressure by turning the pressure release valve to the VENT position. Carefully remove lid when unit has finished releasing pressure.
4. Using silicone-tipped utensils, shred the chicken inside the pot.
5. Add the milk, condensed soup, paprika, and cheese. Stir to combine with the chicken. Season with salt and pepper. Top with the crushed crackers. Close crisping lid.
6. Select AIR CRISP, set temperature to 360°F, and set time to 10 minutes. Select START/STOP to begin.
7. When cooking is complete, open lid and let cool before serving.

Nutrition:
- InfoCalories: 449, Total Fat: 23g, Sodium: 925mg, Carbohydrates: 18g, Protein: 42g.

Chicken With Prunes

Servings: 6
Cooking Time: 55 Min
Ingredients:
- 1 whole chicken, 3 lb/1350g
- ¼ cup packed brown sugar/32.5g
- ½ cup pitted prunes/65g
- 2 bay leaves
- 3 minced cloves of garlic
- 2 tbsp olive oil/30ml
- 2 tbsp capers/30g
- 1 tbsp dried oregano/15g
- 1 tbsp chopped fresh parsley/15g
- 2 tbsp red wine vinegar/30ml
- Salt and black pepper to taste

Directions:
1. In a big and deep bowl, mix the prunes, olives, capers, garlic, olive oil, bay leaves, oregano, vinegar, salt, and pepper.
2. Spread the mixture on the bottom of a baking tray, and place the chicken.
3. Preheat the Foodi to 360°°F or 183°C. Sprinkle a little bit of brown sugar on top of the chicken, close the crisping lid and cook for 45-55 minutes on Air Crisp mode. When ready, garnish with fresh parsley.

Cheesy Chicken & Artichokes

Servings: 4
Cooking Time: 30 Minutes
Ingredients:
- Nonstick cooking spray
- 2 cups baby spinach, chopped & packed
- 1 cup plain yogurt
- 1 cup marinated artichoke hearts, drained & chopped
- ½ tsp garlic powder
- 1 tsp Dijon mustard
- 4 chicken breasts, boneless & skinless
- 8 slices mozzarella cheese

Directions:
1. Spray the cooking pot with cooking spray.
2. In a large bowl, combine spinach, yogurt, artichokes, garlic powder, and mustard, mix well.
3. Place chicken between 2 sheets of plastic wrap and pound out slightly. Place in the cooking pot.
4. Top chicken with spinach mixture. Lay 2 slices of cheese on top of each piece of chicken.
5. Add the tender-crisp lid and set to bake on 400°F. Bake 30 minutes or until chicken is cooked through. Let rest 5 minutes before serving.

Nutrition:
- InfoCalories 602, Total Fat 33g, Total Carbs 7g, Protein 66g, Sodium 348mg.

Italian Turkey & Pasta Soup

Servings: 8
Cooking Time: 10 Minutes
Ingredients:
- 1 lb. ground turkey sausage
- 1 onion, chopped fine
- 5 cloves garlic, chopped fine
- 1 green bell pepper, chopped fine
- 1 tbsp. Italian seasoning
- 2 15 oz. cans tomatoes, diced
- 2 8 oz. cans tomato sauce
- 4 cups chicken broth, low sodium
- 3 cups whole wheat pasta
- ¼ cup parmesan cheese
- ¼ cup mozzarella cheese, grated

Directions:

Ninja Foodi Cookbook

1. Add the sausage,onions,and garlic to the cooking pot.Set to sauté on med-high and cook,breaking sausage up,until meat is no longer pink and onions are translucent.Drain off excess fat.
2. Stir in bell pepper,Italian seasoning,tomatoes,tomato sauce,broth,and pasta,mix well.
3. Add the lid and set to pressure cook on high.Set the timer for 5 minutes.Once the timer goes off,use the natural release for 5-10 minutes,then quick release to remove the pressure.
4. Stir the soup and ladle into bowls.Serve garnished with parmesan and mozzarella cheeses.

Nutrition:
- InfoCalories 294,Total Fat 8g,Total Carbs 37g,Protein 22g,Sodium 841mg.

Garlic-herb Roasted Chicken

Servings:4
Cooking Time:40 Minutes
Ingredients:
- 1 whole chicken
- 1 head garlic
- 2 fresh whole sprigs rosemary
- 2 fresh whole sprigs parsley
- 1 lemon,halved
- ¼cup hot water
- ¼cup white wine
- Juice of 2 lemons
- ¼cup unsalted butter,melted
- 3 tablespoons extra-virgin olive oil
- 5 garlic cloves,minced
- 2 teaspoons minced fresh parsley
- 2 teaspoons minced fresh rosemary
- ½teaspoon sea salt
- ¼teaspoon freshly ground black pepper

Directions:
1. Discard the neck from inside the chicken cavity and remove any excess fat and leftover feathers.Rinse the chicken inside and out under running cold water.Stuff the garlic head into the chicken cavity along with the rosemary and parsley sprigs and lemon halves.Tie the legs together with cooking twine.
2. Add the water,wine,and lemon juice.Place the chicken into the Cook&Crisp Basket and insert the basket in the pot.Assemble pressure lid,making sure the pressure release valve is in the SEAL position.
3. Select PRESSURE and set to HI.Set time to 15 minutes.Select START/STOP to begin.
4. When pressure cooking is complete,quick release the pressure by moving the pressure release valve to the VENT position.Carefully remove lid when the unit has finished releasing pressure.
5. In a small bowl,combine the butter,olive oil,minced garlic,minced parsley,minced rosemary,salt,and pepper.Brush the mixture over the chicken.Close crisping lid.
6. Select AIR CRISP,set temperature to 400°F,and set time to 20 minutes.Select START/STOP to begin.
7. Cooking is complete when the internal temperature of the chicken reaches 165°F on a meat thermometer inserted into the thickest part of the meat(it should not touch the bone).Carefully remove the chicken from the basket using 2 large serving forks.
8. Let the chicken rest for 10 minutes before carving and serving.

Nutrition:
- InfoCalories:693,Total Fat:50g,Sodium:323mg,Carbohydrates:12g,Protein:48g.

Turkey Croquettes

Servings:10
Cooking Time:20 Minutes
Ingredients:
- Nonstick cooking spray
- 2½cups turkey,cooked
- 1 stalk celery,chopped
- 2 green onions,chopped
- ½cup cauliflower,cooked
- ½cup broccoli,cooked
- 1 cup stuffing,cooked
- 1 cup cracker crumbs
- 1 egg,lightly beaten
- 1/8 tsp salt
- 1/8 tsp pepper
- 1 cup French fried onions,crushed

Directions:
1. Spray the fryer basket with cooking spray.
2. Add the turkey,celery,onion,cauliflower,and broccoli to a food processor and pulse until finely chopped.Transfer to a large bowl.
3. Stir in stuffing and 1 cup of the cracker crumbs until combined.
4. Add the egg,salt and pepper and stir to combine.Form into 10 patties.
5. Place the crushed fried onions in a shallow dish.Coat patties on both sides in the onions and place in the basket.Lightly spray the tops with cooking spray.
6. Add the tender-crisp lid and set to air fry on 375°F.Cook 5-7 minutes until golden brown.Flip over and spray with cooking spray again,cook another 5-7 minutes.Serve immediately.

Nutrition:
- InfoCalories 133,Total Fat 4g,Total Carbs 16g,Protein 9g,Sodium 449mg.

Asian Chicken

Servings:4
Cooking Time:35 Min
Ingredients:
- 1 lb.chicken;cut in stripes/450g
- 1 large onion
- 3 green peppers;cut in stripes
- 2 tomatoes;cubed
- 1 pinch fresh and chopped coriander
- 1 pinch ginger
- 1 tbsp mustard/15g
- 1 tbsp cumin powder/15g
- 2 tbsp oil/30ml
- Salt and black pepper

Directions:
1. Heat the oil in a deep pan.Add in the mustard,onion,ginger,cumin and green chili peppers.Sauté the mixture for 2-3 minutes.Then,add the tomatoes,coriander,and salt and keep stirring.
2. Coat the chicken with oil,salt,and pepper and cook for 25 minutes on Air Crisp mode at 380°F or 194°C.Remove from the Foodi and pour the sauce over and around.

Apple Butter Chicken

Servings:4
Cooking Time:35 Minutes
Ingredients:
- Nonstick cooking spray
- 4 chicken breast halves,boneless&skinless
- ½tsp salt
- 1/8 tsp pepper
- ½cup apple butter
- ¼cup cheddar cheese,grated

Directions:
1. Spray cooking pot with cooking spray.
2. Place chicken in the pot and season with salt and pepper.Spread apple butter evenly over the chicken.
3. Add the tender-crisp lid and set to bake on 350°F.Bake 25-30 minutes until chicken is cooked through.
4. Open the lid and sprinkle the cheese over the chicken.Close the lid and bake another 3-5 minutes until cheese is melted.Serve.

Nutrition:
- InfoCalories 344,Total Fat 7g,Total Carbs 28g,Protein 40g,Sodium 426mg.

Chicken Cacciatore

Servings:4
Cooking Time:40 Min
Ingredients:
- 1 pound chicken drumsticks,boneless,skinless/450g
- ½cup dry red wine/125ml
- ¾cup chicken stock/188ml
- 1 cup black olives,pitted and sliced/130g
- 2 bay leaves
- 1 pinch red pepper flakes
- 1 can diced tomatoes/840g
- 1carrot;chopped
- 1 red bell pepper;chopped
- 1 yellow bell pepper;chopped
- 1 onion;chopped
- 4 garlic cloves,thinly sliced
- 2 tsp olive oil/10ml
- 1 tsp dried basil/5g
- 1 tsp dried parsley/5g
- 2 tsp dried oregano/10g
- 1½tsp freshly ground black pepper/7.5g
- 2 tsp salt/10g

Directions:
1. Warm oil on Sear/Sauté.Add pepper and salt to the chicken drumsticks.In batches,sear the chicken for 5-6 minutes until golden-brown.Set aside on a plate.Drain the cooker and remain with 1 tbsp of fat.
2. In the hot oil,sautéonion,garlic,and bell peppers for 4 minutes until softened;add red pepper flakes,basil,parsley,and oregano,and cook for 30 more seconds.Season with salt and pepper.
3. Stir in tomatoes,olives,chicken stock,red wine and bay leaves.
4. Return chicken to the pot.Seal the pressure lid,choose Pressure,set to High,and set the timer to 15 minutes.Press Start.
5. When ready,release the pressure quickly.Divide chicken between four serving bowls;top with tomato mixture before serving.

Chicken Wings With Lemon

Servings:4
Cooking Time:40 Min
Ingredients:
- 8 chicken wings
- ½cup chicken broth/125ml
- 2 lemons,juiced
- ½dried oregano
- 2 tbsp olive oil/30ml
- ½tsp cayenne pepper/2.5g
- ½tsp chili powder/2.5g
- ½tsp garlic powder/2.5g
- ½tsp onion powder/2.5g
- Sea salt and ground black pepper to taste

Directions:
1. Coat the chicken wings with olive oil;season with chili powder,onion powder,salt,oregano,garlic powder,cayenne,and pepper.
2. In the steel pot of the Foodi,add your wings and chicken broth.Seal the pressure lid,choose Pressure,set to High,and set the timer to 4 minutes.Press Start.When ready,do a quick pressure release.Preheat an oven to high.
3. Ontoagreased baking sheet,place the wings in a single layer and drizzle over the lemon juice.Bake for 5 minutes until skin is crispy.

Thyme Chicken With Veggies

Servings:4
Cooking Time:40 Min
Ingredients:
- 4 skin-on,bone-in chicken legs
- ½cup dry white wine/125ml
- 1¼cups chicken stock/312.5ml
- 1 cup carrots,thinly sliced/130g
- 1 cup parsnip,thinly sliced/130g
- 4 slices lemon
- 4 cloves garlic;minced
- 3 tomatoes,thinly sliced
- 2 tbsp olive oil/30ml
- 1 tbsp honey/15ml
- 1 tsp fresh chopped thyme/5g
- salt and freshly ground black pepper to taste
- Fresh thyme;chopped for garnish

Directions:
1. Season the chicken with pepper and salt.Warm oil on Sear/Sauté.Arrange chicken legs into the hot oil;cook for 3 to 5 minutes each side until browned.Place inabowl and set aside.Cook thyme and garlic in the chicken fat for 1 minute until soft and lightly golden.
2. Add wine into the pot to deglaze,scrape the pot's bottom to get rid of any brown bits of food.Simmer the wine for 2 to 3 minutes until slightly reduced in volume.
3. Add stock,carrots,parsnips,tomatoes,pepper and salt into the pot.
4. Lay reversible rack onto veggies.Into the Foodi's steamer basket,arrange chicken legs.Set the steamer basket onto the reversible rack.Drizzle the chicken with honey then top with lemon slices.
5. Seal the pressure lid,choose Pressure,set to High,and set the timer to 12 minutes.Press Start.Release pressure naturally for 10 minutes.Place the chicken onto a bowl.Drain the veggies and place them around the chicken.Garnish with fresh thyme leaves before serving.

Buttermilk Fried Chicken

Servings:4
Cooking Time:30 Minutes
Ingredients:
- 1½pounds boneless,skinless chicken breasts
- 1 to 2 cups buttermilk
- 2 large eggs
- ¾cup all-purpose flour
- ¾cup potato starch
- ½teaspoon granulated garlic,divided
- 1 teaspoon salt,divided
- 2 teaspoons freshly ground black pepper,divided
- 1 cup bread crumbs
- ½cup panko bread crumbs
- Olive oil or cooking spray

Directions:
1. In a large bowl,combine the chicken breasts and buttermilk,turning the chicken to coat.Cover the bowl with plastic wrap and refrigerate the chicken to soak at least 4 hours or overnight.
2. In a medium shallow bowl,whisk the eggs.In a second shallow bowl,stir together the flour,potato starch,¼teaspoon of granulated garlic,½teaspoon of salt,and 1 teaspoon of pepper.In a third shallow bowl,stir together the bread crumbs,panko,remaining¼teaspoon of granulated garlic,remaining½teaspoon of salt,and remaining 1 teaspoon of pepper.
3. Working one piece at a time,remove the chicken from the buttermilk,letting the excess drip into the bowl.Dredge the chicken in the flour mixture,coating well on both sides.Then dip the chicken in the eggs,coating both sides.Finally,dip the chicken in the bread crumb mixture,coating both sides and pressing the crumbs onto the chicken.Spritz both sides of the coated chicken pieces with olive oil.
4. Place the Cook&Crisp Basket into the unit.
5. Select AIR CRISP,set the temperature to 400°F,and set the time to 30 minutes.Select START/STOP to begin and allow to preheat for 5 minutes.
6. Spritz both sides of the coated chicken pieces with olive oil.Working in batches as needed,place the chicken breasts in the Cook&Crisp Basket,ensuring the chicken pieces do not touch each other.
7. After 12 minutes,turn the chicken with a spatula so you don't tear the breading.Close the crisping lid and continue to cook,checking the chicken for an internal temperature of 165°F.
8. When cooking is complete,transfer the chicken to a wire rack to cool.

Nutrition:
- InfoCalories:574,Total Fat:7g,Sodium:995mg,Carbohydrates:67g,Protein:51g.

Fiesta Chicken Casserole

Servings:8
Cooking Time:45 Minutes
Ingredients:
- Nonstick cooking spray
- 12 oz.chicken breast halves,boneless,skinless&cut in strips
- 2 cloves garlic,chopped fine
- 1 tsp chili powder
- 2 tsp olive oil
- 1 onion,halved&sliced thin
- 1 green bell pepper,chopped
- 10 oz.spinach,chopped
- 1½cup salsa
- 4 6-inch corn tortillas,torn in pieces
- ¾cup Monterey Jack cheese,reduced fat,grated
- ½cup cherry tomatoes,chopped
- ½avocado,pitted,peeled&chopped
- ¼cup cilantro,chopped

Directions:
1. Spray a 2-qt casserole dish and the cooking pot with cooking spray.
2. In a medium bowl,combine chicken,garlic,and chili powder.Add to the cooking pot and set to sautéon med-high.Cook 4-6 minutes or until chicken is no longer pink.Transfer to a bowl.
3. Add the oil to the pot and let it get hot.Add onion and pepper and cook 3-5 minutes,stirring frequently until tender.Stir in spinach,transfer to a bowl.
4. Spread½cup salsa on the bottom of the prepared dish.Top with½the tortilla's,½the chicken mixture,and½the vegetable mixture.Pour½the remaining salsa over the vegetables and top with½the cheese.Repeat layers except for the cheese.
5. Place the rack in the cooking pot and add the casserole.Add the tender-crisp lid and set to bake on 350°F.Bake 30-35 minutes.Sprinkle with remaining cheese and let sit 5 minutes.Serve garnished with tomatoes,avocado,and cilantro.

Nutrition:
- InfoCalories 175,Total Fat 7g,Total Carbs 14g,Protein 16g,Sodium 477mg.

Chicken With Bacon And Beans

Servings:4
Cooking Time:45 Min
Ingredients:
- 4 boneless;skinless chicken thighs
- 4 garlic cloves;minced
- 15 ounces red kidney beans,drained and rinsed/450g
- 4 slices bacon,crumbled
- 1 can whole tomatoes/435g
- 1 red bell pepper;chopped
- 1 onion;diced
- 1 cup shredded Monterey Jack cheese/130g
- 1 cup sliced red onion/130g
- ¼cup chopped cilantro/32.5g
- 1 cup chicken broth/250ml
- 1 tbsp tomato paste/15ml
- 1 tbsp olive oil/15ml
- 1 tbsp oregano/15g
- 1 tbsp ground cumin/15g
- 1 tsp chili powder/5g
- ½tsp cayenne pepper/2.5g
- 1 tsp salt/5g
- 1 cup cooked corn/130g

Directions:
1. Warm oil on Sear/Sauté.Sear the chicken for 3 minutes for each side until browned.Set the chicken onaplate.In the same oil,fry bacon until crispy,about 5 minutes and set aside.
2. Add in onions and cook for 2 to 3 minutes until fragrant.Stir in garlic,oregano,cayenne pepper,cumin,tomato

Ninja Foodi Cookbook

paste,bell pepper,and chili powder and cook for 30 more seconds.Pour the chicken broth,salt,and tomatoes and bring to a boil.Press Start/Stop.
3. Take back the chicken and bacon to the pot and ensure it is submerged in the braising liquid.Seal the pressure lid,choose Pressure,set to High,and set the timer to 15 minutes.Press Start.When ready,release the pressure quickly.
4. Pour the kidney beans in the cooker,press Sear/Sautéand bring the liquid toaboil;cook for 10 minutes.Serve topped with shredded cheese and chopped cilantro.

Pizza Stuffed Chicken

Servings:4
Cooking Time:20 Minutes
Ingredients:
- Nonstick cooking spray
- 2 chicken breasts,boneless&skinless
- 2 tbsp.parmesan cheese,divided
- ½tsp oregano
- 12 slices turkey pepperoni
- ½cup mozzarella cheese,grated,divided
- 3 tbsp.whole-wheat bread crumbs
- 4 tbsp.marinara sauce,low sodium

Directions:
1. Place the rack in the cooking pot.Spray the fryer basket with cooking spray.
2. Cut each breast in half horizontally.Place between 2 sheets of plastic wrap and pound out to¼-inch thick.
3. Sprinkle 1 tablespoon of parmesan and the oregano over chicken.Top each cutlet with 3 slices of pepperoni and 1 tablespoon mozzarella.Roll up.
4. In a shallow dish,combine bread crumbs and remaining parmesan,mix well.Coat chicken rolls in bread crumbs and place,seam side down,in the fryer basket.Lightly spray with cooking spray.
5. Add the tender-crisp lid and set to air fry on 400°F.Cook 15 minutes.
6. Open the lid and top each chicken roll with 1 tablespoon marinara sauce and remaining mozzarella.Cook 5-7 minutes until chicken is cooked through and cheese is melted.Serve immediately.

Nutrition:
- InfoCalories 268,Total Fat 8g,Total Carbs 7g,Protein 41g,Sodium 800mg.

Honey Garlic Chicken And Okra

Servings:4
Cooking Time:25 Min
Ingredients:
- 4 boneless;skinless chicken breasts;sliced
- 4 spring onions,thinly sliced
- 6 garlic cloves,grated
- ⅓cup honey/84ml
- 1 cup rice,rinsed/130g
- ¼cup tomato puree/62.5ml
- ½cup soy sauce/125ml
- 2 cups water/500ml
- 2 cups frozen okra/260g
- 1 tbsp cornstarch/15g
- 2 tbsp rice vinegar/30ml
- 1 tbsp olive oil/15ml
- 1 tbsp water/15ml
- 2 tsp toasted sesame seeds/10g
- ½tsp salt/2.5g

Directions:
1. In the inner pot of the Foodi,mix garlic,tomato puree,vinegar,soy sauce,ginger,honey,and oil;toss in chicken to coat.In an ovenproof bowl,mix water,salt and rice.Set the reversible rack on top of chicken.Lower the bowl onto the reversible rack.
2. Seal the pressure lid,choose Pressure,set to High,and set the timer to 10 minutes;press Start.Release pressure naturally for 5 minutes,release the remaining pressure quickly.
3. Useafork to fluff the rice.Lay okra onto the rice.Allow the okra steam in the residual heat for 3 minutes.Take the trivet and bowl from the pot.Set the chicken to a plate.
4. Press Sear/Sauté.Inasmall bowl,mix 1 tbsp of water and cornstarch until smooth;stir into the sauce and cook for 3 to 4 minutes until thickened.
5. Divide the rice,chicken,and okra between 4 bowls.Drizzle sauce over each portion;garnish with spring onions and sesame seeds.

Chicken Meatballs Primavera

Servings:4
Cooking Time:30 Min
Ingredients:
- 1 lb.ground chicken/450g
- ½lb.chopped asparagus/225g
- 1 cup chopped tomatoes/130g
- 1 cup chicken broth/250ml
- 1 red bell pepper,seeded and sliced
- 2 cups chopped green beans/260g
- 1 egg,cracked intoabowl
- 2 tbsp chopped basil+extra to garnish/30g
- 1 tbsp olive oil+½tbsp olive oil/22.5ml
- 6 tsp flour/30g
- 1½tsp Italian Seasoning/7.5g
- Salt and black pepper to taste

Directions:
1. In a mixing bowl,add the chicken,egg,flour,salt,pepper,2 tbsps of basil,1 tbsp of olive oil,and Italian seasoning.Mix them well with hands and make 16 large balls out of the mixture.Set the meatballs aside.
2. Select Sear/Sautémode.Heat half tsp of olive oil,and add peppers,green beans,and asparagus.Cook for 3 minutes,stirring frequently.
3. After 3 minutes,useaspoon the veggies onto a plate and set aside.Pour the remaining oil in the pot to heat and then fry the meatballs in it in batches.Fry them for 2 minutes on each side to brown them lightly.
4. After,put all the meatballs back into the pot as well as the vegetables.Also,pour the chicken broth over it.
5. Close the lid,secure the pressure valve,and select Pressure mode on High pressure for 10 minutes.Press Start/Stop.Doaquick pressure release.Close the crisping lid and select Air Crisp.Cook for 5 minutes at 400°F or 205°C,until nice and crispy.
6. Dish the meatballs with sauce into a serving bowl and garnish it with basil.Serve with over cooked pasta.

Moo Shu Chicken

Servings: 4
Cooking Time: 20 Minutes
Ingredients:
- 1 tbsp. sesame oil
- 1 cup mushrooms, sliced
- 2 cups cabbage, shredded
- ½ cup green onion, sliced thin
- 3 cups chicken, cooked & shredded
- 2 eggs, lightly beaten
- ¼ cup hoisin sauce
- 2 tbsp. tamari
- 2 tsp sriracha sauce

Directions:
1. Add the oil to the cooking pot and set to sauté on med-high heat.
2. Add the mushrooms and cook 5-6 minutes, stirring frequently, until mushrooms have browned and liquid has evaporated.
3. Add cabbage and green onion, cook, stirring, 2 minutes.
4. Stir in chicken and cook 3-5 minutes until heated through.
5. Add the eggs and cook, stirring to scramble, until eggs are cooked.
6. Stir in remaining ingredients. Reduce heat and simmer until heated through. Serve immediately.

Nutrition:
- InfoCalories 378, Total Fat 25g, Total Carbs 15g, Protein 23g, Sodium 1067mg.

Garlic Chicken And Bacon Pasta

Servings: 4
Cooking Time: 10 Minutes
Ingredients:
- 3 strips bacon, chopped
- ½ pound boneless, skinless chicken breast, cut into ½-pieces
- 1 teaspoon dried basil
- 1 teaspoon dried oregano
- ¼ teaspoon sea salt
- 1 tablespoon unsalted butter
- 3 garlic cloves, minced
- 1 cup chicken stock
- 1½ cups water
- 8 ounces dry penne pasta
- ½ cup half-and-half
- ½ cup grated Parmesan cheese, plus more for serving

Directions:
1. Select SEAR/SAUTÉ and set to HI. Select START/STOP to begin. Let preheat for 5 minutes.
2. Add the bacon and cook, stirring frequently, for about 5 minutes or until crispy. Using a slotted spoon, transfer the bacon to a paper towel-lined plate to drain.
3. Season the chicken with the basil, oregano, and salt, coating all the pieces.
4. Add the butter, chicken, and garlic and sauté for 2 minutes, until the chicken begins to brown and the garlic is fragrant.
5. Add the chicken stock, water, and penne pasta. Assemble pressure lid, making sure the pressure release valve is in the SEAL position.
6. Select PRESSURE and set to HI. Set time to 3 minutes. Select START/STOP to begin.
7. When pressure cooking is complete, allow pressure to naturally release for 2 minutes. After 2 minutes, quick release remaining pressure by moving the pressure release valve to the VENT position. Carefully remove lid when unit has finished releasing pressure.
8. Add the half-and-half, cheese, and bacon, and stir constantly to thicken the sauce and melt the cheese. Serve immediately, with additional Parmesan cheese to garnish.

Nutrition:
- InfoCalories: 458, Total Fat: 18g, Sodium: 809mg, Carbohydrates: 45g, Protein: 30g.

Butternut Turkey Stew

Servings: 6
Cooking Time: 4 Hours
Ingredients:
- 1 tbsp. olive oil
- 1 onion, chopped
- 2 carrots, chopped
- 3 cloves garlic, chopped
- 1 butternut squash, peeled & chopped
- 4 cups turkey, cooked & chopped
- 7 cups chicken broth, low sodium
- ½ tsp salt
- ½ tsp pepper
- 1 cup green peas, frozen

Directions:
1. Add oil to the cooking pot and set to sauté on med-high.
2. Add the onions and cook 3-5 minutes until translucent.
3. Set cooker to slow cook on high. Add remaining ingredients, except the peas and stir to mix.
4. Add the lid and cook 4 hours, stirring occasionally. Add the peas in the last 30 minutes of cooking time. Ladle into bowls and serve.

Nutrition:
- InfoCalories 235, Total Fat 8g, Total Carbs 17g, Protein 25g, Sodium 992mg.

Crunchy Chicken & Almond Casserole

Servings: 6
Cooking Time: 30 Minutes
Ingredients:
- Nonstick cooking spray
- 3 cups chicken breast, cooked & chopped
- ¾ cup mozzarella cheese, grated
- 10¾ oz. condensed cream of chicken soup, low fat
- ¼ cup skim milk
- 1 cup red bell pepper, chopped
- ¼ cup celery, chopped
- ¼ cup green onions, sliced
- ¼ tsp pepper
- ¼ cup cornflakes, crushed
- ¼ cup almonds, sliced

Directions:
1. Spray the cooking pot with cooking spray.
2. In a large bowl, combine chicken, cheese, soup, milk, bell pepper, celery, green onions, and pepper. Pour into the pot.
3. In a small bowl, combine cornflakes and almonds, sprinkle over the top of the chicken mixture.

4. Add the tender-crisp lid and set to bake on 400°F. Bake 30 minutes until casserole is hot and bubbly. Turn off the heat and let sit 10 minutes before serving.

Nutrition:
- InfoCalories 266, Total Fat 13g, Total Carbs 7g, Protein 28g, Sodium 526mg.

Lemon Turkey Risotto

Servings: 4
Cooking Time: 40 Min
Ingredients:
- 2 boneless turkey breasts; cut into strips
- 2 cups chicken broth/500ml
- 1 cup Arborio rice, rinsed/130g
- ¼ cup chopped fresh parsley, or to taste/32.5g
- 2 lemons, zested and juiced
- 1 onion; diced
- 8 lemon slices
- 2 garlic cloves; minced
- 1 tbsp dried oregano/15g
- 1½ tbsp olive oil/22.5ml
- ½ tsp sea salt/2.5g
- salt and freshly ground black pepper to taste

Directions:
1. In a ziplock back, mix turkey, oregano, sea salt, garlic, juice and zest of two lemons. Marinate for 10 minutes.
2. Warm oil on Sear/Sauté. Add onion and cook for 3 minutes until fragrant; add rice and chicken broth and season with pepper and salt.
3. Empty the ziplock having the chicken and marinade into the pot. Seal the pressure lid, choose Pressure, set to High, and set the timer to 12 minutes. Press Start. When ready, release the pressure quickly.
4. Divide the rice and turkey between 4 serving bowls; garnish with lemon slices and parsley.

Chicken Cutlets In Dijon Sauce

Servings: 2
Cooking Time: 15 Minutes
Ingredients:
- 2 chicken breasts, boneless & skinless
- 2 tbsp. olive oil, divided
- ½ tsp salt
- ¼ tsp pepper
- ½ tbsp. lemon zest
- 1 clove garlic, chopped fine
- 1 tbsp. fresh rosemary, chopped
- 1 tbsp. fresh parsley, chopped
- 2 tbsp. flour
- Nonstick cooking spray
- 1 shallot, sliced thin
- ½ lemon, juiced
- ½ cup dry white wine
- 1 tsp Dijon mustard

Directions:
1. Place chicken between 2 pieces of plastic wrap and pound to ½-inch thick. Place them in a large bowl.
2. Top the chicken with oil, salt, pepper, zest, garlic, rosemary, and parsley. Cover and refrigerate 1 hour or overnight.
3. Place the flour in a shallow dish and dredge both sides of chicken. Let sit 2-3 minutes.
4. Lightly spray the fryer basket with cooking spray. Place the chicken in the basket and add the tender-crisp lid. Set to air fry on 350°F. Cook chicken 3-5 minutes per side until golden brown and cooked through. Transfer to plate and keep warm.
5. Set cooker to sauté on medium heat. Add the oil and shallot and cook until shallot softens. Stir in lemon juice, wine, and mustard and cook until reduced slightly, about 2-3 minutes.
6. Transfer chicken to serving plates and top with sauce. Serve immediately.

Nutrition:
- InfoCalories 372, Total Fat 23g, Total Carbs 10g, Protein 21g, Sodium 683mg.

Chicken And Quinoa Soup

Servings: 6
Cooking Time: 30 Min
Ingredients:
- 2 large boneless; skinless chicken breasts; cubed
- 6 ounces quinoa, rinsed/180g
- 4 ounces mascarpone cheese, at room temperature/120g
- 1 cup milk/250ml
- 1 cup heavy cream/250ml
- 1 cup red onion; chopped/130g
- 1 cup carrots; chopped/130g
- 1 cup celery; chopped/130g
- 4 cups chicken broth 1000ml
- 2 tbsp butter/30g
- 1 tbsp fresh parsley; chopped/15g
- Salt and freshly ground black pepper to taste

Directions:
1. Melt butter on Sear/Sauté. Add carrot, onion, and celery and cook for 5 minutes until tender. Add chicken broth to the pot; mix in parsley, quinoa and chicken. Add pepper and salt for seasoning.
2. Seal the pressure lid, choose Pressure, set to High, and set the timer to 5 minutes. Press Start. When ready, release the pressure quickly. Press Sear/Sauté.
3. Add mascarpone cheese to the soup and stir well to melt completely; mix in heavy cream and milk. Simmer the soup for 3 to 4 minutes until thickened and creamy.

Salsa Verde Chicken With Salsa Verde

Servings: 4
Cooking Time: 50 Min
Ingredients:
- Salsa Verde:
- 1 jalapeño pepper, deveined and sliced
- ¼ cup extra virgin olive oil/62.5ml
- ¼ cup parsley/32.5g
- ½ cup capers/65g
- 1 lime, juiced
- 1 tsp salt/5g
- Chicken:
- 4 boneless skinless chicken breasts
- 1 cup quinoa, rinsed/130g
- 2 cups water/500ml

Directions:
1. In a blender, mix olive oil, salt, lime juice, jalapeño pepper, capers, and parsley and blend until smooth. Arrange

chicken breasts in the bottom of the Foodi pot.Over the chicken,add salsa verde mixture.
2. In a bowl that can fit in the cooker,mix quinoa and water.Setareversible rack onto chicken and sauce.Set the bowl onto the reversible rack.Seal the pressure lid,choose Pressure,set to High,and set the timer to 20 minutes.Press Start.
3. When ready,release the pressure quickly.Remove the quinoa bowl and reversible rack.Using two forks,shred chicken into the sauce;stir to coat.Divide the quinoa,between plates.Top with chicken and salsa verde before serving.

Butter Chicken

Servings:6
Cooking Time:30 Min
Ingredients:
- 2 pounds boneless;skinless chicken legs/900g
- 3 Roma tomatoes,pureed in a blender
- 1 can coconut milk,refrigerated overnight/435ml
- 1 large onion;minced
- ½cup chopped fresh cilantro;divided/65g
- 2 tbsp Indian curry paste/30ml
- 2 tbsp dried fenugreek/30g
- 1 tbsp Kashmiri red chili powder/15g
- 2 tbsp butter/30g
- 1 tbsp grated fresh ginger/15g
- 1 tbsp minced fresh garlic/15g
- 1 tsp salt/5g
- 2 tsp sugar/10g
- ½tsp ground turmeric/2.5g
- 1 tsp garam masala/5g
- Salt to taste

Directions:
1. Set your Foodi to Sear/Sauté,set to Medium High,and choose Start/Stop to preheat the pot and melt butter.Add in 1 tsp salt and onion.Cook for 2 to 3 minutes until fragrant.Stir in ginger,turmeric,garlic,and red chili powder to coat;cook for 2 more minutes.
2. Place water and coconut cream into separate bowls.Stir the water from the coconut milk can,pureed tomatoes,and chicken with the onion mixture.Seal the pressure lid,choose Pressure,set to High,and set the timer to 8 minutes.Press Start.When ready,release the pressure quickly.
3. Stir sugar,coconut cream,fenugreek,curry paste,half the cilantro,and garam masala through the chicken mixture;apply salt for seasoning.Simmer the mixture and cook for 10 minutes until the sauce thickens,on Sear/Sauté.Garnish with the rest of the cilantro before serving.

Chicken With Mushroom Sauce

Servings:10
Cooking Time:6 Hours
Ingredients:
- 8 oz.tomato sauce
- 1 cup mushrooms,sliced
- ½cup dry white wine
- 1 onion,chopped
- 1 clove garlic,chopped fine
- ¼tsp salt
- ¼tsp pepper
- 3 lbs.chicken pieces,skinless
- 2 tbsp.water
- 1 tbsp.flour

Directions:
1. Add the tomato sauce,mushrooms,wine,onion,garlic,salt and pepper to the cooking pot,stir to mix.
2. Add the chicken and turn to coat well
3. Add the lid and set to slow cook on low heat.Cook 6 hours or until chicken is cooked through and tender.Transfer chicken to a serving plate.
4. In a small bowl,whisk together water and flour until smooth.Stir into the sauce and cook 10-15 minutes,stirring frequently,until sauce thickens.Serve chicken topped with sauce.

Nutrition:
- InfoCalories 176,Total Fat 4g,Total Carbs 4g,Protein 28g,Sodium 164mg.

Country Chicken Casserole

Servings:6
Cooking Time:50 Minutes
Ingredients:
- 1 tbsp.olive oil
- ½cup onion,chopped
- 1 cup mushrooms,sliced
- 1½cups brown rice,cooked
- 2 cups broccoli,steamed&chopped
- 10½oz.cream of chicken soup,low fat
- ½cup sour cream,fat free
- 1¼cup cheddar cheese,reduced fat,grated&divided
- 2 tbsp.Dijon mustard
- 1 tsp garlic powder
- ½tsp pepper
- 2 cups chicken,cooked&chopped

Directions:
1. Add oil to the cooking pot and set to sautéon medium heat.
2. Add the onion and mushrooms and cook 3-5 minutes until they start to soften.
3. Stir in rice and turn off the sautéfunction.Place broccoli in an even layer over the rice mixture.
4. In a medium bowl,combine soup,sour cream,1 cup cheese,mustard,garlic powder,and pepper and mix well.Stir in chicken and spoon over the top of the broccoli.
5. Add the tender-crisp lid and set to bake on 350°F.Bake 35 minutes.
6. Sprinkle the remaining cheese over the top and bake another 5-10 minutes until cheese is melted and bubbly.Serve.

Nutrition:
- InfoCalories 309,Total Fat 15g,Total Carbs 22g,Protein 22g,Sodium 452mg.

Chipotle Raspberry Chicken

Servings:8
Cooking Time:6 Hours
Ingredients:
- Nonstick cooking spray
- 2 lbs.chicken breasts,boneless&skinless
- 1 cup raspberry preserves,sugar free
- 2 tbsp.chipotle in adobo sauce
- 2 tbsp.fresh lime juice
- ½tsp cumin

Directions:

1. Spray the cooking pot with cooking spray and add the chicken.
2. In a medium bowl,combine remaining ingredients.Pour over chicken.
3. Add the lid and set to slow cook on low.Cook 6 hours or until chicken is tender.Stir well before serving.

Nutrition:
- InfoCalories 168,Total Fat 4g,Total Carbs 8g,Protein 26g,Sodium 144mg.

Chicken Stroganoff With Fetucini

Servings:4
Cooking Time:35 Min

Ingredients:
- 2 large boneless skinless chicken breasts
- 8 ounces fettucini/240g
- ½cup sliced onion/65g
- ½cup dry white wine/125ml
- 1 cup sautéed mushrooms/130g
- ¼cup heavy cream/62.5ml
- 1½cups water/375ml
- 2 cups chicken stock/500ml
- 2 tbsp butter/30g
- 1 tbsp flour/15g
- 2 tbsp chopped fresh dill to garnish/30g
- ½tsp Worcestershire sauce/2.5ml
- 1½tsp salt/7.5g

Directions:
1. Season the chicken on both sides with salt and set aside.Choose Sear/Sautéand adjust to Medium.Press Start to preheat the pot.Melt the butter and sautéthe onion until brown,about 3 minutes.
2. Mix in the flour to make a roux,about 2 minutes and gradually pour in the dry white wine while stirring and scraping the bottom of the pot to release any browned bits.Allow the white wine to simmer and to reduce by two-thirds.
3. Pour in the water,chicken stock,1 tbsp or 15g of salt,and fettucini.Mix and arrange the chicken on top of the fettucini.
4. Lock the pressure lid to Seal.Choose Pressure;adjust the pressure to High and the cook time to 5 minutes;press Start.When done pressure-cooking,performaquick pressure release.
5. Transfer the chicken breasts to a cutting board to cool slightly,and then cut into bite-size chunks.Return the chicken to the pot and stir in the Worcestershire sauce and mushrooms.Add the heavy cream and cook until the mixture stops simmering.Ladle the stroganoff into bowls and garnish with dill.

Speedy Fajitas

Servings:4
Cooking Time:15 Minutes

Ingredients:
- Nonstick cooking spray
- 1 clove garlic,chopped fine
- 1 cup onion,sliced
- 1 green bell pepper,cut in strips
- 1 red bell pepper,cut in strips
- 2 chicken breasts,boneless,skinless&cut in strips
- 2 tsp fajita seasoning
- 4 low-carb whole wheat tortillas,warmed

Directions:
1. Spray the cooking pot with cooking spray and set to sautéon medium heat.
2. Add garlic,onion,and bell peppers and cook until tender,about 6-8 minutes.Transfer to a plate.
3. Add the chicken and fajita seasoning and cook until no longer pink,about 5-7 minutes.
4. Return the vegetables to the pot and cook,stirring,2-4 minutes until heated through.
5. Spoon onto serving plates and serve with tortillas and your favorite toppings.

Nutrition:
- InfoCalories 180,Total Fat 5g,Total Carbs 26g,Protein 21g,Sodium 574mg.

Coq Au Vin

Servings:4
Cooking Time:60 Min

Ingredients:
- 4 chicken leg quarters,skin on
- 4 serrano ham slices;cut into thirds
- 1¼cups dry red wine/312.5ml
- ⅓cup chicken stock/84ml
- ½cup sautéed mushrooms/65g
- ¾cup shallots;sliced/98g
- ¼cup brown onion slices/32.5g
- 1 tbsp olive oil/15ml
- 1½tsp tomato puree/7.5ml
- ½tsp brown sugar/2.5g
- 1½tsp salt/7.5g
- Black pepper to taste

Directions:
1. Season the chicken on both sides with 1 tsp of salt and set aside on a wire rack.On the Foodi,choose Sear/Sautéand adjust to Medium.Press Start to preheat the inner pot.
2. Heat the olive oil and place the ham in the pot inasingle layer and cook for 3 to 4 minutes or until browned.Remove the ham to a plate and set aside.
3. Add the chicken quarters to the pot.Cook for 5 minutes or until the skin is golden brown.Turn the chicken over and cook further for 2 minutes;remove toaplate.
4. Carefully pour out almost all the fat leaving about a tbsp to cover the bottom of the pot.Then,stir in the sliced onion and cook until the onion begins to brown.
5. Add½cup of red wine,stir,and scrape the bottom of the pan to let off any browned bits.Then,boil the mixture until the wine reduces by about 1/3,about 2 minutes.
6. Pour the remaining red wine,chicken stock,tomato puree,brown sugar,andafew grinds of black pepper into the pot.Boil the sauce for 1 minute,stirring to make sure the tomato paste is properly mixed.Add the chicken pieces with skin-side up,to the pot.
7. Put the pressure lid in place and lock to seal.Choose Pressure;adjust the pressure to High and the cook time to 12 minutes.Press Start to continue cooking.
8. After cooking,perform a natural pressure release for 10 minutes.Remove the chicken from the pot.Pour the sauce intoabowl and allow sitting until the fat rises to the top and starts firming up.Use a spoon to fetch off the fat on top of the sauce.
9. Pour the sauce back into the pot and stir in the mushrooms and pearl onions.Place the chicken on the sauce with skin side up.Close the crisping lid and select Broil.Adjust the cook time to 7 minutes;press Start.
10. When done cooking,open the lid and transfer the chicken toaserving platter.Spoon the sauce with mushrooms and pearl onions all around the chicken and crumble the reserved ham on top.

Chicken And Broccoli

Servings:4
Cooking Time:20 Minutes
Ingredients:
- 3 pounds boneless chicken,cut into thin strips
- 1 tablespoon olive oil
- 1 yellow onion,peeled and chopped
- 1/2 cup beef stock
- 1-pound broccoli florets
- 2 teaspoons toasted sesame oil
- 2 tablespoons arrowroot
- For Marinade
- 1 cup coconut aminos
- 1 tablespoon sesame oil
- 2 tablespoons fish sauce
- 5 garlic cloves,peeled and minced
- 3 red peppers,dried and crushed
- 1/2 teaspoon Chinese five-spice powder
- Toasted sesame seeds,for serving

Directions:
1. Take a suitable and mix in coconut aminos,fish sauce,1 tablespoon sesame oil,garlic,five-spice powder,crushed red pepper and stir.
2. Stir in chicken strips to the bowl and toss to coat.
3. Keep it on the side for 10 minutes.
4. Select"Sauté"mode on your Ninja Foodi and stir in oil,let it heat up,add onion and stir cook for 4 minutes.
5. Stir in chicken and marinade,stir cook for 2 minutes.
6. Add stock and stir.
7. Lock the pressure lid of Ninja Foodi and cook on"HIGH"pressure for 5 minutes.
8. Release pressure naturally over 10 minutes.
9. Mix arrowroot with 1/4 cup liquid from the pot and gently pour the mixture back to the pot and stir.
10. Place a steamer basket in the Ninja Foodi's pot and stir in broccoli to the steamer rack,Lock and secure the Ninja Foodi's lid.
11. Then cook on"HIGH"pressure mode for 3 minutes more,quick-release pressure.
12. Divide the dish between plates and serve with broccoli,toasted sesame seeds and enjoy.

Nutrition:
- InfoCalories:433;Fat:27g;Carbohydrates:8g;Protein:20g

Chicken Chickpea Chili

Servings:4
Cooking Time:25 Min
Ingredients:
- 1 pound boneless;skinless chicken breast;cubed/450g
- 2 cans chickpeas,drained and rinsed/435g
- 1 jalapeño pepper;diced
- 1 lime;cut into six wedges
- 3 large serrano peppers;diced
- 1 onion;diced
- ½cup chopped fresh cilantro/65g
- ½cup shredded Monterey Jack cheese/65g
- 2½cups water;divided/675ml
- 1 tbsp olive oil/15ml
- 2 tbsp chili powder/30g
- 1 tsp ground cumin/5g
- 1 tsp minced fresh garlic/5g
- 1 tsp salt/5g

Directions:
1. Warm oil on Sear/Sauté.Add in onion,serrano peppers,and jalapeno pepper and cook for 5 minutes until tender;add salt,cumin and garlic for seasoning.
2. Stir chicken with vegetable mixture;cook for 3 to 6 minutes until no longer pink;add 2 cups or 500ml water and chickpeas.
3. Seal the pressure lid,choose Pressure,set to High,and set the timer to 5 minutes.Press Start.Release pressure naturally for 5 minutes.Press Start.Stir chili powder with remaining½cup or 125ml water;mix in chili.
4. Press Sear/Sauté.Boil the chili as you stir and cook until slightly thickened.Divide chili into plates;garnish with cheese and cilantro.Over the chili,squeezealime wedge.

Turkey Enchilada Casserole

Servings:6
Cooking Time:70 Min
Ingredients:
- 1 pound boneless;skinless turkey breasts/450g
- 2 cups shredded Monterey Jack cheese;divided/260g
- 2 cups enchilada sauce/500ml
- 1 yellow onion;diced
- 2 garlic cloves;minced
- 1 can pinto beans,drained and rinsed/450g
- 1 bag frozen corn/480g
- 8 tortillas,each cut into 8 pieces
- 1 tbsp butter/15g
- ¼tsp salt/1.25g
- ¼tsp freshly ground black pepper/1.25g

Directions:
1. Choose Sear/Sautéon the pot and set to Medium High.Choose Start/Stop to preheat the pot.Melt the butter and cook the onion for 3 minutes,stirring occasionally.Stir in the garlic and cook until fragrant,about 1 minute more.
2. Put the turkey and enchilada sauce in the pot,and season with salt and black pepper.Stir to combine.Seal the pressure lid,choose Pressure,set to High,and set the time to 15 minutes.Choose Start/Stop.
3. When done cooking,perform a quick pressure release and carefully open the lid.Shred the turkey with two long forks while being careful not to burn your hands.Mix in the pinto beans,tortilla pieces,corn,and half of the cheese to the pot.Sprinkle the remaining cheese evenly on top of the casserole.
4. Close the crisping lid.Choose Broil and set the time to 5 minutes.Press Start/Stop to begin broiling.When ready,allow the casserole to sit for 5 minutes before serving.

Lime Chicken Chili

Servings:6
Cooking Time:23 Minutes
Ingredients:
- ¼cup cooking wine Keto-Friendly
- ½cup chicken broth
- 1 onion,diced
- 1 teaspoon salt
- ½teaspoon paprika
- 5 garlic cloves,minced
- 1 tablespoon lime juice
- ¼cup butter
- 2 pounds chicken thighs
- 1 teaspoon dried parsley

Ninja Foodi Cookbook

- 3 green chillies,chopped

Directions:
1. Set your Ninja-Foodi to Sautémode and stir in onion and garlic.
2. Sautéfor 3 minutes,add remaining ingredients.
3. Lock and secure the Ninja Foodi's lid and cook on"Medium-High"pressure for 20 minutes.
4. Release pressure naturally over 10 minutes.
5. Serve and enjoy.

Nutrition:
- InfoCalories:282;Fat:15g;Carbohydrates:6g;Protein:27g

Mexican Chicken Soup

Servings:4
Cooking Time:20 Minutes
Ingredients:
- 2 cups chicken,shredded
- 4 tablespoons olive oil
- ½cup cilantro,chopped
- 8 cups chicken broth
- 1/3 cup salsa
- 1 teaspoon onion powder
- ½cup scallions,chopped
- 4 ounces green chillies,chopped
- ½teaspoon habanero,minced
- 1 cup celery root,chopped
- 1 teaspoon cumin
- 1 teaspoon garlic powder
- Black pepper and salt to taste

Directions:
1. Add all ingredients to Ninja Foodi.
2. Stir and lock lid,cook on"HIGH"pressure for 10 minutes.
3. Release pressure naturally over 10 minutes.
4. Serve and enjoy.

Nutrition:
- InfoCalories:204;Fat:14g;Carbohydrates:4g;Protein:14g

Shredded Chicken&Black Beans

Servings:4
Cooking Time:4 Hours
Ingredients:
- 16 oz.fresh salsa
- 15 oz.black beans,rinsed&drained
- 1 lb.chicken thighs,boneless&skinless
- 1/3 cup cheddar cheese,reduced fat,grated
- 1 tsp cumin
- ½tsp chili powder
- 1/8 tsp salt
- 1/8 tsp pepper

Directions:
1. Place the salsa,beans,and chicken in the cooking pot.Add the lid and set to slow cook on high.Cook 3½hours or until chicken is tender.
2. Transfer chicken to a cutting board and use 2 forks to shred.Return to the pot.
3. Stir in remaining ingredients and mix well.Cook another 15 minutes or until cheese is melted.Serve immediately.

Nutrition:
- InfoCalories 283,Total Fat 6g,Total Carbs 25g,Protein 33g,Sodium 1474mg.

Bacon Lime Chicken

Servings:4
Cooking Time:30 Minutes
Ingredients:
- 8 chicken thighs,boneless&skinless
- 1 tsp salt
- 2 tsp honey
- 1 tsp granulated garlic
- 1 tsp granulated onion
- ½tsp pepper
- 2 tsp lime juice
- ¼tsp cayenne pepper
- 8 slices bacon

Directions:
1. Place the chicken and seasonings in a large bowl.Use your hands to mix and rub the seasonings into the meat until chicken is evenly coated.
2. Roll the chicken along the long side and wrap each with a slice of bacon.
3. Place chicken in the fryer basket,with bacon ends on the bottom.Add the tender-crisp lid and set to air fry on 400°F.Cook chicken 25-30 minutes,turning over halfway through cooking time.Serve hot.

Nutrition:
- InfoCalories 371,Total Fat 23g,Total Carbs 6g,Protein 32g,Sodium 878mg.

Chicken Meatballs In Tomato Sauce

Servings:5
Cooking Time:35 Min
Ingredients:
- 1 pound ground chicken/450g
- 1 egg
- 15 ounces canned tomato sauce/450g
- ¼cup bread crumbs/32.5g
- ¼cup Pecorino cheese/32.5g
- 1 cup chicken broth/250ml
- ⅓cup crumbled blue cheese/44g
- 3 tbsp red hot sauce/45ml
- 1 tbsp ranch dressing/15g
- 2 tbsp olive oil/30ml
- 1 tsp dried basil/5g
- A handful of parsley;chopped
- salt and ground black pepper to taste

Directions:
1. Inabowl,mix ground chicken,egg,pecorino,basil,pepper,salt,ranch dressing,blue cheese,3 tbsp or 45ml hot sauce,and bread crumbs;shape the mixture into meatballs.
2. Warm oil on Sear/Sauté.Add in the meatballs and cook for 2 to 3 minutes until browned on all sides.Add in tomato sauce and broth.Seal the pressure lid,choose Pressure,set to High,and set the timer to 7 minutes.Press Start.
3. When ready,release the pressure quickly.Remove meatballs carefully and place to a serving plate;top with parsley and serve.

Turkey Breakfast Sausage

Servings:8
Cooking Time:10 Minutes
Ingredients:
- Nonstick cooking spray

- 1 lb.ground turkey
- ½tsp sage
- ½tsp marjoram
- ¾tsp thyme
- ¼tsp cayenne pepper
- ¼tsp allspice
- ¼tsp black pepper
- ¾tsp salt
- 1 clove garlic,chopped fine
- ¼cup maple syrup

Directions:
1. Spray the fryer basket with cooking spray and place in the cooking pot.
2. In a large bowl,mix all ingredients until combined.Form into 8 patties.
3. Place the sausage patties in the fryer basket in a single layer.Add the tender-crisp lid and set to air fry on 375°F.Cook about 10 minutes until browned on the outside and cooked through,turning over halfway through cooking time.Serve.

Nutrition:
- InfoCalories 126,Total Fat 7g,Total Carbs 7g,Protein 11g,Sodium 252mg.

Creamy Slow Cooked Chicken

Servings:8
Cooking Time:4 Hours
Ingredients:
- 4-5 lb.chicken,whole
- 1 tsp salt
- ½tsp pepper
- 1 tbsp.butter,unsalted
- 1 tbsp.olive oil
- 8 cloves garlic,peeled
- 2 cinnamon sticks
- 2 cups skim milk
- 1 tsp thyme
- Zest of two large oranges

Directions:
1. Season the chicken with salt and pepper.
2. Add the butter and oil to the cooking pot and set to sear on med-high.
3. Add the chicken and brown on all sides,about 4 minutes per side.Transfer to a plate.
4. Add the garlic and cinnamon to the ppot and cook about 2 minutes,stirring frequently.
5. Add the remaining ingredients to the pot and stir to mix.Return the chicken to the pot and turn to coat.
6. Add the lid and set to slow cook on high.Cook 4 hours or until chicken is cooked through and tender.Let sit 5 minutes before serving.

Nutrition:
- InfoCalories 176,Total Fat 10g,Total Carbs 4g,Protein 17g,Sodium 208mg.

Slow Cooked Chicken In White Wine And Garlic

Servings:6
Cooking Time:4 Hours
Ingredients:
- 6 bone-in,skin-on,chicken thighs
- 10 garlic cloves,peeled
- 6 cups chicken broth
- 1 cup dry white wine
- 2 teaspoons dried oregano
- 2 teaspoons kosher salt
- 1 teaspoon freshly ground black pepper
- ¼cup capers,drained
- 1 tablespoon chopped fresh parsley

Directions:
1. Place the chicken,garlic cloves,chicken broth,wine,oregano,salt,and pepper in the cooking pot.
2. Assemble pressure lid,making sure the pressure release valve is in the VENT position.Select SLOW COOK and set to HI.Set time to 4 hours.Select START/STOP to begin.
3. When cooking is complete,carefully remove the lid.Stir in the capers.
4. Serve garnished with fresh parsley.

Nutrition:
- InfoCalories:343,Total Fat:36g,Sodium:578mg,Carbohydrates:4g,Protein:24g.

Chicken Cordon Bleu

Servings:4
Cooking Time:35 Min
Ingredients:
- 2 large boneless skinless chicken breasts
- 12 ounces broccoli;cut into florets/360g
- 4 thin ham slices
- 4 thin slices Emmental cheese
- ⅔cup panko bread crumbs/88g
- ¼cup grated Pecorino Romano cheese/32.5g
- Cooking spray
- 3 tbsp melted butter/45ml
- 4 tsp Dijon mustard/20g
- ¾tsp salt/3.75g

Directions:
1. Put the chicken breasts on a cutting board and slice through the breasts to form two thinner pieces from each breast to make 4 pieces in total.Season the chicken on both sides with½tsp or 2.5g of salt.Pouracup or 250ml of water into the inner pot.Put the reversible rack in the lower position of the pot and lay the broccoli florets on the rack.After,put the chicken on the broccoli.
2. Seal the pressure lid,choose Pressure;adjust the pressure to High and the cook time to 1 minute.Press Start to begin cooking the broccoli and chicken.
3. After cooking,perform a quick pressure release and carefully open the pressure lid.Take out the rack and set aside.Pour the water out of the pot and put the pot back on the base.
4. Place the chicken on the cutting board and the broccoli into the pot.Put 1 tbsp of melted butter on the broccoli florets and sprinkle with the remaining salt.Stir to coat the broccoli with the butter.
5. Grease the reversible rack with cooking spray and fix in the upper position of the pot.Close the crisping lid and Choose Air Crisp;adjust the temperature to 360°F and the time to 4 minutes.Press Start to preheat.
6. Smear 1 tsp of mustard on each chicken piece.Lay each ham slice on each chicken and each Emmental cheese slice on each ham.
7. Inasmall bowl,combine the breadcrumbs,remaining butter,and the Pecorino Romano cheese.Sprinkle the breadcrumb mixture equally over the chicken.

8. Open the crisping lid and carefully transfer the chicken pieces to the rack.Close the crisping lid and choose Air Crisp;adjust the temperature to 360°F or 183°C and the cook time to 10 minutes;press Start.
9. When done cooking,the crumbs should be crisp and have obtained a deep golden brown.Transfer the chicken pieces toaplatter and serve with the broccoli.

Quesadilla Casserole

Servings:8
Cooking Time:30 Minutes
Ingredients:
- Nonstick cooking spray
- 2 cups chicken,cooked&shredded
- ½cup sour cream,fat free
- 1 cup cheddar cheese,reduced fat,grated,divided
- 2 tsp cumin,divided
- 1 tbsp.chili powder,divided
- 1 tsp salt
- ¼tsp pepper,divided
- 1 cup corn
- 15 oz.black beans,drained&rinsed
- 4 large whole grain tortillas

Directions:
1. Spray the cooking pot with cooking spray.
2. In a large bowl,combine chicken,sour cream,half the cheese,half the cumin,half the chili powder,salt,and half the pepper and mix well.
3. In a separate bowl,combine the corn,beans,and remaining spices,mix well.
4. Lay 2 of the tortillas in the bottom of the cooking pot.Spread half the chicken mixture over the tortillas and top with half the bean mixture.Repeat.Sprinkle the remaining cheese over the top.
5. Add the tender-crisp lid and set to bake on 400°F.Bake 25-30 minutes until cheese is melted and casserole is hot.Serve immediately.

Nutrition:
- InfoCalories 354,Total Fat 13g,Total Carbs 35g,Protein 23g,Sodium 533mg.

Pesto Stuffed Chicken With Green Beans.

Servings:4
Cooking Time:20 Min
Ingredients:
- 4 chicken breasts
- ¼cup dry white wine/62.5ml
- 1 cup green beans,trimmed and cut into 1-inch pieces/130g
- ¾cup chicken stock/188ml
- 1 tbsp butter/15g
- 1 tbsp olive oil/15ml
- 1 tsp salt/5g
- For pesto:
- ¼cup Parmesan cheese/32.5g
- ¼cup extra virgin olive oil/62.5ml
- 1 cup fresh basil/130g
- 1 garlic clove,smashed
- 2 tbsp pine nuts/30g

Directions:
1. First make the pesto:in a bowl,mix fresh basil,pine nuts,garlic,salt,pepper and Parmesan and place in food processor.Add in oil and process until the desired consistency is attained.Adjust seasoning.
2. Applyathin layer of pesto to one side of each chicken breast;tightly roll into a cylinder and fasten closed with small skewers.Press Sear/Sauté.Add oil and butter.Cook chicken rolls for 1 to 2 minutes per side until browned.
3. Add in wine cook until the wine has evaporated,about 3-4 minutes.Add stock and salt into the pot.Top the chicken with green beans.
4. Seal the pressure lid,choose Pressure,set to High,and set the timer to 5 minutes.Press Start.When ready,release the pressure quickly.Serve chicken rolls with cooking liquid and green beans.

Apricot Bbq Duck Legs

Servings:6
Cooking Time:8 Hours
Ingredients:
- Nonstick cooking spray
- 2 cups spicy BBQ sauce
- 1 cup apricot preserves
- 1 tsp ginger
- 1 tbsp.garlic powder
- 2 tbsp.Worcestershire sauce
- 4 lbs.duck legs

Directions:
1. Spray the cooking pot with cooking spray.
2. In a medium bowl,whisk together BBQ sauce,preserves,ginger,garlic powder,and Worcestershire until combined.Reserve½cup of the sauce.
3. Add the duck to the cooking pot and pour the sauce over.Stir to coat the duck.
4. Add the lid and select slow cook on low.Cook 6-8 hours or until duck is tender.
5. Add the tender-crisp lid and set to broil.Cook another 2-3 minutes to caramelize the duck legs.Turn the legs over and repeat.Serve.

Nutrition:
- InfoCalories 651,Total Fat 26g,Total Carbs 44g,Protein 61g,Sodium 1027mg.

Buttered Turkey

Servings:6
Cooking Time:25 Min
Ingredients:
- 6 turkey breasts,boneless and skinless
- 1 stick butter,melted
- 2 cups panko breadcrumbs/260g
- ½tsp cayenne pepper/2.5g
- ½tsp black pepper/2.5g
- 1 tsp salt/5g

Directions:
1. Inabowl,combine the panko breadcrumbs,half of the black pepper,the cayenne pepper,and half of the salt.
2. In another bowl,combine the melted butter with salt and pepper.Brush the butter mixture over the turkey breast.
3. Coat the turkey with the panko mixture.Arrange on a lined Foodi basket.Close the crisping lid and cook for 15 minutes at 390°F or 199°C on Air Crisp mode,flipping the meat after 8 minutes.

Lemon, Barley & Turkey Soup

Servings: 6
Cooking Time: 4 Hours
Ingredients:
- 3 tbsp. extra virgin olive oil
- 1 onion, chopped fine
- 3 cloves garlic, chopped fine
- 1 tsp turmeric
- ½ tsp cumin
- ½ tsp ginger
- ½ tsp salt
- ½ tsp pepper
- 6 cups chicken broth, low sodium
- 6-8 strips of lemon peel, pith removed
- 1 cup barley
- 2 cups turkey, cooked & chopped
- 2 tbsp. lemon juice
- ¼ cup fresh parsley, chopped
- ¼ cup cilantro, chopped

Directions:
1. Add the oil to the cooking pot and set to saute on med-heat.
2. Add the onion and cook 2-3 minutes until translucent. Stir in the garlic and cook 1 minute more.
3. Add turmeric, cumin, ginger, and salt, stir to mix. Pour in the broth, zest, and barley. Add the lid and set to slow cook on low. Cook 3-3½ hours until barley is tender.
4. When the barley is cooked, add the turkey, lemon juice, parsley, cilantro, salt, and pepper and cook 30 minutes or until heated through. Discard the lemon peel before serving.

Nutrition:
- InfoCalories 94, Total Fat 4g, Total Carbs 9g, Protein 6g, Sodium 156mg.

Chicken With Bbq Sauce

Servings: 6
Cooking Time: 20 Min
Ingredients:
- 2 pounds boneless skinless chicken breasts/900g
- 1 small onion; minced
- 4 garlic cloves
- 1 cup carrots, thinly sliced/130g
- 1½ cups barbecue sauce/375ml
- 1 tsp salt/5g

Directions:
1. Apply a seasoning of salt to the chicken and place in the inner pot of the Foodi; add onion, carrots, garlic and barbeque sauce. Toss the chicken to coat.
2. Seal the pressure lid, choose Pressure, set to High, and set the timer to 15 minutes. Press Start. Once ready, do a quick release. Use two forks to shred chicken and stir into the sauce.

Chicken Tenders With Broccoli

Servings: 2
Cooking Time: 70 Min
Ingredients:
- 4 boneless; skinless chicken tenders
- 1 head broccoli; cut into florets
- ¼ cup barbecue sauce/62.5ml
- ¼ cup lemon marmalade/32.5g
- 1 cup basmati rice/130g
- 1 cup+2 tbsp water/280ml
- ½ tbsp soy sauce/7.5ml
- 1 tbsp sesame seeds, for garnish/15g
- 2 tbsp sliced green onions, for garnish/30g
- 2 tbsp melted butter; divided/30ml
- ¼ tsp salt/1.25g
- ¼ tsp freshly ground black pepper/1.25g
- Cooking spray

Directions:
1. Pour the rice and water in the pot and stir to combine. Seal the pressure lid, choose Pressure, set to High, and the timer to 2 minutes. Press Start/Stop to boil the rice.
2. Meanwhile, in a medium bowl, toss the broccoli with 1 tbsp of melted butter, and season with the salt and black pepper. When done cooking, perform a quick pressure release, and carefully open the lid.
3. Place the reversible rack in the higher position inside the pot, which will be over the rice. Then, spray the rack with cooking spray. Lay the chicken tenders on the rack and brush with the remaining 1 tbsp of melted butter. Arrange the broccoli around the chicken tenders.
4. Close the crisping lid. Choose Air Crisp, set the temperature to 400°F, and set the time to 10 minutes. Press Start/Stop to begin. In a bowl, mix the barbecue sauce, lemon marmalade, and soy sauce until well combined. When done crisping, coat the chicken with the lemon sauce.
5. Use tongs to turn the chicken over and apply the lemon sauce in the other side. Close the crisping lid, select Broil and set the time to 5 minutes; press Start/Stop.
6. After cooking is complete, check for your desired crispiness and remove the rack from the pot. Spoon the rice into serving plates with the chicken and broccoli. Garnish with the sesame seeds and green onions and serve.

Ninja Foodi Cookbook

Beef, Pork & Lamb

Asian Beef

Servings: 6
Cooking Time: 15 Minutes
Ingredients:
- 1/4 cup soy sauce
- 1/2 cup beef broth
- 1 tablespoon sesame oil
- 1/4 cup brown erythritol, packed
- 4 cloves garlic, minced
- 1 teaspoon hot sauce
- 1 tablespoon rice wine vinegar
- 1 tablespoon ginger, grated
- 1/2 teaspoon onion powder
- 1/2 teaspoon pepper
- 3 lb. boneless beef chuck roast, cubed
- 3 tablespoons corn starch dissolved in 1 teaspoon water

Directions:
1. Mix all the seasonings in a suitable bowl except the chuck roast and corn starch.
2. Pour the mixture into the Ninja Foodi. Stir in the beef. Seal the pot.
3. Select pressure. Cook at "HIGH" pressure for 15 minutes.
4. Do a quick pressure release. Stir in the corn starch.
5. Select sauté setting to thicken the sauce.

Nutrition:
- InfoCalories: 482; Fat: 16.6g; Carbohydrate: 8.4g; Protein: 70.1g

Crunchy Cashew Lamb Rack

Servings: 4
Cooking Time: 30 Min
Ingredients:
- 1½ lb. rack of lamb/675g
- 3 oz. chopped cashews/90g
- 1 garlic clove; minced
- 1 egg, beaten
- 1 tbsp chopped rosemary/15g
- 1 tbsp olive oil/15ml
- 1 tbsp breadcrumbs/15g
- Salt and pepper, to taste

Directions:
1. Combine the olive oil with the garlic and brush this mixture onto the lamb. Combine the rosemary, cashews, and breadcrumbs, in a small bowl. Brush the egg over the lambs, and then coat it with the cashew mixture.
2. Place the lamb in the Foodi, close the crisping lid and cook for 25 minutes on Air Crisp at 320°F or 160°C. Then increase to 390°F or 199°C, and cook for 5 more minutes. Cover with a foil and let sit for a couple of minutes before serving.

Tender Beef & Onion Rings

Servings: 6
Cooking Time: 25 Minutes
Ingredients:
- 2 lb. chuck roast, cubed
- ¼ cup soy sauce, low sodium
- 1 tbsp. lemon juice
- ½ tsp pepper
- 1 cup water
- 3 tbsp. olive oil
- 3 cloves garlic, chopped fine
- 1 onion, sliced & separated in rings

Directions:
1. In a large bowl, combine beef, soy sauce, lemon juice, and pepper, mix well. Cover and let sit 1 hour.
2. Add the beef mixture to the cooking pot. Stir in water. Add the lid and set to pressure cook on high. Set timer for 20 minutes. When the timer goes off, use natural release to remove the pressure.
3. Use a slotted spoon to transfer beef to a bowl.
4. Set cooker to sauté on medium heat. Cook until sauce reduces and thickens, about 3-4 minutes.
5. Stir in oil and garlic. Add the beef back to the pot and cook until sauce turns a light brown, about 4-5 minutes. Add the onion rings and cook 2 minutes, or until onions are almost soft. Serve.

Nutrition:
- InfoCalories 529, Total Fat 29g, Total Carbs 4g, Protein 62g, Sodium 1059mg.

Cheese Burgers In Hoagies

Servings: 4
Cooking Time: 65 Min
Ingredients:
- 1 lb. chuck beef roast/450g
- 1 can French onion soup/420ml
- 3 slices Provolone cheese
- 3 hoagies, halved
- 1 onion; sliced
- 2 Cups beef broth/500ml
- 1 tbsp olive oil/15ml
- 2 tbsp Worcestershire sauce/30ml
- 1 tsp garlic powder/5g
- 3 tsp mayonnaise/15ml
- Salt and black pepper to taste

Directions:
1. Season the beef with garlic powder, salt, and pepper. On Foodi, select Sear/Sauté mode. Heat the olive oil and brown the beef on both sides for about 5 minutes. Remove the meat onto a plate.
2. Into the pot, add the onions and cook until soft. Then, pour the beef broth and stir, while scraping bottom off every stuck bit. Add the onion soup, Worcestershire sauce, and beef. Close the lid, secure the pressure valve, and select Pressure mode on High pressure for 20 minutes. Press Start/Stop.
3. Once the timer has stopped, do a natural pressure release for 10-15 minutes, and then a quick pressure release to let out any remaining steam.
4. Use two forks to shred the meat. Close the crisping lid and cook on Bake/Roast for 10 minutes at 350°F or 177°C. When ready, open the lid and strain the juice of the pot through a sieve into a bowl. Assemble the burgers by slathering mayo on halved hoagies, spoon the shredded meat over and top each hoagie with cheese.

Ninja Foodi Cookbook

Pork Chops With Broccoli

Servings:6
Cooking Time:45 Min
Ingredients:
- Pork Chops:
- 6 boneless pork chops
- 1 broccoli head,broken into florets
- ¼cup butter,melted/62.5ml
- 1 cup chicken stock/250ml
- ¼cup milk/62.5ml
- 1 tsp garlic powder/5g
- 1 tsp onion powder/5g
- 1 tsp red pepper flakes/5g
- 1½tsp salt/7.5g
- 1 tsp ground black pepper/5g
- Gravy:
- ½cup heavy cream/125ml
- 3 tbsp flour/45g
- salt and ground black pepper to taste

Directions:
1. Combine salt,garlic powder,red pepper flakes,onion powder,and black pepper;rub the mixture to the pork chops.Place stock and broccoli into the Foodi.Lay the pork chops on top.
2. Seal the pressure lid,choose Pressure,set to High,and set the timer to 15 minutes.Press Start.When ready,release the pressure quickly.
3. Transfer the pork chops and broccoli toaplate.Press Sear/Sautéand simmer the liquid remaining in the pot.Mix cream and flour;pour into the simmering liquid and cook for 5 to 7 minutes until thickened and bubbly;season with pepper and salt.Top the chops with gravy before,drizzle melted butter over broccoli and serve.

Beef Bourguignon(2)

Servings:4
Cooking Time:45 Min
Ingredients:
- 2 lb.stewing beef;cut in large chunks/900g
- ½lb.mushrooms;sliced/225g
- 2 carrots,peeled and chopped
- 1 onion;sliced
- 2 cloves garlic,crushed
- 1 cup red wine/250ml
- ½cup cognac/65g
- 2 cups beef broth/500ml
- 1 bunch thyme
- ¼cup pearl onion/3.5g
- 2½tbsp olive oil/37.5ml
- 2 tbsp flour/30g
- 3 tsp tomato paste/15g
- ¼tsp red wine vinegar/1.25ml
- Salt and pepper,to taste

Directions:
1. Select Sear/Sautémode.Season the beef with salt,pepper,andalight sprinkle of flour.Heat the oil in the pot,and brown the meat on all sides.Pour the cognac into the pot and stir the mixture with a spoon to deglaze the bottom.Stir in thyme,red wine,broth,paste,garlic,mushrooms,onion,and pearl onions.
2. Close the lid,secure the pressure valve,and select Pressure mode on High for 25 minutes.Press Start/Stop.
3. Once the timer is off,doanatural pressure release for 10 minutes,then a quick pressure release to let out the remaining steam.Close the crisping lid and cook for 10 minutes on Broil mode.When ready,open the lid.
4. Use the spoon to remove the thyme,adjust the taste with salt and pepper,and add the vinegar.Stir the sauce and serve hot,withaside of rice.

Mongolian Beef

Servings:2
Cooking Time:11 Minutes
Ingredients:
- 1 lb.flank steak,sliced
- 1/4 cup corn starch
- Sauce:
- 2 teaspoon vegetable oil
- 1/2 teaspoon ginger,minced
- 1 tablespoon garlic,minced
- 1/2 cup soy sauce
- 1/2 cup water
- 3/4 cup brown erythritol

Directions:
1. Coat the beef with corn starch.Put in the Ninja Foodi basket.
2. Seal the crisping lid.Set it to air crisp.
3. Cook at 390°F for about 10 minutes per side.
4. Remove and set aside.Set the pot to sauté.Stir in the vegetable oil.
5. Sautéthe ginger and garlic for 1 minute.Stir in the soy sauce,water and brown erythritol.
6. Pour the prepared sauce on top of the beef.

Nutrition:
- InfoCalories:399;Fat:11.7g;Carbohydrate:39g;Protein:33.7g

Flank Steak With Bell Pepper Salsa

Servings:6
Cooking Time:30 Minutes
Ingredients:
- 2 tbsp.soy sauce,low sodium
- 4 tbsp.apple cider vinegar,divided
- 5 cloves garlic,chopped fine,divided
- 4 tbsp.olive oil,divided
- ¼tsp pepper
- 2 lb.flank steak
- 1 green bell pepper,chopped fine
- 4 green onions,sliced thin
- 2 tbsp.fresh basil,chopped
- ¼tsp red pepper flakes
- Salt&pepper to taste

Directions:
1. In a large bowl,combine soy sauce,2 tablespoons vinegar,4 cloves of garlic,2 tablespoons oil,and pepper,mix well.Place the steak in the bowl and turn to coat.Let sit 20 minutes.
2. In a medium bowl,combine bell pepper,green onions,1 clove garlic,basil,pepper flakes,remaining vinegar and oil,mix well.Salt and pepper to taste.Cover until ready to use.
3. Spray the rack with cooking spray and place in the cooking pot.

Ninja Foodi Cookbook

4. Lay the steak on the rack. Add the tender-crisp lid and set to broil. Cook steak 3-4 minutes per side, for rare, 5-6 minutes per side for medium rare, or to desired doneness.
5. Transfer meat to a cutting board and tent with foil. Let rest 10-15 minutes before slicing.
6. Slice against the grain and top with salsa to serve.

Nutrition:
- InfoCalories 161, Total Fat 10g, Total Carbs 2g, Protein 15g, Sodium 312mg.

Pesto Pork Chops & Asparagus

Servings: 4
Cooking Time: 20 Minutes
Ingredients:
- Nonstick cooking spray
- 4 pork chops, bone-in, 1-inch thick
- 1 tsp salt, divided
- 1 tsp pepper, divided
- 1 bunch asparagus, trimmed
- 1 cup cherry tomatoes
- 3 tbsp. extra-virgin olive oil, divided
- ¼ cup pesto
- ¼ cup fresh basil, chopped

Directions:
1. Spray the rack with cooking spray and place it in the cooking pot.
2. Rub chops with 2 tablespoons oil and sprinkle with ½ teaspoon salt and pepper on both sides. Cover and let sit 20 minutes.
3. Place chops on the rack and add the tender-crisp lid. Set to broil. Cook chops 6-8 minutes per side or until they reach desired doneness. Remove to serving plate.
4. Place the asparagus and tomatoes in a large bowl and add remaining oil, salt, and pepper, toss to coat. Place the vegetables on the rack and broil 6-8 minutes until asparagus is tender-crisp and tomatoes start to char, turning vegetables every couple of minutes.
5. Place pork chops and vegetables on serving plates, drizzle with pesto and sprinkle with basil. Serve immediately.

Nutrition:
- InfoCalories 332, Total Fat 24g, Total Carbs 4g, Protein 25g, Sodium 647mg.

Cuban Pork

Servings: 8
Cooking Time: 2 Hr 30 Min
Ingredients:
- 3 pounds pork shoulder/1350g
- ¼ cup lime juice/62.5ml
- ½ cup orange juice/125ml
- ¼ cup canola oil/62.5ml
- ¼ cup chopped fresh cilantro/32.5g
- 8 cloves garlic; minced
- 1 tbsp fresh oregano/15g
- 1 tbsp ground cumin/15g
- 1 tsp red pepper flakes/5g
- 2 tsp ground black pepper/10g
- 1 tsp salt/5g

Directions:
1. In a bowl, mix orange juice, olive oil, cumin, salt, pepper, oregano, lime juice, and garlic; add into a large plastic bag alongside the pork. Seal and massage the bag to ensure the marinade covers the pork completely.
2. Place in the refrigerator for an hour to overnight. In the Foodi, set your removed pork from bag. Add the marinade on top. Seal the pressure lid, choose Pressure, set to High, and set the timer to 50 minutes. Press Start.
3. Release pressure naturally for 15 minutes. Transfer the pork to a cutting board; use a fork to break into smaller pieces.
4. Skim and get rid of the fat from liquid in the cooker. Serve the liquid with pork and sprinkle with cilantro.

Sticky Barbeque Baby Back Ribs

Servings: 4
Cooking Time: 35 Min
Ingredients:
- 1 rack baby back ribs; cut into quarters/1350g
- 1 cup beer/250ml
- 1 cup barbecue sauce/250ml
- 3 tbsp brown sugar/45g
- 1½ tbsp smoked paprika/22.5g
- 1 tbsp salt/15g
- 1 tbsp black pepper/15g
- 2 tsp garlic powder/10g

Directions:
1. In a bowl, mix the paprika, brown sugar, garlic, salt, and black pepper. Season all sides of the ribs with the rub. Pour the beer into the pot, put the ribs in the Crisping Basket, and place the basket in the pot. Seal the pressure lid, choose Pressure, set to High, and set the time to 10 minutes. Choose Start/Stop.
2. When done cooking, perform a quick pressure release, and carefully the open the lid. Close the crisping lid. Choose Air Crisp, set the temperature to 400°F or 205°C, and the time to 15 minutes. Choose Start/Stop to begin crisping.
3. After 10 minutes, open the lid, and brush the ribs with the barbecue sauce. Close the lid to cook further for 5 minutes.

Beef Broccoli

Servings: 6
Cooking Time: 16 Minutes
Ingredients:
- 1-1/2 lb. beef chuck roast boneless, trimmed and sliced
- Black pepper and salt to taste
- 2 teaspoons olive oil
- 1 onion, chopped
- 4 cloves garlic, minced
- 3/4 cup beef broth
- 1/2 cup soy sauce
- 1/3 cup erythritol
- 2 tablespoons sesame oil
- 1 lb. broccoli florets
- 3 tablespoons water
- 3 tablespoons corn starch

Directions:
1. Season the beef strips with black pepper and salt.
2. Stir in the olive oil to the Ninja Foodi. Switch it to sauté.
3. Add the onion and saute for 1 minute. Stir in the garlic and cook for 30 seconds.
4. Stir in the beef and cook in batches until brown on both sides.
5. Deglaze the pot with broth and soy sauce.
6. Stir in the erythritol and sesame oil. Cover the pot.

7. Set it to pressure. Cook at "HIGH" pressure for 12 minutes.
8. Release the pressure naturally. Stir in the broccoli. Seal the pot.
9. Cook at "HIGH" pressure for 3 minutes. Release the pressure quickly.
10. Mix corn starch with water and add to the pot.
11. Simmer until the sauce has thickened.
12. Serve warm.

Nutrition:
- InfoCalories:563;Fat:38.1g;Carbohydrate:10.7g;Protein:34.1g

Honey Short Ribs With Rosemary Potatoes

Servings:4
Cooking Time:105 Min
Ingredients:
- 4 bone-in beef short ribs, silver skin
- 2 potatoes, peeled and cut into 1-inch pieces
- ½ cup beef broth/125ml
- 3 garlic cloves; minced
- 1 onion; chopped
- 2 tbsp olive oil/30ml
- 2 tbsp honey/30ml
- 2 tbsp minced fresh rosemary/30ml
- 1 tsp salt/5g
- 1 tsp black pepper/5g

Directions:
1. Choose Sear/Sauté on the pot and set to High. Choose Start/Stop to preheat the pot. Season the short ribs on all sides with ½ tsp or 2.5g of salt and ½ tsp or 2.5g of pepper. Heat 1 tbsp of olive oil and brown the ribs on all sides, about 10 minutes total. Stir in the onion, honey, broth, 1 tbsp of rosemary, and garlic.
2. Seal the pressure lid, choose Pressure, set to High, and set the time to 40 minutes. Choose Start/Stop to begin. In a large bowl, toss the potatoes with the remaining oil, rosemary, salt, and black pepper.
3. When the ribs are ready, perform a quick pressure release and carefully open the lid.
4. Fix the reversible rack in the higher position of the pot, which is over the ribs. Put the potatoes on the rack. Close the crisping lid. Choose Bake/Roast, set the temperature to 350°F or 177°C, and set the time to 15 minutes. Choose Start/Stop to begin roasting.
5. Once the potatoes are tender and roasted, use tongs to pick the potatoes and the short ribs into a plate; set aside. Choose Sear/Sauté and set to High. Simmer the sauce for 5 minutes and spoon the sauce into a bowl.
6. Allow sitting for 2 minutes and scoop off the fat that forms on top. Serve the ribs with the potatoes and sauce.

Baked Bacon Macaroni And Cheese

Servings:6
Cooking Time:30 Minutes
Ingredients:
- 4 strips bacon, chopped
- 5 cups water
- 1 box elbow pasta
- 2 tablespoons unsalted butter
- 1 tablespoon ground mustard
- 1 can evaporated milk
- 8 ounces Cheddar cheese, shredded
- 8 ounces Gouda, shredded
- Sea salt
- Freshly ground black pepper
- 2 cups panko or Italian bread crumbs
- 1 stick(½cup)butter, melted

Directions:
1. Select SEAR/SAUTÉ and set temperature to HI. Select START/STOP to begin. Let preheat for 5 minutes.
2. Add the bacon and cook, stirring frequently, for about 6 minutes or until crispy. Using a slotted spoon, transfer the bacon to a paper towel-lined plate to drain.
3. Add the water, pasta, 2 tablespoons of butter, and mustard. Assemble pressure lid, making sure the pressure release valve is in the SEAL position.
4. Select PRESSURE and set to LO. Set time to 0 minutes. Select START/STOP to begin.
5. When pressure cooking is complete, allow pressure to naturally release for 10 minutes. After 10 minutes, quick release remaining pressure by moving the pressure release valve to the VENT position. Carefully remove lid when unit has finished releasing pressure.
6. Add the evaporated milk, Cheddar cheese, Gouda cheese and the bacon. Season with salt and pepper. Stir well to melt the cheeses and ensure all ingredients are combined.
7. In a medium bowl, stir together the bread crumbs and melted butter. Cover the pasta evenly with the mixture. Close crisping lid.
8. Select AIR CRISP, set temperature to 360°F, and set time to 7 minutes. Select START/STOP to begin.
9. When cooking is complete, serve immediately.

Nutrition:
- InfoCalories:721,Total Fat:45g,Sodium:1213mg,Carbohydrates:44g,Protein:35g.

Char Siew Pork Ribs

Servings:6
Cooking Time:4 Hours 55 Min
Ingredients:
- 2 lb. pork ribs/900g
- 2 tbsp char siew sauce/30ml
- 2 tbsp minced ginger/30g
- 2 tbsp hoisin sauce/30ml
- 2 tbsp sesame oil/30ml
- 1 tbsp honey/15ml
- 4 garlic cloves; minced
- 1 tbsp soy sauce/15ml

Directions:
1. Whisk together all marinade ingredients, in a small bowl. Coat the ribs well with the mixture. Place in a container with a lid, and refrigerate for 4 hours.
2. Place the ribs in the basket but do not throw away the liquid from the container. Close the crisping lid and cook for 40 minutes on Air Crisp at 350°F or 177°C. Stir in the liquid, increase the temperature to 350°F or 177°C, and cook for 10 minutes.

Ninja Foodi Cookbook

Pepper Crusted Tri Tip Roast

Servings: 6
Cooking Time: 45 Minutes

Ingredients:
- 1 tbsp. salt
- 1 tbsp. pepper
- 1 tbsp. garlic powder
- 1 tbsp. onion powder
- 1 tsp cayenne pepper
- 1 tbsp. oregano
- 1 tsp rosemary
- ½ tsp sage
- 3 lb. tri-tip roast
- Nonstick cooking spray

Directions:
1. In a small bowl, combine all the spices until mixed.
2. Place the roast on baking sheet and massage the rub mix into all sides. Cover and let sit 1 hour.
3. Lightly spray the cooking pot with cooking spray. Set to sear.
4. Add the roast and brown all sides. Add the tender-crisp lid and set to roast on 300°F.
5. Cook until meat thermometer reaches desired temperature for doneness, 120°F for a rare roast, 130°F for medium-rare and 140°F for medium, about 20-40 minutes.
6. Remove roast from cooking pot, tent with foil and let rest 10-15 minutes. Slice across the grain and serve.

Nutrition:
- InfoCalories 169, Total Fat 8g, Total Carbs 7g, Protein 19g, Sodium 2300mg.

Beef Stew With Beer

Servings: 4
Cooking Time: 60 Min

Ingredients:
- 2 lb. beef stewed meat; cut into bite-size pieces/900g
- 1 packet dry onion soup mix
- 2 cloves garlic; minced
- 2 cups beef broth/500ml
- ¼ cup flour/32.5g
- 1 medium bottle beer
- 3 tbsp butter/45g
- 2 tbsp Worcestershire sauce/30ml
- 1 tbsp tomato paste/15g
- Salt and black pepper to taste

Directions:
1. In a zipper bag, add beef, salt, all-purpose flour, and pepper. Close the bag up and shake it to coat the meat well with the mixture. Select Sear/Sauté mode on the Foodi. Melt the butter, and brown the beef on both sides, for 5 minutes.
2. Pour the broth to deglaze the bottom of the pot. Stir in tomato paste, beer, Worcestershire sauce, and the onion soup mix.
3. Close the lid, secure the pressure valve, and select Pressure mode on High pressure for 25 minutes. Press Start/Stop to start cooking.
4. Once the timer is done, do a natural pressure release for 10 minutes, and then a quick pressure release to let out any remaining steam.
5. Open the pressure lid and close the crisping lid. Cook on Broil mode for 10 minutes. Spoon the beef stew into serving bowls and serve with overabed of vegetable mash with steamed greens.

Bacon-wrapped Hot Dogs

Servings: 4
Cooking Time: 15 Minutes

Ingredients:
- 4 beef hot dogs
- 4 bacon strips
- Cooking spray
- 4 bakery hot dog buns, split and toasted
- ½ red onion, chopped
- 1 cup sauerkraut, rinsed and drained

Directions:
1. Place Cook&Crisp Basket in pot. Close crisping lid. Select AIR CRISP, set temperature to 360°F, and set time to 5 minutes. Select START/STOP to begin preheating.
2. Wrap each hot dog with 1 strip of bacon, securing it with toothpicks as needed.
3. Once unit has preheated, open lid and coat the basket with cooking spray. Place the hot dogs in the basket in a single layer. Close crisping lid.
4. Select AIR CRISP, set temperature to 360°F, and set time to 15 minutes. Select START/STOP to begin.
5. After 10 minutes, open lid and check doneness. If needed, continue cooking until it reaches your desired doneness.
6. When cooking is complete, place the hot dog in the buns with the onion and sauerkraut. Top, if desired, with condiments of your choice, such as yellow mustard, ketchup, or mayonnaise.

Nutrition:
- InfoCalories: 336, Total Fat: 17g, Sodium: 1297mg, Carbohydrates: 27g, Protein: 20g.

Pork Asado

Servings: 6
Cooking Time: 1 Hour

Ingredients:
- 1½ lbs. pork picnic or shoulder, cut in 2-inch cubes
- ¼ cup soy sauce
- ½ cup lemon juice
- 1½ cups water
- ¼ cup olive oil
- 1 onion, peeled & sliced into ¼-inch thick rings
- 2 potatoes, peeled & sliced in ½-inch thick strips
- Salt and pepper to taste

Directions:
1. Add the pork, soy sauce, lemon juice, and water to the cooking pot. Set to sauté on med-high heat and bring to a boil.
2. Add lid and set to pressure cook on high. Set timer for 10 minutes. When timer goes off, use quick release to remove the pressure. Transfer pork and cooking liquid to a bowl.
3. Add the oil to the cooking pot and set to sauté on med-high. Add onions and cook about 1 minute. Use a slotted spoon to transfer them to a bowl.
4. Add potatoes to the pot and cook until tender and lightly browned. Transfer to bowl with onions.
5. Return just the pork to the pot and cook until browned. Drain off fat. Add the reserved cooking liquid and bring to a boil. Season with salt and pepper. Cook about 5 minutes until liquid is reduced.
6. Place pork on a serving platter and place potatoes and onions around it. Pour the sauce over all and serve.

Nutrition:
- InfoCalories 327, Total Fat 13g, Total Carbs 25g, Protein 27g, Sodium 882mg.

Crusted Pork Chops

Servings: 6
Cooking Time: 12 Minutes
Ingredients:
- Cooking spray
- 6 pork chops
- Black pepper and salt to taste
- 1/2 cup bread crumbs
- 2 tablespoons Parmesan cheese, grated
- 1/4 cup cornflakes, crushed
- 1-1/4 teaspoon sweet paprika
- 1/2 teaspoon onion powder
- 1/2 teaspoon garlic powder
- 1/4 teaspoon chilli powder
- 1 egg, beaten

Directions:
1. Season the pork chops liberally with black pepper and salt.
2. In a suitable, mix the rest of the ingredients except the egg.
3. Beat the egg in a suitable. Dip the pork chops in the egg.
4. Coat the pork with the breading. Place the pork on the Ninja Foodi basket.
5. Set it to air crisp and close the crisping lid.
6. Cook at 400°F for about 12 minutes, flipping halfway through.

Nutrition:
- InfoCalories: 310; Fat: 21.3g; Carbohydrate: 8.2g; rotein: 20.3g

Beef Tips & Mushrooms

Servings: 8
Cooking Time: 5 Hours
Ingredients:
- 2 tbsp. olive oil
- 3 lbs. beef stew meat
- Salt & pepper, to taste
- 3 cups beef broth, low sodium
- 1 pkg. dry onion soup mix
- 1 tbsp. Worcestershire sauce
- 1 onion chopped
- 2 cups mushrooms, sliced
- 3 cloves garlic, chopped fine
- ¼ cup water
- 3 tbsp. cornstarch

Directions:
1. Add the oil to the cooking pot and set to sauté on med-high heat.
2. Season the beef with salt and pepper. Add to the pot, in batches, and cook until browned on all sides. Transfer to a bowl until all the beef has been seared.
3. Return all the beef to the pot and add broth, soup mix, onions, mushrooms, and garlic, stir to combine.
4. Add the lid and set to slow cook on low. Cook 5-6 hours until beef is tender.
5. 30 minutes before the beef tips are done, whisk together the water and cornstarch until smooth and stir into the beef mixture. Stir well before serving over noodles, mashed potatoes or mashed cauliflower to keep it low carb.

Nutrition:
- InfoCalories 285, Total Fat 11g, Total Carbs 9g, Protein 40g, Sodium 1178mg.

Beef Brisket

Servings: 4
Cooking Time: 1 Hour, 10 Minutes
Ingredients:
- 3 pounds beef brisket, quartered
- 1 onion, cut into quarters
- 2 cups beef broth
- Splash Worcestershire sauce
- 1 teaspoon kosher salt

Directions:
1. Select SEAR/SAUTÉ and set temperature to MD:HI. Select START/STOP to begin and allow to preheat for 5 minutes.
2. Add the brisket (fat side down) into the cooking pot and sear for 5 minutes. Using tongs, carefully flip the brisket over and sear on the other side for an additional 5 minutes.
3. In the cooking pot, combine the onion, beef broth, Worcestershire sauce, and salt.
4. Assemble the pressure lid, making sure the pressure release valve is in the SEAL position.
5. Select PRESSURE and set to HI. Set the time to 60 minutes. Select START/STOP to begin.
6. When pressure cooking is complete, allow the pressure to naturally release for 20 minutes. After 20 minutes, quick release any remaining pressure by moving the pressure release valve to the VENT position. Carefully remove lid when unit has finished releasing pressure.
7. Shred or slice the meat, as desired for serving.

Nutrition:
- InfoCalories: 486, Total Fat: 20g, Sodium: 782mg, Carbohydrates: 3g, Protein: 72g.

Carne Guisada

Servings: 4
Cooking Time: 45 Minutes
Ingredients:
- 3 pounds beef stew
- 3 tablespoon seasoned salt
- 1 tablespoon oregano chilli powder
- 1 tablespoon cumin
- 1 pinch crushed red pepper
- 2 tablespoons olive oil
- 1/2 medium lime, juiced
- 1 cup beef bone broth
- 3 ounces tomato paste
- 1 large onion, sliced

Directions:
1. Trim the beef stew to taste into small bite-sized portions.
2. Toss the beef stew pieces with dry seasoning.
3. Select "Sauté" mode on your Ninja Foodi and stir in oil; allow the oil to heat up.
4. Add seasoned beef pieces and brown them.
5. Combine the browned beef pieces with the rest of the ingredients.
6. Lock the Ninja foodi's lid and cook on "HIGH" pressure for 3 minutes.
7. Release the pressure naturally.
8. Enjoy.

Nutrition:
- InfoProtein: 33g; Carbohydrates: 11g; Fats: 12g; Calories: 274

Ninja Foodi Cookbook

Pork Medallions With Dijon Sauce

Servings: 4
Cooking Time: 10 Minutes
Ingredients:
- 1 lb.pork tenderloin,cut in 1-inch-thick slices
- ¼tsp salt
- ¼tsp pepper
- 1 tbsp.olive oil
- ¼cup half-and-half
- 1 tbsp.Dijon mustard

Directions:
1. Place the pork slices between 2 sheets of plastic wrap and pound out to¼-inch thick.Season with salt and pepper.
2. Add the oil to the cooking pot and set to sautéon med-high.
3. Add the pork and cook until browned on both sides,about 2-3 minutes per side.Transfer to a plate and keep warm.
4. Reduce the heat to low and add half and half and mustard stirring to combine.Cook 1-2 minutes until heated through.
5. Place pork medallions on serving plates and top with sauce.Serve immediately.

Nutrition:
- InfoCalories 165,Total Fat 6g,Total Carbs 2g,Protein 24g,Sodium 263mg.

Hamburger&Macaroni Skillet

Servings: 4
Cooking Time: 20 Minutes
Ingredients:
- 1 tbsp.olive oil
- 1 lb.lean ground beef
- 1 onion,chopped
- ½tsp seasoned salt
- 1/8 tsp red pepper flakes
- ½tsp celery seed
- 28 oz.tomatoes,diced,undrained
- 2 tbsp.Worcestershire sauce
- 2 cups macaroni,cooked&drained,reserve½cup pasta water
- 1/4 cup chopped fresh parsley

Directions:
1. Add the oil to the cooking pot and set to sautéon med-high heat.
2. Add the ground beef and cook,breaking up slightly with a spatula,until meat is no longer pink.
3. Add the onions and cook another 4-6 minutes until they are soft.Stir in seasonings,tomatoes,and Worcestershire.Simmer 5 minutes.
4. Add the macaroni and parsley,if the mixture is too dry,stir in the reserved water from the pasta.Cook,stirring occasionally,5 minutes until heated through.Salt and pepper to taste and serve.

Nutrition:
- InfoCalories 156,Total Fat 9g,Total Carbs 12g,Protein 6g,Sodium 235mg.

Smoky Sausage&Potato Soup

Servings: 4
Cooking Time: 4 Hours
Ingredients:
- 1 lb.smoked sausage,cut in bite-sized pieces
- 1½cups onion,chopped fine
- 2 carrots,peeled&chopped
- 2 stalks celery,chopped
- 2 russet potatoes,cut in 1-inch cubes
- 2 cup chicken broth,low sodium
- 1 cup skim milk
- 2 cup baby spinach,chopped

Directions:
1. Add the sausage,onion,carrot,celery,potatoes and broth to the cooking pot.Add the lid and set to slow cook on high.Cook 4 hours,or until sausage and vegetables are tender.
2. About 10 minutes before the end of cooking time,add½cup cooking liquid to a small bowl and stir in the milk.
3. Add the milk mixture to the pot along with the spinach and cook until spinach wilts.Serve immediately.

Nutrition:
- InfoCalories 572,Total Fat 23g,Total Carbs 47g,Protein 22g,Sodium 1578mg.

Beef Brisket&Carrots

Servings: 10
Cooking Time: 8 Hours 15 Minutes
Ingredients:
- 4-5 lb.beef brisket,
- 1½tsp salt
- 3 onions,sliced
- 6 cloves garlic,chopped fine
- 1 sprig thyme
- 1 sprig rosemary
- 4 bay leaves
- 2 cups beef broth,low sodium
- 3 carrots,peeled&sliced½-inch thick
- 1 tbsp.mustard

Directions:
1. Use a sharp knife and score the fat side of the brisket in parallel lines,being careful to only slice through the fat,not the meat.Repeat to create a cross-hatch pattern.Sprinkle with salt and let sit 30 minutes.
2. Set the cooker to sear on med-high and lay brisket,fat side down,in the pot.Cook 5-8 minutes to render the fat.Turn the brisket over and brown the other side.Transfer to a plate.
3. Add the onions and season with salt.Cook,stirring frequently,until onions are browned,about 5-8 minutes.Add the garlic and cook 1 minute more.
4. Stir in remaining ingredients.Add the brisket back to the pot,pushing it down to cover as much as possible by the broth.
5. Add the lid and set to slow cook on low.Cook 8-9 hours or until brisket is tender.Transfer brisket to cutting board and tent with foil.Let rest 10-15 minutes.Slice across the grain to serve with carrots,onions and some of the cooking liquid.

Nutrition:
- InfoCalories 143,Total Fat 10g,Total Carbs 2g,Protein 10g,Sodium 833mg.

Baked Rigatoni With Beef Tomato Sauce

Servings: 4
Cooking Time: 75 Min
Ingredients:
- 2 pounds ground beef/900g
- 2 cans tomato sauce/720ml
- 16-ounce dry rigatoni/480g
- 1 cup cottage cheese/130g
- 1 cup shredded mozzarella cheese/130g
- ½cup chopped fresh parsley/65g
- 1 cup water/250ml
- 1 cup dry red wine/250ml
- 1 tbsp butter/15g
- ½tsp garlic powder/2.5g
- ½tsp salt/2.5g

Directions:
1. Choose Sear/Sauté and set to High. Choose Start/Stop to preheat the pot. Melt the butter, add the beef and cook for 5 minutes, or until browned and cooked well. Stir in the tomato sauce, water, wine, and rigatoni; season with the garlic powder and salt.
2. Put the pressure lid together and lock in the Seal position. Choose Pressure, set to Low, and set the time to 2 minutes. Choose Start/Stop to begin cooking.
3. When the timer is done, perform a natural pressure release for 10 minutes, then a quick pressure release and carefully open the lid. Stir in the cottage cheese and evenly sprinkle the top of the pasta with the mozzarella cheese. Close the crisping lid.
4. Choose Broil, and set the time to 3 minutes. Choose Start/Stop to begin. Cook for 3 minutes, or until the cheese has melted, slightly browned, and bubbly. Garnish with the parsley and serve immediately.

Teriyaki Pork Noodles

Servings: 4
Cooking Time: 60 Min
Ingredients:
- 1 pork tenderloin, trimmed and cut into 1-inch pieces
- 1 pound green beans, trimmed/450g
- 1 cup teriyaki sauce/250ml
- 8 ounces egg noodles/240g
- 1 tbsp olive oil/15ml
- ¼tsp salt/1.25g
- ¼tsp black pepper/1.25g
- Cooking spray
- Sesame seeds, for garnish

Directions:
1. Pour the egg noodles and cover with enough water in the pot. Seal the pressure lid, choose Pressure, set to High, and set the time to 2 minutes. Choose Start/Stop.
2. In a large bowl, toss the green beans with the olive oil, salt, and black pepper. In another bowl, toss the pork with the teriyaki sauce. When the egg noodles are ready, perform a quick pressure release, and carefully open the lid.
3. Fix the reversible rack in the upper position of the pot, which will be over the egg noodles. Oil the rack with cooking spray and place the pork in the rack. Also, lay the green beans around the pork.
4. Close the crisping lid. Choose Broil and set the time to 12 minutes. Press Start/Stop to begin cooking the pork and vegetables.
5. When done cooking, check for your desired crispiness and take the rack out of the pot. Serve the pork and green beans over the drained egg noodles and garnish with sesame seeds.

Ranch Pork With Mushroom Sauce

Servings: 4
Cooking Time: 22 Min
Ingredients:
- 4 pork loin chops
- 1 oz. Ranch Dressing and Seasoning mix/30g
- 1 can mushroom soup cream/450ml
- ½cup chicken broth/125ml
- Chopped parsley to garnish

Directions:
1. Add pork, mushroom soup cream, ranch dressing and seasoning mix, and chicken broth, inside the inner pot of your Foodi. Close the lid, secure the pressure valve, and select Pressure mode on High pressure for 10 minutes. Press Start/Stop.
2. Once the timer has ended, do a natural pressure release for 10 minutes, then a quick pressure release to let the remaining steam out.
3. Close the crisping lid and cook for 5 minutes on Broil mode, until tender. Serve with well-seasoned sautéed cremini mushrooms, and the sauce.

Beef Stroganoff

Servings: 6
Cooking Time: 55 Minutes
Ingredients:
- 2 tablespoons unsalted butter
- 1 yellow onion, diced
- 4 cups cremini mushrooms, sliced
- 2 pounds beef stew meat, cut in 1-to 2-inch cubes
- 2 teaspoons freshly ground black pepper
- 2 sprigs fresh thyme
- 2 tablespoons soy sauce
- 2 cups chicken stock
- 1 package egg noodles
- 2 tablespoons cornstarch
- 2 tablespoons water
- ½cup sour cream

Directions:
1. Select SEAR/SAUTÉ and set to MED. Select START/STOP to begin. Let preheat for 3 minutes.
2. Add the butter, onion, and mushrooms and sauté for 5 minutes.
3. Add the beef, black pepper, thyme, soy sauce, and chicken stock. Simmer for 2 to 3 minutes. Assemble pressure lid, making sure the pressure release valve is in the SEAL position.
4. Select PRESSURE and set to HI. Set time to 10 minutes. Select START/STOP to begin.
5. When pressure cooking is complete, quick release the pressure by turning the pressure release valve to the VENT position. Carefully remove lid when unit has finished releasing pressure.
6. Add the egg noodles. Stir well. Assemble pressure lid, making sure the pressure release valve is in the SEAL position.
7. Select PRESSURE and set to HI. Set time to 5 minutes. Select START/STOP to begin.

8. In a small bowl,mix the cornstarch and water until smooth.
9. When pressure cooking is complete,quick release the pressure by turning the pressure release valve to the VENT position.Carefully remove lid when unit has finished releasing pressure.
10. Stir in cornstarch until incorporated.Stir in the sour cream.Serve immediately.

Nutrition:
- InfoCalories:448,Total Fat:16g,Sodium:605mg,Carbohydrates:35g,Protein:41g.

Sausage With Celeriac And Potato Mash

Servings:4
Cooking Time:45 Min
Ingredients:
- 4 potatoes,peeled and diced
- 4 pork sausages
- 1 onion
- 2 cups vegetable broth/500ml
- 1 cup celeriac;chopped/130g
- ¼cup milk/62.5ml
- ½cup water/125ml
- 1 tbsp heavy cream/15ml
- 1 tbsp olive oil/15ml
- 2 tbsp butter/30g
- 1 tsp Dijon mustard/5g
- ½tsp dry mustard powder/2.5g
- Fresh flat-leaf parsley;chopped
- salt and ground black pepper to taste

Directions:
1. Warm oil on Sear/Sauté.Add in sausages and cook for 1 to 2 minutes for each side until browned.Set the sausages to a plate.To the same pot,add onion and cook for 3 minutes until fragrant.
2. Add sausages on top of onions and pour water and broth over them.Placeatrivet over onions and sausages.Put potatoes and celeriac in the steamer basket and transfer it to the trivet.
3. Seal the pressure lid,choose Pressure,set to High,and set the timer to 11 minutes.Press Start.When ready,release the pressure quickly.
4. Transfer potatoes and celeriac to a bowl and set sausages on a plate and cover them with aluminum foil.Usingapotato masher,mash potatoes and celeriac together with black pepper,milk,salt and butter until mash becomes creamy and fluffy.Adjust the seasonings.
5. Set your Foodi to Sear/Sauté.Add the onion mixture and bring to a boil.Cook for 5 to 10 minutes until the mixture is reduced and thickened.Into the gravy,stir in dry mustard,salt,pepper,mustard and cream.Place the mash in 4 bowls in equal parts,top withasausage or two,and gravy.Add parsley for garnishing.

Bacon Strips

Servings:2
Cooking Time:7 Minutes
Ingredients:
- 10 bacon strips
- 1/4 teaspoon chilli flakes
- 1/3 teaspoon salt
- 1/4 teaspoon basil,dried

Directions:
1. Rub the bacon strips with chilli flakes,dried basil,and salt.
2. Turn on your air fryer and place the bacon on the rack.
3. Lower the air fryer lid.Cook the bacon at 400°F for 5 minutes.
4. Cook for 3 minutes more if the bacon is not fully cooked.Serve and enjoy.

Nutrition:
- InfoCalories:500;Fat:46g;Carbohydrates:0g;Protein:21g

Swedish Meatballs With Mashed Cauliflower

Servings:6
Cooking Time:1 Hr
Ingredients:
- ¾pound ground pork/337.5g
- ¾pound ground beef/337.5g
- 1 head cauliflower;cut into florets
- 1 large egg,beaten
- ½onion;minced
- 1¾cup heavy cream;divided/438ml
- ¼cup bread crumbs/32.5g
- ¼cup sour cream/62.5ml
- 2 cups beef stock/500ml
- ¼cup fresh chopped parsley/32.5g
- 1 tbsp water/15ml
- 4 tbsp butter;divided/60g
- 3 tbsp flour/45g
- ½tsp red wine vinegar/2.5ml
- salt and freshly ground black pepper to taste

Directions:
1. In a mixing bowl,mix ground beef,onion,salt,bread crumbs,ground pork,egg,water,and pepper;shape meatballs.Warm 2 tbsp or 30g of butter on Sear/Sauté.
2. Add meatballs and cook until browned,about 5-6 minutes.Set aside toaplate.Pour beef stock in the pot to deglaze,scrape the pan to get rid of browned bits of food.
3. Stir vinegar and flour with the liquid in the pot until smooth;bring to a boil.Stir¾cup heavy cream into the liquid.Arrange meatballs into the gravy.Place trivet onto meatballs.Arrange cauliflower florets onto the trivet.
4. Seal the pressure lid,choose Pressure,set to High,and set the timer to 8 minutes.Press Start.When ready,release the pressure quickly.
5. Set the cauliflower inamixing bowl.Add in the remaining 1 cup or 250ml heavy cream,pepper,sour cream,salt,and 2 or 30g tbsp butter and use a potato masher to mash the mixture until smooth.
6. Spoon the mashed cauliflower onto serving bowls;placeatopping of gravy and meatballs.Add parsley for garnishing.

Beef Sirloin Steak

Servings:4
Cooking Time:17 Minutes
Ingredients:
- 3 tablespoons butter
- 1/2 teaspoon garlic powder
- 1-2 pounds beef sirloin steaks
- Black pepper and salt to taste
- 1 garlic clove,minced

Directions:

1. Select "Sauté" mode on your Ninja Foodi and add butter; let the butter melt.
2. Stir in beef sirloin steaks.
3. Sauté for 2 minutes on each side.
4. Add garlic powder, garlic clove, salt, and pepper.
5. Lock and secure the Ninja Foodi's lid and cook on "Medium-High" pressure for 15 minutes.
6. Release pressure naturally over 10 minutes.
7. Transfer prepare Steaks to a serving platter, enjoy.

Nutrition:
- Info Calories: 246; Fat: 13g; Carbohydrates: 2g; Protein: 31g

Chunky Pork Meatloaf With Mashed Potatoes

Servings: 4
Cooking Time: 55 Min

Ingredients:
- 2 pounds potatoes; cut into large chunks/900g
- 12 ounces pork meatloaf/360g
- 2 garlic cloves; minced
- 2 large eggs
- 12 individual saltine crackers, crushed
- 1¾ cups full cream milk; divided/438ml
- 1 cup chopped white onion/130g
- ½ cup heavy cream/125ml
- ¼ cup barbecue sauce/62.5ml
- 1 tbsp olive oil/15ml
- 3 tbsp chopped fresh cilantro/45g
- 3 tbsp unsalted butter/45g
- ¼ tsp dried rosemary/1.25g
- 1 tsp yellow mustard/5g
- 1 tsp Worcestershire sauce/5ml
- 2 tsp salt/10g
- ½ tsp black pepper/2.5g

Directions:
1. Select Sear/Sauté and adjust to Medium. Press Start to preheat the pot for 5 minutes. Heat the olive oil until shimmering and sauté the onion and garlic in the oil. Cook for about 2 minutes until the onion softens. Transfer the onion and garlic to a plate and set aside.
2. In a bowl, crumble the meatloaf mix into small pieces. Sprinkle with 1 tsp of salt, the pepper, cilantro, and thyme. Add the sautéed onion and garlic. Sprinkle the crushed saltine crackers over the meat and seasonings.
3. In a small bowl, beat ¼ cup of milk, the eggs, mustard, and Worcestershire sauce. Pour the mixture on the layered cracker crumbs and gently mix the ingredients in the bowl with your hands. Shape the meat mixture into an 8-inch round.
4. Cover the reversible rack with aluminum foil and carefully lift the meatloaf into the rack. Pour the remaining 1½ cups of milk and the heavy cream into the inner pot. Add the potatoes, butter, and remaining salt. Place the rack with meatloaf over the potatoes in the upper position in the pot.
5. Seal the pressure lid, choose Pressure; adjust the pressure to High and the cook time to 25 minutes; press Start. After cooking, perform a quick pressure release, and carefully open the pressure lid. Brush the meatloaf with the barbecue sauce.
6. Close the crisping lid; choose Broil and adjust the cook time to 7 minutes. Press Start to begin grilling. When the top has browned, remove the rack, and transfer the meatloaf to a serving platter. Mash the potatoes in the pot. Slice the meatloaf and serve with the mashed potatoes.

Mexican Pot Roast

Servings: 8
Cooking Time: 8 Hours

Ingredients:
- 3 lb. beef chuck roast
- 4 cups lemon-lime soda
- 1 tsp chili powder
- 1 tsp salt
- 3 cloves garlic, chopped
- 2 limes juiced

Directions:
1. Place the roast in the cooking pot and pour the soda over the top. Sprinkle with chili powder, salt, and garlic.
2. Add the lid and set to slow cook on low. Cook 8 hours or until roast is tender.
3. Transfer roast to a large bowl and use 2 forks to shred. Pour the lime juice over the meat and serve hot.

Nutrition:
- Info Calories 367, Total Fat 14g, Total Carbs 14g, Protein 46g, Sodium 449mg.

Beef And Cabbage Stew

Servings: 4
Cooking Time: 30 Min

Ingredients:
- 1 lb. ground beef/450g
- 1 large head cabbage; cut in chunks
- 1 cup diced tomatoes/130g
- 1½ cup beef broth/375ml
- ¼ cup Plain vinegar/62.5ml
- 1 cup rice/130g
- ½ cup chopped onion/65g
- 4 cloves garlic; minced
- 1 bay leaf
- 2 tbsp Worcestershire sauce/30ml
- 2 tbsp butter/30g
- 1 tbsp paprika powder/15g
- 1 tbsp dried oregano/15g
- Salt and black pepper to taste
- Chopped parsley to garnish

Directions:
1. Set the Foodi on Sear/Sauté mode. Melt the butter and add the beef. Brown it for about 6 minutes and add in the onions, garlic, and bay leaf. Stir and cook for 2 more minutes.
2. Stir in the oregano, paprika, salt, pepper, rice, cabbage, vinegar, broth, and Worcestershire sauce. Cook for 3 minutes, stirring occasionally.
3. Add the tomatoes but don't stir. Close the lid, secure the pressure valve, and select Pressure Cook mode on High for 5 minutes. Press Start/Stop.
4. Once the timer is done, let the pot sit closed for 5 minutes and then do a quick pressure. Open the lid. Stir the sauce, remove the bay leaf, and adjust the seasoning with salt. Dish the cabbage sauce in serving bowls and serve with bread rolls.

Philippine Pork Chops

Servings: 6
Cooking Time: 2 Hours 20 Min

Ingredients:
- 2 lb. pork chops/900g
- 5 garlic cloves, coarsely chopped

- 2 bay leaves
- 1 tbsp peanut oil/15ml
- 2 tbsp soy sauce/30ml
- 1 tbsp peppercorns/15g
- 1 tsp salt/5g

Directions:
1. Combine the bay leaves,soy sauce,garlic,salt,peppercorns,and oil,in a bowl.Rub the mixture onto meat.Wrap the pork with a plastic foil and refrigerate for 2h.
2. Place the pork in the Foodi,close the crisping lid and cook for 10 minutes on Air Crisp mode at 350°F or 177°C.Increase the temperature to 370°F or 188°C,flip the chops,and cook for another 10 minutes.Discard bay leaves before serving.

Braised Short Ribs With Mushrooms

Servings:4
Cooking Time:1 Hr
Ingredients:
- 2 pounds beef short ribs/900g
- 1 small onion;sliced
- 1 bell pepper;diced
- 4 garlic cloves,smashed
- ⅓cup beef broth/88ml
- 1 cup beer/250ml
- 1 cup crimini mushrooms;sliced/130g
- 1 tbsp olive oil/15ml
- 1 tbsp soy sauce/15ml
- 1 tsp smoked paprika/5g
- ½tsp dried oregano/2.5g
- ½tsp cayenne pepper/2.5g
- salt and ground black pepper to taste

Directions:
1. In a small bowl,combine pepper,paprika,cayenne pepper,salt,and oregano.Rub the seasoning mixture on all sides of the short ribs.
2. Warm oil on Sear/Sauté.Add mushrooms and cook until browned,about 6-8 minutes;set aside.Add short ribs to the Foodi,and cook for 3 minutes for each side until browned;set aside on a plate.
3. Throw in garlic and onion to the oil and stir-fry for 2 minutes until fragrant.Add in beer to deglaze,scrape the pot's bottom to get rid of any browned bits of food;bring to a simmer and cook for 2 minutes until reduced slightly.
4. Stir in soy sauce,bell pepper and beef broth.Dip short ribs into the liquid in a single layer.Seal the pressure lid,choose Pressure,set to High,and set the timer to 40 minutes.Press Start.Release pressure naturally for about 10 minutes.Divide the ribs with the sauce into bowls and top with fried mushrooms.

Korean Pork Chops

Servings:4
Cooking Time:10 Minutes
Ingredients:
- ½cup soy sauce,low sodium
- 4 tbsp.honey
- 12 cloves garlic,chopped
- 4 tsp ginger
- 2 tsp sesame oil
- 2 tbsp.sweet chili sauce
- 4 top loin pork chops
- 2 tsp olive oil

Directions:
1. In a medium bowl,whisk together soy sauce,honey,garlic,ginger,sesame oil,and chili sauce until smooth.Reserve½the marinade for later.
2. Add the pork chops to the bowl and turn to coat.Let sit 10 minutes.
3. Add the olive oil to the cooking pot and set to sauté on med-high heat.
4. Add the pork chops and cook 5 minutes until browned.Turn the chops over and add the reserved marinade to the pot.Cook another 5 minutes or until chops are cooked through.Let rest 3 minutes before serving.

Nutrition:
- InfoCalories 364,Total Fat 8g,Total Carbs 24g,Protein 46g,Sodium 2218mg.

Bolognese Pizza

Servings:4
Cooking Time:70 Min
Ingredients:
- ½lb.ground pork,meat cooked and crumbled/225g
- 1 cup shredded mozzarella cheese/130g
- ½cup canned crushed tomatoes/65g
- 1 yellow bell pepper;sliced;divided
- 4 pizza crusts
- 1 tbsp chopped fresh basil,for garnish/15g
- 1 tsp red chili flakes;divided/5g
- Cooking spray

Directions:
1. Place the reversible rack in the pot.Close the crisping lid;choose Air Crisp,set the temperature to 400°F or 205°C,and the time to 5 minutes.
2. Grease one side of a pizza crust with cooking spray and lay on the preheated rack,oiled side up.Close the crisping lid.Choose Air Crisp,set the temperature to 400°F,and set the time to 4 minutes.Choose Start/Stop to begin baking.
3. Remove the crust from the rack and flip so the crispy side is down.Top the crust with 2 tbsps of crushed tomatoes,a quarter of bell pepper,2 ounces or 60g of ground pork,¼cup or 32.5g of mozzarella cheese,and¼tbsp or 1.25g of red chili flakes.
4. Close the crisping lid.Choose Broil and set the time to 3 minutes.Choose Start/Stop to continue baking.When done baking and crispy as desired,remove the pizza from the rack.Repeat with the remaining pizza crusts and ingredients.Top each pizza with some basil and serve.

Tex Mex Beef Stew

Servings:10
Cooking Time:25 Minutes
Ingredients:
- 2 tsp cumin
- 1 tsp salt
- 1 tsp garlic powder
- 2 tbsp.coconut oil
- 1 lb.lean ground beef
- 1 lb.beef chuck,boneless&cut in 1-inch cubes
- 2 cups sweet onions,chopped
- 1 yellow bell pepper,seeded&chopped
- 1 orange bell pepper,seeded&chopped
- 1 sweet potato,peeled&chopped

Ninja Foodi Cookbook

- 2 28 oz.cans tomatoes,crushed
- 1 cup beef broth,low sodium
- 3 chipotle peppers in adobo sauce,chopped
- ¼ cup cilantro,chopped,divided

Directions:
1. In a small bowl,combine cumin,salt,and garlic powder.
2. Add oil to the cooking pot and set to sautéon med-high heat.
3. Add the ground beef and half the spice mixture.Cook until beef is no longer pink.Use a slotted spoon to transfer beef to a bowl.
4. Add beef chuck and remaining spice mixture and cook until meat is browned on all sides.
5. Add the ground beef back to the pot.Add remaining ingredients,except cilantro,and stir to mix.
6. Add the lid and set to pressure cook on high.Set timer for 12 minutes.When the timer goes off,use manual release to remove the pressure.Stir in 2 tablespoons cilantro.Ladle into bowls and garnish with remaining cilantro.Serve.

Nutrition:
- InfoCalories 261,Total Fat 11g,Total Carbs 18g,Protein 24g,Sodium 461mg.

Beef Stir Fry

Servings:4
Cooking Time:11 Minutes
Ingredients:
- 1 lb.beef sirloin,sliced into strips
- 1 tablespoon vegetable oil
- 1-1/2 lb.broccoli florets
- 1 red bell pepper,sliced into strips
- 1 yellow pepper,sliced into strips
- 1 green bell pepper,sliced into strips
- 1/2 cup onion,sliced into strips
- Marinade:
- 1/4 cup of hoisin sauce
- 1 teaspoon sesame oil
- 2 teaspoons garlic,minced
- 1 teaspoon of ground ginger
- 1 tablespoon soy sauce
- 1/4 cup of water

Directions:
1. Put all the marinade ingredients in a suitable.Divide it in half.
2. Soak the beef in the marinade for 20 minutes.Toss the vegetables in the other half.
3. Place the vegetables in the Ninja Foodi basket.Seal the crisping lid.
4. Select air crisp.Cook at 200°F for 5 minutes.
5. Remove the vegetables and set them aside.Put the meat on the basket.
6. Seal and cook at 360°For 6 minutes.

Nutrition:
- InfoCalories:390;Fat:13g;Carbohydrate:28.9g;Protein:41.3g

Hawaiian Pork Meal

Servings:8
Cooking Time:15 Minutes
Ingredients:
- 20 oz.pineapple chunks,undrained
- 2 tablespoons water
- 1 tablespoon corn starch
- 2 tablespoons soy sauce
- 3 tablespoons choc zero maple syrup
- 1 tablespoon ginger,grated
- 2 tablespoons brown erythritol
- 3 cloves garlic,minced
- 2 tablespoons olive oil
- 1 onion,chopped
- 2 lb.pork stew meat
- Black pepper and salt to taste
- 1 teaspoon oregano

Directions:
1. Mix the pineapple juice,soy sauce,choc zero maple syrup,ginger,erythritol and garlic in a suitable.Set aside.Set the Ninja Foodi to sauté.Stir in half of the oil.Saute onion for 1 minute.
2. Add the remaining oil.Brown the pork on both sides.
3. Stir in the pineapple chunks,oregano and pineapple juice mixture.
4. Cover the pot.Set it to pressure.Cook at"HIGH"pressure for 10 minutes.
5. Release the pressure naturally.
6. Serve warm.

Nutrition:
- InfoCalories:384;Fat:27g;Carbohydrates:13g;Protein:20g

Lamb Chops And Potato Mash

Servings:8
Cooking Time:40 Min
Ingredients:
- 5 potatoes,peeled and chopped
- 4 cilantro leaves,for garnish
- 8 lamb cutlets
- 1 green onion;chopped
- ⅓ cup milk/88ml
- 1 cup beef stock/250ml
- 3 sprigs rosemary leaves;chopped
- 3 tbsp butter,softened/45g
- 1 tbsp olive oil/15ml
- 1 tbsp tomato puree/15ml
- salt to taste

Directions:
1. Rub rosemary leaves and salt to the lamb chops.Warm oil and 2 tbsp or 30g of butter on Sear/Sauté.Add in the lamb chops and cook for 1 minute for each side until browned;set aside onaplate.
2. In the pot,mix tomato puree and green onion;cook for 2-3 minutes.Add beef stock into the pot to deglaze,scrape the bottom to get rid of any browned bits of food.
3. Return lamb cutlets alongside any accumulated juices to the pot.Set a reversible rack on lamb cutlets.Place steamer basket on the reversible rack.Arrange potatoes in the steamer basket.
4. Seal the pressure lid,choose Pressure,set to High,and set the timer to 4 minutes.Press Start.
5. When ready,release the pressure quickly.Remove trivet and steamer basket from pot.Inahigh speed blender,add potatoes,milk,salt,and remaining tbsp butter.Blend well until you obtain a smooth consistency.
6. Divide the potato mash between serving dishes.Lay lamb chops on the mash.Drizzle with cooking liquid obtained from pressure cooker;apply cilantro sprigs for garnish.

Ninja Foodi Cookbook

Maple Glazed Pork Chops

Servings:4
Cooking Time:12 Minutes
Ingredients:
- 2 tablespoons choc zero maple syrup
- 4 tablespoons mustard
- 2 tablespoons garlic,minced
- Black pepper and salt to taste
- 4 pork chops
- Cooking spray

Directions:
1. Mix the choc zero maple syrup,mustard,garlic,black pepper and salt in a suitable.
2. Marinate the choc zero maple syruped pork chops in the mixture for 20 minutes.
3. Place the pork chops on the Ninja Foodi basket.
4. Put the basket inside the pot.Seal with the crisping lid.
5. Set it to air crisp.Cook at 350°F for about 12 minutes,flipping halfway through.

Nutrition:
- InfoCalories:348;Fat:23.3g;Carbohydrate:14g;Protein:21.1g

Bacon&Sauerkraut With Apples

Servings:6
Cooking Time:30 Minutes
Ingredients:
- ¼lb.apple-wood smoked bacon
- 1 onion,chopped fine
- 2 Granny Smith apples,peeled,cored,&grated
- 2 cloves garlic,chopped fine
- 1 tsp caraway seeds,ground
- 3 cups apple juice,unsweetened
- ¼cup white wine vinegar
- 2 lbs.refrigerated sauerkraut,drained

Directions:
1. Add the bacon to the cooking pot and set to sautéon medium heat.Cook until bacon has browned and fat is rendered.Transfer to paper towel lined plat.Drain all but 1 tablespoon of the fat.
2. Add the onions and apples to the pot and cook 6-7 minutes,until onions are translucent.Add the garlic and caraway and cook 1 minute more.
3. Stir in apple juice and vinegar,increase heat to med-high and bring to a boil.Let boil about 5 minutes until liquid is reduced to a syrup.
4. Chop the bacon and add it and the sauerkraut to the pot,stir to mix.Reduce heat to low and cook 10 minutes until heated through and sauerkraut is tender.Salt and pepper to taste and serve.

Nutrition:
- InfoCalories 58,Total Fat 2g,Total Carbs 9g,Protein 1g,Sodium 170mg.

Cheddar Cheeseburgers

Servings:4
Cooking Time:20 Min
Ingredients:
- 1 lb.ground beef/900g
- 1 packet dry onion soup mix/30g
- 4 burger buns
- 4 tomato slices
- 4 Cheddar cheese slices
- 4 small leaves lettuce
- 1 cup water/250ml
- Mayonnaise
- Ketchup
- Mustard

Directions:
1. In a bowl,add beef and onion mix,and mix well with hands.Shape in 4 patties and wrap each in foil paper.Pour the water into the inner steel insert of Foodi,and fit in the steamer rack.Place the wrapped patties on the trivet,close the lid,and secure the pressure valve,and cook on 10 minutes on Pressure mode on High pressure.
2. Once the timer has stopped,doanatural pressure release for 5 minutes,then a quick pressure release to let out the remaining steam.
3. Useaset of tongs to remove the wrapped beef onto a flat surface and carefully unwrap the patties.
4. To assemble the burgers:
5. In each half of the buns,putalettuce leaf,then a beef patty,aslice of cheese,and a slice of tomato.Top it with the other halves of buns.Serve with some ketchup,mayonnaise,and mustard.

Lime Glazed Pork Tenderloin

Servings:8
Cooking Time:45 Minutes
Ingredients:
- ¼cup honey
- 1/3 cup lime juice
- 1 tsp lime zest,grated
- 2 cloves garlic,chopped fine
- 2 tbsp.yellow mustard
- ½tsp salt
- ½tsp pepper
- 2 pork tenderloins,1 lb.each,fat trimmed
- Nonstick cooking spray

Directions:
1. In a large Ziploc bag combine,honey,lime juice,zest,garlic,mustard,salt,and pepper.Seal the bag and shake to mix.
2. Add the tenderloins and turn to coat.Refrigerate overnight.
3. Spray the rack with cooking spray and add it to the cooking pot.
4. Place the tenderloins on the rack,discard marinade.Add the tender-crisp lid and set to roast on 400°F.Cook tenderloins 40-45 minutes or until they reach desired doneness.Transfer to serving plate and let rest 10 minutes before slicing and serving.

Nutrition:
- InfoCalories 162,Total Fat 3g,Total Carbs 10g,Protein 24g,Sodium 249mg.

Mexican Pork Stir Fry

Servings:4
Cooking Time:15 Minutes
Ingredients:
- 12 oz.pork tenderloin
- 4 slices hickory bacon,chopped
- 1 chipotle chili,chopped
- 1 tbsp.olive oil
- 1 tsp cumin

- 1 tsp oregano
- 2 cloves garlic,chopped
- 1 red bell pepper,cut in strips
- 1 onion,halved&sliced thin
- 3 cups lettuce,chopped

Directions:
1. Slice tenderloin in half lengthwise,and then cut crosswise thinly.Toss pork,bacon and chipotle pieces together in small bowl;set aside.
2. Add oil,cumin,oregano,and garlic to the cooking pot.Set to sauté on med-high heat.
3. Add bell pepper and onion and cook,stirring frequently,3-4 minutes until tender-crisp.Transfer to a bowl.
4. Add pork mixture to the pot and cook,stirring frequently,3-4 minutes until bacon is crisp and pork is no longer pink.
5. Return vegetables to the pot and cook until heated through.Serve over a bed of lettuce.

Nutrition:
- InfoCalories 322,Total Fat 18g,Total Carbs 5g,Protein 34g,Sodium 192mg.

Ham,Ricotta&Zucchini Fritters

Servings:4
Cooking Time:10 Minutes
Ingredients:
- 1½tbsp.butter,unsalted
- 1/3 cup milk
- ½cup ricotta cheese
- 2 eggs
- 1½tsp baking powder
- ½tsp salt
- ¼tsp pepper
- 1 cup flour
- ¼cup fresh basil,chopped
- 3 oz.ham,cut in strips
- ½zucchini,cut into matchsticks

Directions:
1. Spray the fryer basket with cooking spray.Place in the cooking pot.
2. Place the butter in a large microwave safe bowl and microwave until melted.
3. Whisk milk and ricotta into melted butter until smooth.Whisk in eggs until combined.
4. Stir in baking powder,salt,and pepper until combined.Stir in flour,until combined.
5. Fold in basil,ham and zucchini until distributed evenly.Drop batter by¼cups into fryer basket,these will need to be cooked in batches.
6. Add the tender-crisp lid and set to air fry on 375°F.Cook fritters 4-5 minutes per side until golden brown and cooked through.Serve immediately.

Nutrition:
- InfoCalories 180,Total Fat 10g,Total Carbs 15g,Protein 7g,Sodium 451mg.

Lone Star Chili

Servings:8
Cooking Time:8 Hours
Ingredients:
- 2 tbsp.flour
- 2 lbs.lean beef chuck,cubed
- 1 tbsp.olive oil
- 1 onion,chopped fine
- 2 jalapeño peppers,chopped
- 4 cloves garlic,chopped fine
- 1 tbsp.cumin
- 4 oz.green chilies,drained&chopped
- 3 tbsp.Ancho chili powder
- 1 tsp crushed red pepper flakes
- 1 tsp oregano
- 3 cups beef broth,fat-free&low-sodium
- 28 oz.tomatoes,diced,undrained
- ¼cup Greek yogurt,fat free
- 3 tbsp.green onions,chopped

Directions:
1. Place the flour in a large Ziploc bag.Add the beef and toss to coat.
2. Add the oil to the cooking pot and set to sauté on med-high.
3. Add the beef and cook,stirring occasionally,until browned on all sides.Add the onions and jalapenos and cook until soft.Stir in the garlic and cook 1 minute more.
4. Stir in remaining ingredients,except yogurt and green onions,mix well.Add the lid and set to slow cook on low.Cook 7-8 hours until chili is thick and beef is tender.
5. Ladle into bowls and top with a dollop of yogurt and green onions.Serve.

Nutrition:
- InfoCalories 267,Total Fat 9g,Total Carbs 8g,Protein 36g,Sodium 317mg.

Brisket Chili Verde

Servings:4
Cooking Time:19 Minutes
Ingredients:
- 1 tablespoon vegetable oil
- ½white onion,diced
- 1 jalapeño pepper,diced
- 1 teaspoon garlic,minced
- 1 pound brisket,cooked
- 1 can green chile enchilada sauce
- 1 can fire-roasted diced green chiles
- Juice of 1 lime
- 1 teaspoon seasoning salt
- ½teaspoon ground chipotle pepper

Directions:
1. Select SEAR/SAUTÉ and set temperature to HI.Select START/STOP to begin and allow to preheat for 5 minutes.
2. Add oil to the pot and allow to heat for 1 minute.Add the onion,jalapeño,and garlic.Sauté for 3 minutes or until onion is translucent.
3. Add the brisket,enchilada sauce,green chiles,lime juice,salt,and chipotle powder.Mix well.
4. Assemble the pressure lid,making sure the pressure release valve is in the SEAL position.
5. Select PRESSURE and set to HI.Set the time to 15 minutes.Select START/STOP to begin.
6. When cooking is complete,quick release the pressure by turning the pressure release valve to the VENT position.Carefully remove the lid when the unit has finished releasing pressure.

Nutrition:
- InfoCalories:427,Total Fat:16g,Sodium:1323mg,Carbohydrates:30g,Protein:41g.

Beef & Broccoli Casserole

Servings: 4
Cooking Time: 40 Minutes
Ingredients:
- 12 oz. broccoli florets
- 1 lb. extra lean ground beef
- 14 oz. tomato sauce
- 1 stalk celery, chopped fine
- 1 tsp salt
- 1 tsp garlic powder
- ¼ tsp cayenne pepper
- 1¾ cup cheddar cheese, grated, divided
- ¼ cup parmesan cheese

Directions:
1. Add the broccoli to large microwave safe bowl, cover and microwave about 5 minutes until tender. Dump onto paper towel lined baking sheet to drain.
2. Add the beef to the cooking pot and set to sauté on med-high heat. Cook, breaking meat up with a spatula, about 5 minutes or until no longer pink.
3. Add tomato sauce, celery, salt, garlic powder, and cayenne stir well. Simmer 10 minutes or until sauce thickens.
4. Add the broccoli and half the cheddar cheese and stir to combine. Sprinkle remaining cheddar and parmesan over the top.
5. Add the tender-crisp lid and set to bake on 375°F. Bake 20 minutes until hot and bubbling. Let rest 10 minutes before serving.

Nutrition:
- InfoCalories 432, Total Fat 25g, Total Carbs 13g, Protein 42g, Sodium 1590mg.

Cuban Marinated Pork

Servings: 8
Cooking Time: 10 Hours
Ingredients:
- 4 lb. pork shoulder, bone in
- 1½ tsp salt
- 1 tsp pepper
- ½ cup fresh lime juice
- ¾ cup fresh orange juice
- Zest of 1 orange
- Zest of 1 lime
- ½ cup olive oil
- 8 cloves garlic, chopped fine
- 2 tsp oregano
- 2 tsp cumin
- ¼ cup cilantro, chopped

Directions:
1. Use a sharp knife to score the pork.
2. Add remaining ingredients to the cooking pot and stir to mix. Top with pork.
3. Add the lid and set to slow cook on low. Cook 8-10 hours or until meat is almost tender.
4. Line a baking sheet with foil and place the pork on it. Drain cooking liquid into a large bowl.
5. Add the pork back to the pot and add the tender-crisp lid. Set to roast on 400°F. Cook pork 15-20 minutes until browned.
6. Transfer pork to a cutting board and let rest 10 minutes. Slice and serve topped with some of the reserved cooking liquid.

Nutrition:
- InfoCalories 452, Total Fat 24g, Total Carbs 6g, Protein 50g, Sodium 575mg.

Bunless Burgers

Servings: 4
Cooking Time: 10 Minutes
Ingredients:
- ¼ teaspoon onion powder
- ¼ teaspoon garlic powder
- ¼ teaspoon Italian seasoning
- Dash Himalayan pink salt
- 1 pound ground beef

Directions:
1. Place the Cook & Crisp Basket into the cooking pot. Select AIR CRISP, set the temperature to 375°F, and set the time to 5 minutes to preheat. Select START/STOP to begin.
2. In a small bowl, stir together the onion powder, garlic powder, Italian seasoning, and salt.
3. Divide the ground beef into 4 equal portions and shape each into a patty. Season both side of the patties with the seasoning mix and place them on a sheet of parchment paper.
4. Once the unit is preheated, add the burgers to the basket, working in batches as needed. Close the crisping lid.
5. Select AIR CRISP, set the temperature to 375°F, and set the time to 8 to 10 minutes. Select START/STOP to begin. Cook the burgers until cooking is complete; no need to flip the burgers!

Nutrition:
- InfoCalories: 172, Total Fat: 8g, Sodium: 82mg, Carbohydrates: 0g, Protein: 23g.

Pork Sandwiches With Slaw

Servings: 8
Cooking Time: 20 Min
Ingredients:
- 2 lb. chuck roast/900g
- 1 white onion; sliced
- 2 cups beef broth/500ml
- ¼ cup sugar/32.5g
- 1 tsp Spanish paprika/5g
- 1 tsp garlic powder/5g
- 2 tbsp apple cider vinegar/30ml
- Salt to taste
- Assembling:
- 4 Buns, halved
- 1 cup red cabbage, shredded/130g
- 1 cup white cabbage, shredded/130g
- 1 cup white Cheddar cheese, grated/130g
- 4 tbsp mayonnaise/60ml

Directions:
1. Place the pork roast on a clean flat surface and sprinkle with paprika, garlic powder, sugar, and salt. Use your hands to rub the seasoning on the meat.
2. Open the Foodi, add beef broth, onions, pork, and apple cider vinegar. Close the lid, secure the pressure valve, and select Pressure mode on High pressure for 12 minutes. Press Start/Stop.
3. Once the timer has ended, do a quick pressure release. Remove the roast to a cutting board, and use two forks to shred them. Return to the pot, close the crisping lid, and cook for 3 minutes on Air Crisp at 300°F or 149°C.
4. In the buns, spread the mayo, add the shredded pork, some cooked onions from the pot, and shredded red and white cabbage. Top with the cheese.

Chipotle Beef Brisket

Servings: 4
Cooking Time: 1 Hr 10 Min
Ingredients:
- 2 pounds, beef brisket/900g
- 1 cup beef broth/250ml
- ¼ cup red wine/62.5ml
- 2 tbsp olive oil/30ml
- 1 tbsp Worcestershire sauce/15ml
- ½ tsp ground cumin/2.5g
- ½ tsp garlic powder/2.5g
- 1 tsp chipotle powder/5g
- ¼ tsp cayenne pepper/1.25g
- 2 tsp smoked paprika/10g
- ½ tsp dried oregano/2.5g
- ½ tsp salt/2.5g
- ½ tsp ground black pepper/2.5g
- A handful of parsley; chopped

Directions:
1. In a bowl, combine oregano, cumin, cayenne pepper, garlic powder, salt, paprika, pepper, Worcestershire sauce and chipotle powder; rub the seasoning mixture on the beef to coat. Warm olive oil on Sear/Sauté. Add in beef and cook for 3 to 4 minutes each side until browned completely. Pour in beef broth and red wine.
2. Seal the pressure lid, choose Pressure, set to High, and set the timer to 50 minutes. Press Start. Release the pressure naturally, for about 10 minutes.
3. Place the beef on a cutting board and Allow cooling for 10 minutes before slicing. Arrange the beef slices on a serving platter, pour the cooking sauce over and scatter with parsley to serve.

Cauliflower & Bacon Soup

Servings: 4
Cooking Time: 3 Hours
Ingredients:
- 1 head cauliflower, chopped
- 3 cloves garlic, chopped
- 1 onion, chopped
- 4 cups vegetable broth, low sodium
- 4 slices bacon, chopped

Directions:
1. Add the bacon to the cooking pot and set to sauté on med-high. Cook until bacon is crisp, about 3-4 minutes. Transfer to a paper towel lined plate. Drain off the fat.
2. Add the cauliflower, garlic, onion, and broth to the cooking pot, stir well to combine.
3. Add the lid and cook on high for 3 hours, or until cauliflower is tender.
4. Use an immersion blender, or transfer soup in batches to a regular blender, and process until smooth. If using a regular blender return the soup to the pot and cook just until heated through.
5. Ladle into bowls and top with bacon. Serve.

Nutrition:
- InfoCalories 148, Total Fat 11g, Total Carbs 10g, Protein 5g, Sodium 1084mg.

Korean-style Barbecue Meatloaf

Servings: 4
Cooking Time: 30 Minutes
Ingredients:
- 1 pound beef, pork, and veal meatloaf mix
- 1 large egg
- 1 cup panko bread crumbs
- ½ cup whole milk
- ⅓ cup minced onion
- ¼ cup chopped cilantro
- 1 garlic clove, grated
- 1 tablespoon grated fresh ginger
- ½ tablespoon fish sauce
- 1½ teaspoons sesame oil
- 1 tablespoon, plus 1 teaspoon
- soy sauce
- ¼ cup, plus 1 tablespoon
- gochujang
- 1 cup water
- 1 tablespoon honey

Directions:
1. In a large bowl, stir together the beef, egg, bread crumbs, milk, onion, cilantro, garlic, ginger, fish sauce, sesame oil, 1 teaspoon of soy sauce, and 1 tablespoon of gochujang.
2. Place the meat mixture in the Ninja Loaf Pan or an 8½-inch loaf pan and cover tightly with aluminum foil.
3. Pour the water into the pot. Place the loaf pan on the Reversible Rack, making sure the rack is in the lower position. Place the rack with pan in the pot. Assemble pressure lid, making sure the pressure release valve is in the SEAL position.
4. Select PRESSURE and set to HI. Set time to 15 minutes. Select START/STOP to begin.
5. When pressure cooking is complete, quick release the pressure by moving the pressure release valve to the VENT position. Carefully remove lid when unit has finished releasing pressure.
6. Carefully remove the foil from the pan. Close crisping lid.
7. Select BAKE/ROAST, set temperature to 360°F, and set time to 15 minutes. Select START/STOP to begin.
8. In a small bowl stir together the remaining ¼ cup of gochujang, 1 tablespoon of soy sauce, and honey.
9. After 7 minutes, open lid and top the meatloaf with the gochujang barbecue mixture. Close lid and continue cooking.
10. When cooking is complete, open lid and remove meatloaf from the pot. Let cool for 10 minutes before serving.

Nutrition:
- InfoCalories: 389, Total Fat: 22g, Sodium: 887mg, Carbohydrates: 24g, Protein: 31g.

Roasted Pork With Apple Gravy

Servings: 6
Cooking Time: 3 Hours 30 Minutes
Ingredients:
- 1 tbsp. fennel seeds, toasted
- 2 tsp peppercorns
- 2 tbsp. fresh thyme, chopped
- 2 tbsp. fresh rosemary, chopped
- 4 cloves garlic, chopped
- 2 tsp salt
- 4 tbsp. olive oil, divided
- 4-5 lbs. pork shoulder, boneless & fat trimmed
- 4 Fuji apples, peeled, cored & cut in wedges

Ninja Foodi Cookbook

- 1 onion,cut in 12 wedges
- ½cup dry white wine
- ½cup water
- ½tsp Dijon mustard

Directions:
1. Place fennel seeds,peppercorns,thyme,rosemary,garlic,and 2 teaspoons salt into a spice or coffee grinder and grind to a paste.
2. Transfer to a small bowl and stir in 2 tablespoons olive oil.Rub mixture evenly over the pork.Wrap with plastic wrap and refrigerate overnight.
3. Place the apples and onions in the cooking pot and drizzle with remaining oil,toss to coat.Place the pork on top of the apples and onions.
4. Add the tender-crisp lid and set to roast on 450°F.Cook 30 minutes.
5. Remove the lid and add the wine.Cover roast with foil.Add the tender-crisp lid and reduce heat to 325°F.Cook 2½-3 hours or until pork falls apart when stuck with a fork.
6. Transfer pork to a serving plate and tent with foil to keep warm.
7. Transfer apples and onions to a blender.Add½cup water and the mustard and pulse to puree.Mixture should be the consistency of gravy,if not add more water.
8. Slice the pork and serve topped with gravy.

Nutrition:
- InfoCalories 111,Total Fat 3g,Total Carbs 4g,Protein 15g,Sodium 229mg.

Simple Beef&Shallot Curry

Servings:4
Cooking Time:40 Minutes
Ingredients:
- 1 lb.beef stew meat
- ¼tsp salt
- 1/8 tsp turmeric
- 2 tbsp.olive oil
- 2 tbsp.shallots,sliced
- 1 tbsp.fresh ginger,grated
- 1 tbsp.garlic,chopped fine
- 3 cups water
- 2 tsp fish sauce
- 8 shallots,peeled&left whole
- ½tsp chili powder

Directions:
1. In a large bowl,combine beef,salt,and turmeric,use your fingers to massage the seasonings into the meat.Cover and refrigerate 1 hour.
2. Add the oil to the cooking pot and set to sautéon med-high.
3. Add the sliced shallot and cook until golden brown,6-8 minutes.Transfer to a bowl.
4. Add the garlic and ginger to the pot and cook 1 minute or until fragrant.
5. Add the beef and cook until no pink shows,about 5-6 minutes.Stir in the water and fish sauce until combined.
6. Add the lid and set to pressure cook on high.Set the timer for 20 minutes.When the timer goes off,use manual release to remove the pressure.
7. Set back to sautéon med-high and add the fried shallots,whole shallots,and chili powder.Cook,stirring frequently,until shallots are soft and sauce has thickened,about 10 minutes.Serve.

Nutrition:
- InfoCalories 70,Total Fat 9g,Total Carbs 4g,Protein 7g,Sodium 130mg.

Beef Jerky

Servings:4
Cooking Time:20 Minutes
Ingredients:
- 1/2-pound beef,sliced into 1/8-inch-thick strips
- 1/2 cup of soy sauce
- 2 tablespoons Worcestershire sauce
- 2 teaspoons black pepper
- 1 teaspoon onion powder
- 1/2 teaspoon garlic powder
- 1 teaspoon salt

Directions:
1. Add listed ingredient to a large-sized Ziploc bag,seal it shut.
2. Shake well,seal and leave it in the fridge overnight.
3. Lay strips on dehydrator trays,making sure not to overlap them.
4. Lock Air Crisping Lid and Set its cooking temperature to 135°F,cook for 7 hours.

Nutrition:
- InfoCalories:62;Fat:7g;Carbohydrates:2g;Protein:9g

Southern Sweet Ham

Servings:12
Cooking Time:8 Hours
Ingredients:
- 5½lb.ham,bone-in&cooked
- 1 cup apple cider
- ½cup dark brown sugar
- 1/3 cup bourbon
- ¼cup honey
- ¼cup Dijon mustard
- 4 sprigs fresh thyme

Directions:
1. Place the ham in the cooking pot.
2. In a small bowl,whisk together cider,brown sugar,bourbon,honey,and mustard until smooth.Pour over the ham.Scatter the thyme around the ham.
3. Add the lid and set to slow cook on low.Cook 8 hours or until ham is very tender.Transfer ham to cutting board and let rest 10-15 minutes.
4. Pour the cooking liquid through fine mesh sieve into a bowl.Pour back into the cooking pot.Set to sautéon med-high heat and bring to a simmer,cook 10 minutes or until reduced,stirring occasionally.
5. Slice the ham and serve topped with sauce.

Nutrition:
- InfoCalories 372,Total Fat 10g,Total Carbs 20g,Protein 45g,Sodium 2000mg.

Baby Back Ribs With Barbeque Sauce

Servings:4
Cooking Time:45 Min
Ingredients:
- 2 pounds baby back pork ribs/900g
- Juice from 1 lemon
- 4 cups orange juice/1000ml
- For BBQ sauce:
- ½cup ketchup/125ml

- Juice from ½ lemon
- 1 tbsp Worcestershire sauce/15ml
- 2 tbsp honey/30ml
- 2 tsp paprika/10g
- ½ tsp cayenne pepper/2.5g
- 1 tsp mustard/5g
- Salt to taste

Directions:
1. Mix all the BBQ sauce ingredients in a bowl until well incorporated. Set aside. Place ribs in your Foodi pot; add in lemon juice and orange juice.
2. Seal the pressure lid, choose Pressure, set to High, and set the timer to 20 minutes. Press Start. Release pressure naturally for 15 minutes. Meanwhile, preheat oven to 400°°F or 205°C. Line the sheet pan with aluminum foil.
3. Transfer the ribs to the prepared sheet. Do away with the cooking liquid. Onto both sides of ribs, brush barbecue sauce. Bake ribs in the oven for 10 minutes until sauce is browned and caramelized; set the ribs aside and cut into individual bones to serve.

Sour And Sweet Pork

Servings: 4
Cooking Time: 40 Min
Ingredients:
- 1 pound pork loin; cut into chunks/450g
- 15 ounces canned peaches/450g
- ¼ cup water/62.5ml
- ¼ cup beef stock/62.5ml
- 2 tbsp sweet chili sauce/30ml
- 2 tbsp soy sauce/30ml
- 2 tbsp cornstarch/30g
- 2 tbsp white wine/30ml
- 2 tbsp honey/30ml

Directions:
1. Into the pot, mix soy sauce, beef stock, white wine, juice from the canned peaches, and sweet chili sauce; stir in pork to coat.
2. Seal the pressure lid, choose Pressure, set to High, and set the timer to 5 minutes. Press Start. Release pressure naturally for 10 minutes, then release the remaining pressure quickly. Remove the pork to serving plate. Chop the peaches into small pieces.
3. In a bowl, mix water and cornstarch until cornstarch dissolves completely; stir the mixture into the pot. Press Sear/Sauté and cook for 5 more minutes until you obtain the desired thick consistency; add in the chopped peaches and stir well. Serve the pork topped with peach sauce and enjoy.

Zucchini & Beef Lasagna

Servings: 4
Cooking Time: 1 Hour
Ingredients:
- 2 zucchini, cut lengthwise in ½-thick slices
- ½ tsp salt
- Nonstick cooking spray
- 3 tomatoes
- 1 cup onion, chopped
- 2 cloves garlic, chopped fine
- 1 serrano chili, chopped fine
- 1½ cups mushrooms, chopped
- 1 lb. lean ground beef
- ½ cube chicken bouillon
- 1 tsp paprika
- 1 tsp thyme
- 1 tsp basil
- ½ tsp salt
- ¼ tsp pepper
- ½ cup mozzarella cheese, grated

Directions:
1. Place zucchini in a large bowl, sprinkle with salt and let sit 10 minutes.
2. Spray the rack with cooking spray and add it to the cooking pot. Pat zucchini dry with paper towels and lay them on the rack, these will need to be done in batches. Add the tender-crisp lid and set to broil, cook zucchini 3 minutes. Transfer to a paper-towel lined baking sheet.
3. Bring a pot of water to a boil. Cut the ends off the tomatoes and make an X insertion on the top. Place in boiling water for 2-3 minutes. Transfer to bowl of ice water and remove the skin. Chop the tomatoes.
4. Spray the cooking pot with cooking spray and set to sauté on med-high heat. Add onion, garlic, and chili and cook 1 minute. Add the tomatoes and mushrooms and cook 3-4 minutes or until almost tender. Transfer to a bowl.
5. Add the beef to the cooking pot and cook, breaking up with a spatula, until no longer pink.
6. Add the vegetables to the beef along with the bouillon and remaining spices. Reduce heat to low and simmer 25 minutes, stirring occasionally.
7. Spray an 8x8-inch baking dish with cooking spray. Lay 1/3 of the zucchini across the bottom. Top with 1/3 of the meat mixture. Repeat layers two more times. Sprinkle cheese evenly over the top.
8. Add the rack back to the cooking pot and place lasagna on it. Add the tender-crisp lid and set to bake on 375°F. Bake 35 minutes. Transfer to cutting board and let rest 10 minutes before serving.

Nutrition:
- InfoCalories 309, Total Fat 18g, Total Carbs 9g, Protein 28g, Sodium 775mg.

Beef Lasagna

Servings: 4
Cooking Time: 10-15 Minutes
Ingredients:
- 2 small onions
- 2 garlic cloves, minced
- 1-pound ground beef
- 1 large egg
- 1 and 1/2 cups ricotta cheese
- 1/2 cup parmesan cheese
- 1 jar 25 ounces0 marinara sauce
- 8 ounces mozzarella cheese, sliced

Directions:
1. Select "Sauté" mode on your Ninja Foodi and stir in beef, brown the beef.
2. Add onion and garlic.
3. Add parmesan, ricotta, egg in a small dish and keep it on the side.
4. Stir in sauce to browned meat, reserve half for later.
5. Sprinkle mozzarella and half of ricotta cheese into the browned meat.
6. Top with remaining meat sauce.
7. For the final layer, add more mozzarella cheese and the remaining ricotta.
8. Stir well.

9. Cover with a foil transfer to Ninja Foodi.
10. Lock and secure the Ninja Foodi's lid,then cook on"HIGH"pressure for 8-10 minutes.
11. Quick-release pressure.
12. Drizzle parmesan cheese on top.
13. Enjoy.

Nutrition:
- InfoCalories:365;Fats:25g;Carbohydrates:6g;Protein:25g

Smoky Horseradish Spare Ribs

Servings:4
Cooking Time:55 Min
Ingredients:
- 1 spare rack ribs
- 1 cup smoky horseradish sauce/250ml
- 1 tsp salt/5g

Directions:
1. Season all sides of the rack with salt and cut into 3 pieces.Cut the rack into 3 pieces.Pour 1 cup of water into the Foodi's inner pot.Fix the reversible rack in the pot in the lower position and put the ribs on top,bone-side down.
2. Seal the pressure lid,choose Pressure;adjust the pressure to High and the cook time to 18 minutes.Press Start.After cooking,perform a quick pressure release and carefully open the lid.
3. Take out the rack with ribs and pour out the water from the pot.Return the inner pot to the base.Set the reversible rack and ribs in the pot in the lower position.Close the crisping lid and Choose Air Crisp;adjust the temperature to 400°F or 205°C and the cook time to 20 minutes.Press Start.
4. After 10 minutes,open the lid and turn the ribs.Lightly baste the bony side of the ribs with the smoky horseradish sauce and close the lid to cook further.After 4 minutes,open the lid and turn the ribs again.Baste the meat side with the remaining sauce and close the lid to cook until the ribs are done.

Spanish Lamb & Beans

Servings:8
Cooking Time:6 Hours
Ingredients:
- 2 tbsp.olive oil,divided
- 2 onions,sliced
- ½red hot pepper,chopped fine
- 1 chorizo sausage,chopped
- 2 lbs.lamb,cubed
- 2 cups beef broth,low sodium
- 2 cups water
- 4 cloves garlic,chopped fine
- 2 tsp Worcestershire sauce
- 2 tbsp.balsamic vinegar
- ¼tsp oregano
- ¼tsp pepper
- 3 tbsp.tomato paste
- 1 zucchini,sliced
- 2 carrots,sliced
- 15 oz.cannellini beans,drained&rinsed

Directions:
1. Add half the oil to the cooking pot and set to sautéon med-high heat.
2. Add the onions and cook 3 minutes,stirring occasionally.Add the pepper and chorizo and cook 5-6 minutes or until chorizo is cooked through.Transfer to a bowl.
3. Add remaining oil to the pot and let it get hot.Add the lamb and cook until browned on the outside.
4. Return the chorizo mixture along with the broth,water,garlic,Worcestershire,vinegar,oregano,and pepper,stir to mix.
5. Add the lid and set to slow cook on low.Cook 4 hours.
6. Add the tomato paste,zucchini,carrots,and beans,stir to combine.Recover and cook another 2 hours until lamb and vegetables are tender.Serve.

Nutrition:
- InfoCalories 710,Total Fat 54g,Total Carbs 21g,Protein 36g,Sodium 890mg.

Jamaican Pork

Servings:4
Cooking Time:25 Minutes
Ingredients:
- 1 tbsp.butter
- 1 tsp curry powder
- 2 bananas,sliced½-inch thick
- 1 lb.pork tenderloin,cubed
- ½tsp salt
- ½cup pineapple juice,unsweetened
- ¼cup onion,chopped fine
- ¼cup coconut flakes,unsweetened

Directions:
1. Add butter to the cooking pot and set to sautéon medium heat.
2. Once the butter has melted,stir in curry powder until foamy.
3. Add bananas and cook until golden brown,about 3-5 minutes.Transfer to a plate.
4. Add pork and cook until golden brown,about 6-8 minutes.Season with salt.
5. Stir in pineapple juice and onion.Cover,reduce heat,and simmer 10 minutes until pork is tender.
6. Stir in coconut and bananas and toss gently to combine.Serve over cooked rice.

Nutrition:
- InfoCalories 247,Total Fat 7g,Total Carbs 21g,Protein 25g,Sodium 100mg.

Healthier Meatloaf

Servings:4
Cooking Time:6 Hours
Ingredients:
- Nonstick cooking spray
- 1 lb.lean ground pork
- 1 cup oats
- 8 oz.tomato sauce,divided
- 1 onion,chopped fine
- ½cup zucchini,grated&excess liquid squeezed out
- 1 clove garlic,chopped fine
- 1 egg,lightly beaten
- 1 tsp salt
- 1/8 tsp pepper
- ½tsp Italian seasoning

Directions:
1. Spray the cooking pot with cooking spray.

2. In a large bowl,combine pork,oats,half the tomato sauce,onion,zucchini,garlic,egg,salt,pepper,and Italian seasoning,mix well.
3. Fold a large sheet of foil in half,then in half again.Place along the bottom up two sides of the cooking pot.
4. Add the pork mixture and form into a loaf shape.Spoon remaining tomato sauce over the top.
5. Add the lid and set to slow cook on low.Cook 6 hours or until meatloaf is cooked through.
6. Use the foil sling to remove the meatloaf from the cooking pot.Let rest 5 minutes before slicing and serving.
Nutrition:
- InfoCalories 335,Total Fat 7g,Total Carbs 36g,Protein 33g,Sodium 947mg.

Beef In Basil Sauce

Servings:4
Cooking Time:15 Minutes
Ingredients:
- 2 tbsp.olive oil
- 2 shallots,sliced thin
- 7 cloves garlic sliced
- 1 tbsp.fresh ginger,peeled&grated
- 1/2 red bell pepper,sliced thin
- 1 lb.lean ground beef
- 2 tsp brown sugar
- 2 tbsp.fish sauce
- 6 tbsp.soy sauce,low sodium
- 3 tsp oyster sauce
- 2 tbsp.Asian garlic chili paste
- ½cup beef broth,low sodium
- ¼cup water
- 1 tsp cornstarch
- 1 cup basil leaves,chopped
- Cooked Jasmine rice for serving

Directions:
1. Add the oil to the cooking pot and set to sautéon med-high heat.
2. Add the shallots,garlic,ginger,and bell peppers to the pot and cook,stirring frequently,3 minutes.Use a slotted spoon to transfer mixture to a bowl.
3. Increase heat to high and add the ground beef,cook,breaking it up with a spoon until beef is no longer pink.
4. In a small bowl,whisk together brown sugar,fish sauce,soy sauce,oyster sauce,cornstarch,broth,and water until smooth.
5. Add the pepper mixture back to the pot and pour the sauce over.Cook,stirring,2 minutes until sauce has thickened.
6. Stir in basil and cook until wilted,about 2 minutes.Serve over hot rice.
Nutrition:
- InfoCalories 359,Total Fat 20g,Total Carbs 10g,Protein 34g,Sodium 1785mg.

Creole Dirty Rice

Servings:6
Cooking Time:15 Minutes
Ingredients:
- 1 tbsp.olive oil
- 1 lb.lean ground beef
- 1 stalk celery,sliced
- ½green bell pepper,chopped
- 2 tbsp.garlic,chopped fine
- 1 onion,chopped
- 4 tbsp.fresh parsley,chopped
- 2 tbsp.creole seasoning
- 5 cups brown rice,cooked

Directions:
1. Add the oil to the cooking pot and set to sautéon med-high heat.
2. Add the beef,celery,bell pepper,garlic,and onion and cook,breaking up beef with a spatula,until meat is no longer pink and vegetables are tender,about 6-8 minutes.
3. Add the parsley and Creole seasoning and mix well.
4. Add the rice and cook,stirring occasionally,about 5 minutes or until heated through.Serve.
Nutrition:
- InfoCalories 386,Total Fat 15g,Total Carbs 43g,Protein 19g,Sodium 57mg.

Italian Pot Roast

Servings:8
Cooking Time:8 Hours
Ingredients:
- 1 tsp salt
- ½tsp pepper
- 1 tsp garlic powder
- 1 tsp onion powder
- 2 tsp Italian seasoning
- 6 oz.tomato paste
- 2 lb.beef sirloin roast
- 1 onion,sliced thin
- 1 green bell pepper,sliced thin
- 1 banana pepper,sliced thin
- ½cup beef broth,low sodium

Directions:
1. In a small bowl,combine salt,pepper,garlic powder,onion powder,Italian seasoning,and tomato paste,mix well.
2. Coat the roast,on all sides,with spice mixture and place in the cooking pot.Place the onions and peppers on top of the roast and pour in the broth.
3. Add the lid and set to slow cook on low.Cook 7-8 hours or until beef is tender.
4. You can slice the beef and serve topped with the onions and peppers.Or,you can shred the beef and use it to make sandwiches.
Nutrition:
- InfoCalories 270,Total Fat 16g,Total Carbs 6g,Protein 24g,Sodium 392mg.

Beef And Pumpkin Stew

Servings:6
Cooking Time:35 Min
Ingredients:
- 2 pounds stew beef;cut into 1-inch chunks/900g
- 3 carrots;sliced
- 1 onion;chopped
- 3 whole cloves
- 1 bay leaf
- ½butternut pumpkin;sliced
- 1 cup red wine/250ml
- 2 tbsp cornstarch/30g
- 2 tbsp canola oil/30ml
- 3 tbsp water/45ml

- 1 tsp garlic powder/5g
- 1 tsp salt/5g

Directions:
1. Warm oil on Sear/Sauté.Add beef and brown for 5 minutes on each side.Deglaze the pot with wine,scrape the bottom to get rid of any browned beef bits.Add in onion,salt,bay leaf,cloves,and garlic powder.Seal the pressure lid,choose Pressure,set to High,and set the timer to 15 minutes.Press Start.
2. When ready,release the pressure quickly.Add in pumpkin and carrots without stirring.Seal the pressure lid again,choose Pressure,set to High,and set the timer to 5 minutes.Press Start.
3. When ready,release the pressure quickly.Inabowl,mix water and cornstarch until cornstarch dissolves completely;mix into the stew.Allow the stew to simmer while uncovered on Keep Warm for 5 minutes until you attain the desired thickness.

Pork And Ricotta Meatballs With Cheesy Grits

Servings:8
Cooking Time:26 Minutes
Ingredients:
- 2 pounds ground pork
- 1 cup whole milk ricotta cheese
- 2 eggs
- 1 cup panko bread crumbs
- 4 garlic cloves,minced
- ¼cup parsley,minced,plus more for garnishing
- 1½cups grated Parmesan cheese,divided
- 2 tablespoons kosher salt,divided
- 1 teaspoon freshly ground black pepper
- 2 tablespoons canola oil
- 4 cups whole milk
- 1 cup coarse ground grits

Directions:
1. In a large bowl,combine the pork,ricotta,eggs,bread crumbs,garlic,parsley,½cup of Parmesan,1 tablespoon of salt,and pepper.Use your hands or a sturdy spatula to mix well.
2. Use a 3-ounce ice cream scoop to portion the mixture into individual meatballs.Use your hands to gently form them into balls.
3. Select SEAR/SAUTÉand set to HI.Select START/STOP to begin.Let preheat for 5 minutes.
4. Add the oil.Add half the meatballs and sear for 6 minutes,flipping them after 3 minutes.Remove from the pot and repeat with the remaining meatballs.Remove the second batch of meatballs from the pot.
5. Add the milk,grits,and remaining 1 tablespoon of salt and stir.Gently place meatballs back in the pot.They will sink slightly when placed in the milk.Assemble pressure lid,making sure pressure release valve is in the SEAL position.
6. Select PRESSURE and set to HI.Set time to 6 minutes.Select START/STOP to begin.
7. When pressure cooking is complete,quick release the pressure by moving the pressure release valve to the VENT position.Carefully remove lid when unit has finished releasing pressure.
8. Sprinkle the remaining 1 cup of Parmesan cheese over the top of the grits and meatballs.Close crisping lid.
9. Select BROIL and set time to 8 minutes.Select START/STOP to begin.
10. When cooking is complete,serve immediately.

Nutrition:
- InfoCalories:544,Total Fat:32g,Sodium:763mg,Carbohydrates:28g,Protein:37g.

Meatballs With Spaghetti Sauce

Servings:6
Cooking Time:20 Min
Ingredients:
- 2 lb.ground beef/900g
- 1 cup grated Parmesan cheese/130g
- 4 cups spaghetti sauce/1000ml
- 1 cup breadcrumbs/130g
- 1 cup water/250ml
- 2 cloves garlic;minced
- 2 eggs,cracked into a bowl
- 1 onion,finely chopped
- 3 tbsp milk/45ml
- 1 tbsp olive oil/15ml
- 1 tsp dried oregano/5g
- Salt and pepper,to taste

Directions:
1. Inabowl,add beef,onion,breadcrumbs,parmesan,eggs,garlic,milk,salt,oregano,and pepper.Mix well with hands and shape bite-size balls.
2. Open the pot,and add the spaghetti sauce,water and the meatballs.Close the lid,secure the pressure valve,and select Steam mode on High pressure for 6 minutes.Press Start/Stop.
3. Once the timer is done,do a natural pressure release for 5 minutes,then doaquick pressure release to let out any extra steam,and open the lid.Dish the meatball sauce over cooked pasta and serve.

Garlicky Pork Chops

Servings:2
Cooking Time:10 Minutes
Ingredients:
- 1 tablespoon coconut butter
- 1 tablespoon coconut oil
- 2 teaspoons cloves garlic,grated
- 2 teaspoons parsley,chopped
- Black pepper and salt to taste
- 4 pork chops,sliced into strips

Directions:
1. Combine all the ingredients except the pork strips.Mix well.
2. Marinate the pork in the mixture for 1 hour.Put the pork on the Ninja Foodi basket.
3. Set it inside the pot.Seal with the crisping lid.Choose air crisp function.
4. Cook at 400°For 10 minutes.

Nutrition:
- InfoCalories:388;Fat:23.3g;Carbohydrate:0.5g;Protein:18.1g

Ninja Foodi Cookbook

Traditional Beef Stroganoff

Servings: 6
Cooking Time: 1 Hr 15 Min

Ingredients:
- 2 pounds beef stew meat/900g
- 8 ounces sour cream/240g
- 2 garlic cloves; minced
- 1 onion; chopped
- 3 cups fresh mushrooms; chopped/390g
- 1 cup long-grain rice, cooked/130g
- 1 cup beef broth/250ml
- ¼ cup flour/32.5g
- 2 tbsp olive oil/30ml
- 1 tbsp chopped fresh parsley/15g
- salt and ground black pepper to taste

Directions:
1. In a large bowl, combine salt, pepper and flour. Add beef and massage to coat beef in flour mixture. Warm oil on Sear/Sauté. Brown the beef for 4 to 5 minutes. Add garlic and onion and cook for 3 minutes until fragrant. Add beef broth to the pot.
2. Seal the pressure lid, choose Pressure, set to High, and set the timer to 35 minutes. Press Start. When ready, release the pressure quickly.
3. Open the lid and stir mushrooms and sour cream into the beef mixture. Seal the pressure lid again, choose Pressure, set to High, and set the timer to 2 minutes. Press Start.
4. When ready, release the pressure quickly. Season the stroganoff with pepper and salt; scoop over cooked rice before serving.

Beef Mole

Servings: 8
Cooking Time: 8 Hours

Ingredients:
- 2 lbs. beef stew meat, cut in 1-inch cubes
- 3 tsp salt, divided
- 2 tbsp. olive oil
- 2 onions, chopped fine
- 4 cloves garlic, chopped fine
- 1 chili, seeded & chopped fine
- 3 tsp chili powder
- 1 tsp ancho chili powder
- 2 tsp oregano
- 2 tsp cumin
- 1 tsp paprika
- 1 lb. dried red beans, soaked in water overnight, drained
- 5 cups water
- 2 cups beer
- 2 15 oz. tomatoes, crushed
- 1 tbsp. brown sugar
- 2 oz. unsweetened chocolate, chopped
- 1 bay leaf
- 3 tbsp. lime juice

Directions:
1. Place the beef in a large Ziploc bag with 1½ teaspoons salt, seal and rub gently to massage the salt into the meat. Refrigerate overnight.
2. Add the oil to the cooking pot and set to sauté on med-high heat.
3. Working in batches, add the beef and cook until deep brown on all sides. Transfer to a bowl.
4. Add the onions to the pot and cook about 5 minutes or until softened. Stir in garlic, chilies, remaining salt, chili powders, oregano, cumin, and paprika and cook 1 minute more.
5. Stir in beans, water, beer, tomatoes, brown sugar, and chocolate and mix well. Stir in the beef and add the bay leaf.
6. Add the lid and set to slow cook on low. Cook 8 hours or until beef is tender. Stir in lime juice and serve.

Nutrition:
- InfoCalories 127, Total Fat 8g, Total Carbs 7g, Protein 7g, Sodium 310mg.

Pulled Pork Tacos

Servings: 5
Cooking Time: 1 Hr 25 Min

Ingredients:
- 2 pounds pork shoulder, trimmed; cut into chunks/900g
- 3 cups shredded cabbage/390g
- 5 taco tortillas
- 1 cup beer/250ml
- 1 cup vegetable broth/250ml
- 1/4 cup plus 2 tbsp lemon juice/92.5ml
- 1/4 cup mayonnaise/62.5ml
- 3 tbsp sugar/45g
- 2 tbsp honey/30ml
- 3 tsp taco seasoning/15g
- 1 tsp ground black pepper/5g
- 2 tsp mustard/10g

Directions:
1. In a bowl, combine sugar, taco seasoning, and black pepper; rub the mixture onto pork pieces to coat well. Allow to settling for 30 minutes. Into the Foodi, add 1/4 cup or 62.5ml lemon juice, broth, pork and beer.
2. Seal the pressure lid, choose Pressure, set to High, and set the timer to 50 minutes. Press Start. Meanwhile in a large bowl, mix mayonnaise, mustard, 2 tbsp lemon juice, cabbage and honey until well coated.
3. Release pressure naturally for 15 minutes before doing a quick release. Transfer the pork to a cutting board and Allow cooling before using two forks to shred. Skim and get rid of fat from liquid in the pressure cooker. Return pork to the pot and mix with the liquid. Top the pork with slaw on taco tortillas before serving.

Beef Pho With Swiss Chard

Servings: 6
Cooking Time: 1 Hr 10 Min

Ingredients:
- 2 pounds Beef Neck Bones/900g
- 10 ounces sirloin steak/300g
- 8 ounces rice noodles/240g
- 1 yellow onion, quartered
- A handful of fresh cilantro; chopped
- 2 scallions; chopped
- 2 jalapeño peppers; sliced
- ¼ cup minced fresh ginger/32.5g
- 9 cups water/2250ml
- 2 cups Swiss chard; chopped/260g
- 2 tsp coriander seeds/10g
- 2 tsp ground cinnamon/10g
- 2 tsp ground cloves/10g

Ninja Foodi Cookbook

- 2 tbsp coconut oil/30ml
- 3 tbsp sugar/45g
- 2 tbsp fish sauce/30ml
- 2½ tsp kosher salt/12.5g
- Freshly ground black pepper to taste

Directions:
1. Melt the oil on Sear/Sauté. Add ginger and onions and cook for 4 minutes until the onions are softened. Stir in cloves, cinnamon and coriander seeds and cook for 1 minute until soft. Add in water, salt, beef meat and bones.
2. Seal the pressure lid, choose Pressure, set to High, and set the timer to 30 minutes. Press Start. Release pressure naturally for 10 minutes.
3. Transfer the meat to a large bowl; cover with it enough water and soak for 10 minutes. Drain the water and slice the beef. In hot water, soak rice noodles for 8 minutes until softened and pliable; drain and rinse with cold water. Drain liquid from cooker into a separate pot through a fine-mesh strainer; get rid of any solids.
4. Add fish sauce and sugar to the broth; transfer into the Foodi and simmer on Sear/Sauté. Place the noodles in four separate soup bowls. Top with steak slices, scallions, swiss chard; sliced jalapeño pepper, cilantro, red onion, and pepper. Spoon the broth over each bowl to serve.

Pork Chops With Squash Purée And Mushroom Gravy

Servings: 4
Cooking Time: 45 Min
Ingredients:
- 4 pork chops
- 1 pound butternut squash; cubed/450g
- 2 sprigs rosemary, leaves removed and chopped
- 2 sprigs thyme, leaves removed and chopped
- 4 cloves garlic; minced
- 1 cup mushrooms; chopped/130g
- 1 cup chicken broth/250ml
- 1 tbsp olive oil/15ml
- 2 tbsp olive oil/30ml
- 1 tbsp soy sauce/15ml
- 1 tsp cornstarch 5g

Directions:
1. Set on Sear/Sauté, set to Medium High, and choose Start/Stop to preheat the pot and heat rosemary, thyme and 1 tbsp or 15ml of olive oil. Add the pork chops and sear for 1 minute for each side until lightly browned.
2. Sauté garlic and mushrooms in the pressure cooker for 5-6 minutes until mushrooms are tender. Add soy sauce and chicken broth. Transfer pork chops to a wire trivet and place it into the pressure cooker. Over the chops, place a cake pan. Add butternut squash in the pot and drizzle with 1 tbsp olive oil.
3. Seal the pressure lid, choose Pressure, set to High, and set the timer to 10 minutes. Press Start. When ready, release the pressure quickly. Remove the pan and trivet from the pot. Stir cornstarch into the mushroom mixture for 2 to 3 minutes until the sauce thickens.
4. Transfer the mushroom sauce to an immersion blender and blend until you attain the desired consistency. Scoop sauce into a cup with a pour spout. Smash the squash into a purée. Set pork chops on a plate and ladle squash puree next to them. Top the pork chops with gravy.

Soups & Stews

Italian Sausage, Potato, And Kale Soup

Servings: 8
Cooking Time: 18 Minutes
Ingredients:
- 1 tablespoon extra-virgin olive oil
- 1½ pounds hot Italian sausage, ground
- 1 pound sweet Italian sausage, ground
- 1 large yellow onion, diced
- 2 tablespoons minced garlic
- 4 large Russet potatoes, cut in ½-inch thick quarters
- 5 cups chicken stock
- 2 tablespoons Italian seasoning
- 2 teaspoons crushed red pepper flakes
- Salt
- Freshly ground black pepper
- 6 cups kale, chopped
- ½ cup heavy (whipping) cream

Directions:
1. Select SEAR/SAUTÉ. Set temperature to MD:HI. Select START/STOP to begin. Let preheat for 5 minutes.
2. Add the olive oil and hot and sweet Italian sausage. Cook, breaking up the sausage with a spatula, until the meat is cooked all the way through, about 5 minutes.
3. Add the onion, garlic, potatoes, chicken stock, Italian seasoning, and crushed red pepper flakes. Season with salt and pepper. Stir to combine. Assemble pressure lid, making sure the pressure release valve is in the SEAL position.
4. Select PRESSURE and set to HI. Set time to 10 minutes. Select START/STOP to begin.
5. When pressure cooking is complete, quick release the pressure by turning the pressure release valve to the VENT position. Carefully remove lid when the unit has finished releasing pressure.
6. Stir in the kale and heavy cream. Serve.

Nutrition:
- Info Calories: 689, Total Fat: 45g, Sodium: 1185mg, Carbohydrates: 38g, Protein: 33g.

Chickpea, Spinach, And Sweet Potato Stew

Servings: 6
Cooking Time: 23 Minutes
Ingredients:
- 1 tablespoon extra-virgin olive oil
- 1 yellow onion, diced
- 4 garlic cloves, minced
- 4 sweet potatoes, peeled and diced
- 4 cups vegetable broth
- 1 can fire-roasted diced tomatoes, undrained
- 2 cans chickpeas, drained
- 1½ teaspoons ground cumin
- 1 teaspoon ground coriander
- ½ teaspoon paprika
- ½ teaspoon sea salt
- ½ teaspoon freshly ground black pepper
- 4 cups baby spinach

Directions:
1. Select SEAR/SAUTÉ and set to MD:HI. Select START/STOP to begin. Allow the pot to preheat for 5 minutes.
2. Combine the oil, onion, and garlic in the pot. Cook, stirring occasionally, for 5 minutes.
3. Add the sweet potatoes, vegetable broth, tomatoes, chickpeas, cumin, coriander, paprika, salt, and black pepper to the pot. Assemble the pressure lid, making sure the pressure release valve is in the SEAL position.
4. Select PRESSURE and set to HI. Set the time to 8 minutes, then select START/STOP to begin.
5. When pressure cooking is complete, quick release the pressure by moving the pressure release valve to the VENT position. Carefully remove the lid when the unit has finished releasing pressure.
6. Add the spinach to the pot and stir until wilted. Serve.

Nutrition:
- Info Calories: 220, Total Fat: 4g, Sodium: 593mg, Carbohydrates: 42g, Protein: 7g.

Coconut And Shrimp Bisque

Servings: 4
Cooking Time: 15 Minutes
Ingredients:
- ¼ cup red curry paste
- 2 tablespoons water
- 1 tablespoon extra-virgin olive oil
- 1 bunch scallions, sliced
- 1 pound medium shrimp, peeled and deveined
- 1 cup frozen peas
- 1 red bell pepper, diced
- 1 can full-fat coconut milk
- Kosher salt

Directions:
1. In a small bowl, whisk together the red curry paste and water. Set aside.
2. Select SEAR/SAUTÉ and set to MED. Select START/STOP to begin. Let preheat for 3 minutes.
3. Add the oil and scallions. Cook for 2 minutes.
4. Add the shrimp, peas, and bell pepper. Stir well to combine. Stir in the red curry paste. Cook for 5 minutes, until the peas are tender.
5. Stir in coconut milk and cook for an additional 5 minutes until shrimp is cooked through and the bisque is thoroughly heated.
6. Season with salt and serve immediately.

Nutrition:
- Info Calories: 460, Total Fat: 32g, Sodium: 902mg, Carbohydrates: 16g, Protein: 29g.

Fish Chowder And Biscuits

Servings: 8
Cooking Time: 30 Minutes
Ingredients:
- 5 strips bacon, sliced
- 1 white onion, chopped
- 3 celery stalks, chopped
- 4 cups chicken stock
- 2 Russet potatoes, rinsed and cut in 1-inch pieces
- 4 frozen haddock fillets
- Kosher salt
- ½ cup clam juice
- ⅓ cup all-purpose flour
- 2 cans evaporated milk
- 1 tube refrigerated biscuit dough

Directions:

1. Select SEAR/SAUTÉ and set to HI. Select START/STOP to begin. Let preheat for 5 minutes.
2. Add the bacon and cook, stirring frequently, for 5 minutes. Add the onion and celery and cook for an additional 5 minutes, stirring occasionally.
3. Add the chicken stock, potatoes, and haddock filets. Season with salt. Assemble pressure lid, making sure the pressure release valve is in the SEAL position.
4. Select PRESSURE and set to HI. Set time to 5 minutes. Select START/STOP to begin.
5. Whisk together the clam juice and flour in a small bowl, ensuring there are no flour clumps in the mixture.
6. When pressure cooking is complete, quick release the pressure by moving the pressure release valve to the VENT position. Carefully remove lid when unit has finished releasing pressure.
7. Select SEAR/SAUTÉ and set to MED. Select START/STOP to begin. Add the clam juice mixture, stirring well to combine. Add the evaporated milk and continue to stir frequently for 3 to 5 minutes, until chowder has thickened to your desired texture.
8. Place the Reversible Rack in the pot in the higher position. Place the biscuits on the rack; it may be necessary to tear the last biscuit or two into smaller pieces in order to fit them all on the rack. Close crisping lid.
9. Select BAKE/ROAST, set temperature to 350°F, and set time to 12 minutes. Select START/STOP to begin.
10. After 10 minutes, check the biscuits for doneness. If desired, cook for up to an additional 2 minutes.
11. When cooking is complete, open lid and remove rack from pot. Serve the chowder and top each portion with biscuits.

Nutrition:
- InfoCalories:518, Total Fat:22g, Sodium:1189mg, Carbohydrates:49g, Protein:33g.

Tex-mex Chicken Tortilla Soup

Servings:8
Cooking Time:20 Minutes
Ingredients:
- 1 tablespoon extra-virgin olive oil
- 1 onion, chopped
- 1 pound boneless, skinless chicken breasts
- 6 cups chicken broth
- 1 jar salsa
- 4 ounces tomato paste
- 1 tablespoon chili powder
- 2 teaspoons cumin
- ½ teaspoon sea salt
- ½ teaspoon freshly ground black pepper
- 1 pinch of cayenne pepper
- 1 can black beans, rinsed and drained
- 2 cups frozen corn
- Tortilla strips, for garnish

Directions:
1. Select SEAR/SAUTÉ and set to temperature to HI. Select START/STOP to begin. Let preheat for 5 minutes.
2. Place the olive oil and onions into the pot and cook, stirring occasionally, for 5 minutes.
3. Add the chicken breast, chicken broth, salsa, tomato paste, chili powder, cumin, salt, pepper, and cayenne pepper. Assemble pressure lid, making sure the pressure release valve is in the SEAL position.
4. Select PRESSURE and set to HI. Set time to 10 minutes. Select START/STOP to begin.
5. When pressure cooking is complete, allow pressure to naturally release for 10 minutes. After 10 minutes, quick release remaining pressure by moving the pressure release valve to the VENT position. Carefully remove lid when unit has finished releasing pressure.
6. Transfer the chicken breasts to a cutting board and shred with two forks. Set aside.
7. Add the black beans and corn. Select SEAR/SAUTÉ and set to MD. Select START/STOP to begin. Cook until heated through, about 5 minutes.
8. Add shredded chicken back to the pot. Garnish with tortilla strips, serve, and enjoy!

Nutrition:
- InfoCalories:186, Total Fat:4g, Sodium:783mg, Carbohydrates:23g, Protein:19g.

Chicken Potpie Soup

Servings:6
Cooking Time:1 Hour
Ingredients:
- 4 chicken breasts
- 2 cups chicken stock
- 2 tablespoons unsalted butter
- 1 yellow onion, diced
- 16 ounces frozen mixed vegetables
- 1 cup heavy (whipping) cream
- 1 can condensed cream of chicken soup
- 2 tablespoons cornstarch
- 2 tablespoons water
- Salt
- Freshly ground black pepper
- 1 tube refrigerated biscuit dough

Directions:
1. Place the chicken and stock in the pot. Assemble pressure lid, making sure the pressure release valve is in the SEAL position.
2. Select PRESSURE and set to HI. Set time to 15 minutes. Select START/STOP to begin.
3. Once pressure cooking is complete, quick release the pressure by turning the pressure release valve to the VENT position. Carefully remove lid when the unit has finished releasing pressure.
4. Using a silicone-tipped utensil, shred the chicken.
5. Select SEAR/SAUTÉ and set to MED. Add the butter, onion, mixed vegetables, cream, and condensed soup and stir. Select START/STOP to begin. Simmer for 10 minutes.
6. In a small bowl, whisk together the cornstarch and water. Slowly whisk the cornstarch mixture into the soup. Set temperature to LO and simmer for 10 minutes more. Season with salt and pepper.
7. Carefully arrange the biscuits on top of the simmering soup. Close crisping lid.
8. Select BAKE/ROAST, set temperature to 325°F, and set time to 15 minutes. Select START/STOP to begin.
9. When cooking is complete, remove the biscuits. To serve, place a biscuit in a bowl and ladle soup over it.

Nutrition:
- InfoCalories:731, Total Fat:26g, Sodium:1167mg, Carbohydrates:56g, Protein:45g.

Butternut Squash, Apple, Bacon And Orzo Soup

Servings: 8
Cooking Time: 28 Minutes
Ingredients:
- 4 slices uncooked bacon, cut into ½-inch pieces
- 12 ounces butternut squash, peeled and cubed
- 1 green apple, cut into small cubes
- Kosher salt
- Freshly ground black pepper
- 1 tablespoon minced fresh oregano
- 2 quarts chicken stock
- 1 cup orzo

Directions:
1. Select SEAR/SAUTÉ and set temperature to HI. Select START/STOP to begin. Let preheat for 5 minutes.
2. Place the bacon in the pot and cook, stirring frequently, about 5 minutes, or until fat is rendered and the bacon starts to brown. Using a slotted spoon, transfer the bacon to a paper towel-lined plate to drain, leaving the rendered bacon fat in the pot.
3. Add the butternut squash, apple, salt, and pepper and sauté until partially soft, about 5 minutes. Stir in the oregano.
4. Add the bacon back into the pot along with the chicken stock. Bring to a boil for about 10 minutes, then add the orzo. Cook for about 8 minutes, until the orzo is tender. Serve.

Nutrition:
- InfoCalories: 247, Total Fat: 7g, Sodium: 563mg, Carbohydrates: 33g, Protein: 12g.

Chicken Enchilada Soup

Servings: 8
Cooking Time: 30 Minutes
Ingredients:
- 1 tablespoon extra-virgin olive oil
- 1 small red onion, diced
- 2 cans fire-roasted tomatoes with chiles
- 1 can corn
- 1 can black beans, rinsed and drained
- 1 can red enchilada sauce
- 1 can tomato paste
- 3 tablespoons taco seasoning
- 2 tablespoons freshly squeezed lime juice
- 2 boneless, skinless chicken breasts
- Salt
- Freshly ground black pepper

Directions:
1. Select SEAR/SAUTÉ and set temperature to MD:HI. Select START/STOP to begin. Let preheat for 5 minutes.
2. Place the olive oil and onion in the pot. Cook until the onions are translucent, about 2 minutes.
3. Add the tomatoes, corn, beans, enchilada sauce, tomato paste, taco seasoning, lime juice, and chicken. Season with salt and pepper and stir. Assemble pressure lid, making sure the pressure release valve is in the SEAL position.
4. Select PRESSURE and set to HI. Set time to 9 minutes. Select START/STOP to begin.
5. When pressure cooking is complete, allow pressure to naturally release for 10 minutes. After 10 minutes, quick release remaining pressure by moving the pressure release valve to the VENT position. Carefully remove lid when unit has finished releasing pressure.
6. Transfer the chicken breasts to a cutting board. Using two forks, shred the chicken. Return the chicken back to the pot and stir. Serve in a bowl with toppings of choice, such as shredded cheese, crushed tortilla chips, sliced avocado, sour cream, cilantro, and lime wedges, if desired.

Nutrition:
- InfoCalories: 257, Total Fat: 4g, Sodium: 819mg, Carbohydrates: 37g, Protein: 20g.

Lasagna Soup

Servings: 8
Cooking Time: 16 Minutes
Ingredients:
- 1 tablespoon extra-virgin olive oil
- 16 ounces Italian sausage
- 1 small onion, diced
- 4 garlic cloves, minced
- 1 jar marinara sauce
- 2 cups water
- 1 cup vegetable broth
- 1 teaspoon dried basil
- 1 teaspoon dried oregano
- ½ teaspoon dried thyme
- Freshly ground black pepper
- 8 ounces lasagna noodles, broken up
- 1 cup ricotta cheese
- ½ cup grated Parmesan cheese
- 1 teaspoon dried parsley
- ½ cup heavy (whipping) cream
- 1 cup shredded mozzarella cheese

Directions:
1. Select SEAR/SAUTÉ and set to HI. Select START/STOP to begin. Let preheat for 5 minutes.
2. Add the oil and sausage and cook for about 5 minutes. Using a wooden spoon, break apart the sausage and stir.
3. Add the onions and cook, stirring occasionally, for 3 minutes. Add the garlic and cook for 2 minutes, or until the meat is no longer pink.
4. Add the marinara sauce, water, vegetable broth, basil, oregano, thyme, pepper, and lasagna noodles. Assemble pressure lid, making sure the pressure release valve is in the SEAL position.
5. Select PRESSURE and set to HI. Set time to 6 minutes. Select START/STOP to begin.
6. In a medium bowl, combine the ricotta cheese, Parmesan cheese, and parsley. Cover and refrigerate.
7. When pressure cooking is complete, quick release the pressure by turning the pressure release valve to the VENT position. Carefully remove lid when unit has finished releasing pressure.
8. Stir in the heavy cream. Add the cheese mixture and stir. Top the soup with the mozzarella. Close crisping lid.
9. Select BROIL and set time to 5 minutes. Select START/STOP to begin.
10. When cooking is complete, serve immediately.

Nutrition:
- InfoCalories: 398, Total Fat: 22g, Sodium: 892mg, Carbohydrates: 29g, Protein: 23g.

Chicken Chili

Servings: 8
Cooking Time: 30 Minutes
Ingredients:
- 1 tablespoon extra-virgin olive oil
- 1 yellow onion, chopped
- 4 garlic cloves, minced
- 2 pounds boneless chicken breast, cut in half crosswise
- 4 cups chicken broth
- 1 green bell pepper, seeded and chopped
- 2 jalapeños, seeded and chopped
- 1½ tablespoons ground cumin
- 1 tablespoon coriander
- 1 teaspoon dried oregano
- 1 teaspoon sea salt
- 1 teaspoon freshly ground black pepper
- 2 cans cannellini beans, rinsed and drained
- Shredded Monterey Jack cheese, for garnish
- Chopped cilantro, for garnish
- Lime wedge, for garnish

Directions:
1. Select SEAR/SAUTÉ and set to HI. Select START/STOP to begin. Let preheat for 5 minutes.
2. Add the oil and onions and cook, stirring occasionally, for 3 minutes. Add the garlic and cook for 2 minutes.
3. Add the chicken breast, chicken broth, green bell pepper, jalapeño, cumin, coriander, oregano, salt, and black pepper. Assemble pressure lid, making sure the pressure release valve is in the SEAL position.
4. Select PRESSURE and set to HI. Set time to 15 minutes. Select START/STOP to begin.
5. When pressure cooking is complete, quick release the pressure by turning the pressure release valve to the VENT position. Carefully remove lid when unit has finished releasing pressure.
6. Remove the chicken from the soup and shred it using two forks. Set aside.
7. Add the cannellini beans. Select SEAR/SAUTÉ and set to MED. Select START/STOP to begin. Cook until heated through, about 5 minutes.
8. Add shredded chicken back to the pot. Serve, garnished with the cheese, cilantro, and lime wedge (if using).

Nutrition:
- InfoCalories: 279, Total Fat: 9g, Sodium: 523mg, Carbohydrates: 18g, Protein: 32g.

Creamy Pumpkin Soup

Servings: 8
Cooking Time: 23 Minutes
Ingredients:
- ¼ cup unsalted butter
- ½ small onion, diced
- 1 celery stalk, diced
- 1 carrot, diced
- 2 garlic cloves, minced
- 1 can pumpkin purée
- 1½ teaspoons poultry spice blend
- 3 cups chicken stock
- 1 package cream cheese
- 1 cup heavy (whipping) cream
- ¼ cup maple syrup
- Sea salt
- Freshly ground black pepper

Directions:
1. Select SEAR/SAUTÉ and set to HI. Select START/STOP to begin. Let preheat for 5 minutes.
2. Add the butter. Once melted, add the onions, celery, carrot, and garlic. Cook, stirring occasionally, for 3 minutes.
3. Add the pumpkin, poultry spice, and chicken stock. Assemble pressure lid, making sure the pressure release valve is in the SEAL position.
4. Select PRESSURE and set to HI. Set time to 15 minutes. Select START/STOP to begin.
5. When pressure cooking is complete, quick release the pressure by turning the pressure release valve to the VENT position. Carefully remove lid when the unit has finished releasing pressure.
6. Whisk in the cream cheese, heavy cream, and maple syrup. Season with salt and pepper. Using an immersion blender, purée the soup until smooth.

Nutrition:
- InfoCalories: 334, Total Fat: 28g, Sodium: 266mg, Carbohydrates: 17g, Protein: 6g.

Loaded Potato Soup

Servings: 6
Cooking Time: 30 Minutes
Ingredients:
- 5 slices bacon, chopped
- 1 onion, chopped
- 3 garlic cloves, minced
- 4 pounds Russet potatoes, peeled and chopped
- 4 cups chicken broth
- 1 cup whole milk
- ½ teaspoon sea salt
- ½ teaspoon freshly ground black pepper
- 1½ cups shredded Cheddar cheese
- Sour cream, for serving (optional)
- Chopped fresh chives, for serving (optional)

Directions:
1. Select SEAR/SAUTÉ and set to HI. Select START/STOP to begin. Let preheat for 5 minutes.
2. Add the bacon, onion, and garlic. Cook, stirring occasionally, for 5 minutes. Set aside some of the bacon for garnish.
3. Add the potatoes and chicken broth. Assemble pressure lid, making sure the pressure release valve is in the SEAL position.
4. Select PRESSURE and set to HI. Set time to 10 minutes, then select START/STOP to begin.
5. When pressure cooking is complete, quick release the pressure by moving the pressure release valve to the VENT position. Carefully remove lid when unit has finished releasing pressure.
6. Add the milk and mash the ingredients until the soup reaches your desired consistency. Season with the salt and black pepper. Sprinkle the cheese evenly over the top of the soup. Close crisping lid.
7. Select BROIL and set time to 5 minutes. Select START/STOP to begin.
8. When cooking is complete, top with the reserved crispy bacon and serve with sour cream and chives (if using).

Nutrition:
- InfoCalories: 468, Total Fat: 19g, Sodium: 1041mg, Carbohydrates: 53g, Protein: 23g.

Jamaican Jerk Chicken Stew

Servings: 6
Cooking Time: 28 Minutes
Ingredients:
- 2 tablespoons canola oil
- 6 boneless, skinless chicken thighs, cut in 2-inch pieces
- 2 tablespoons Jamaican jerk spice
- 1 white onion, peeled and chopped
- 2 red bell peppers, chopped
- ½ head green cabbage, core removed and cut into 2-inch pieces
- 1½ cups wild rice blend, rinsed
- 4 cups chicken stock
- ½ cup prepared Jamaican jerk sauce
- Kosher salt

Directions:
1. Select SEAR/SAUTÉ and set to HI. Select START/STOP to begin. Let preheat for 5 minutes.
2. Add the oil, chicken, and jerk spice and stir. Cook for 5 minutes, stirring occasionally.
3. Add the onions, bell pepper, and cabbage and stir. Cook for 5 minutes, stirring occasionally.
4. Add the wild rice and stock, stirring well to combine. Assemble pressure lid, making sure the pressure release valve is in the SEAL position.
5. Select PRESSURE and set to HI. Set time to 18 minutes. Select START/STOP to begin.
6. When pressure cooking is complete, allow pressure to naturally release for 10 minutes. After 10 minutes, quick release any remaining pressure by moving the pressure release valve to the VENT position. Carefully remove lid when unit has finished releasing pressure.
7. Add the jerk sauce to pot, stirring well to combine. Let the stew sit for 5 minutes, allowing it to thicken. Season with salt and serve.

Nutrition:
- InfoCalories: 404, Total Fat: 10g, Sodium: 373mg, Carbohydrates: 53g, Protein: 29g.

Mushroom And Wild Rice Soup

Servings: 6
Cooking Time: 30 Minutes
Ingredients:
- 5 medium carrots, chopped
- 5 celery stalks, chopped
- 1 onion, chopped
- 3 garlic cloves, minced
- 1 cup wild rice
- 8 ounces fresh mushrooms, sliced
- 6 cups vegetable broth
- 1 teaspoon kosher salt
- 1 teaspoon poultry seasoning
- ½ teaspoon dried thyme

Directions:
1. Place all the ingredients in the pot. Assemble pressure lid, making sure the pressure release valve is in the SEAL position.
2. Select PRESSURE and set to HI. Set time to 30 minutes. Select START/STOP to begin.
3. When pressure cooking is complete, quick release the pressure by turning the pressure release valve to the VENT position. Carefully remove lid when unit has finished releasing pressure.
4. Serve.

Nutrition:
- InfoCalories: 175, Total Fat: 2g, Sodium: 723mg, Carbohydrates: 30g, Protein: 11g.

Goulash (hungarian Beef Soup)

Servings: 6
Cooking Time: 55 Minutes
Ingredients:
- ½ cup all-purpose flour
- 1 tablespoon kosher salt
- ½ teaspoon freshly ground black pepper
- 2 pounds beef stew meat
- 2 tablespoons canola oil
- 1 medium red bell pepper, seeded and chopped
- 4 garlic cloves, minced
- 1 large yellow onion, diced
- 2 tablespoons smoked paprika
- 1½ pounds small Yukon Gold potatoes, halved
- 2 cups beef broth
- 2 tablespoons tomato paste
- ¼ cup sour cream
- Fresh parsley, for garnish

Directions:
1. Select SEAR/SAUTÉ and set to HI. Select START/STOP to begin. Let preheat for 5 minutes.
2. Mix together the flour, salt, and pepper in a small bowl. Dip the pieces of beef into the flour mixture, shaking off any extra flour.
3. Add the oil and let heat for 1 minute. Place the beef in the pot and brown it on all sides, about 10 minutes.
4. Add the bell pepper, garlic, onion, and smoked paprika. Sauté for about 8 minutes or until the onion is translucent.
5. Add the potatoes, beef broth, and tomato paste and stir. Assemble pressure lid, making sure the pressure release valve is in the SEAL position.
6. Select PRESSURE and set to LO. Set time to 30 minutes. Select START/STOP to begin.
7. When pressure cooking is complete, quick release the pressure by moving the pressure release valve to the VENT position. Carefully remove lid when unit has finished releasing pressure.
8. Add the sour cream and mix thoroughly. Garnish with parsley, if desired, and serve immediately.

Nutrition:
- InfoCalories: 413, Total Fat: 13g, Sodium: 432mg, Carbohydrates: 64g, Protein: 37g.

Desserts

Chocolate Cheesecake

Servings:10
Cooking Time:20 Minutes
Ingredients:
- For Crust
- ¼cup coconut flour
- ¼cup almond flour
- 2½tablespoons cacao powder
- 1½tablespoons Erythritol
- 2 tablespoons butter,melted
- For Filling
- 16 ounces cream cheese,softened
- 1/3 cup cacao powder
- ½teaspoon powdered Erythritol
- ½teaspoon stevia powder
- 1 large egg
- 2 large egg yolks
- 6 ounces unsweetened dark chocolate,melted
- ¾cup heavy cream
- ¼cup sour cream
- 1 teaspoon vanilla extract

Directions:
1. For the crust:in a suitable,mix together flours,cacao powder and Erythritol.
2. Stir in the melted butter and mix until well combined.
3. Stir in the mixture into a parchment paper-lined 7-inch springform pan evenly,and with your fingers,press evenly.
4. For filling:in a food processor,add the cream cheese,cacao powder,monk fruit powder and stevia and pulse until smooth.
5. Stir in the egg and egg yolks and pulse until well combined.
6. Add the rest of the ingredients and pulse until well combined.
7. Place the prepared filling mixture on top of the crust evenly and with a rubber spatula,smooth the surface.
8. With a piece of foil,cover the springform pan loosely.
9. In the Ninja Foodi's insert,place 2 cups of water.
10. Set a"Reversible Rack"in the Ninja Foodi's insert.
11. Place the springform pan over the"Reversible Rack".
12. Close the Ninja Foodi's lid with a pressure lid and place the pressure valve in the"Seal"position.
13. Select"Pressure"mode and set it to"High"for 20 minutes.
14. Press the"Start/Stop"button to initiate cooking.
15. Switch the pressure valve to"Vent"and do a"Natural"release.
16. Place the pan onto a wire rack to cool completely.
17. Refrigerate for about 6-8 hours before serving.

Nutrition:
- InfoCalories:385;Fats:35.6g;Carbohydrates:9.8g;Proteins:8.9g

Cinnamon Apple Cake

Servings:10
Cooking Time:40 Minutes
Ingredients:
- Butter flavored cooking spray
- ½cup coconut oil,soft
- ½cup+1 tbsp.honey,divided
- 1 egg
- 1 tsp vanilla
- 1¼cups+2 tbsp.whole wheat flour,divided
- 1 tsp baking powder
- ½tsp baking soda
- 2 tsp cinnamon,divided
- ½tsp salt
- 2 cups apple,chopped
- ¼cup oats
- ½cup pecans,chopped

Directions:
1. Spray an 8-inch cake pan with cooking spray.
2. In a large bowl,beat together oil,½cup honey,egg,and vanilla until smooth.
3. In a medium bowl,stir together 1¼cups flour,baking powder,baking soda,1 teaspoon cinnamon,and salt.
4. Add apples to dry ingredients and toss to combine.And mixture to wet ingredients and mix well.Pour into prepared pan.
5. In a small bowl,combine remaining flour,cinnamon,oats,pecans,and 1 tablespoon honey and mix well.Sprinkle over the top of the cake batter.
6. Add the cake to the cooking pot along with the tender-crisp lid.Set to bake on 325°F.Bake 35-40 minutes until edges begin to brown.
7. Transfer to a wire rack and let cool in the pan 10 minutes.Then invert onto serving plate and let cool completely before serving.

Nutrition:
- InfoCalories 267,Total Fat 16g,Total Carbs 31g,Protein 3g,Sodium 111mg.

Portuguese Honey Cake

Servings:8
Cooking Time:15 Minutes
Ingredients:
- Butter flavored cooking spray
- 3 egg yolks,room temperature
- 2 eggs,room temperature
- 2 tbsp.powdered sugar
- ¼cup honey
- 4½tbsp.cake flour

Directions:
1. Place the rack in the cooking pot.Spray an 8-inch round baking dish with cooking spray and lightly coat with flour.
2. In a large bowl,beat egg yolks,eggs,and powdered sugar until combined.
3. In a small saucepan over medium heat,heat honey until it starts to simmer.Let simmer 2 minutes.
4. With mixer running,slowly beat in the hot honey.Beat mixture 8-10 minutes until pale and thick and doubled in size.Gently tap the bowl on the counter to remove any air bubbles.
5. Sift flour into mixture and gently fold in to combine.Pour the batter into the pan and tap again to remove air bubbles.Place the cake on the rack.
6. Add the tender-crisp lid and set to bake on 350°F.Bake the cake 15 minutes,center should still be soft.
7. Transfer to a wire rack and let cool in pan 30 minutes.Invert onto serving plate and serve.

Nutrition:
- InfoCalories 97,Total Fat 3g,Total Carbs14 g,Protein 3g,Sodium 23mg.

Poached Peaches

Servings: 4
Cooking Time: 15 Min
Ingredients:
- 4 Peaches,peeled,pits removed
- 1 cup Freshly Squeezed Orange Juice/250ml
- ½cup Black Currants/65g
- 1 Cinnamon Stick

Directions:
1. Place black currants and orange juice in a blender.Blend until the mixture becomes smooth.Pour the mixture in your Foodi,and add the cinnamon stick.
2. Add the peaches to the steamer basket and then insert the basket into the pot.Seal the pressure lid,select Pressure,and set to 5 minutes at High pressure.When done,doaquick pressure release.Serve the peaches drizzled with sauce,to enjoy!

Coconut Lime Snack Cake

Servings: 8
Cooking Time: 20 Minutes
Ingredients:
- Butter flavored cooking spray
- 2 eggs
- ½cup coconut milk
- 3 tbsp.honey
- 1 tsp vanilla
- ¼cup+1 tbsp.fresh lime juice,divided
- 1 tbsp.+1 tsp lime zest,divided
- 2¼cup almond flour,sifted
- 1 tsp baking soda
- ½cup coconut,unsweetened&shredded
- ½cup powdered Stevia

Directions:
1. Place the rack in the cooking pot.Spray an 8-inch baking pan with cooking spray.
2. In a large bowl,beat eggs,milk,honey,vanilla,¼cup lime juice and tablespoon zest until thick and frothy,about 6-8 minutes.
3. Fold in flour,baking soda,and coconut just until combined.Pour into prepared pan.
4. Place the cake on the rack and add the tender-crisp lid.Set to bake on 350°F.Bake 15-20 minutes or until cake passes the toothpick test.
5. Let cool in the pan for 10 minutes,then invert onto a serving plate.
6. In a small bowl,whisk together powdered sugar,remaining tablespoon lime juice,and remaining teaspoon lime zest.Drizzle over the top of cooled cake.Serve.

Nutrition:
- InfoCalories 183,Total Fat 13g,Total Carbs 28g,Protein 5g,Sodium 35mg.

Pecan Pie Bars

Servings: 16
Cooking Time: 25 Minutes
Ingredients:
- Butter flavored cooking spray
- 1/3 cup+4 tbsp.butter soft
- ¾cup Stevia brown sugar,packed,divided
- ¼cup almond flour
- ¼tsp salt
- ¼cup maple syrup
- ¼cup milk
- ¼tsp vanilla
- 1½cups pecans,chopped

Directions:
1. Place the rack in the cooking pot.Line an 8x8-inch baking pan with foil,leaving some overlap over the sides and spray with cooking spray.
2. In a medium bowl,beat 1/3 cup butter and¼cup Stevia until light and fluffy.
3. Add the flour and salt,beat until combined.Press evenly on the bottom of the prepared pan.
4. Place pan on the rack and add the tender-crisp lid.Set to bake on 350°F.Bake 10-13 minutes.
5. In a medium saucepan over medium heat,combine butter,remaining Stevia,syrup,and milk.Bring to a simmer,stirring occasionally.Cook 1 minute.
6. Remove butter mixture from heat and stir in vanilla and pecans.Pour evenly over crust.Bake another 10-12 minutes or until bubbling,center will still be soft.
7. Transfer to wire rack and cool completely.Once the bars are room temperature,cover and refrigerate until ready to serve.

Nutrition:
- InfoCalories 177,Total Fat 17g,Total Carbs 17g,Protein 2g,Sodium 84mg.

Almond Milk

Servings: 4
Cooking Time: 20 Min
Ingredients:
- 1 cup raw almonds;soaked overnight,rinsed and peeled/130g
- 2 dried apricots;chopped
- 1 cup cold water/250ml
- 4 cups water/1000ml
- 1 vanilla bean
- 2 tbsp honey/30ml

Directions:
1. In the pot,mixacup of cold water with almonds and apricots.Seal the pressure lid,choose Pressure,set to High,and set the timer to 1 minute.
2. When ready,release the pressure quickly.Open the lid.The almonds should be soft and plump,and the water should be brown and murky.Use a strainer to drain almonds;rinse with cold water for 1 minute.
3. Toahigh-speed blender,add the rinsed almonds,vanilla bean,honey,and 4 cups or 1000ml water.Blend for 2 minutes until well combined and frothy.Line a cheesecloth to the strainer.
4. Place the strainer over a bowl and strain the milk.Useawooden spoon to press milk through the cheesecloth and get rid of solids.Place almond milk in an airtight container and refrigerate.

Maply Soufflés

Servings: 4
Cooking Time: 10 Minutes
Ingredients:
- Butter flavored cooking spray
- 1/3 cup maple syrup
- 2 eggs,separated
- ½tsp vanilla
- 2 tbsp.flour
- 1/8 tsp salt

Ninja Foodi Cookbook

- Powdered sugar for dusting

Directions:
1. Spray 4 ramekins with cooking spray.
2. In a medium bowl, beat syrup, egg yolks, and vanilla until thickened, about 1 minute.
3. Add flour and beat until combined.
4. In a large bowl, beat egg whites until stiff peaks form, about 2 minutes. Gently fold ¼ of the egg whites into syrup mixture just until combined. Fold the syrup mixture into the remaining egg whites just until combined. Divide evenly among ramekins.
5. Place ramekins in the cooking pot and add the tender-crisp lid. Set to bake on 375°F. Bake 10-12 minutes, or until puffed and golden brown. Dust with powdered sugar and serve immediately.

Nutrition:
- InfoCalories 119, Total Fat 2g, Total Carbs 21g, Protein 3g, Sodium 116mg.

Vanilla Cheesecake(1)

Servings: 6
Cooking Time: 2 Hours
Ingredients:
- For Crust:
- 1 cup almonds, toasted
- 1 egg
- 2 tablespoons butter
- 4-6 drops liquid stevia
- For Filling:
- 2 8-ounce packages of cream cheese, softened
- 4 tablespoons heavy cream
- 2 eggs
- 1 tablespoon coconut flour
- 1 teaspoon liquid stevia
- 1 teaspoon vanilla extract

Directions:
1. For the crust: in a high-speed food processor, stir in almonds and pulse until a flour-like consistency is achieved.
2. In a suitable, add ground almond, egg, butter and stevia and mix until well combined.
3. In the bottom of a 1½-quart oval pan, place the crust mixture and press to smooth the top surface, leaving a little room on each side.
4. For the filling: in a suitable, stir in all ingredients and with an immersion blender, blend until well combined.
5. Place the prepared filling mixture over the crust evenly.
6. In the Ninja Foodi's insert, place 1 cup of water.
7. Carefully set the pan in the Ninja Foodi's insert.
8. Close the Ninja Foodi's lid with a crisping lid and select "Slow Cooker".
9. Set on "Low" for 2 hours.
10. Press the "Start/Stop" button to initiate cooking.
11. Place the pan onto a wire rack to cool.
12. Refrigerate to chill for at least 6-8 hours before serving.

Nutrition:
- InfoCalories:446; Fats:42.9g; Carbohydrates:7.2g; Proteins:10.6g

Pecan Stuffed Apples

Servings: 6
Cooking Time: 20 Min
Ingredients:
- 3½ pounds Apples, cored/1575g
- 1¼ cups Red Wine/312.5ml
- ¼ cup Pecans; chopped/32.5g
- ¼ cup Graham Cracker Crumbs/32.5g
- ½ cup dried Apricots; chopped/65g
- ¼ cup Sugar/32.5g
- ½ tsp grated Nutmeg/2.5g
- ½ tsp ground Cinnamon/2.5g
- ¼ tsp Cardamom/1.25g

Directions:
1. Lay the apples at the bottom of your cooker, and pour in the red wine. Combine the other ingredients, except the crumbs.
2. Seal the pressure lid, and cook at High pressure for 15 minutes. Once ready, do a quick pressure release. Top with graham cracker crumbs and serve!

Cheese Babka

Servings: 8
Cooking Time: 30 Minutes
Ingredients:
- FOR THE DOUGH
- 1 packet dry active yeast
- ¼ cup water, warmed to 110°F
- ¼ cup, plus ¼ teaspoon granulated sugar, divided
- 2 cups all-purpose flour
- 2 large eggs, divided
- ½ teaspoon kosher salt
- 3 tablespoons unsalted butter, at room temperature
- ¼ cup milk
- FOR THE FILLING
- 8 ounces cream cheese
- ¼ cup granulated sugar
- 1 tablespoon sour cream
- 1 tablespoon all-purpose flour
- ½ teaspoon vanilla extract
- Zest of 1 lemon
- Cooking spray
- All-purpose flour, for dusting
- 3 tablespoons water
- TO MAKE THE DOUGH

Directions:
1. In a small bowl, combine the yeast, warm water, and ¼ teaspoon of sugar. Let sit 10 minutes until foamy.
2. Place the flour, yeast mixture, remaining ¼ cup of sugar, 1 egg, salt, butter, and milk into the bowl of stand mixer. Using the dough hook attachment, mix on medium-low speed until the dough is smooth and elastic, about 10 minutes.
3. TO MAKE THE FILLING
4. In a medium bowl, whisk together all the filling ingredients until smooth.
5. TO MAKE THE BABKA
6. Spray the cooking pot with the cooking spray. Place the dough in the pot. Cover the dough with plastic wrap and let it rise in a warm place until doubled in size, about 1 hour.
7. Spray the Ninja Multi-Purpose Pan or 8-inch baking pan with cooking spray.
8. Turn the dough out onto a floured work surface. Punch down the dough. Using a rolling pin, roll it out into a 10-by-12-inch rectangle. Spread the cheese filling evenly on top of the dough. From the longer edge of the dough, roll it up like a jelly roll.
9. Cut the roll evenly into 12 pieces. Place each piece cut-side up in the prepared pan. The rolls should be touching but with visible gaps in between.

10. Beat the remaining egg with 1 teaspoon of water. Gently brush the tops of the rolls with this egg wash.
11. Place the remaining 3 tablespoons of water in the pot. Place the pan on the Reversible Rack, making sure the rack is in the lower position. Then place the rack with pan in the pot.
12. Select SEAR/SAUTÉ and set to LO. Select START/STOP to begin.
13. After 5 minutes, select START/STOP to turn off the heat. Let the rolls rise for another 15 minutes in the warm pot.
14. Remove the rack and pan from the pot. Close crisping lid.
15. Select BAKE/ROAST, set temperature to 325°F, and set time to 30 minutes. Select START/STOP to begin. Let preheat for 5 minutes.
16. Place the rack with pan in the pot. Close lid and cook for 25 minutes.
17. Once cooking is complete, open lid and remove rack and pan. Let the babka completely cool before serving.

Nutrition:
- InfoCalories:325,Total Fat:16g,Sodium:286mg,Carbohydrates:38g,Protein:7g.

Chocolate Chip Brownies

Servings:16
Cooking Time:20 Minutes
Ingredients:
- Butter flavored cooking spray
- 3 bananas,mashed
- 1 egg
- ½tsp vanilla
- ¼cup dark cocoa powder
- ¼cup chocolate chips,sugar free

Directions:
1. Place the rack in the cooking pot. Spray an 8x8-inch baking pan with cooking spray.
2. In a large bowl, combine bananas, egg, vanilla, and cocoa powder, mix well. Fold in chocolate chips and spread evenly in prepared pan.
3. Place the pan on the rack and add tender-crisp lid. Set to bake on 350°F. Bake 15-20 minutes or until top is firm.
4. Transfer to wire rack and let cool completely. Cover and refrigerate at least one hour before cutting.

Nutrition:
- InfoCalories 91,Total Fat 5g,Total Carbs 10g,Protein 2g,Sodium 7mg.

Vanilla Chocolate Spread

Servings:16
Cooking Time:25 Min
Ingredients:
- 1¼pounds Hazelnuts,halved/562.5g
- ½cups icing Sugar,sifted/65g
- ½cup Cocoa Powder/65g
- 10 ounces Water/300ml
- 1 tsp Vanilla Extract/5ml
- ¼tsp Cardamom,grated/1.25g
- ¼tsp Cinnamon powder/1.25g
- ½tsp grated Nutmeg/2.5g

Directions:
1. Place the hazelnut in a blender and blend until you obtain a paste. Place in the cooker along with the remaining ingredients.
2. Seal the pressure lid, choose Pressure, set to High, and set the time to 15 minutes. Press Start. Once the cooking is over, allow for a natural pressure release, for 10 minutes.

Peach Cobbler

Servings:6
Cooking Time:35 Minutes
Ingredients:
- Nonstick cooking spray
- 5 fresh peaches,peeled,pitted&sliced
- 3 tbsp.Stevia
- 1 tsp coconut flour
- ¼tsp cinnamon
- 1/8 tsp nutmeg
- ½cup almond flour,sifted
- 1 cup oats,ground fine
- 1½tsp baking powder
- ¼cup almond milk,unsweetened
- 1 tsp almond extract
- 2 tbsp.honey

Directions:
1. Place the rack in the cooking pot. Spray an 8-inch baking dish with cooking spray.
2. In a large bowl, toss peaches with Stevia, coconut flour, cinnamon, and nutmeg. Place in prepared baking dish.
3. In a medium bowl, combine almond flour, oats, baking powder, milk, almond extract, and honey, mix well. Drop by large spoonful over the top of the peaches. Place in the cooking pot.
4. Add the tender-crisp lid and set to air fry on 350°F. Bake 35-40 minutes until top is lightly browned. Serve warm.

Nutrition:
- InfoCalories 204,Total Fat 7g,Total Carbs 39g,Protein 7g,Sodium 11mg.

Cheat Apple Pie

Servings:9
Cooking Time:30 Min
Ingredients:
- 4 apples;diced
- 1 egg,beaten
- 3 large puff pastry sheets
- 2 oz.sugar/60g
- 1 oz.brown sugar/30g
- 2 oz.butter,melted/60ml
- 2 tsp cinnamon/10g
- ¼tsp salt/1.25g

Directions:
1. Whisk the white sugar, brown sugar, cinnamon, salt, and butter together. Place the apples in a baking dish and coat them with the mixture.
2. Slide the dish into the Foodi and cook for 10 minutes on Roast at 350°F or 177°C.
3. Meanwhile, roll out the pastry on a floured flat surface, and cut each sheet into 6 equal pieces. Divide the apple filling between the parts.
4. Brush the edges of the pastry squares with the egg. Fold and seal the edges with a fork. Place on a lined baking sheet and cook in the fryer at 350°F or 177°C for 8 minutes on Roast. Flip over, increase the temperature to 390°F or 177°C, and cook for 2 more minutes.

Pecan Apple Crisp

Servings:6
Cooking Time:35 Minutes
Ingredients:
- Butter flavored cooking spray
- 3 apples,peeled&diced
- 1 tbsp.sugar
- 1 3/8 tsp cinnamon,divided
- ¼cup+½tbsp.almond flour,divided
- ½cup oats
- ¼cup pecans,chopped
- 1/8 tsp salt
- 1/8 cup coconut oil,melted
- 1/8 cup honey

Directions:
1. Place the rack in the cooking pot.Spray an 8x8-inch baking pan with cooking spray.
2. In a large bowl,combine apples,sugar,1 teaspoon cinnamon,and½tablespoon almond flour,toss to coat the apples.Pour into prepared pan.
3. In a medium bowl,combine oats,remaining flour,pecans,remaining cinnamon,salt,oil,and honey.Use a fork to mix until mixture resembles fine crumbs.Pour over apples.
4. Place on the rack and add the tender-crisp lid.Set to bake on 350°F.Bake 30-35 minutes,or until apples are tender and topping is golden brown.
5. Transfer to a wire rack to cool slightly before serving.

Nutrition:
- InfoCalories 293,Total Fat 18g,Total Carbs 30g,Protein 7g,Sodium 62mg.

Chocolate Fondue

Servings:12
Cooking Time:5 Min
Ingredients:
- 10 ounces Milk Chocolate;chopped into small pieces/300g
- 1½cups Lukewarm Water/375ml
- 8 ounces Heavy Whipping Cream/240ml
- 2 tsp Coconut Liqueur/60ml
- ¼tsp Cinnamon Powder/1.25g
- A pinch of Salt

Directions:
1. Melt the chocolate in a heat-proof recipient.Add the remaining ingredients,except for the liqueur.Transfer this recipient to the metal reversible rack.Pour 1½cups or 375ml of water into the cooker,and placeareversible rack inside.
2. Seal the pressure lid,choose Pressure,set to High,and set the time to 5 minutes.Press Start.Once the cooking is complete,do a quick pressure release.Pull out the container with tongs.Mix in the coconut liqueur and serve right now.Enjoy!

Strawberry Crumble

Servings:5
Cooking Time:2 Hours
Ingredients:
- 1 cup almond flour
- 2 tablespoons butter,melted
- 10 drops liquid stevia
- 4 cups fresh strawberries,hulled and sliced
- 1 tablespoon butter,chopped

Directions:
1. Lightly,grease the Ninja Foodi's insert.
2. In a suitable,stir in the flour,melted butter and stevia and mix until a crumbly mixture form.
3. In the pot of the prepared Ninja Foodi,place the strawberry slices and dot with chopped butter.
4. Spread the flour mixture on top evenly
5. Close the Ninja Foodi's lid with a crisping lid and select"Slow Cooker".
6. Set on"Low"for 2 hours.
7. Press the"Start/Stop"button to initiate cooking.
8. Place the pan onto a wire rack to cool slightly.
9. Serve warm.

Nutrition:
- InfoCalories:233;Fats:19.2g;Carbohydrates:10.7g;Proteins:0.7g

Coconut Rice Pudding

Servings:6
Cooking Time:8 Minutes
Ingredients:
- ¾cup arborio rice
- 1 can unsweetened full-fat coconut milk
- 1 cup milk
- 1 cup water
- ¾cup granulated sugar
- ½teaspoon vanilla extract

Directions:
1. Rinse the rice under cold running water in a fine-mesh strainer.
2. Place the rice,coconut milk,milk,water,sugar,and vanilla in the pot and stir.Assemble pressure lid,making sure the pressure release valve is in the SEAL position.
3. Select PRESSURE and set to HI.Set time to 8 minutes.Select START/STOP to begin.
4. When pressure cooking is complete,allow pressure to naturally release for 10 minutes.After 10 minutes,quick release remaining pressure by moving the pressure release valve to the VENT position.Carefully remove lid when unit has finished releasing pressure.
5. Press a layer of plastic wrap directly on top of the rice(it should be touching)to prevent a skin from forming on top of the pudding.Let pudding cool to room temperature,then refrigerate overnight to set.

Nutrition:
- InfoCalories:363,Total Fat:18g,Sodium:31mg,Carbohydrates:50g,Protein:5g.

Lime Blueberry Cheesecake

Servings:6
Cooking Time:30 Minutes
Ingredients:
- ¼cup 1 teaspoon Erythritol
- 8 ounces cream cheese,softened
- 1/3 cup Ricotta cheese
- 1 teaspoon fresh lime zest,grated
- 2 tablespoons fresh lime juice
- ½teaspoon vanilla extract
- 1 cup blueberries
- 2 eggs
- 2 tablespoons sour cream

Directions:

Ninja Foodi Cookbook

1. In a suitable, stir in ¼ cup of Erythritol and remaining ingredients except for eggs and sour cream and with a hand mixer, beat on high speed until smooth.
2. Stir in the eggs and beat on low speed until well combined, then fold in blueberries.
3. Transfer the mixture into a 6-inch greased springform pan evenly.
4. With a piece of foil, cover the pan.
5. In the Ninja Foodi's insert, place 2 cups of water.
6. Set a "Reversible Rack" in the Ninja Foodi's insert.
7. Place the springform pan over the "Reversible Rack".
8. Close the Ninja Foodi's lid with a pressure lid and place the pressure valve in the "Seal" position.
9. Select "Pressure" mode and set it to "High" for 30 minutes.
10. Press the "Start/Stop" button to initiate cooking.
11. Switch the pressure valve to "Vent" and do a "Natural" release.
12. Place the pan onto a wire rack to cool slightly.
13. Meanwhile, in a small bowl, stir in the sour cream and remaining erythritol and beat until well combined.
14. Spread the cream mixture on the warm cake evenly.
15. Refrigerate for about 6-8 hours before serving.

Nutrition:
- InfoCalories:182;Fats:16.6g;Carbohydrates:2.1g;Proteins:6.4g

Coconut Cream Dessert Bars

Servings:10
Cooking Time:2 Hour
Ingredients:
- Butter flavored cooking spray
- 1 cup heavy cream
- ¾ cup powdered Stevia
- 4 eggs
- ½ cup coconut milk, full fat
- ¼ cup butter, melted
- 1 cup coconut, unsweetened, grated
- 3 tbsp. coconut flour
- ½ tsp baking powder
- ½ tsp vanilla
- ½ tsp salt

Directions:
1. Spray cooking pot with cooking spray.
2. Place cream, Stevia, and coconut milk in a food processor or blender. Pulse until combined.
3. Add remaining ingredients and pulse until combined.
4. Pour mixture into cooking pot. Place two paper towels over the top. Add the lid and set to slow cooking on high. Cook 1-3 hours or until center is set.
5. Carefully remove lid so no moisture gets on the bars. Transfer cooking pot to a wire rack and let cool 30 minutes.
6. Refrigerate, uncovered at least 1 hour. Cut into 10 squares or bars and serve.

Nutrition:
- InfoCalories 190, Total Fat 17g, Total Carbs 24g, Protein 4g, Sodium 236mg.

Key Lime Pie

Servings:8
Cooking Time:15 Minutes
Ingredients:
- 1 cup water
- Butter flavored cooking spray
- ¾ cup graham-cracker crumbs
- 3 tbsp. butter, unsalted, melted
- 1 tbsp. sugar
- 14 oz. sweetened condensed milk
- 4 egg yolks
- ½ cup fresh key lime juice*
- 1/3 cup sour cream
- 2 tbsp. key lime zest, grated

Directions:
1. Place the trivet in the cooking pot and add the water. Spray a 7-inch springform pan with cooking spray.
2. In a small bowl, combine cracker crumbs, butter, and sugar, mix well. Press evenly on the bottom and up sides of the pan. Freeze 10 minutes.
3. In a large bowl, beat egg yolks until they are light yellow.
4. Slowly beat in condensed milk until thickened.
5. Slowly beat in lime juice until smooth. Stir in sour cream and zest until combined. Pour into crust. Cover tightly with foil and place on the trivet.
6. Secure the lid and set to pressure cooking on high. Set timer for 15 minutes. When timer goes off, use natural release to remove the lid. Pie is done when the middle is set, if not done, cook another 5 minutes.
7. Transfer to wire rack and remove foil to cool. Wrap with plastic wrap and refrigerate at least 4 hours before serving.

Nutrition:
- InfoCalories 246, Total Fat 11g, Total Carbs 32g, Protein 6g, Sodium 92mg.

Fried Snickerdoodle Poppers

Servings:6
Cooking Time:30 Min
Ingredients:
- 1 box instant vanilla Jell-O
- 1½ cups cinnamon sugar/195g
- 1 can of Pillsbury Grands Flaky Layers Biscuits
- Melted butter, for brushing

Directions:
1. Unroll the flaky biscuits and cut them into fourths. Roll each ¼ into a ball. Arrange the balls on a lined baking sheet, and cook in the Foodi for 7 minutes, or until golden, on Air Crisp mode at 350°F or 177°C.
2. Prepare the Jell-O following the package's instructions. Using an injector, inject some of the vanilla pudding into each ball. Brush the balls with melted butter and then coat them with cinnamon sugar.

Chocolate Peanut Butter And Jelly Puffs

Servings:4
Cooking Time:15 Minutes
Ingredients:
- 1 tube prepared flaky biscuit dough
- 2 milk chocolate bars
- Cooking spray
- 16 teaspoons (about ⅓ cup) creamy peanut butter
- 1 cup confectioners' sugar
- 1 tablespoon whole milk
- ¼ cup raspberry jam

Directions:
1. Remove biscuits from tube. There is a natural widthwise separation in each biscuit. Gently peel each biscuit in half using this separation.

2. Break the chocolate into 16 small pieces.
3. Spray a baking sheet with cooking spray.
4. Using your hands,stretch a biscuit half until it is about 3-inches in diameter.Place a teaspoon of peanut butter in center of each biscuit half,then place piece of chocolate on top.Pull an edge of dough over the top of the chocolate and pinch together to seal.Continue pulling the dough over the top of the chocolate and pinching until the chocolate is completely covered.The dough is pliable,so gently form it into a ball with your hands.Place on the prepared baking sheet.Repeat this step with the remaining biscuit dough,peanut butter,and chocolate.
5. Place the baking sheet in the refrigerator for 5 minutes.
6. Place Cook&Crisp Basket in pot.Close crisping lid.Select AIR CRISP,set temperature to 360°F,and set time to 20 minutes.Select START/STOP to begin.Let preheat for 5 minutes.
7. Remove the biscuits from the refrigerator and spray the tops with cooking spray.Open lid and spray the basket with cooking spray.Place 5 biscuit balls in the basket.Close lid and cook for 5 minutes.
8. When cooking is complete,remove the biscuit balls from the basket.Repeat step 7 two more times with remaining biscuit balls.
9. Mix together the confectioners'sugar,milk,and jam in a small bowl to make a frosting.
10. When the cooked biscuit balls are cool enough to handle,dunk the top of each into the frosting.As frosting is beginning to set,garnish with any toppings desired,such as sprinkles,crushed toffee or candy,or mini marshmallows.

Nutrition:
- InfoCalories:663,Total Fat:25g,Sodium:1094mg,Carbohydrates:101g,Protein:14g.

Lemon And Blueberries Compote

Servings:4
Cooking Time:10 Min+Chilling Time
Ingredients:
- 2 cups Blueberries/260g
- ½cup Water+2 tbsp./155ml
- ¾cups Coconut Sugar/98g
- 2 tbsp Cornstarch/30g
- Juice of½Lemon

Directions:
1. Place blueberries,lemon juice,½cup or 125ml water,and coconut sugar in your cooker.Seal the pressure lid,choose Steam and set the timer to 3 minutes at High pressure.Press Start.Once done,do a quick pressure.
2. Meanwhile,combine the cornstarch and water,inabowl.Stir in the mixture into the blueberries and cook until the mixture thickens,pressure lid off,on Sear/Sauté.Transfer the compote to a bowl and let cool completely before refrigerating for 2 hours.

Strawberry And Lemon Ricotta Cheesecake

Servings:6
Cooking Time:35 Min
Ingredients:
- 10 strawberries,halved to decorate
- 10 oz.cream cheese/300g
- 1½cups water/375ml
- ¼cup sugar/32.5f
- ½cup Ricotta cheese/65f
- One lemon,zested and juiced
- 2 eggs,cracked into a bowl
- 3 tbsp sour cream/45ml
- 1 tsp lemon extract/5g

Directions:
1. In the electric mixer,add the cream cheese,quarter cup of sugar,ricotta cheese,lemon zest,lemon juice,and lemon extract.Turn on the mixer and mix the ingredients untilasmooth consistency is formed.Adjust the sweet taste to liking with more sugar.
2. Reduce the speed of the mixer and add the eggs.Fold it in at low speed until it is fully incorporated.Make sure not to fold the eggs in high speed to prevent a cracker crust.Grease the spring form pan with cooking spray and useaspatula to spoon the mixture into the pan.Level the top with the spatula and cover it with foil.
3. Open the Foodi,fit in the reversible rack,and pour in the water.Place the cake pan on the rack.Close the lid,secure the pressure valve,and select Pressure mode on High pressure for 15 minutes.Press Start/Stop.
4. Meanwhile,mix the sour cream and one tbsp of sugar.Set aside.Once the timer has gone off,do a natural pressure release for 10 minutes,thenaquick pressure release to let out any extra steam,and open the lid.
5. Remove the rack with pan,place the spring form pan on a flat surface,and open it.Useaspatula to spread the sour cream mixture on the warm cake.Refrigerate the cake for 8 hours.Top with strawberries;slice it into 6 pieces and serve while firming.

Churro Bites

Servings:7
Cooking Time:12 Minutes
Ingredients:
- Cooking spray
- 1 box cinnamon swirl crumb cake and muffin mix,brown sugar mix packet removed and reserved
- 2 large eggs
- 1 cup buttermilk
- 1 teaspoon ground cinnamon,divided
- ¼cup packed light brown sugar
- 1½cups water
- 1 tablespoon granulated sugar
- Chocolate sauce,for serving(optional)
- Caramel sauce,for serving(optional)
- Strawberry sauce,for serving(optional)
- Whipped topping,for serving(optional)
- Peanut butter,for serving(optional)

Directions:
1. Lightly coat 2 egg bite molds with cooking spray and set aside.
2. In a large bowl,combine the cake mix,brown sugar mix packet,eggs,buttermilk,and½teaspoon of cinnamon.Mix until evenly combined.
3. Using a cookie scoop,transfer the batter to the prepared mold,filling each three-quarters full.Tightly cover the molds with aluminum foil,or with the silicone cover that came with the egg molds.
4. Pour the water into the cooking pot.Place the egg molds onto the Reversible Rack in the lower steam position and lower into the pot.
5. If using a foil sling(see TIP),ensure the foil cover is tight enough to support the egg mold that will sit on

top. Rotate the top egg mold slightly to ensure that the molds do not press into one another.
6. Assemble the pressure lid, making sure the pressure release valve is in the SEAL position.
7. Select PRESSURE and set to HI. Set the time to 12 minutes. Select START/STOP to begin.
8. When pressure cooking is complete, allow the pressure to naturally release for 10 minutes. After 10 minutes, quick release any remaining pressure by moving the pressure release valve to the VENT position. Carefully remove the lid when the unit has finished releasing pressure.
9. In a small bowl, stir together the brown sugar, granulated sugar, and remaining ½ teaspoon of cinnamon. Set aside.
10. Using the sling, remove the egg molds from the pot and let cool for 5 minutes.
11. One at a time, place a plate over the egg mold and flip the mold over. Gently press on the mold to release the churro bites.
12. Roll the warm churro bites in the brown sugar mixture, and sprinkle any remaining brown sugar on top. Serve with your favorite dipping sauce.

Nutrition:
- Info.

Coconut Cream "custard" Bars

Servings: 8
Cooking Time: 20 Minutes

Ingredients:
- 1¼ cups all-purpose flour
- 6 tablespoons unsalted butter, melted
- 2 tablespoons granulated sugar
- ½ cup unsweetened shredded coconut, divided
- ½ cup chopped almonds, divided
- Cooking spray
- 1 package instant vanilla pudding
- 1 cup milk
- 1 cup heavy (whipping) cream
- 4 tablespoons finely chopped dark chocolate, divided

Directions:
1. Select BAKE/ROAST, set temperature to 375°F, and set time to 15 minutes. Select START/STOP to begin. Let preheat for 5 minutes.
2. To make the crust, combine the flour, butter, sugar, ¼ cup of coconut, and ¼ cup of almonds in a large bowl and stir until a crumbly dough forms.
3. Grease the Ninja Multi-Purpose Pan or an 8-inch round baking dish with cooking spray. Place the dough in the pan and press it into an even layer covering the bottom.
4. Once unit has preheated, place pan on Reversible Rack, making sure the rack is in the lower position. Open lid and place rack in pot. Close crisping lid. Reduce temperature to 325°F.
5. Place remaining ¼ cup each of almonds and coconut in a Ninja Loaf Pan or any small loaf pan and set aside.
6. When cooking is complete, remove rack with pan and let cool for 10 minutes.
7. Quickly place the loaf pan with coconut and almonds in the bottom of the pot. Close crisping lid.
8. Select AIR CRISP, set temperature to 350°F, and set time to 10 minutes. Select START/STOP to begin.
9. While the nuts and coconut toast, whisk together the instant pudding with the milk, cream, and 3 tablespoons of chocolate.
10. After 5 minutes, open lid and stir the coconut and almonds. Close lid and continue cooking for another 5 minutes.
11. When cooking is complete, open lid and remove pan from pot. Add the almonds and coconut to the pudding. Stir until fully incorporated. Pour this in a smooth, even layer on top of the crust.
12. Refrigerate for about 10 minutes. Garnish with the remaining 1 tablespoon of chocolate, cut into wedges, and serve.

Nutrition:
- InfoCalories: 476, Total Fat: 33g, Sodium: 215mg, Carbohydrates: 39g, Protein: 6g.

Flourless Chocolate Cake

Servings: 8
Cooking Time: 40 Minutes

Ingredients:
- Unsalted butter, at room temperature, for greasing the pan
- 9½ tablespoons unsalted butter, melted and cooled
- 4 large eggs, whites and yolks separated
- 1 cup granulated sugar, divided
- ½ cup unsweetened cocoa powder
- ¼ teaspoon vanilla extract
- ¼ teaspoon sea salt
- 1 cup plus 2 tablespoons semisweet chocolate chips, melted
- OPTIONAL TOPPINGS:
- Whipped cream
- Fruit sauce

Directions:
1. Grease a Ninja Multi-Purpose Pan or an 8-inch baking pan with butter and line the pan with a circle of parchment paper. Grease the parchment paper with butter.
2. Close crisping lid. Select BAKE/ROAST, set temperature to 350°F, and set time to 5 minutes. Select START/STOP to begin preheating.
3. In a large bowl, beat the melted butter and egg yolks. Add ½ cup of sugar, cocoa powder, vanilla extract, and salt. Slowly add the melted chocolate and stir.
4. In a medium bowl, beat the egg whites until soft peaks form. Add the remaining ½ cup of sugar and beat until stiff peaks form.
5. Gently fold the egg white mixture into the chocolate mixture. Pour the batter into the prepared pan.
6. When unit has preheated, place pan on Reversible Rack, making sure the rack is in the lower position. Open lid and place rack with pan in pot. Close crisping lid.
7. Select BAKE/ROAST, set temperature to 350°F, and set time to 40 minutes. Select START/STOP to begin.
8. After 30 minutes, check for doneness. If a toothpick inserted into the cake comes out clean, the cake is done. If not, close lid and continue baking until done.
9. When cooking is complete, carefully remove pan from pot and place it on a cooling rack for 5 minutes, then serve.

Nutrition:
- InfoCalories: 437, Total Fat: 29g, Sodium: 109mg, Carbohydrates: 49g, Protein: 7g.

Cranberry Almond Rice Pudding

Servings: 6
Cooking Time: 40 Minutes
Ingredients:
- 1 tbsp. almonds
- 1 cup brown rice, short grain
- 2½ cups almond milk, unsweetened
- 1 tbsp. Stevia
- 2 tsp vanilla
- ½ tsp cinnamon
- ¼ cup dried cranberries, chopped

Directions:
1. Set cooker to sauté on low heat. Add almonds and toast 3-5 minutes. Transfer to cutting board and chop.
2. Increase heat to med-high. Add the rice, milk, Stevia, and vanilla and stir to mix. Bring to a boil stirring frequently.
3. Reduce heat to low and simmer, 35-40 minutes or until rice is cooked through.
4. To serve, ladle into bowls or dessert dishes. Sprinkle with cinnamon and top with almonds and cranberries.

Nutrition:
- InfoCalories 200, Total Fat 4g, Total Carbs 36g, Protein 6g, Sodium 49mg.

Mini Vanilla Cheesecakes

Servings: 4
Cooking Time: 10 Minutes
Ingredients:
- ¾ cup Erythritol
- 2 eggs
- 1 teaspoon vanilla extract
- ½ teaspoon fresh lemon juice
- 16 ounces cream cheese, softened
- 2 tablespoon sour cream

Directions:
1. Set the "Air Crisp Basket" in the Ninja Foodi's insert.
2. Close the Ninja Foodi's lid with a crisping lid and select "Air Crisp".
3. Set its cooking temperature to 350°F for 5 minutes.
4. Press the "Start/Stop" button to initiate preheating.
5. In a blender, stir in the Erythritol, eggs, vanilla extract and lemon juice and pulse until smooth.
6. Stir in the cream cheese along with sour cream and pulse until smooth.
7. Stir in the mixture into 2-4-inch springform pans evenly.
8. After preheating, Open the Ninja Foodi's lid.
9. Place the pans into the "Air Crisp Basket".
10. Close the Ninja Foodi's lid with a crisping lid and select "Air Crisp".
11. Set its cooking temperature to 350°F for 10 minutes.
12. Press the "Start/Stop" button to initiate cooking.
13. Place the pans onto a wire rack for 10 minutes.
14. Refrigerator overnight before serving.

Nutrition:
- InfoCalories: 436; Fats: 21g; Carbohydrates: 3.2g; Proteins: 13.1g

Pumpkin Crème Brulee

Servings: 4
Cooking Time: 3:00 Hours
Ingredients:
- 1 egg yolk
- 1 egg, lightly beaten
- ¾ cup heavy cream
- 4 tbsp. pumpkin puree
- 1 tsp vanilla
- 4 tbsp. sugar, divided
- ¾ tsp pumpkin pie spice

Directions:
1. In a medium bowl, whisk together egg yolk and beaten egg, mix well.
2. Whisk in cream, slowly until combined.
3. Stir in pumpkin and vanilla and mix until combined.
4. In a small bowl, stir together 2 tablespoons sugar and pie spice. Add to pumpkin mixture and stir to blend.
5. Fill 4 small ramekins with mixture and place in the cooking pot. Carefully pour water around the ramekins, it should reach halfway up the sides.
6. Add the lid and set to slow cooking on low. Cook 2-3 hours or until custard is set.
7. Sprinkle remaining 2 tablespoons over the top of the custards. Add the tender-crisp lid and set to broil on 450°F. Cook another 2-3 minutes or until sugar caramelizes, be careful not to let it burn. Transfer ramekins to wire rack to cool before serving.

Nutrition:
- InfoCalories 334, Total Fat 21g, Total Carbs 30g, Protein 6g, Sodium 59mg.

Filling Coconut And Oat Cookies

Servings: 4
Cooking Time: 30 Min
Ingredients:
- 5½ oz. flour/165g
- 3 oz. sugar/90g
- 1 small egg, beaten
- ¼ cup coconut flakes/32.5g
- ½ cup oats/65g
- 1 tsp vanilla extract/5ml
- Filling:
- 4 oz. powdered sugar/120g
- 1 oz. white chocolate, melted/30ml
- 2 oz. butter/60g
- 1 tsp vanilla extract/5ml

Directions:
1. Beat all cookie ingredients, with an electric mixer, except the flour. When smooth, fold in the flour. Drop spoonfuls of the batter onto a prepared cookie sheet. Close the crisping lid and cook in the Foodi at 350°F or 177°C for about 18 minutes on Air Crisp mode; let cool.
2. Prepare the filling by beating all ingredients together. Spread the mixture on half of the cookies. Top with the other halves to make cookie sandwiches.

Vanilla Hot Lava Cake

Servings: 8
Cooking Time: 40 Min
Ingredients:
- 1½ cups chocolate chips/195g
- 1½ cups sugar/195g
- 1 cup butter/130g
- 1 cup water/250ml
- 5 eggs
- 7 tbsp flour/105g

- 4 tbsp milk/60ml
- 4 tsp vanilla extract/20ml
- Powdered sugar to garnish

Directions:
1. Grease the cake pan with cooking spray and set aside.Open the Foodi,fit the reversible rack at the bottom of it,and pour in the water.Inamedium heatproof bowl,add the butter and chocolate and melt them in the microwave for about 2 minutes.Remove it from the microwave.
2. Add sugar and use a spatula to stir it well.Add the eggs,milk,and vanilla extract and stir again.Finally,add the flour and stir it until even and smooth.
3. Pour the batter into the greased cake pan and use the spatula to level it.Place the pan on the trivet in the pot,close the lid,secure the pressure valve,and select Pressure on High for 15 minutes.Press Start/Stop.
4. Once the timer has gone off,doanatural pressure release for 10 minutes,then a quick pressure release,and open the lid.
5. Remove the rack with the pan on it and place the pan onaflat surface.Put a plate over the pan and flip the cake over into the plate.Pour the powdered sugar inafine sieve and sift it over the cake.Use a knife to cut the cake into 8 slices and serve immediately(while warm).

Peanut Butter Pie

Servings:8
Cooking Time:30 Minutes
Ingredients:
- 10 peanut butter cookies,crushed
- 3 tablespoons unsalted butter,melted
- 2 packages cream cheese,at room temperature
- ¾cup granulated sugar
- 2 eggs
- ⅓cup creamy peanut butter
- 10 chocolate peanut butter cups,chopped
- 2 cups water
- 1 tub whipped cream topping

Directions:
1. In a small bowl,mix together peanut butter cookie crumbs and melted butter.Press the mixture into the bottom of the Ninja Multi-Purpose Pan or 8-inch baking dish.
2. In a medium bowl,use an electric hand mixer to combine the cream cheese,sugar,eggs,and peanut butter.Mix on medium speed for 5 minutes.
3. Place the chopped chocolate peanut butter cups evenly on top of crust in the pan.Pour the batter on top.Cover tightly with aluminum foil.
4. Place the water in the pot.Insert Reversible Rack into pot,making sure it is on the lower position.Place covered multipurpose pan onto rack.Assemble pressure lid,making sure the pressure release valve is in the SEAL position.
5. Select PRESSURE and set to HI.Set time to 25 minutes.Press START/STOP to begin.
6. When pressure cooking is complete,allow pressure to naturally release for 15 minutes.After 15 minutes,quick release remaining pressure by moving the pressure release valve to the VENT position.Carefully remove lid when unit has finished releasing pressure.
7. Remove the pan and chill in the refrigerator for at least 3 hours or overnight before serving topped with whipped cream.

Nutrition:
- InfoCalories:645,Total Fat:47g,Sodium:383mg,Carbohydrates:48g,Protein:13g.

Vanilla Pound Cake

Servings:8
Cooking Time:45 Minutes
Ingredients:
- Nonstick cooking spray
- 1 cup butter,unsalted,soft
- 1 cup sugar
- 4 eggs
- 2 tsp vanilla
- ½tsp salt
- 2 cups flour

Directions:
1. Add the rack to the cooking pot.Spray a loaf pan with cooking spray.
2. In a large bowl,on high speed,beat butter and sugar until fluffy.
3. Beat in eggs,one at a time,until combined.Stir in vanilla and salt.
4. Turn mixer to low and add flour a 1/3 at a time.Beat just until combined.Pour into prepared pan.
5. Place the pan on the rack and add the tender-crisp lid.Set to bake on 350°F.Bake 45-50 minutes or until cake passes the toothpick test.
6. Let cool in pan 15 minutes then invert onto a wire rack and let cool completely.

Nutrition:
- InfoCalories 389,Total Fat 18g,Total Carbs 49g,Protein 7g,Sodium 192mg.

Blueberry Peach Crisp

Servings:8
Cooking Time:40 Minutes
Ingredients:
- 1 cup blueberries
- 6 peaches,peeled,cored&cut in½-inch pieces
- ½cup+3 tbsp.flour
- ¾cups Stevia,divided
- ½tsp cinnamon
- ¼tsp salt,divided
- Zest&juice of 1 lemon
- 1 cup oats
- 1/3 cup coconut oil,melted

Directions:
1. Place the rack in the cooking pot.
2. In a large bowl,combine blueberries,peaches,3 tablespoons flour,¼cup Stevia,cinnamon,and 1/8 teaspoon salt,toss to coat fruit.Stir in lemon zest and juice just until combined.Pour into an 8-inch baking dish.
3. In a medium bowl,combine oats,½cup Stevia,coconut oil,remaining flour and salt and mix with a fork until crumbly.Sprinkle over the top of the fruit.
4. Place the dish on the rack and add the tender-crisp lid.Set to bake on 350°F.Bake 35-40 minutes until filling is bubbly and top is golden brown.Serve warm.

Nutrition:
- InfoCalories 265,Total Fat 11g,Total Carbs 44g,Protein 6g,Sodium 74mg.

Molten Lava Cake

Servings:4
Cooking Time:20 Min
Ingredients:
- 3½oz.butter,melted/105ml
- 3½oz.dark chocolate,melted/105ml
- 2 eggs
- 3½tbsp sugar/52.5g
- 1½tbsp self-rising flour/22.5g

Directions:
1. Grease 4 ramekins with butter.Beat the eggs and sugar until frothy.Stir in the butter and chocolate.
2. Gently fold in the flour.Divide the mixture between the ramekins and bake in the Foodi for 10 minutes on Air Crisp mode at 370°F or 188°C.Let cool for 2 minutes before turning the lava cakes upside down onto serving plates.

Rhubarb,Raspberry,And Peach Cobbler

Servings:6
Cooking Time:40 Minutes
Ingredients:
- 1 cup all-purpose flour,divided
- ¾cup granulated sugar
- ½teaspoon kosher salt,divided
- 2½cups diced fresh rhubarb
- 2½cups fresh raspberries
- 2½cups fresh peaches,peeled and sliced into¾-inch pieces
- Cooking spray
- ¾cup brown sugar
- ½cup oat flakes(oatmeal)
- 1 teaspoon cinnamon
- Pinch ground nutmeg
- 6 tablespoons unsalted butter,sliced,at room temperature
- ½cup chopped pecans or walnuts

Directions:
1. Select BAKE/ROAST,set temperature to 400°F,and set time to 30 minutes.Select START/STOP to begin.Let preheat for 5 minutes.
2. In a large bowl,whisk together¼cup of flour,granulated sugar,and¼teaspoon of salt.Add the rhubarb,raspberries,and peach and mix until evenly coated.
3. Grease a Ninja Multi-Purpose Pan or a 1½-quart round ceramic baking dish with cooking spray.Add the fruit mixture to the pan.
4. Place pan on Reversible Rack,making sure the rack is in the lower position.Cover pan with aluminum foil.
5. Once unit has preheated,place rack in pot.Close crisping lid and adjust temperature to 375°F.Cook for 25 minutes.
6. In a medium bowl,combine the remaining¾cup of flour,brown sugar,oat flakes,cinnamon,remaining¼teaspoon of salt,nutmeg,butter,and pecans.Mix well.
7. When cooking is complete,open lid.Remove the foil and stir the fruit.Spread the topping evenly over the fruit.Close crisping lid.
8. Select BAKE/ROAST,set temperature to 400°F,and set time to 15 minutes.Select START/STOP to begin.Cook until the topping is browned and the fruit is bubbling.
9. When cooking is complete,remove rack with pan from pot and serve.

Nutrition:
- InfoCalories:476,Total Fat:19g,Sodium:204mg,Carbohydrates:76g,Protein:6g.

Almond Banana Dessert

Servings:1
Cooking Time:8 Min
Ingredients:
- 1 Banana;sliced
- 2 tbsp Almond Butter/30g
- 1 tbsp Coconut oil/15ml
- ½tsp Cinnamon/2.5g

Directions:
1. Melt oil on Sear/Sautémode.Add banana slices and fry them for a couple of minutes,or until golden on both sides.Top the fried bananas with almond butter and sprinkle with cinnamon.

Buttery Cranberry Cake

Servings:8
Cooking Time:40 Minutes
Ingredients:
- Butter flavored cooking spray
- 2 eggs
- 1 cup sugar
- 3/8 cup butter,softened
- ½tsp vanilla
- 1 cup flour
- 6 oz.fresh cranberries

Directions:
1. Set cooker to bake on 350°F.Spray an 8-inch baking pan with cooking spray.
2. In a large bowl,beat eggs and sugar until light in color and slightly thickened,about 5-7 minutes.
3. Add butter and vanilla and continue beating another 2 minutes.
4. Stir in flour just until combined.Gently fold in cranberries.
5. Spread batter in prepared pan and place in the cooking pot.Add the tender-crisp lid and bake 35-40 minutes or until the cake passes the toothpick test.
6. Remove from cooker and let cool in pan 10 minutes before transferring to a wire rack to cool completely.

Nutrition:
- InfoCalories 259,Total Fat 10g,Total Carbs 40g,Protein 3g,Sodium 88mg.

Carrot Raisin Cookie Bars

Servings:16
Cooking Time:15 Minutes
Ingredients:
- Butter flavored cooking spray
- ½cup brown sugar
- ½cup sugar
- ½cup coconut oil,melted
- ½cup applesauce,unsweetened
- 2 eggs
- 1 tsp vanilla
- ½cup almond flour
- 1 tsp baking soda
- 1 tsp baking powder
- ¼tsp salt
- 1 tsp cinnamon
- ½tsp nutmeg

- ½tsp ginger
- 2 cups oats
- 1½cups carrots,finely grated
- 1 cup raisins

Directions:
1. Place the rack in the cooking pot.Spray an 8x8-inch pan with cooking spray.
2. In a large bowl,combine sugars,oil,applesauce,eggs,and vanilla,mix well.
3. Stir in dry ingredients until combined.Fold in carrots and raisins.Press evenly in prepared pan.
4. Place the pan on the rack and add the tender-crisp lid.Set to bake on 350°F.Bake 12-15 minutes or until golden brown and cooked through.
5. Remove to wire rack to cool before cutting and serving.

Nutrition:
- InfoCalories 115,Total Fat 7g,Total Carbs 19g,Protein 3g,Sodium 56mg.

Banana Coconut Pudding

Servings:8
Cooking Time:10 Minutes
Ingredients:
- ¼cup cornstarch
- ¼tsp salt
- 1/3 cup honey
- 2 egg yolks,lightly beaten
- 1½cups lite coconut milk,canned
- 1 teaspoon vanilla extract
- ½cup coconut flakes,unsweetened
- 2 bananas,sliced½-inch thick

Directions:
1. Add the cornstarch and salt to the cooking pot and stir to mix.
2. Whisk in honey and egg yolks until combined.
3. Set to sautéon med-low heat.Slowly whisk in milk until combined.
4. Cook,stirring constantly,8-10 minutes or until pudding reaches desired thickness.
5. Remove from heat and stir in coconut and vanilla.Layer pudding and banana slices in dessert dishes.Let cool 15 minutes before serving.

Nutrition:
- InfoCalories 212,Total Fat 12g,Total Carbs 26g,Protein 2g,Sodium 97mg.

Mixed Berry Cobbler

Servings:4
Cooking Time:40 Min
Ingredients:
- 2 bags frozen mixed berries
- 1 cup sugar/130g
- 3 tbsps arrowroot starch/45g
- For the topping
- 1 cup self-rising flour/130g
- ⅔cup crème fraiche,plus more as needed/177ml
- 1 tbsp melted unsalted butter/15ml
- 1 tbsp whipping cream/15ml
- 5 tbsps powdered sugar;divided/75g
- ¼tsp cinnamon powder/1.25g

Directions:
1. To make the base,pour the blackberries into the inner pot along with the arrowroot starch and sugar.Mix to combine.Seal the pressure lid,choose Pressure;adjust the pressure to High and the cook time to 3 minutes;press Start.After cooking,perform a quick pressure release and carefully open the lid.
2. To make the topping,inasmall bowl,whisk the flour,cinnamon powder,and 3 tbsps of sugar.In a separate small bowl,whisk the crème fraiche with the melted butter.
3. Pour the cream mixture on the dry ingredients and combine evenly.If the mixture is too dry,mix in 1 tbsp of crème fraiche atatime until the mixture is soft.
4. Spoon 2 to 3 tbsps of dough on top over the peaches and spread out slightly on top.Brush the topping with the whipping cream and sprinkle with the remaining sugar.
5. Close the crisping lid and Choose Bake/Roast;adjust the temperature to 325°F or 163°Cand the cook time to 12 minutes.Press Start.Check after 8 minutes;if the dough isn't cooking evenly,rotate the pot about 90,and continue cooking.
6. When ready,the topping should be cooked through and lightly browned.Allow cooling before slicing.Serve warm.

Tres Leches Cake

Servings:8
Cooking Time:38 Minutes
Ingredients:
- 1 box of yellow cake mix
- Cooking spray
- 1 can evaporated milk
- 1 can sweetened condensed milk
- 1 cup heavy(whipping)cream

Directions:
1. Close crisping lid.Select BAKE/ROAST,set temperature to 400°F,and set time to 43 minutes.Select START/STOP to begin.Let preheat for 5 minutes.
2. Prepare the cake batter according to the box instructions.
3. Grease a Ninja Multi-Purpose Pan or a 1½-quart round baking dish with cooking spray.Pour the batter into the pan.Place the pan on Reversible Rack,making sure rack is in the lower position.
4. Once unit has preheated,open lid and place rack with pan in pot.Close lid,and reduce temperature to 315°F.Cook for 38 minutes.
5. In a medium bowl whisk together the evaporated milk,condensed milk,and heavy cream.
6. When cooking is complete,remove rack with pan from pot and let cool for 10 minutes.
7. Remove pan from the rack.Using a long-pronged fork,poke holes every inch or so across the surface of the cake.Slowly pour the milk mixture over the cake.Refrigerate for 1 hour.
8. Once the cake has cooled and absorbed the milk mixture,slice and serve.If desired,top with whipped cream and strawberries.

Nutrition:
- InfoCalories:644,Total Fat:28g,Sodium:574mg,Carbohydrates:89g,Protein:12g.

Milk Dumplings In Sweet Sauce

Servings:20
Cooking Time:30 Min
Ingredients:
- 2½cups Sugar/325g
- 6 cups Milk/1500ml
- 6 cups Water/1500ml

- 3 tbsp Lime Juice/45ml
- 1 tsp ground Cardamom/5g

Directions:
1. Bring toaboil the milk,on Sear/Sauté,and stir in the lime juice.The solids should start to separate.Pour milk through a cheesecloth-lined colander.Drain as much liquid as you can.Place the paneer onasmooth surface.Form a ball and divide into 20 equal pieces.
2. Pour water in the Foofi and bring toaboil on Sear/Sauté.Add in sugar and cardamom and cook until dissolved.Shape the dumplings into balls,and place them in the syrup.
3. Seal the pressure lid and choose Pressure,set to High,and set the time to 5 minutes.Press Start.Once done,do a quick pressure release.Let cool and refrigerate for at least 2 hours.

Yogurt Cheesecake

Servings:8
Cooking Time:40 Minutes
Ingredients:
- 4 cups plain Greek Yogurt
- 1 cup Erythritol
- ½teaspoon vanilla extract

Directions:
1. Line a cake pans with Parchment paper.
2. In a suitable,stir in the yogurt and Erythritol and with a hand mixer,mix well.
3. Stir in vanilla extract and mix to combine.
4. Add the mixture into the prepared pan and cover with a paper kitchen towel.
5. Then with a piece of foil,cover the pan tightly.
6. In the Ninja Foodi's insert,place 1 cup of water.
7. Set a"Reversible Rack"in the Ninja Foodi's insert.
8. Place the ramekins over the"Reversible Rack".
9. Close the Ninja Foodi's lid with a pressure lid and place the pressure valve to the"Seal"position.
10. Select"Pressure"mode and set it to"High"for 40 minutes.
11. Press the"Start/Stop"button to initiate cooking.
12. Switch the pressure valve to"Vent"and do a"Quick"release.
13. Place the pan onto a wire rack and remove the foil and paper towel.
14. Again,cover the pan with a new paper towel and refrigerate to cool overnight.

Nutrition:
- InfoCalories:88;Fats:1.5g;Carbohydrates:8.7g;Proteins:7g

Brownie Bites

Servings:10
Cooking Time:45 Minutes
Ingredients:
- Cooking spray
- 1 box brownie mix,prepared to package instructions
- Confectioners'sugar,for garnish
- Carmel sauce,for garnish

Directions:
1. Coat a silicone egg mold with nonstick cooking spray and set aside.
2. In a large bowl,prepare the brownie mix according to package instructions.Using a cookie scoop,transfer the batter to the prepared mold.
3. Place 1 cup water in the pot.Place the filled molds onto the Reversible Rack in the lower steam position,and lower into the pot.
4. Assemble the pressure lid,making sure the pressure release valve is in the SEAL position.
5. Select PRESSURE and set to HI.Set the time to 45 minutes.Select START/STOP to begin.
6. When pressure cooking is complete,allow the pressure to naturally release for 10 minutes.After 10 minutes,quick release any remaining pressure by moving the pressure release valve to the VENT position.Carefully remove the lid when the unit has finished releasing pressure.
7. Carefully remove the mold from the cooker and let cool for 5 minutes.
8. Flip the brownie onto a plate and garnish with confectioners'sugar and caramel sauce.

Nutrition:
- InfoCalories:288,Total Fat:5g,Sodium:168mg,Carbohydrates:43g,Protein:2g.

Red Velvet Cheesecake

Servings:8
Cooking Time:25 Minutes
Ingredients:
- 2 cups Oreo cookie crumbs
- 3 tablespoons unsalted butter,melted
- 2 packages cream cheese,at room temperature
- ½cup granulated sugar
- ½cup buttermilk
- 2 tablespoons unsweetened cocoa powder
- 1 teaspoon vanilla extract
- 2 tablespoons red food coloring
- ½teaspoon white vinegar
- 1 cup water

Directions:
1. In a small bowl,combine the cookie crumbs and butter.Press this mixture into the bottom of the Ninja Multi-Purpose Pan or 8-inch baking pan.
2. In a large bowl,use an electric hand mixer to combine the cream cheese,sugar,buttermilk,cocoa powder,vanilla,food coloring,and vinegar for 3 minutes.Pour this over the cookie crust.Cover the pan tightly with aluminum foil.
3. Place the water in the pot.Insert Reversible Rack into pot,making sure it is in the lower position.Place the covered multi-purpose pan onto the rack.Assemble pressure lid,making sure the pressure release valve is in the SEAL position.
4. Select PRESSURE on HI.Set time to 25 minutes.Press START/STOP to begin.
5. When pressure cooking is complete,allow pressure to naturally release for 15 minutes.After 15 minutes,quick release remaining pressure by moving the pressure release valve to the VENT position.Carefully remove lid when unit has finished releasing pressure.
6. Remove cheesecake from the pot.Refrigerate for 3 hours,or overnight if possible before serving.

Nutrition:
- InfoCalories:437,Total Fat:31g,Sodium:338mg,Carbohydrates:36g,Protein:7g.

Cranberry Cheesecake

Servings: 8
Cooking Time: 1 Hr
Ingredients:
- 1/3 cup dried cranberries/44g
- 1 cup water/250ml
- ½ cup sugar/65g
- 1 cup coarsely crumbled cookies/130g
- 1 cup mascarpone cheese, room temperature/130g
- 2 eggs, room temperature
- 2 tbsp sour cream/30ml
- 2 tbsp butter, melted/30ml
- ½ tsp vanilla extract/2.5ml

Directions:
1. Fold a 20-inch piece of aluminum foil in half lengthwise twice and set on the pressure cooker. In a bowl, combine melted butter and crushed cookies; press firmly to the bottom and about 1/3 of the way up the sides of a 7-inch springform pan. Freeze the crust while the filling is being prepared.
2. In a separate bowl, beat together mascarpone cheese and sugar to obtain a smooth consistency; stir in vanilla extract and sour cream. Beat one egg and add into the cheese mixture to combine well; do the same with the second egg.
3. Stir cranberries into the filling. Transfer the filling into the crust. Into the pot, add water and set the reversible rack at the bottom. Center the springform pan onto the prepared foil sling. Use the sling to lower the pan onto the reversible rack.
4. Fold foil strips out of the way of the lid. Close the crisping lid and select Bake/Roast; adjust the temperature to 250°F or 122°C and the cook time to 40 minutes. Press Start.
5. When the time is up, open the lid and let to cool the cheesecake. When, transfer the cheesecake to a refrigerator for 2 hours or overnight.
6. Use a paring knife to run along the edges between the pan and cheesecake to remove the cheesecake and set to the plate.

Chocolate Mousse

Servings: 12
Cooking Time: 25 Minutes
Ingredients:
- Nonstick cooking spray
- 8 oz. semisweet chocolate chips
- 8 eggs, separated
- 1 teaspoon vanilla
- ¼ cup+2 tbsp. powdered sugar

Directions:
1. Spray an 8-inch springform pan with cooking spray. Line the bottom with parchment paper.
2. Melt the chocolate in a microwave safe bowl in 30 second intervals.
3. Beat the egg yolks until thick and pale. Slowly beat in the melted chocolate until combined. Fold in the vanilla.
4. Beat the egg whites with ¼ cup of sugar until soft peaks form. Fold ¼ of the egg whites into the chocolate mixture just until combined. Gently fold in remaining egg whites. Pour into the prepared pan.
5. Place the rack in the cooking pot and place the mousse on it. Add the tender-crisp lid and set to bake on 350°F. Bake 20-25 minutes until almost set, the mousse will still be a little jiggly in the middle.
6. Transfer mousse to a wire rack and let cool completely. Cover and refrigerate at least 4 hours. Dust with remaining sugar before serving.

Ninja Foodi Cookbook

Nutrition:
- InfoCalories 154, Total Fat 8g, Total Carbs 15g, Protein 5g, Sodium 48mg.

Cinnamon Butternut Squash Pie

Servings: 4
Cooking Time: 30 Min
Ingredients:
- 1-pound Butternut Squash; diced/450g
- ¼ cup Honey/62.5ml
- 1 cup Water/250ml
- ½ cup Milk/125ml
- 1 Egg
- ½ tbsp Cornstarch/7.5g
- ½ tsp Cinnamon/2.5g
- A pinch of Sea Salt

Directions:
1. Pour the water inside your Foodi and add a reversible rack. Lower the butternut squash onto the reversible rack. Seal the pressure lid, and cook on Pressure for 4 minutes at High pressure.
2. Meanwhile, whisk all remaining ingredients in a bowl. Do a quick pressure. Drain the squash and add it to the milk mixture. Pour the batter into a greased baking dish. Place in the cooker, and seal the pressure lid.
3. Choose Pressure, set to High, and set the time to 10 minutes. Press Start. Do a quick pressure release. Transfer pie to wire rack to cool.

Spiced Poached Pears

Servings: 4
Cooking Time: 4 Hours
Ingredients:
- 4 ripe pears, peeled
- 2 cups fresh orange juice
- ¼ cup maple syrup
- 5 cardamom pods
- 1 cinnamon stick, broke in 2
- 1-inch piece ginger, peeled & sliced

Directions:
1. Slice off the bottom of the pears so they stand upright. Carefully remove the core with a paring knife. Stand in the cooking pot.
2. In a small bowl, whisk together orange juice and syrup. Pour over pears and add the spices.
3. Add the lid and set to slow cooking on low. Cook 3-4 hours or until pears are soft. Baste the pears every hour or so.
4. Serve garnished with whipped cream and chopped walnuts if you like, or just serve them as they are sprinkled with a little cinnamon.

Nutrition:
- InfoCalories 219, Total Fat 1g, Total Carbs 53g, Protein 2g, Sodium 6mg.

Chocolate Brownie Cake

Servings: 6
Cooking Time: 35 Minutes.
Ingredients:
- ½ cup 70% dark chocolate chips
- ½ cup butter
- 3 eggs
- ¼ cup Erythritol
- 1 teaspoon vanilla extract

Directions:
1. In a microwave-safe bowl, stir in the chocolate chips and butter and microwave for about 1 minute, stirring after every 20 seconds.
2. Remove from the microwave and stir well.
3. Set a "Reversible Rack" in the pot of the Ninja Foodi.
4. Close the Ninja Foodi's lid with a crisping lid and select "Air Crisp".
5. Set its cooking temperature to 350°F for 5 minutes.
6. Press the "Start/Stop" button to initiate preheating.
7. In a suitable, add the eggs, Erythritol and vanilla extract and blend until light and frothy.
8. Slowly add in the chocolate mixture and beat again until well combined.
9. Add the mixture into a lightly greased springform pan.
10. After preheating, Open the Ninja Foodi's lid.
11. Place the springform pan into the "Air Crisp Basket".
12. Close the Ninja Foodi's lid with a crisping lid and select "Air Crisp".
13. Set its cooking temperature to 350°F for 35 minutes.
14. Press the "Start/Stop" button to initiate cooking.
15. Place the hot pan onto a wire rack to cool for about 10 minutes.
16. Flip the baked and cooled cake onto the wire rack to cool completely.
17. Cut into desired-sized slices and serve.

Nutrition:
- InfoCalories:302;Fats:28.2g;Carbohydrates:5.6g;Proteins:5.6g

Blueberry Lemon Pound Cake

Servings:12
Cooking Time:1 Hour 5 Minutes
Ingredients:
- Butter flavored cooking spray
- 1¾cups+2 tsp flour, divided
- 2 tsp baking powder
- ½tsp salt
- 1½cups blueberries
- ¾cup butter, unsalted, soft
- 1 cup ricotta cheese, room temperature
- 1½cups sugar
- 3 eggs, room temperature
- 1 tsp vanilla
- 1 tbsp. lemon zest

Directions:
1. Spray a loaf pan with cooking spray
2. In a medium bowl, combine flour, baking powder, and salt, mix well.
3. Add the blueberries to a bowl and sprinkle 2 tsp flour over them, toss to coat.
4. In a large bowl, beat together butter, ricotta, and sugar on high speed, until pale and fluffy.
5. Reduce speed to medium and beat in eggs, one at a time. Beat in zest and vanilla.
6. Stir in dry ingredients, a fourth at a time, until combined. Fold in blueberries and pour into prepared pan.
7. Add the rack to the cooking pot and place the pan on it. Add the tender-crisp lid and set to bake on 325°F. Bake 1 hour 10 minutes or until cake passes the toothpick test. After 40 minutes, cover the cake with foil.
8. Transfer to wire rack and let cool in pan 15 minutes. Then invert and let cool completely before serving.

Nutrition:
- InfoCalories 303, Total Fat 17g, Total Carbs 32g, Protein 6g, Sodium 147mg.

Double Chocolate Cake

Servings:12
Cooking Time:1 Hour
Ingredients:
- ½cup coconut flour
- 1½cups Erythritol
- 5 tablespoons cacao powder
- 1 teaspoon baking powder
- ½teaspoon salt
- 3 eggs
- 3 egg yolks
- ½cup butter, melted and cooled
- 1 teaspoon vanilla extract
- ½teaspoon liquid stevia
- 4 ounces 70% dark chocolate chips
- 2 cups hot water

Directions:
1. Grease the Ninja Foodi's insert.
2. In a large bowl, stir in the flour, 1¼cups of Erythritol, 3 tablespoons of cacao powder, baking powder and salt.
3. In a suitable bowl, add the eggs, egg yolks, butter, vanilla extract and liquid stevia and beat until well combined.
4. Stir in the egg mixture into the flour mixture and mix until just combined.
5. In a small bowl, add hot water, remaining cacao powder and Erythritol and beat until well combined.
6. In the prepared Ninja Foodi's insert, stir in the mixture evenly and top with chocolate chips, followed by the water mixture.
7. Close the Ninja Foodi's lid with a crisping lid and select "Slow Cooker".
8. Set on "Low" for 3 hours.
9. Press the "Start/Stop" button to initiate cooking.
10. Transfer the pan onto a wire rack for about 10 minutes.
11. Flip the baked and cooled cake onto the wire rack to cool completely.
12. Cut into desired-sized slices and serve.

Nutrition:
- InfoCalories:169;Fats:15.4g;Carbohydrates:4.4g;Proteins:3.9g

Caramel Apple Bread Pudding

Servings:6
Cooking Time:35 Minutes
Ingredients:
- 2 cups water
- Butter flavored cooking spray
- ½cup applesauce, unsweetened
- ½cup almond milk, unsweetened
- ¼cup molasses
- 2 eggs
- ½tsp vanilla
- ½tsp cinnamon
- 1/8 tsp nutmeg
- 2½cups whole wheat bread, cut in 1-inch cubes
- ½cup apple, peeled & cut in 1-inch cubes

Directions:
1. Place rack in the cooking pot and pour the water in. Spray an 8x8-inch baking dish with cooking spray.

Ninja Foodi Cookbook

2. In a large bowl, whisk together everything except the bread and apples.
3. Lay the bread cubes in the prepared dish and top with apples. Pour applesauce mixture, ¼ at a time, over apples. Let sit 5 minutes, then pour another ¼ liquid mixture. Repeat process until liquid and bread are 1/4-inch from top of the dish.
4. Place the dish on the rack and add the tender-crisp lid. Set to bake on 325°F. Bake 30-35 minutes or until the bread pudding passes the toothpick test and top is golden brown.
5. Transfer to wire rack and let cool 10 minutes before serving.

Nutrition:
- InfoCalories 199, Total Fat 3g, Total Carbs 33g, Protein 8g, Sodium 233mg.

Strawberry Cheesecake

Servings: 8
Cooking Time: 20 Minutes
Ingredients:
- Butter flavored cooking spray
- 16 oz. cream cheese, soft
- 2/3 cup powdered Stevia
- 1 tsp vanilla
- 2 eggs, room temperature
- 1 cup strawberries, chopped

Directions:
1. Place the trivet in the cooking pot and add enough water to cover bottom by 1 inch. Spray an 8-inch springform pan with cooking spray.
2. In a large bowl, beat cream cheese until smooth.
3. Beat in Stevia and vanilla until combined.
4. Beat in eggs, one at a time and beat until thoroughly combined.
5. Pour into prepared pan. Cover bottom and sides of pan with foil to prevent any water from leaking in. Place the pan on the trivet.
6. Add the lid and select pressure cooking on high. Set timer for 20 minutes.
7. When the timer goes off, use natural release to remove the lid. Transfer cheesecake to wire rack to cool completely.
8. Cover and refrigerate 8 hours or overnight. Top with chopped strawberries before serving.

Nutrition:
- InfoCalories 219, Total Fat 21g, Total Carbs 20g, Protein 5g, Sodium 225mg.

Chocolate Cake

Servings: 16
Cooking Time: 30 Minutes
Ingredients:
- Butter flavored cooking spray
- 8 Eggs
- 1 lb. semi-sweet chocolate chips
- 1 cup butter

Directions:
1. Place the rack in the cooking pot. Line the bottom of an 8-inch springform pan with parchment paper. Spray with cooking spray and wrap foil around the outside of the pan.
2. In a large bowl, beat eggs until double in size, about 6-8 minutes.
3. Place the chocolate chips and butter in a microwave safe bowl. Microwave at 30 second intervals until melted and smooth.
4. Fold 1/3 of the eggs into chocolate, folding gently just until eggs are incorporated. Repeat two more times.
5. Pour the batter into the prepared pan. Pour 1½ cups water into the cooking pot. Place the cake on the rack.
6. Add the tender-crisp lid and set to air fry on 325°F. Bake 25-30 minutes or until center is set.
7. Transfer to wire rack to cool. When cool, invert onto serving plate, top with fresh berries if desired. Slice and serve.

Nutrition:
- InfoCalories 302, Total Fat 25g, Total Carbs 15g, Protein 5g, Sodium 130mg.

Citrus Steamed Pudding

Servings: 8
Cooking Time: 1 Hour
Ingredients:
- Butter flavored cooking spray
- 3½ cups water, divided
- 3 tbsp.+1 tsp butter, soft
- 1 cup sugar, divided
- 2 tsp orange zest, finely grated
- 1 tbsp.+2 tsp lemon zest, finely grated
- 2 eggs
- ¼ cup milk
- ¼ cup+1 tbsp. orange juice, unsweetened, divided
- 2 cups self-rising flour, sifted
- 1 orange, peel & pith removed, chopped
- 1½ tbsp. cornstarch

Directions:
1. Spray a 6-cup oven-safe bowl with cooking spray. Pour 2 cups water in the cooking pot and add the steamer rack.
2. In a large bowl, beat 3 tablespoons butter, ½ cup sugar, and 4 teaspoons orange and lemon zest until smooth.
3. Beat in eggs, one at a time, and beating well after each addition.
4. In a small bowl, stir together milk and ¼ cup orange juice.
5. Fold flour, orange pieces, and milk mixture into butter mixture, alternating between ingredients, begin and end with flour.
6. Pour into prepared bowl and tent with foil. Tie with kitchen string and place on the steamer rack. Add the lid and set to steam. Cook 1 hour or until the pudding passes the toothpick test. Transfer to wire rack.
7. Drain any remaining water from the cooking pot. Set cooker to saute on medium heat.
8. Add remaining sugar and cornstarch to the pot. Slowly pour in 1½ cups water, stirring constantly until combined. Cook 5 minutes, or until thickened.
9. Stir in tablespoon of lemon juice, tablespoon orange juice, tablespoon lemon zest, and teaspoon butter and cook until butter has melted and mixture is smooth.
10. To serve: invert pudding onto serving plate and drizzle sauce over the top. Slice and serve.

Nutrition:
- InfoCalories 305, Total Fat 8g, Total Carbs 54g, Protein 5g, Sodium 68mg.

RECIPE INDEX

A
Almond Banana Dessert ... 135
Almond Crusted Haddock ... 55
Almond Lover's Bars ... 27
Almond Milk ... 126
Almond Quinoa Porridge ... 30
Apple Butter Chicken ... 85
Apple Pecan Cookie Bars ... 22
Apple Walnut Quinoa ... 40
Applesauce Pumpkin Muffins ... 28
Apricot Bbq Duck Legs ... 95
Apricot Snack Bars ... 23
Arroz Con Cod ... 47
Artichoke Lasagna Rolls ... 60
Artichoke With Mayo ... 70
Artichoke&Spinach Casserole ... 73
Asian Beef ... 97
Asian Chicken ... 84
Asparagus Fries With Chipotle Dip ... 13
Asparagus With Feta ... 68
Avocado Cups ... 34

B
Baby Back Ribs With Barbeque Sauce ... 113
Baby Porcupine Meatballs ... 66
Bacon And Gruyère Egg Bites ... 41
Bacon Lime Chicken ... 93
Bacon Strips ... 105
Bacon&Cranberry Stuffed Turkey Breast ... 82
Bacon&Egg Poppers ... 30
Bacon&Sauerkraut With Apples ... 109
Bacon-wrapped Halloumi Cheese ... 13
Bacon-wrapped Hot Dogs ... 101
Baked Bacon Macaroni And Cheese ... 100
Baked Cajun Turnips ... 64
Baked Cod Casserole ... 57
Baked Eggs In Spinach ... 40
Baked Linguine ... 60
Baked Rigatoni With Beef Tomato Sauce ... 104
Banana Coconut Loaf ... 39
Banana Coconut Pudding ... 136
Banana Custard Oatmeal ... 28
Banana Nut Muffins ... 36
Bbq Chicken Sandwiches ... 33
Beef And Cabbage Stew ... 106
Beef And Pumpkin Stew ... 116
Beef Bourguignon(2) ... 98
Beef Brisket ... 102
Beef Brisket&Carrots ... 103
Beef Broccoli ... 99
Beef In Basil Sauce ... 116
Beef Jerky ... 113
Beef Lasagna ... 114
Beef Mole ... 118
Beef Pho With Swiss Chard ... 118
Beef Sirloin Steak ... 105
Beef Stew With Beer ... 101
Beef Stir Fry ... 108
Beef Stroganoff ... 104
Beef Tips&Mushrooms ... 102
Beef&Broccoli Casserole ... 111
Bell Pepper Frittata ... 32
Bell Peppers Mix ... 61
Blackened Salmon ... 52
Blueberry Lemon Pound Cake ... 139
Blueberry Peach Crisp ... 134
Bok Choy And Zoddle Soup ... 64
Bolognese Pizza ... 107
Braised Short Ribs With Mushrooms ... 107
Breakfast Burrito Bake ... 38
Breakfast Pies ... 36
Brisket Chili Verde ... 110
Broccoli Cauliflower ... 75
Brownie Bites ... 137
Bunless Burgers ... 111
Burrito Bowls ... 62
Butter Chicken ... 90
Buttered Turkey ... 95
Butter-flower Medley ... 15
Buttermilk Chicken Thighs ... 79
Buttermilk Fried Chicken ... 86
Butternut Breakfast Squash ... 29
Butternut Squash,Apple,Bacon And Orzo Soup ... 122
Butternut Turkey Stew ... 88
Buttery Chicken Meatballs ... 18
Buttery Cranberry Cake ... 135

C
Cabbage With Bacon ... 73
Cajun Shrimp ... 56
Caponata ... 26
Caprese Pasta Salad ... 60
Caramel Apple Bread Pudding ... 139
Caramelized Cauliflower With Hazelnuts ... 27
Caramelized Salmon ... 52
Caribbean Chicken Skewers ... 13
Carne Guisada ... 102
Carrot Cake Oats ... 35
Carrot Gazpacho ... 69
Carrot Raisin Cookie Bars ... 135
Carrots Walnuts Salad ... 76
Cashew Cream ... 17
Cauliflower Enchiladas ... 65
Cauliflower Gratin ... 23
Cauliflower Nuggets ... 25
Cauliflower Steaks&Veggies ... 61
Cauliflower&Bacon Soup ... 112
Char Siew Pork Ribs ... 100
Charred Broccoli With Mustard Cream Sauce ... 14
Cheat Apple Pie ... 128
Cheddar Cheeseburgers ... 109
Cheese Babka ... 127
Cheese Burgers In Hoagies ... 97
Cheeseburger Boats ... 22
Cheesecake French Toast ... 41
Cheesy Bacon Brussel Sprouts ... 21

Cheesy Baked Spinach ... 63
Cheesy Chicken And Broccoli Casserole ... 83
Cheesy Chicken Dip ... 22
Cheesy Chicken&Artichokes ... 83
Cheesy Chilies ... 70
Cheesy Fried Risotto Balls ... 14
Cheesy Green Beans With Nuts ... 70
Cheesy Meat Omelet ... 38
Cheesy Squash Tart ... 65
Cheesy Stuffed Mushroom ... 19
Cheesy Stuffed Onions ... 20
Cheesy Tangy Arancini ... 15
Chicken And Broccoli ... 92
Chicken And Quinoa Soup ... 89
Chicken Bites ... 25
Chicken Cacciatore ... 85
Chicken Carnitas ... 81
Chicken Chickpea Chili ... 92
Chicken Chili ... 123
Chicken Cordon Bleu ... 94
Chicken Cutlets In Dijon Sauce ... 89
Chicken Enchilada Soup ... 122
Chicken In Thai Peanut Sauce ... 77
Chicken Lettuce Wraps ... 26
Chicken Meatballs In Tomato Sauce ... 93
Chicken Meatballs Primavera ... 87
Chicken Meatballs With Dill Dipping Sauce ... 18
Chicken Omelet ... 34
Chicken Pasta With Pesto Sauce ... 77
Chicken Potpie Soup ... 121
Chicken Stroganoff With Fetucini ... 91
Chicken Tenders With Broccoli ... 96
Chicken Wings With Lemon ... 85
Chicken With Bacon And Beans ... 86
Chicken With Bbq Sauce ... 96
Chicken With Mushroom Sauce ... 90
Chicken With Prunes ... 83
Chicken With Tomatoes And Capers ... 81
Chickpea,Spinach,And Sweet Potato Stew ... 120
Chili Cheese Quiche ... 28
Chipotle Beef Brisket ... 112
Chipotle Raspberry Chicken ... 90
Chipotle-lime Chicken Wings ... 24
Chocolate Brownie Cake ... 138
Chocolate Cake ... 140
Chocolate Cheesecake ... 125
Chocolate Chip And Banana Bread Bundt Cake ... 37
Chocolate Chip Brownies ... 128
Chocolate Fondue ... 129
Chocolate Mousse ... 138
Chocolate Peanut Butter And Jelly Puffs ... 130
Chorizo Mac And Cheese ... 68
Chunky Pork Meatloaf With Mashed Potatoes ... 106
Churro Bites ... 131
Cinnamon Apple Bread ... 38
Cinnamon Apple Cake ... 125
Cinnamon Bun Oatmeal ... 39
Cinnamon Butternut Squash Pie ... 138
Cinnamon Crumb Donuts ... 41
Cinnamon Sugar Donuts ... 29
Cinnamon Sugar French Toast Bites ... 35
Citrus Glazed Halibut ... 46
Citrus Steamed Pudding ... 140

Clam&Corn Chowder ... 54
Classic Crab Imperial ... 51
Coconut And Shrimp Bisque ... 120
Coconut Cream Dessert Bars ... 130
Coconut Cream"custard"Bars ... 132
Coconut Lime Snack Cake ... 126
Coconut Rice Pudding ... 129
Coconut Shrimp With Pineapple Rice ... 45
Coq Au Vin ... 91
Country Chicken Casserole ... 90
Crab Cake Casserole ... 54
Crab Cakes ... 51
Cran-apple Turkey Cutlets ... 79
Cranberry Almond Rice Pudding ... 133
Cranberry Cheesecake ... 138
Cranberry Lemon Quinoa ... 30
Cranberry Vanilla Oatmeal ... 37
Creamy Chicken Carbonara ... 81
Creamy Crab Soup ... 55
Creamy Golden Casserole ... 62
Creamy Polenta&Mushrooms ... 66
Creamy Pumpkin Soup ... 123
Creamy Slow Cooked Chicken ... 94
Creamy Tuscan Chicken Pasta ... 80
Crème De La Broc ... 60
Creole Dirty Rice ... 116
Crispy Cheesy Straws ... 16
Crispy Chicken Skin ... 21
Crispy Delicata Squash ... 15
Crispy Sesame Shrimp ... 11
Crunchy Cashew Lamb Rack ... 97
Crunchy Chicken Schnitzels ... 79
Crunchy Chicken&Almond Casserole ... 88
Crusted Pork Chops ... 102
Cuban Marinated Pork ... 111
Cuban Pork ... 99
Cumin Baby Carrots ... 22
Curried Salmon&Sweet Potatoes ... 53

D

Dill Butter ... 19
Double Chocolate Cake ... 139

E

Eggplant Casserole ... 76
Enchilada Bites ... 18

F

Farfalle Tuna Casserole With Cheese ... 44
Fiesta Chicken Casserole ... 86
Filling Coconut And Oat Cookies ... 133
Fish Broccoli Stew ... 50
Fish Chowder And Biscuits ... 120
Flank Steak With Bell Pepper Salsa ... 98
Flaxseeds Granola ... 37
Flounder Oreganata ... 56
Flounder Veggie Soup ... 49
Flourless Chocolate Cake ... 132
Fried Beef Dumplings ... 12
Fried Salmon ... 45
Fried Snickerdoodle Poppers ... 130

G

Garlic Chicken And Bacon Pasta 88
Garlic Potatoes 76
Garlic Shrimp And Veggies 58
Garlic Shrimp 51
Garlic Turkey Breasts 82
Garlic-herb Roasted Chicken 84
Garlicky Pork Chops 117
Gingered Butternut Squash 25
Glazed Carrots 41
Glazed Lemon Muffins 34
Goulash(hungarian Beef Soup) 124
Greek Chicken With Potatoes 82
Green Cream Soup 74
Green Minestrone 67
Green Squash Gruyere 73
Grilled Broccoli 35
Grilled Cheese 63

H

Haddock With Sanfaina 52
Ham Breakfast Casserole 38
Ham&Hash Brown Casserole 28
Ham,Ricotta&Zucchini Fritters 110
Hamburger&Macaroni Skillet 103
Hassel Back Chicken 78
Hawaiian Pork Meal 108
Healthier Meatloaf 115
Healthy Chicken Stew 77
Hearty Breakfast Muffins 32
Hearty Veggie Soup 59
Herb Roasted Mixed Nuts 12
Herbed Cauliflower Fritters 17
Herby Fish Skewers 23
Homemade Vanilla Yogurt 31
Honey Bourbon Wings 20
Honey Garlic Chicken And Okra 87
Honey Short Ribs With Rosemary Potatoes 100
Hot Crab Dip 12

I

Italian Baked Zucchini 59
Italian Flounder 44
Italian Pita Crisps 18
Italian Pot Roast 116
Italian Sausage With Garlic Mash 64
Italian Sausage,Potato,And Kale Soup 120
Italian Turkey&Pasta Soup 83

J

Jalapeno Salsa 26
Jamaican Jerk Chicken Stew 124
Jamaican Pork 115

K

Key Lime Pie 130
Korean Pork Chops 107
Korean-style Barbecue Meatloaf 112
Kung Pao Shrimp 56

L

Lamb Chops And Potato Mash 108
Lasagna Soup 122
Lemon And Blueberries Compote 131
Lemon Cod Goujons And Rosemary Chips 49
Lemon Turkey Risotto 89
Lemon,Barley&Turkey Soup 96
Lettuce Carnitas Wraps 80
Lime Blueberry Cheesecake 129
Lime Chicken Chili 92
Lime Glazed Pork Tenderloin 109
Loaded Potato Soup 123
Lone Star Chili 110
Louisiana Crab Dip 14

M

Maple Dipped Asparagus 31
Maple Giant Pancake 37
Maple Glazed Pork Chops 109
Maply Soufflés 126
Mashed Broccoli With Cream Cheese 76
Mashed Potatoes With Spinach 75
Meatballs With Spaghetti Sauce 117
Mexican Chicken Soup 93
Mexican Pork Stir Fry 109
Mexican Pot Roast 106
Mexican Street Corn 11
Milk Dumplings In Sweet Sauce 136
Minestrone With Pancetta 71
Mini Crab Cakes 20
Mini Shrimp Tacos 17
Mini Steak Kebabs 16
Mini Vanilla Cheesecakes 133
Mixed Berry Cobbler 136
Molten Lava Cake 135
Mongolian Beef 98
Moo Shu Chicken 88
Morning Pancakes 36
Mushroom And Wild Rice Soup 124
Mushroom Brown Rice Pilaf 68
Mushroom Goulash 64
Mushrooms Stuffed With Veggies 27
Mussel Chowder With Oyster Crackers 52
Mustard And Apricot-glazed Salmon With Smashed
Potatoes 53

N

New England Lobster Rolls 46
Noodles With Tofu And Peanuts 67
Nutmeg Peanuts 13
Nutmeg Pumpkin Porridge 33

O

Okra Stew 62
Olives And Rice Stuffed Mushrooms 71
Orange Glazed Cod&Snap Peas 48

P

Palak Paneer 75
Paneer Cutlet 66
Paprika Buttered Chicken 77
Paprika Chicken 80
Paprika Hard-boiled Eggs 42

Parmesan Butternut Crisps 22
Parmesan Stuffed Mushrooms 16
Parmesan Tilapia 51
Parsley Mashed Cauliflower 74
Pasta Veggie Toss 69
Peach Cobbler 128
Peanut Butter Pie 134
Pecan Apple Crisp 129
Pecan Pie Bars 126
Pecan Stuffed Apples 127
Penne All Arrabbiata With Seafood And Chorizo 50
Pepper And Sweet Potato Skewers 75
Pepper Crusted Tri Tip Roast 101
Pesto Pork Chops&Asparagus 99
Pesto Stuffed Chicken With Green Beans. 95
Pesto With Cheesy Bread 70
Philippine Pork Chops 106
Pistachio Crusted Mahi Mahi 43
Pistachio Crusted Salmon 44
Pizza Stuffed Chicken 87
Poached Flounder With Mango Salsa 58
Poached Peaches 126
Pomegranate Radish Mix 62
Popcorn Chicken 21
Pork And Ricotta Meatballs With Cheesy Grits 117
Pork Asado 101
Pork Chops With Broccoli 98
Pork Chops With Squash Purée And Mushroom Gravy ... 119
Pork Medallions With Dijon Sauce 103
Pork Sandwiches With Slaw 111
Pork Shank 24
Portuguese Honey Cake 125
Potato Filled Bread Rolls 68
Prosciutto Egg Bake 31
Pull Apart Cheesy Garlic Bread 14
Pulled Pork Tacos 118
Pumpkin Coconut Breakfast Bake 35
Pumpkin Crème Brulee 133
Pumpkin Pecan Oatmeal 34
Pumpkin Soup 72
Pumpkin Steel Cut Oatmeal 30

Q
Quesadilla Casserole 95
Quick Indian-style Curry 71
Quinoa Pesto Bowls With Veggies 62
Quinoa Protein Bake 29

R
Radish Apples Salad 59
Ranch Pork With Mushroom Sauce 104
Red Velvet Cheesecake 137
Rhubarb,Raspberry,And Peach Cobbler 135
Ricotta Raspberry Breakfast Cake 32
Roasted Bbq Shrimp 46
Roasted Pork With Apple Gravy 112
Roasted Vegetable Salad 69
Rosemary Potato Fries 21
Rosemary Sweet Potato Medallions 68

S
Salmon Chowder 50

Salmon With Creamy Grits 43
Salmon With Dill Chutney 48
Salmon With Dill Sauce 44
Salmon,Cashew&Kale Bowl 47
Salsa Chicken With Feta 78
Salsa Verde Chicken With Salsa Verde 89
Sausage With Celeriac And Potato Mash 105
Sausage Wrapped Scotch Eggs 31
Sausage&Broccoli Frittata 36
Seafood Gumbo 55
Sesame Radish 65
Sesame Tuna Steaks 55
Shredded Chicken And Wild Rice 78
Shredded Chicken With Lentils And Rice 79
Shredded Chicken&Black Beans 93
Shrimp And Sausage Paella 56
Shrimp Etouffee 45
Shrimp Fried Rice 47
Shrimp&Asparagus Risotto 47
Shrimp&Zoodles 48
Simple Beef&Shallot Curry 113
Simple Salmon&Asparagus 57
Slow Cooked Chicken In White Wine And Garlic 94
Smoky Horseradish Spare Ribs 115
Smoky Sausage&Potato Soup 103
Sour And Sweet Pork 114
Sour Cream&Onion Frittata 74
South Of The Border Corn Dip 16
Southern Grits Casserole 42
Southern Pineapple Casserole 67
Southern Sweet Ham 113
Southwest Chicken Bake 80
Spanish Lamb&Beans 115
Spanish Potato And Chorizo Frittata 38
Spanish Rice 70
Spanish Steamed Clams 53
Speedy Clams Pomodoro 54
Speedy Fajitas 91
Spiced Poached Pears 138
Spiced Red Snapper 57
Spicy Black Bean Dip 23
Spicy Grilled Shrimp 57
Spicy Shrimp Pasta With Vodka Sauce 49
Spicy"grilled"Catfish 46
Spinach Casserole 42
Spinach Gratin&Eggs 72
Spinach Hummus 26
Spinach Turkey Cups 29
Spinach,Tomatoes,And Butternut Squash Stew 61
Steamed Artichokes With Lemon Aioli 74
Steamed Sea Bass With Turnips 54
Sticky Barbeque Baby Back Ribs 99
Stir Fried Veggies 67
Strawberry And Lemon Ricotta Cheesecake 131
Strawberry Cheesecake 140
Strawberry Crumble 129
Strawberry Oat Breakfast Bars 30
Strawberry Snack Bars 25
Stuffed Baked Tomatoes 40
Stuffed Manicotti 59
Stuffed Mushrooms 72
Stuffed Summer Squash 74
Swedish Meatballs With Mashed Cauliflower 105

Sweet Bread Pudding	33
Sweet Pickled Cucumbers	11
Sweet Potato And Beetroot Chips	12
Sweet Potato Fries	16
Sweet Potato Skins	19
Sweet Potato,Sausage,And Rosemary Quiche	40
Sweet Potatoes&Fried Eggs	39
Sweet&Spicy Shrimp Bowls	58
Sweet&Spicy Shrimp	51
Swiss Bacon Frittata	33

T

Tangy Jicama Chips	24
Tasty Acorn Squash	72
Tender Beef&Onion Rings	97
Teriyaki Pork Noodles	104
Teriyaki Salmon	50
Tex Mex Beef Stew	107
Tex-mex Chicken Tortilla Soup	121
Three-layer Taco Dip	24
Thyme Chicken With Veggies	85
Thyme Turkey Nuggets	82
Tofu&Carrot Toss	73
Tomato Bisque	61
Traditional Beef Stroganoff	118
Tres Leches Cake	136
Tuna&Avocado Patties	45
Turkey Breakfast Sausage	93
Turkey Croquettes	84
Turkey Enchilada Casserole	92
Turkey Meatballs	78
Turkey Scotch Eggs	11
Tuscan Chicken&Pasta	79
Tuscan Cod	43

V

Vanilla Cheesecake(1)	127
Vanilla Chocolate Spread	128
Vanilla Hot Lava Cake	133
Vanilla Pound Cake	134
Vegan Split Pea Soup	61
Veggie Lasagna	63
Veggie Loaded Pasta	66
Veggie Lover's Pizza	67
Veggie Skewers	69

W

Walnut Orange Coffee Cake	32
Wrapped Asparagus In Bacon	19

Y

Yogurt Cheesecake	137

Z

Zesty Brussels Sprouts With Raisins	18
Zesty Meatballs	20
Zucchini Chips	17
Zucchini Muffins	11
Zucchini&Beef Lasagna	114

Printed in Great Britain
by Amazon